Psychedelic Popular Music

MUSICAL MEANING AND INTERPRETATION
Robert S. Hatten, editor

A Theory of Musical Narrative	BYRON ALMÉN
Approaches to Meaning in Music	BYRON ALMÉN AND EDWARD PEARSALL
Voicing Gender: Castrati, Travesti, and the Second Woman in Early Nineteenth-Century Italian Opera	NAOMI ANDRÉ
The Italian Traditions and Puccini: Compositional Theory and Practice in Nineteenth-Century Opera	NICHOLAS BARAGWANATH
Debussy Redux: The Impact of His Music on Popular Culture	MATTHEW BROWN
Music and Embodied Cognition: Listening, Moving, Feeling, and Thinking	ARNIE COX
Music and the Politics of Negation	JAMES R. CURRIE
Il Trittico, Turandot, *and Puccini's Late Style*	ANDREW DAVIS
Neil Young and the Poetics of Energy	WILLIAM ECHARD
Reconfiguring Myth and Narrative in Contemporary Opera: Osvaldo Golijov, Kaija Saariaho, John Adams, and Tan Dun	YAYOI UNO EVERETT
Interpreting Musical Gestures, Topics, and Tropes: Mozart, Beethoven, Schubert	ROBERT S. HATTEN
Musical Meaning in Beethoven: Markedness, Correlation, and Interpretation	ROBERT S. HATTEN
Intertextuality in Western Art Music	MICHAEL L. KLEIN
Music and the Crises of the Modern Subject	MICHAEL L. KLEIN
Music and Narrative since 1900	MICHAEL L. KLEIN AND NICHOLAS REYLAND
Musical Forces: Motion, Metaphor, and Meaning in Music	STEVE LARSON
Is Language a Music? Writings on Musical Form and Signification	DAVID LIDOV

Pleasure and Meaning in the Classical Symphony   MELANIE LOWE

*Breaking Time's Arrow: Experiment and Expression
in the Music of Charles Ives*   MATTHEW MCDONALD

*Decorum of the Minuet, Delirium of the Waltz:
A Study of Dance-Music Relations in $\frac{3}{4}$ Time*   ERIC MCKEE

The Musical Topic: Hunt, Military, Pastoral   RAYMOND MONELLE

*Musical Representations, Subjects, and Objects: The Construction
of Musical Thought in Zarlino, Descartes, Rameau, and Weber*   JAIRO MORENO

The Rite of Spring *at 100*   SEVERINE NEFF, MAUREEN CARR, AND GRETCHEN HORLACHER, WITH JOHN REEF

Meaning and Interpretation of Music in Cinema   DAVID NEUMEYER

*Deepening Musical Performance through Movement:
The Theory and Practice of Embodied Interpretation*   ALEXANDRA PIERCE

*Expressive Intersections in Brahms:
Essays in Analysis and Meaning*   HEATHER PLATT AND PETER H. SMITH

*Expressive Forms in Brahms's Instrumental Music:
Structure and Meaning in His Werther Quartet*   PETER H. SMITH

Music as Philosophy: Adorno and Beethoven's Late Style   MICHAEL SPITZER

Death in Winterreise:
Musico-Poetic Associations in Schubert's Song Cycle   LAURI SUURPÄÄ

*Music and Wonder at the Medici Court:
The 1589 Interludes for* La pellegrina   NINA TREADWELL

Reflections on Musical Meaning and Its Representations   LEO TREITLER

Debussy's Late Style: The Compositions of the Great War   MARIANNE WHEELDON

WILLIAM ECHARD

Psychedelic Popular Music
A History through Musical Topic Theory

INDIANA UNIVERSITY PRESS

This book is a publication of

Indiana University Press
Office of Scholarly Publishing
Herman B Wells Library 350
1320 East 10th Street
Bloomington, Indiana 47405 USA

iupress.indiana.edu

© 2017 by William Echard

All rights reserved

No part of this book may be reproduced or utilized in any form or by any means, electronic or mechanical, including photocopying and recording, or by any information storage and retrieval system, without permission in writing from the publisher. The Association of American University Presses' Resolution on Permissions constitutes the only exception to this prohibition.

The paper used in this publication meets the minimum requirements of the American National Standard for Information Sciences—Permanence of Paper for Printed Library Materials, ANSI Z39.48-1992.

Manufactured in the United States of America

Library of Congress Cataloging-in-Publication Data

Names: Echard, William, author.
Title: Psychedelic popular music : a history through
    musical topic theory / William Echard.
Other titles: Musical meaning and interpretation.
Description: Bloomington : Indiana University Press,
    2017. | Series: Musical meaning and interpretation
Identifiers: LCCN 2016059651 (print) | LCCN 2017000758 (ebook) |
    ISBN 9780253026453 (pbk. : alk. paper) | ISBN 9780253025661
    (hardcover : alk. paper) | ISBN 9780253026590 (ebook)
Subjects: LCSH: Psychedelic rock music—History and criticism.
Classification: LCC ML3534 .E25 2017 (print) |
    LCC ML3534 (ebook) | DDC 781.64—dc23
LC record available at https://lccn.loc.gov/2016059651

1 2 3 4 5   22 21 20 19 18 17

Contents

Acknowledgments   ix

Introduction   1

1. Delineating Psychedelia:
   Topic Theory and Popular Music Cultures   5
2. Developments through 1966   29
3. The Later 1960s   104
4. The 1970s   199
5. The 1980s and On   228

Epilogue: Conclusions and Prospects   264

Appendix A: The Sample and Discography   267

Appendix B: The San Francisco Poster Sample   273

Appendix C: Some Notes on the Transcriptions   275

List of References   277

Index   285

Acknowledgments

Much of the early work on this book was supported by a research grant from the Social Sciences and Humanities Research Council of Canada. I am also grateful for financial support received from the Faculty of Arts and Social Sciences, Carleton University. As always, special thanks are due to my family, especially to Lillian, Morgan, Siân, and my parents. Your unwavering patience with the long stretches of work and your interest in the results have been absolutely essential to seeing this project through.

Psychedelic Popular Music

Introduction

> An hour later, with ten more miles and the visit to the World's Biggest Drug Store safely behind us, we were back at home, and I had returned to that reassuring but profoundly unsatisfactory state known as "being in one's right mind."
>
> —Aldous Huxley, *The Doors of Perception*, 1954

There are a lot of things this book does not get into. For any writer on music, that is a familiar situation, because it is notoriously difficult to fit even a small part of the listening experience into words. A few seconds of listening will uncover countless nuances that were not even hinted at, no matter how thorough the author aims to be. This rift is heightened when music is tied to personal experiences and states of mind and feeling that are ineffable, profoundly atypical, and ultimately inexpressible. This book does not try to analyze the aesthetic and emotional landscape of psychedelic music, let alone psychedelic experience. It is about something else: how psychedelia developed as an interlinked family of styles, a set of conventional codes and typical features. It is in turn about how psychedelia drew upon preexisting styles and codes, capitalizing on their existing meanings and forging new ones. Aldous Huxley talks about the world of daily life, how it frames and reabsorbs the transient psychedelic experience. He presents this mainly as a loss or a missed opportunity. However, in that framing world and in those framing discourses, a whole language of styles and signs grows up, which can be a fascinating area of study on its own.

Issues of this sort also arise for a different reason, because music signifies in a variety of different ways simultaneously. Some musical meaning is highly affective, linked to tantalizingly ineffable gestures and emotions. While we are listening to or performing music, these gestures and emotions can feel entirely clear and distinct, yet they evade verbalization. At the same time, some musical meanings are more like words, highly conventional signifiers linked to clearly delineated cultural concepts. This second sort of meaning has been theorized in various ways, but one of the most powerful and current of its models is the theory of *musical topics*. Topic theory is explained in chapter 1, but briefly, a topic is a highly conventional musical figure that signifies a broad cultural concept. The topical signifier originally gains its meaning through direct historical and contextual connection with the cultural concept, then over time the sign becomes less historically and socially specific. For example, hunting horns were originally used in pastoral situations and so could become a generalized signifier for the pastoral as a concept. Similarly, certain distinctive guitar licks were originally connected to Chuck Berry as part of his personal style; later, they became generalized as topical signifiers of 1950s rock and roll along with all of the connotations of that era and subculture.

Topic theory was developed in connection with the study of Western art music, but it bears a strong resemblance to theories of musical meaning in popular music studies. One purpose of this book is to explore those areas of overlap. I chose psychedelia as my case study not because of anything to do with psychedelic experience itself but because it is a genre with good credentials for studying topicality. It is fairly recent in origin, so we can look at questions of how topics emerge. Psychedelia drew from a wide range of preexisting topics and at the same time transformed them, and so it can expand our understanding of topical change and dynamism. Finally, the psychedelic genre has existed long enough to have reached a crucial turning point. This book is being written in an era when some kinds of psychedelic music are stylistically quite new and current but are also becoming historically self-reflexive and standardized. Psychedelia is still an actively changing and expanding topical field, but at the same time it affords chances to study how topics solidify. Overall, psychedelia offers a rich set of possibilities for research into topicality, and this book has two purposes. For readers interested in the history of popular music style, the book offers a survey of the main signs, styles, and codes that went into the formation of psychedelia and its proliferation of substyles from the mid-1960s into the 1990s. On a theoretical level, it explores topic theory in a way that aims to enrich both popular music studies and musical semiotics overall.

Scope and Sample

Because this book is centered on topic theory, there are many aspects of psychedelic style that will be mentioned only briefly or not at all. It is not a comprehensive study of psychedelic music but only of those aspects most relevant to topicality. I have aimed only to touch the highlights, and although this is not a short book, it is still in some ways a pilot project, not only with respect to psychedelia itself but also with respect to the broader work of mapping the overall topical field of rock, funk, soul, and related popular musics of the twentieth and early twenty-first centuries.

One of the greatest methodological challenges facing a study of this sort is to delineate the sample. Since topics are defined in part by their broad distribution, a wide variety of recordings need to be consulted in order to make sure that particular features really are ubiquitous enough to warrant inclusion. I also needed a fairly large sample because I wanted to cover a broad historical period (the 1960s through the 1990s) and a range of styles (rock, folk, soul, funk, and their many relevant subgenres). At the same time, topical analysis requires a considerable amount of time-consuming musical transcription and analysis, which puts limits on the size of the sample that could be realistically addressed. I decided early to limit myself almost entirely to artists from the United States and the United Kingdom. This was not an easy choice, because psychedelia has been a transnational and translocal genre from the start. But there was already more than enough to do in dealing with these core regions. The next decision was temporal, and the main consideration was to be able to cover everything from the early roots of psychedelia through the appearance and then standardization of electronic dance music variants such as Goa trance, along with several generations of neopsychedelic rock music. In the end, this meant the mid-1960s to the early 1990s. Finally, the selection of individual songs went through a funnel procedure, where I listened to and took informal notes on as much repertoire as possible and gradually identified those recordings and artists that seemed to give the best examples of general trends or had the most interesting and illustrative idiosyncrasies. I cannot claim too much systematicity for this process, but my hope is that most readers will accept the final list of recordings as reasonably representative of all the main trends in psychedelia. Appendix A gives a full accounting of which songs made up the sample. These songs are a formal sample in the sense that they were all subjected to some degree of transcription and/or musical analysis, and their topical features were cataloged.

In summary, when I generalize about broad trends in psychedelic topicality there are concentric rings of formality involved. In some instances I will refer specifically to examples from this sample, and in most cases the sample is what I am generalizing about. Beyond that, I sometimes refer to trends that I noticed while pursuing the larger listening project that led to the selection of the sample. And least formally, I sometimes rely on my own instincts and biases, shaped by decades of participation in popular music culture. Wherever possible I aim to stay with assertions that can be analytically demonstrated through the formal sample, but there is no escaping the fact that this sort of writing is sometimes more a critical and intuitive art than a science.

Plan of the Book

At the level of the chapter, the book is largely chronological in design, with each chapter based around a particular period. That decision was made because the historical development of topics is a key theme throughout. However, in some instances a chronological layout imposes a frustrating amount of jumping around and cross-referencing, so I have occasionally broken out of the chronological presentation and pursued thematic or theoretical digressions when it seemed easiest to keep discussion of a particular topic or stylistic feature contained in a single passage. Within each chapter, the chronological model is not entirely absent but is followed much more weakly. The chapters are internally organized around key artists and key recordings, sequenced in a way that generally follows chronology. There is also a difference between earlier and later chapters in terms of how comprehensive they aim to be. Chapter 2 is the only one that attempts a complete overview of its period, because 1965–66 was the crucial era in which most aspects of psychedelic topicality were established. Subsequent chapters become increasingly less comprehensive and place more emphasis on single artists and recordings that either modify earlier topics or introduce new topical areas. Throughout, there are four tasks being pursued in parallel: (1) identify preexisting topics and styles taken up by psychedelia, saying how these were used and transformed; (2) identify style components of psychedelia that support these topics; (3) identify style components of psychedelia that may not have been fully topical in their original use but that later became so; and (4) pay special attention to dynamism, change, and dialogic properties of the overall topical field.

Chapter 1 contains the bulk of the theoretical material and explores the problem of delineating psychedelia. That chapter also introduces topic theory in detail, arguing that when studying contemporary and emergent topical fields, it is desirable to adopt a dialogical and pluralistic view of musical competency. Chapter 2 begins the specific overview of repertoire and psychedelic topicality, developing a comprehensive overview of the period 1965–66. This was the foundational era for psychedelia, and so the chapter is especially dense with specifics and examples. Later chapters become increasingly more selective, since they have the luxury of commenting on changes relative to the framework established in the earlier period. Chapter 3 deals with the later 1960s, including a detailed discussion of early psychedelic soul and funk, the San Francisco scene, the Beatles, the Incredible String Band, and early Pink Floyd. Chapter 4 is focused on two major developments of the early 1970s: space rock's emergence as a freestanding genre and Afrofuturist psychedelic funk. Chapter 5 completes the historical overview with a study of developments from the 1980s through the early 1990s, touching on 1980s neopsychedelic rock, the free festival scene, the appearance of new psychedelic imaginaries, rock-rave crossovers, and psychedelic electronic dance musics. Finally, the conclusion returns to the question of popular music topicality more generally, exploring how the particular case of psychedelia lays the groundwork and offers lessons for a broader agenda of studying the topical fields of popular music in the twentieth and early twenty-first centuries.

1 Delineating Psychedelia: Topic Theory and Popular Music Cultures

They would have been fresh in so many ways, those first fourteen seconds. The sonics alone would have stood out: stinging, droning chords with a soaring, catchy hook over the top. The sound of the lead guitar would have drawn special attention, cutting melodic fuzz at a time when that was still a new thing. This was only the second Yardbirds single to venture far from their blues roots and just their fourth overall. Swept along by the guitar hero wave that was just gathering strength, the song would have carried the energy of a new scene. And finally, most remarkably, the lead guitar hook sounded like a sitar. It had even been played on a sitar in an earlier working recording. As a result, "Heart Full of Soul," released in June 1965, is often said to have marked the arrival of raga rock, a sound that would not only proliferate over the next few years but also be pivotal in shaping the look and sound of 1960s psychedelia. It was followed in July by the gentler, more understated "See My Friends" from the Kinks, and by the end of the year the Beatles had publicly aligned themselves with the new style. The peak was 1966, with landmark releases from the Byrds ("Eight Miles High"), the Beatles (*Revolver*), and many others. Rock music was, for a time, broadly garlanded with tablas, sitars, and other trappings of India. But the trend was waning. Although some interesting new directions continued to be found, for example, by the Incredible String Band, which blended raga rock with British folk traditions, the momentum was tapering off by the fall of 1967, and a few months after that, raga rock was a thing of the past.

Like any pop fad, raga rock's signifiers were at first blush clear-cut. The minimum you needed to get on board was a drone (tambura or otherwise), or a few sitar flourishes (actual or imitated), or some tabla-like hand drumming. During the mid-1960s many tracks did little to go beyond these surface details. On the other hand, some artists explored Indian aesthetics and techniques more extensively. That was one kind of depth, perhaps best exemplified by George Harrison's commitment to become a student of Ravi Shankar. There was also another, focusing on the multimedia scope of the thing, extending beyond musical sound. As a full participant, you might well have been listening while sitting on a Persian carpet, an incense stick smoldering in the corner and morning sunlight filtering through the paisley shawl draped across your window. The individual signs were separate and specific, but they were subsumed in a more amorphous web of resemblances and connections. This was true not only for raga rock itself but for the ways it reached out and linked with other fashions of the time. The kaleidoscope is a nineteenth-century Scottish invention, but it fit right in, next to the rugs and mandalas. The shirt might have been paisley, or it might have been tie-dye, which gets us from India to pretty much anywhere else (tie-dye having roots in Africa, East Asia, and pre-Columbian America, to name a few places). Following the circles of association as they spread outward, we might notice that much of the Orientalist imagery is also to some degree Victorian or Edwardian, blending smoothly into a belle époque British nostalgia. Sometimes the sitars and tamburas rubbed shoulders with the classical avant-garde, as in the tape loops of "Tomorrow Never Knows" by the Beatles. And the whole thing could be piled together with other styles from radically different times and places, like country music and electric blues.

In later chapters we will examine raga rock in detail. For now, I evoke the associations of its style because they offer a vivid example of this book's core concept: musical topicality. The word "topic" will be used in two related but distinct senses. First, in the narrower sense, "topic" is shorthand for "topical signifier." The sitar-like quality of the lead guitar in "Heart Full of Soul" is an example, as are the recognizable graphical motifs of any design that immediately evokes the concept of a Persian carpet. These are signifiers insofar as they are like spoken or written words: discrete and portable configurations, clearly recognizable, that evoke fairly standardized meanings. Because of this self-contained property, any given signifier can be deployed in a wide range of contexts and combinations. For example, in "Heart Full of Soul" the sitar-like guitar serves as an Indian topical signifier, but it is layered with an acoustic guitar that is more country and western in its implications. Each of these signifiers appears in other songs in very different combinations. Similarly, a visual signifier of Egypt such as the eye of Horus can easily be combined with images evoking science fiction and outer space.

So sometimes a topic refers to a particular signifier, pinpointing the exact sound or other configuration that carries a particular meaning. But not all signifiers are topical. Why apply the name to these signifiers when used in these ways? This brings us to the second, broader sense of topic: a conceptual area for contemplation and discussion, for elaboration, for exploration. Orientalist conceptions of India form a topic, as do concepts like the martial, or the pastoral, or 1950s rock-and-roll culture. A topic is a field of meaning that is specific enough to be recognizable and coherent but broad enough to wander around in. The important topics in a culture are explored in a wide range of media. For example, you can find Orientalist India not only in music but also in literature, visual art, philosophy, industrial design, and many other places. Each medium in which a topic is explored houses a relatively distinct version of the topic, but they all link together into an overarching topical field. And topics interpenetrate in myriad ways. The Indian topic evoked by raga rock, when seen in the broader context of psychedelia as a whole, intersects with many other topics, such as Victorian British nostalgia, blues culture, pastoralism, and others.

The musical topic is a straightforward concept to introduce, but it becomes continually more complex on reflection. It suggests a range of supporting concepts and terminology, and rather than explain these one at a time over the course of the book, I have opted to put all of them into this first chapter. Readers who would rather not start with theory may skip ahead and come back to it later as needed to help explain subsequent terms.

But for those who like to know where their authors are coming from, this chapter explores my own position on certain controversial points of semiotics and topic theory. One overarching goal of my work, both here and elsewhere, is to explore zones of contact between semiotic theory as it has typically been used in the study of Western art music and the slightly different priorities and applications that have become more common in popular music studies (Echard 2005, 2006a, 2006b, 2008). This is not because of any preexisting agenda on my part but rather because I find use for elements of both and was surprised that so few authors in either area acknowledged one another or made regular use of each other's work. One reason there has not been more exchange between these theoretical camps is that in some cases they proceed from different assumptions and agendas regarding the ontology of the musical work and the role of social theory in musical interpretation. The divide is far from absolute, and I am far from the only person to situate myself in the middle. But I believe there is still work to be done in making explicit some of the underlying issues and differences of emphasis. Overall, chapter 1 argues that when studying contemporary and emergent topical fields it is desirable to adopt a dialogical and pluralistic view of musical competency. By *dialogical* I mean a perspective that takes special interest in the way that meanings and interpretive practices emerge from ongoing negotiations of power and identity between different individuals and groups within an interpretive community.

In terms of topic theory this chapter has three purposes: (1) to provide an introduction for those readers who may need it; (2) to define terms and concepts used in later chapters; and (3) to stake out a position in some of the underlying debates in the hope that this may help show how sometimes separate schools of thought in musical interpretation can be brought into a productive relationship. The other major goal, partly theoretical and partly historical, is to say what I mean by *psychedelic* and, in the course of that, to define a few terms and concepts that will be useful when thinking about how new styles and genres grow out of older ones. One methodological question not touched on in the introduction was how I decided in the first place that certain recordings and artists should be considered psychedelic. By explaining my own delineation of psychedelia in this chapter, I can explain those choices while at the same time providing a broad historical overview. So this chapter begins with a discussion of what I mean by psychedelic, along with the development of a few related theoretical ideas. After that there is a general introduction to topic theory, followed by a discussion of how my own version of topic theory differs from some other versions. Finally, there will be a summary of how these broad theoretical arguments are reflected in the rest of the book.

Delineating Psychedelia: The Multiplicity

A topic such as the pastoral or the psychedelic can be found in film, literature, visual art, and many other areas. Any given topic connotes and participates in a particular cultural field that extends far beyond music. In the case of psychedelia, this is especially evident given its strong expression in visual art and design, not only in a countercultural way but also in mainstream culture of the 1960s and beyond. In this respect, psychedelic style was one element in a midcentury design boom:

> As the domestic goods consumer boom developed, product design moved outside the bounds of both traditional good taste and . . . the determination of form by function. . . . In such a climate, experimentation in form and exuberance in colour developed in as diverse a range of objects as clothes, furniture, goods packaging, electrical goods, transistor radios and cars. . . . Perhaps above all it was in the fields of graphic design, glossy display advertising and the photographic image that the pattern of simultaneous overlap and stark antagonism between "straight" and "psychedelic" culture may be most clearly observed. (Laing 2005, 31–32)

This complex situation reflects many of the same tendencies we will need to track in terms of musical psychedelia. The psychedelic style is special, but at the same time it is a product of its times, borrowing a great deal from other styles and practices. The signs of psychedelic style developed in close connection to particular countercultures and ideologies, but they also circulated outside of them. There is no clear-cut moment at which particular signifiers clearly became psychedelic or clearly stopped being psychedelic, but there are various details of translation and transformation that can be tracked. In terms of musical sound, an instructive example is offered by Russell Reising and Jim LeBlanc: "With today's recording techniques and the widespread, routine use of synthesized sounds, a great deal of twenty-first-century pop music could be construed in some way as psychedelic. This was not the case in 1967, however, in an era when four-track recording techniques and the association of 'flower power' and colourful imagery with LSD and other spiritual intoxicants were commonplace" (2008, 107).

The complication here is different—having to do with musical sound and the passage of time—but similar in that the core issue is how signifiers shift in scope. Many other examples could be added, but for now the point is that when seeking to delineate the psychedelic we will need to define our terms in such a way that they narrow the field but still take these sorts of subtleties into account. Even when we narrow our attention to participants in psychedelic countercultures of the 1960s, it is important to remember that experiences, agendas, and understandings varied widely. Although clichés center on countercultural styles of San Francisco and the London Underground, neither of these scenes was monolithic, and there were many other variants of psychedelia besides. For example, there is what Joe Boyd (2006, 115, 117) called the "beer-drinker's psychedelia" of the Move, rooted in pub rock, and there is also substantial overlap between psychedelic rock and mainstream pop. Even within the emerging canon and dominant clichés we find alternative perspectives. For example, Barry Miles suggests that "in reality the Floyd were neither psychedelic nor underground" (2006, 65).

We also need to consider the wide range of reactions psychedelic experience might engender. Throughout the various eras of psychedelia there were a substantial number of curious thrill seekers and spectators who might be drawn to the novelty of psychedelic styles without having any insider knowledge of psychedelic experience or countercultures. Consider the young *Revolver* listeners hypothesized by Nick Bromell: "The album appeared at least a year before psychedelics irrupted into American youth culture. The vast majority of young listeners heard *Revolver* with prepsychedelic innocence, and it sounded bizarre." For such listeners, the album "was an enigma they would understand only gradually, through many listenings and over many months" (Bromell 2000, 89, 94).

We have gradually been narrowing our focus: from the whole sweep of cultural products, to music in particular, to the unstable mixture of countercultural and broader versions of musical psychedelia. At every step we encounter a multiplicity of perspectives. This complexity does not diminish even if we look at the history of European American engagement with psychoactive drugs in particular.[1] Early European exploration and colonization, from at least the fifteenth century, produced reports and myths of drug use among indigenous populations. These reports form one important source for European American concepts of what would eventually be regarded as psychedelic drugs. But they did so in a context where such practices were cast as completely other to European experiences and values. By contrast, in the eighteenth and nineteenth centuries there began to appear sporadic interest in psychoactive drugs among European artists, writers, occultists, and scientists, who still regarded these drugs as exotic but approached them in an exploratory and appropriating mode. By the late nineteenth century we find the beginning of medical and anthropological study, especially of peyote. Some early workers in this area, for example, Silas Weir Mitchell, mostly confined themselves to description. But in some cases there was outright advocacy of psychoactive drugs as beneficial in certain circumstances; the work of Havelock Ellis is an early case in point. In turn, the first years of the twentieth century saw the beginning of detailed psychological studies of psychoactive drugs, the first production of synthetic versions of the relevant organic compounds (e.g., mescaline in 1919), and eventually entirely new chemicals, most famously LSD, whose psychoactive properties were discovered in 1943. In all of these instances, scientific and otherwise, psychoactive substances were, on the one hand, regarded as important and of interest but, on the other hand, associated with the exotic, psychosis, and a breakdown of norms. The situation was further complicated in the period immediately following World War II, which saw widespread criminalization and mainstream shunning of any form of recreational drug use.

It was in the period from the early 1950s to the early 1960s that psychedelic ideas and practices as such began to emerge. Key moments include 1951–52, Gordon Wasson and Al Hubbard became active in the field; the spring of 1954, Aldous Huxley published *The Doors of Perception*; 1956, the term "psychedelic" was coined by Aldous Huxley and Humphry Osmond; May 1957, Gordon Wasson published a widely read article in *Life* magazine about psychoactive fungi; circa 1959–61, various figures who would become leaders in the 1960s countercultures tried psychedelics for the first time; the summer of 1962, various US governmental agencies began implementing measures against LSD use and research; and roughly 1963, the street-level LSD trade began. In 1963 Timothy Leary founded his first extra-academic psychedelic group and the entourage that would evolve into the Merry Pranksters began to gather around Ken Kesey. The period 1964–65 marked the earliest appearance of popular music groups explicitly devoted to psychedelics, and the Summer of Love in 1967 is generally acknowledged as the peak of the countercultural psychedelic era. So by the middle of the 1960s there had been at least four important and distinct eras in the development of psychedelic attitudes and practices: (1) the era of early European exploration; (2) the colonial and Romantic era, during which various kinds of experimentation began but within a strong framework of exoticism and Orientalism; (3) the early psychedelic era as such, mostly limited to elites who defined their agendas relative to values of institutional science and high culture; and (4) the appearance of popular-culture psychedelia, which corresponded to a breakdown of any remaining mainstream tolerance or endorsement of recreational drug use.

Given such complex roots, it is not surprising that the psychedelic movement of the 1960s was not in any way monolithic. A web of similarities and differences both united and divided psychedelic insiders. As a result, there are many different ways of grouping them and understanding their relationships. One option is to look at the main outcomes hoped for by different advocates of psychedelic drugs: scientific (positive knowledge gained through structured theory and research), humanistic (self-improvement, enlightenment), hedonistic (sensation as an end in itself), and political (social disruption as a tool of change). Simply listing the names of selected key players can also illustrate their diversity: the Diggers, Aldous Huxley, the "lab madness" researchers and clinicians, Timothy Leary, LSD therapists, the Merry Pranksters, Hunter S. Thompson, the White Panthers, and the Yippies. After the 1960s, various spin-off psychedelic movements appeared with a fair degree of regularity, but few attained the same degree of prominence as the earlier ones, with the possible exception of rave culture in the late 1980s.

Are You Experienced? The Question of Drugs

Musicology offers very few definitions of psychedelia, and all of them are constrained in ways that reflect particular research agendas. This is not meant as a criticism, but it does mean that none of the available definitions and discussions will touch on all the points necessary to my own study. The earliest extended musicological study of psychedelia is that of Sheila Whiteley (1992). Her general approach, focused as it was on psychedelic coding and norms of style, is a useful starting point for topic theory, but it will require expansion. Whiteley summarizes her model as follows: "Musically psychedelic coding focuses on *alternative meanings* and involves a correlation of drug experience and stylistic characteristics" (8). In speaking of alternative meanings, she has in mind both the desire to explore altered states of consciousness and the way in which psychedelia frequently borrowed stylistic components and signs from other sources. The one aspect of Whiteley's work that will require the most refinement is the direct correlation drawn between psychedelic style and drug experience. Other theorists have offered more nuanced approaches in this area. For example, Arun Saldanha (2007, 6) in his work on Goa trance speaks in the plural of "psychedelics," a family of practices for self-transformation: "Practices are psychedelic to the extent that they invoke a core as a site for investment and transformation, opposing what elders and the law have to say about it. The psychedelic self isn't at all purified of the social; rather, it seriously plays around with what the environment has to offer" (15). This resembles Whiteley's approach insofar as psychedelics are marked by conscious experimentation with alternative meanings. But while drug use is still an essential component of psychedelics for Saldanha, the emphasis has shifted away from a simple correlation between drugs and stylistic features and toward an engagement with the purposes and complex results of these practices. To go one step further, the broadest possible view would be that psychedelia is not inherently about drug use at all but rather can include any form of art or practice explicitly concerned with the expansion and exploration of consciousness. This position has been taken by several authors. To cite just one: "The term itself, in fact, contains no etymological reference to drugs: *psyche-delia* means simply to 'make clear' or 'visible' the mind" (Harris 2005, 10). This is not to deny that drug use was an important part of psychedelic cultures. But an advantage of the broad view is that it can draw attention to the wider range of histories and practices with which psychedelia is cognate. Jonathan Harris continues: "This desire to experience mind and body again as a new and changing reality had precedents of countless kinds, and drug-taking as a means to achieve it also has a long history. . . . Psychedelia as socio-cultural style, then, is partly a matter of highly eclectic borrowings and restorations" (11).

Another advantage of exploring a broader delineation of psychedelia—one in which the drug connection is not denied but is also not considered primary—is that it takes into account the manner in which psychedelia came to function, in some cases, as style. Jim DeRogatis puts the point succinctly: "As psychedelic rock evolved, it developed a code of *sonic* requirements. . . . Many artists told me that they used drugs in the process of making those sounds, and many told me that they did not" (2003, xiii–xiv, emphasis mine). This aspect of psychedelia, as style rather than experience, is also relevant to reception in many instances: "Equally significant, LSD had captured the popular imagination by 1966 to the point where people who never had a psychedelic experience *thought* they had a fairly good idea what one was like" (10, emphasis in original). The overall message is that the importance and nature of the drug connection vary widely, depending on whose experiences are being considered.

Drugs are themselves a complex cultural product marked as much by their symbolic aspects as by their material effects. Marcus Boon (2002, 4), for example, suggests that for the cultural analyst or historian, clinical descriptions of drug effects are less relevant than how the drug is valued and understood in different times and places. Paul Manning offers another version of the same argument: "It is not the pharmacological power of particular drugs that provides the key to understanding the social and cultural practices associated with drug consumption but, rather, ... the social and cultural practices that lend *meaning* to the perceived physiological effects of drugs" (2007, 9, emphasis in original). He goes on to argue that "the critique of pharmacological determinism had been firmly established for at least half a century," citing foundational work by Howard Becker, Mary Douglas, and others (10–12). Seen in this light, drugs can be understood as a form of technology, and the critique of pharmacological determinism proceeds along lines similar to the critique of technological determinism (Gilbert and Pearson 1999, 138).

In the context of topic theory, I will offer a semiotic perspective on how these complex relationships are mediated. In sociological terms, a relevant concept is *normalization*, the process by which certain drugs and certain practices become incorporated as unremarkable features within particular contexts. Andrew Blake (2007, 103), while acknowledging that the idea of normalization is controversial, argues that drug use has been normalized in most popular music cultures and that these cultures have been influential in fostering normalization in society more generally. Normalization is not equivalent to whitewashing. In connection with 1960s and 1970s rock culture, Blake argues that "normal or not, the drugs' dark side was acknowledged. Indeed, a number of variations on the Faustian theme emerged during and after the 1960s" (109). I raise the idea of normalization and the critique of pharmacological determinism not in an attempt to evade the medical, legal, and social downsides of drug-related practices but because an understanding of these sociological nuances will be helpful when we arrive at our main task of asking how particular topical meanings arise and are mediated.

Before laying out my own delineation of psychedelia, we should return once more to a question raised in the introduction: What does it mean to study representations of experiences that many believed were unrepresentable? To consider one influential early formulation of the psychedelic, Boon argues that Aldous Huxley was significant in large part because he championed direct experience over any form of representation: "This shift was to have profound implications for art, politics, and religion that would begin to be realized in the 1960s.... The new value and interest accorded to the psychedelics had everything to do with [the] broad shift away from an aesthetic of the symbol towards one of experience" (2002, 251). Or, as Harris summarizes: "Psychedelia, then, was self-consciousness and body-consciousness, and a new *social* consciousness too. To see the mind afresh, or the body or the world, involved the fiction that one could or would or should abstract and 'get out of one's mind' via intense sensual and cognitive stimulation. But, by definition, those experiences then *cannot* be recouped: that is, there can be no direct ex post facto knowledge of psychedelia's experiences" (2005, 11).

This conundrum is not so different from that of lived aesthetic experience in any area. The ineffability of psychedelic experience may have been given special ideological weight, but the underlying technical problem is not specific to psychedelia. And as we will see, one of the crucial themes in topic theory is precisely the manner in which direct experience and historical specificity drift toward standardized symbolism over time. This is true to a degree of all musical signification, but it is especially true of topics. The essential point is in Raymond Monelle's (2000, 15–16) suggestion that topics are distinguished from other kinds of musical signs in part because they signify by learned codes rather than by more internal aesthetic experiences. To deal with topicality is to deal with convention, with signs of experience rather than with raw experience itself. This is one reason that the seemingly ineffable experience of psychedelia was so amenable to being expressed through conventions and signs that frequently had their origin in other times and in connection with other ideologies. It has become commonplace to note that 1960s countercultures not only challenged hegemonic values but also reinscribed such values. Some writers have come up with striking phrases for this, as when George Lipsitz remarked that the rock counterculture embodied "alternative rather than oppositional" impulses (1994, 222) or when, in a slightly different context, David Farber said that "the Beats' songs of adventure . . . were both remarkably familiar and familiarly remarkable" (1994, 173). Along similar lines, David Lenson argues that "at its heart the counterculture was a conservative movement, a reaction back into the old individualistic idealism of the American nineteenth century. As such it was a Romantic revival, and arguably the last gasp of a dying Modernism" (1995, 10).

Looking specifically at literary and artistic symbolism, it is striking that while we find drug-related themes, there is little that would amount to a clear-cut drug topic. Boon is getting at this when he shows that representations of psychedelic experience generally overlapped with broader conceptions of the imaginal and so can be linked with many early fantasy literatures (2002, 218–22). A similar point was made much earlier by Alethea Hayter: "A survey of imagery in opium visions has to take into account which images were general property at the time and which were special to the opium landscape, if any of them were. In fact what happened was probably more like an unconscious selection, among standard images, some of which could be made to bear the weight of the special emotions of the opium rêverie" (1968, 84–85).

Just as I would not want to take the idea of normalization or the critique of pharmacological determinism so far as a blanket apologetic for drug use, I would also not want to take arguments about the borrowing of signifiers and style elements so far as to deny that there was a truly distinct topical field that emerged in connection with psychedelia. But as we now move on, to try and delineate that field, we need to keep all of the preceding complexities in mind, aiming for a model that is sufficiently nuanced but still retains useful powers of distinction.

A Working Model

My approach to delineating psychedelia hinges on the shifting relationship between three main elements: psychedelic *experience*, which formed a basis for attributions of psychedelic *intent*, which led over time to conventions of *style*. Psychedelic experience refers both to a particular kind of experience, usually drug related, and to the cultural/historical contexts within which that experience was valued and understood. In turn, psychedelic intent does not refer to authorial intent but rather to a judgment made by listeners that the music seems to have been intended to induce, describe, guide, or enhance psychedelic experience. What is crucial here is that the interpreter thinks of the music in this way. A milder version of the same thing occurs when a listener feels that a piece of music is *appropriate* to psychedelic experience, regardless of whether that listener goes so far as to attribute intent. Finally, psychedelic style refers to how certain features and signifiers were frequently attributed to, or perceived as appropriate to, psychedelic intent. Over time these traits cluster, forming coherent styles. Psychedelic styles retain symbolic connections to psychedelic experience and intent but at the same time become so conventionalized as to have no further necessary attachment to them. Since a psychedelic style comes to exist through correlations established in a particular historical context, it can become, among other things, a sign of that context. For post-1960s cases we will find a multitude of options in terms of how the originating historical moment is understood and represented.

When exploring specific elements that went into psychedelic style, we will find that some of them were recycled wholesale from preexisting styles, some were alterations of preexisting materials, and some were comparatively novel. We will need a vocabulary for describing such relationships. One suggestive idea, following Whiteley (1992, 36), is that of a *base style*. A base style is one that either preexisted psychedelia or was parallel with it and that many psychedelic performances adopted as an overarching framework. Whiteley does not expand on the idea, but it is a crucial feature of psychedelic music and deserves elaboration. In my own application, a *base style* is one that is not inherently psychedelic. Listeners would be willing to accept a piece of music as a token of that style without any psychedelic dimensions being present. Or to put it another way, listeners would not expect any psychedelic dimensions to be present if all you told them ahead of time was that they were going to hear an example of that style. This is the situation with styles such as psychedelic country, psychedelic folk, and psychedelic funk. Such names indicate that we are dealing with a psychedelically inflected example of a piece that is strongly associated with a base style. This sort of arrangement is so common that early psychedelia might best be seen not as a coherent style of its own but rather as a way of altering already-established styles. In this respect, psychedelic music resembled early jazz. Taking a longer view, at a certain point there are new jazz compositions, and similarly there are pieces of music in which the psychedelic signifiers are so numerous and foregrounded as to almost occlude the base style. But do such instances cohere into a style of their own, as jazz eventually did? I think this is an open question.

There are two different but related senses in which a style may be a base style relative to its psychedelic use. In a *temporal* sense, certain styles had achieved a strong identity before ever being put to psychedelic use and in many cases before psychedelia as such even existed. In a *distributional* sense, certain styles have many more nonpsychedelic than psychedelic examples and are often primarily supported by communities of listeners and musicians without psychedelic involvement. We should also make a distinction between a base style and what could be called a *donor style*. A donor style is one from which psychedelic-friendly signifiers are drawn but that does not form the overarching framework for the piece. This is a matter of fine judgments and is highly sensitive to the particular expectations of different listeners. Nonetheless, the distinction can be clarified by a few examples. "Trip to Your Heart" by Sly and the Family Stone could be appropriately called psychedelic funk, which is to say a psychedelically inflected funk song. It is likely to be heard as properly a funk song, just one with a particular flavor, and so funk is the base style in this case. By contrast, "Norwegian Wood" by the Beatles is not likely to be heard as Indian classical music. It is not a token of that style, and so Indian music is in this case the donor style rather than the base style. A similar pair of examples might be "Uncle John's Band" by the Grateful Dead (folk/country as base style) versus "Who Are the Brain Police" by Frank Zappa (musique concrète as donor style).

The final thing I would like to note about base styles and donor styles is that they almost always appear to have been chosen because they are somehow *cognate* with psychedelic intent or psychedelic style. There are at least three different ways in which a style may be cognate with psychedelia. *Cognate by intent* refers to style traits associated with practices that are intended to transform consciousness but do not have psychedelic intent (e.g., Buddhism, Hinduism, surrealism). *Cognate by formal affect* refers to styles that are formally amenable to psychedelic use. Formal affect and intent often go together (Indian classical music has both) but not always (musique concrète has cognate formal affect but not cognate intent). *Cognate by context* refers to styles that are implicated through a temporal or spatial connection to psychedelia. Some may formally invite the link (e.g., Yardbirds-style rave-ups), and some may not (e.g., country music, pre-1960s blues). One important area for attention is how styles and genres interact when hybridized in this way. In the context of topic theory, Robert Hatten (2014) has summarized a range of possible resulting effects—metaphor, irony, contradiction, commentary, parody, and satire—along with a range of different sorts of relationship between an imported style feature and its new context, including *compatibility* (which encompasses as well different sorts of incompatibility), *dominance*, *creativity* (the generation of strikingly fresh meanings), and *productivity* (with respect to the generation of meanings over the trajectory of a larger work).

An Introduction to Topic Theory

Topic theory was first presented by Leonard Ratner in his work on the Classic style: "From its contacts with worship, poetry, drama, entertainment, dance, ceremony, the military, the hunt, and the life of the lower classes, music in the early 18th century developed a thesaurus of characteristic figures, which formed a rich legacy for classic composers. . . . They are designated here as topics—subjects for musical discourse" (1980, 9). While Ratner did not mention semiotics, topic theory is compatible with a semiotic interpretation and was taken up and expanded along those lines by V. Kofi Agawu (1991), Monelle (2000, 2006), and Hatten (1994, 2004, 2014), among others. Topic theory has developed into a lively and rich area of study, but there has been surprisingly little debate among the key theorists regarding underlying assumptions and methodologies. This may be in part because topic theory, at least under that name, has been applied almost exclusively to the study of Western art musics. But as already noted in the introduction, there are other areas of musical semiotics that bear a strong resemblance to topic theory, especially in popular music studies and ethnomusicology. One unique contribution that topic theory can make to the broader discussion is a refined and powerful model of the underlying semiotic processes in this sort of musical signification. In turn, what related approaches from popular music studies can add is a more socially grounded understanding of the contexts and practices through which these semiotic processes unfold. I will first describe topic theory as developed in its original context and then show how some of its ontological and epistemological assumptions can be altered in order to better correspond to the context of psychedelia as an emergent topical field. Throughout, I will engage most closely with the work of Raymond Monelle, followed closely by Robert Hatten. They are the two theorists who have done the most to develop a semiotic model of the inner workings of topicality. Monelle, in particular, has offered the clearest exposition of certain underlying assumptions. I will need to question those assumptions not by way of critique but by way of understanding how different repertoires and different historical situations can require different theoretical models.

For most people, the most familiar kind of sign is the word. The single word in natural language provided a central template for the semiological model of Ferdinand de Saussure (1959), and in his formulation a sign has three hallmarks: (1) signifiers, which can be clearly defined (there is usually little confusion about which word you are hearing or reading); (2) signifieds, which show a high level of consistency within an interpretive community (most people agree on the basic core meaning of most words); and (3) obvious dependence on contingent historical and social factors (meanings change as habits of speaking, writing, and interpreting change). Many kinds of musical signs are not well described by a Saussurean model, since musical meanings are often subjective and ineffable. But topics are an exception, being one of the few kinds of musical signs that show the three Saussurean hallmarks. Topical signifiers are, on the one hand, very clear and conventionalized; there is often little doubt when one is hearing a characteristic figure such as waltz time, or a hunting horn, or a Chuck Berry–style guitar solo. On the other hand, it can be quite challenging to precisely delineate in formal terms the necessary and sufficient features that identify any particular topical signifier. This has been noted in one way or another by most topic theorists (see, e.g., Monelle 2006, 4–7). This situation is not unique to topics, and an ongoing theme in most musical semiotics is the difficulty in offering precise descriptions of musical signifiers. For the purposes of my own work, the two most salient features of topical signifiers are, first, that they are easily recognized as such by listeners and, second, that at least some of their features are strongly conventionalized. But the attribution of topicality cannot be made on the basis of the signifier alone: far more important are properties of the signified. The crucial thing about the topical signified is that while it constitutes a relatively bounded and coherent cultural field, it is also widely distributed and open-ended. As Monelle puts it: "In describing a musical topic, it is not enough to identify a motive, give it a label, and then move on to the next. Each topic may signify a large semantic world, connected to aspects of contemporary society, literary themes, and older traditions" (2000, 79). It can be very tempting to approach topical analysis as an occasion for list making and taxonomy, and in one respect that is a useful contribution. On the other hand, topic theory must also be an opening onto historical and cultural analysis if we are to realize its full potential.

Following Monelle, I consider two features essential for a musical sign to be a topic: (1) it must be highly conventionalized within a listening community, and (2) it must rely for a large part of its meaning on indexicality of the content (Monelle 2000, 17, 80). These two properties are separable. Many signs display one or the other, but only topics display both. Indexicality here is meant in the Peircean sense. An index is a sign that functions by virtue of direct contextual connection, as in the case of smoke signifying fire or footprints signifying the prior passage of an individual. In the case of musical topics, sitar-like timbres and melodies signify India because they originally came from there. By virtue of this connectedness, indexicality often serves a pointing function, as when a pointing finger is an index of the location of the moon. By contrast, a symbol is a sign that functions entirely by convention—for example, when a red octagon signifies "stop." In practice, the line between the index and the symbol is a moving target, because very often indices become symbols over time. And indeed this is a crucial feature of topicality.[2] In order for a sign to function as a topic, it must be removed from its original stylistic frame, or the entire stylistic frame must be removed from its original context, a point underscored recently by Hatten (2014). When sitars remain embedded in Indian contexts and musical practices, they do not have the necessary distance to topically symbolize India as part of raga rock. This transposition of signifiers into a new context also by necessity represents an abandonment, or at least a transformation, of any originally indexical aspects they may have had.

When Monelle speaks of the indexicality of content, he is providing a semiotic model for two distinct but related aspects of topicality. First, attention is drawn to the way in which topical signs gain their meaning through embeddedness in particular historical situations. For example, certain drum patterns were actually used in military exercises, and certain guitar riffs were actually part of the idiolect of Chuck Berry. This is an indexical connection. But as the sign becomes conventionalized, it becomes more symbolic, referring to the broader cultural concepts associated with those original contexts: the martial in general, or 1950s rock and roll in general. The indexicality remains important but is now one link in a chain connecting a more broadly distributed symbol to a more general set of concepts. Second, and more abstractly, indexicality of content refers to how the topic is embedded in a web of larger significations. For example, in the Baroque theory of affects a descending minor second signifies a sigh in certain harmonic and metrical contexts. This connection is iconic insofar as the gestural and energetic profile of a descending minor second resembles the sagging sensation of a sigh. It is also iconic with the sigh's high-to-low pitch profile. However, the *pianto* as a topic does not primarily signify a sigh as such but rather all of the emotions, histories, and cultural concepts associated with a sigh—those with which sighing is usually thought to be connected and toward which sighing tends to direct our attention. So while the signifier in this case is an icon, the topic overall has a necessary indexical aspect because it is embedded within the whole indexically related field of cultural meanings bearing on those emotions (Monelle 2000, 17).

In popular music studies, the closest parallel to topic theory is Philip Tagg's theory of musemes.[3] I am using "parallel" here in a narrow sense, because many aspects of popular music semiotics overlap topic theory in rather general ways. For example, theories of competency and levels of code could all be mobilized as useful contributions to the discussion. Tagg was one of many popular music scholars who, since the late 1970s, have developed models of musical meaning rooted in Saussurean semiotics and in critical social theory (an overview of the field can be found in Middleton 1990). While a broader study would need to engage with a wider range of this literature, for my immediate purposes I focus on Tagg's theory both because it is the most detailed and rigorous in semiotic terms and because it is most similar to topic theory in the sense of identifying very specific signifiers, analyzing their prototypical sonic tokens, and placing emphasis on how they participate in broader but well-specified fields of cultural meaning.

Tagg's core concept is the museme, defined as follows: "A *museme* shall be taken to mean the basic unit of musical expression which in the framework of one given musical system is not further divisible without destruction of meaning" (2000b, 108). While this formulation may seem a bit literal relative to its inspiration in phonology, Tagg immediately goes on to note that the continuous nature of musical signifiers makes it difficult in some cases to draw boundaries between the levels of such a hierarchy. He also points out that musemes are rarely meaningful in isolation but are much clearer in their signification when heard together in the form of *museme stacks* or *museme strings* (Tagg 2000b, 108–109). Tagg reports that over the course of his research "the museme . . . has become an increasingly elusive entity. Museme stacks and museme strings, on the other hand . . . became increasingly useful as work on this project progressed because . . . listener connotations tended to correspond much more to identifiable *combinations* of musical structures and *parameters of musical expression* . . . than to the individual constituent parts of those combinations" (Tagg and Clarida 2003, 94). As we will see, topic theorists have also increasingly moved toward the study of how topics combine and elaborate one another.

One crucial difference between Tagg's work and other topic theory can be seen in his reference to listeners. Tagg makes a point of refining his interpretations by conducting tests with a range of listeners, adjusting his model depending on what they report. Other topic theorists also base their interpretations on extensive cultural research, but they do not generally go so far as to conduct interviews or tests with live listeners. This is a point to which we will return when we consider monological versus dialogical views of musical competency. But differences aside, both Tagg's work and topic theory are essentially lexical in emphasis. And both at their best strive to avoid the reductionism that marred earlier lexical theories. One important difference is that while musematic analysis as practiced by Tagg connects in direct ways to ideological and political analysis, topic theory has mostly avoided such things. On this front, then, I would hope that the encounter between topic theory and musematic analysis could be one of mutual enrichment. They can be conceived as two parts of a more comprehensive theory of musical code in social context.

Although the basic idea of topicality is straightforward, topical analysis in practice needs to come to terms with many complexities. One factor, already noted, is that the exact demarcation of any particular topical signifier can be complex. There is no sharp line, for example, between a clear-cut waltz and other $\frac{3}{4}$ metrical frameworks. Similarly, there is no sharp line dividing a sitar-like electric guitar timbre from other bright, clean, but not necessarily Orientalist examples. For the most part, these sorts of judgments need to be explored case by case and with careful attention to context. Perhaps more interesting on a theoretical level is that topics almost never appear in isolation. Most musical textures mobilize several different topics either simultaneously, in sequence, or both. Following Hatten (1994, 2004, 2014), I use the term *troping* to refer to the combination of distinct topics. In more elaborated cases, the movement from one trope or topic to another can create meanings that are dependent on change-of-state schemas unfolding in time. Hatten's concept of *expressive genre* (1994) is one way to approach such structures, as is Byron Almén's work on narrative (2008). Similarly, when we shift our attention from individual texts to the semantic resources available to an entire culture, we can think in terms of *topical fields*, which are not unlike Pierre Bourdieu's notion of cultural fields in that they provide a set of common reference points, resources, and constraints within which individuals can orient and improvise their practices of production and reception.

Although topic theory along these lines does consider the dynamism of topical meaning to some degree, it still tends to treat individual topics as somewhat fixed and atomic. Topics are combined into tropes, and time-dependent forms such as expressive genre and narrative allow movement from one topic or trope to another. But the topics themselves are rarely treated as dynamic and changeable. In such theories, it is the relative fixity of topics that is relied on as a framework against which various forms of combination and movement are analyzed. For example, Almén argues that "as a locus for a network of correlations, topic is expressively static. By contrast, as a manifestation of the playing-out of a fundamental opposition, narrative is expressively dynamic" (2008, 75). It is not that theorists in this area deny that topics change over time—Monelle, especially, has offered exemplary studies of topical history—but simply that this aspect is rarely foregrounded or treated in a particularly theorized manner. For example, Monelle's own work in many ways can be read as an attempt to get past the atomic approach to topics through an emphasis on historical context, textuality, and cultural units. But Monelle makes other choices that put strict limits on how far such topical dynamism can be extended. For example, he frequently asserts that topics are defined by complete conventionality: a topical signifier evokes the same cultural unit for competent listeners wherever it occurs. This is not to say that Monelle fails to study the varieties of meaning and changes in meaning associated with topics as they develop but that his ultimate perspective is removed from such multiplicity. The diverging and partial reports of contemporaries are discussed but then sublated within a holistic perspective, and though the competency he ultimately describes is based on consensus, that consensus is often tacit.

It is in this area of monological versus dialogical views of competency that my own approach diverges most sharply from established topic theory and where I am influenced most strongly by approaches from popular music studies and ethnomusicology. In existing topic theory, historical meanings are generally treated at a high level of generality, one at which individual differences in interpretive practice are melded into a single, transpersonal competency. Hatten summarizes some of the key points: "I maintain that we still have access to *relatively objective* (by which I mean *intersubjectively defensible*) historical meanings. . . . I do not claim there must be one and only one musical meaning . . . but rather that we can propose plausible, contemporaneous meanings, at an appropriate level of generality" (2004, 6–7). But what constitutes the appropriate level of generality in any given case? The currently dominant preference among most topic theorists is to posit an extremely high level of generality, even universality. This choice makes sense relative to the field's linguistic and semiotic origins, where generalized competencies are taken as a given. But it also creates a tension with the particularistic and nuanced description of specific historical situations, also invited by topic theory. In the next section I go deeper into this question, making the case for viewing competencies as multiple and inherently dialogical.

Epistemic Authority and Multiple Competencies

When identifying topical moments in music, the question of musical versus extramusical meanings becomes important. The literature in this area is vast, and the issues are complex, but the core areas of discussion can be summarized fairly easily. Consider a song like "Yellow Submarine" by the Beatles (discussed in depth in chapter 2). There are certain clear meanings evoked. These meanings include a mood of playful nostalgia and childlike wonder and also specific references to other art forms (especially cinema) and other musical styles (especially British music hall and brass bands), which in turn suggest particular historical eras, character types, narratives, and so forth. Some of these meanings come from the lyrics, some are raised more by musical sounds, and many are connected to both. When speaking about extramusical meanings in a case like this, there are two questions being evoked at once. First, what are the meanings ultimately about? Second, what factors are needed to explain them? If the meanings are ultimately thought to be about things other than music (e.g., about a mood itself or about a particular historical era), then they would be characterized as extramusical. Similarly, if we think that the meanings can only be explained by discussing nonmusical features such as lyrics, or album art, or contextual knowledge about the artists or subculture, then the meanings would be extramusical in at least those senses. By contrast, when the music seems to be mostly evoking other music, or when the meanings are explained entirely as the effect of musical sounds with minimal or no other explanatory factors being evoked, then the meanings are claimed to be musical rather than extramusical.

The task of defining exactly what might be meant by musical meaning removed from other kinds of meanings is extremely difficult and tied up with a range of philosophical and practical issues. For our immediate purposes it is enough to note that the question has been contentious for centuries and remains so. More importantly, we need to notice that topic theory stands in an interesting relationship to this question, because in order to explain the operation of musical topics we need to keep both modes of signification in sight. If meanings or mechanisms were entirely musical, with no significant extramusical involvement, then they could not have the cultural scope necessary for topicality. On the other hand, if we want to understand specifically *musical* topicality, then we need to look at ways that music can uniquely express and develop a topic using resources that are not available in any other medium. Most existing work in topic theory displays a strong tendency to view meanings as intrinsic to structural features of the music.[4] Contextual features are not ignored altogether, but there is a pervasive sense that they are to be treated as framing and secondary rather than as constituting a core feature of the analysis. We can see such tendencies in some of the more subtle distinctions made by Monelle, for example, when he writes:

> The signified of a musical topic is a textural feature or cultural unit, not a feature of the real world (or even of the world physically contemporary with the signifier, since topics often refer to older cultural traditions). . . . Music does not signify society. It does not signify literature. And most of all, it does not signify "reality." Musical codes are proper to music, as the other codes are proper to their respective spheres. Codes signify each other, however; between literature and society, reading and life, there are the sorts of semiotic relations that permit each medium to make sense. (2000, 13, 19)

On one level this is entirely defensible. Semiotics is founded, in both its Saussurean and its Peircean versions, on the idea that a sign points to other signs and not directly to an outside world. Nonetheless, the vigor with which Monelle seeks to maintain boundaries between different signifying regimes and different spheres of practice is noteworthy, especially since topic theory draws special attention to the frequent blurring and renegotiation of such boundaries. The attempt to limit attention in such a way has important consequences on several levels. Melanie Lowe (2007) notes that many musical semioticians, in response to the perceived danger of a completely open and undisciplined interpretive practice, focus inquiry on meanings they believe to be highly intersubjective. This is a particularly subtle response to the question raised earlier: do we need to evoke contextual and extramusical factors to explain why particular pieces of music mean what they do? Few semioticians are so mystical as to deny the importance of context altogether, because it is clear that things only have meaning in accordance with readings made by actual people, and those people are influenced by a range of factors outside the music itself. So for a music semiotician who needs to acknowledge this fact but still wishes to maintain as much agency as possible for the music itself, the typical theoretical move has been to assert that the relevant cultural knowledge and reading habits are so widely distributed and so standardized that we can consider them as shared by all members of the relevant community. This makes them much more like a fixed element of the music itself. As a result, attention to social context is often minimal, since it is the broader context that introduces many of the factors that can cause meanings to become highly complex and less clearly intersubjective. While the theoretical benefits of this move have been impressive, it is not without drawbacks. As Lowe puts it: "To limit contextualization, while perhaps prudent, creates as many theoretical questions as practical answers it provides. For one, limiting context draws firm boundaries around the text as well, sustaining the problematic text/context binary.... Moreover, by constraining context and allowing a text to embrace only 'relevant' intertextual relationships, the main mechanism of intertextuality itself—context becoming text—can ultimately fail to operate.... Equally problematic is the question of who decides which 'some' things outside of the text 'ascend' to be part of the text" (2007, 76–77).

It is significant that Lowe makes these arguments from within the tradition of art music semiotics. Another theorist of Western art music who makes similar arguments is Mark Bonds (2008). Critiques of this sort have been commonly heard from popular music scholars, ethnomusicologists, and others since the 1970s and even earlier. But we can see that an awareness of the issue is also alive within art music semiotics itself, and so the debate should not be framed as one between subdisciplines of musicology so much as between different sets of research questions and priorities. That being said, it is still striking to note the contrast between the kind of text-centric approach dominant in topic theory, on the one hand, and the work of Tagg, on the other. Tagg (2000b, 112) fundamentally relies on two main methods for discovery and verification of his musemes: *intersubjective comparison* and *interobjective comparison*. Interobjective comparison is quite similar to what all music semioticians do: they compare features of a wide range of pieces in order to establish norms. But intersubjective comparison is more sociological, because it is based on tests in which listeners respond to various musical materials and report on their associated meanings. Similarly, it is commonplace for workers in popular music studies and ethnomusicology to test and develop their semiotic models against the judgments of those who produce and consume the music. I do not raise this point to suggest that such listener-based theories are inherently superior to a more interpreter-based approach but to highlight the differences of perspective and agenda that can come into play when a study like my own finds itself drawing from theories and methods found in both camps.

Aside from the social and even political reasons for adopting a more dialogic point of view, I believe there are technical and logical reasons for doing so as well. Consider *competency*, defined as the set of all knowledge and skills necessary to produce and interpret statements in a given sign system (language, music, visual art, etc.). Competency is one of the central concepts in topic theory and in musical semiotics more generally (for style competency, see Hatten 1994). It is often taken as a given that a semiotic study should assume all members of a particular interpretive community share the same competency and that this intersubjective competency is the proper object of study. Competency here does not refer to a level of achievement but to a specific set of basic, often tacit abilities and items of knowledge. The idea that such semiotic competency is singular and monological is rooted in the belief that it resembles linguistic competency as defined by Noam Chomsky. For Chomsky, linguistic competency could be treated as a human universal because it is a reasonable hypothesis that every human being, in order to be considered normally functional in his or her community, needs to have the ability to produce and understand language. The object of study in such a model is the ideal speaker in a homogeneous community. So at first it seems entirely reasonable that a theory of music-semiotic competency would be similarly universalist. But as early as the 1960s, doubts were raised with respect to the idea of a general musical competency and the question of how closely it can resemble linguistic competency. For example, even though ethnomusicologists such as John Blacking were excited by the parallel, they also noted that music competency is nowhere near as evenly distributed as is linguistic competency. You do not need musical competency in order to function in a socially normal fashion. Similarly, while productive and interpretive competencies are not generally separable in the case of language, they are very commonly separated in the case of music. It is not uncommon for a person to be very adept at interpreting music but almost completely unable to produce it.

With respect to topic theory more specifically, there are other important respects in which the analogy with linguistic competency fails to operate. First, the frame of reference for topic theory is not all music, or even all musics within a particular culture, but rather certain substyles. A kind of universality is asserted when topic theory treats a competency as being the same for all members of a community (and therefore does not take individual listener variations into account); but this is difficult to justify, in that true universality has already been set aside by choosing a fairly constrained object of study (usually a musical style that is quite specific in its historical and social scope). Second, while aesthetic and social value judgments are outside the scope of Chomskyan linguistic competency, they are an important part of music-semiotic competency. I therefore characterize the view of musical competency typical of existing topic theory as monological in two related senses, first, in the assumption that stylistic competency is singular and universally distributed within a culture, and, second, in the assumption that such competency includes consensus on certain judgments of aesthetic and social value. I have described a contradiction in the first sense of monologism, since it tries to be particular and universal at the same time. Especially when working with contemporary cultures, such a position is problematic not only for reasons of epistemological politics but also for simple methodological reasons. It is too difficult to pry apart the obviously intertwined stylistic and interpretive frameworks active in the present moment. If we accept this analysis of the first sense of monologism, then we have much less reason to sustain the second.

My suggestion is that when doing analysis on contemporary music-semiotic practices, including the study of emergent topics, it is necessary to recognize that the kind of competency involved is like competency in a single language or even a dialect and therefore not a universal competency. Furthermore, discursive struggles over authority can be productively understood as a clash of competing competencies. None of this requires denying the presence of widespread consensus and standardized meaning where they apply: we also need to attend to the fact that any such competency will include strategies for negotiating with and translating between competing competencies, such that over time the interaction between several of them may well produce competencies of greater generality and more widespread distribution. This drift toward monological authority, typical in many interpretive communities, is crucial to bear in mind. But widespread and standardized competencies need to be analyzed as a result of dynamic historical trajectories, rather than taken as a starting point for interpretation.

Topic theory in its present form was developed in order to study music at a significant historical remove, and its subsequent major developments and applications have similarly been focused on music of the nineteenth century and earlier. For music of such time periods it has proven methodologically effective to proceed as if the object of study is a single competency, universal to the culture in question. By contrast, the relatively contemporary nature of twentieth-century popular music provides an opportunity to examine the process of topic formation close up, not only because many of the participants are still alive but, more interestingly, because topics in this area may still be in the process of coalescing. With respect to the early years of psychedelia, it is clear that the relevant competencies were multiple and under negotiation. But it is also clear that processes of canonization and discursive control were beginning to emerge.

None of the foregoing should be taken as criticism of existing topic theory, let alone rejection. In the last analysis, I will often analyze psychedelic topicality as if it represented a widespread, intersubjectively shared set of signifying resources. But it is nonetheless important to note the difference of emphasis. Because I am studying topics still in the process of emerging, I will frequently need to treat competencies as multiple and to emphasize ways in which the meanings of a particular topic are in flux or under negotiation. That being said, many of the theoretical models and concepts from existing topic theory can be adapted to this sort of dynamic context with little alteration, as in the short examples that follow.

A Few Sample Extensions

In order to illustrate the kind of multiperspective analysis I have in mind and to show how existing models can be pressed into service, I would like to consider a few extensions to the idea of indexicality of content in a psychedelic context. All three of these examples are structured after Monelle's (2000, 18) diagramming of topical structure but with various extensions and alternative interpretations.

Table 1.1 gives two cases that conform closely to Monelle's model. Readings of this sort rely on correlations and interpretive habits that have been widely standardized. The example also shows, in structural terms, how the link between the signifier and the immediate object can be of various types, but the connection back to topical signification is always indexical. I will frequently have occasion to use the unaltered model of topicality in such ways. However, the same basic model can also be useful in showing how meanings can be contested or divergent. Table 1.2 offers two ways of reading the same signifier, both of them topical (based on indexicality of content) and both likely consistent with the interpretive priorities of different groups of listeners.

In both of these readings, raga rock is seen as a style with direct connections to a broader psychedelic agenda. It is valued as "authentically" psychedelic. The difference is in whether the particular token of the raga rock style offered by the Hollies is felt to be in turn an authentic part of the genre (an index) or rather a cynical copy (an icon). In this example, it is possible that two disagreeing interpreters would both self-identify as insiders to rock culture. Similar divergences, or even greater ones, could be possible between self-identified subcultural insiders and outsiders. For example, consider a disagreement over whether a loose improvisatory approach to music ultimately represents social and artistic progress or social and artistic degeneration. It is important to note that in some cases holders of the different views not only disagree but fundamentally perceive different situations. Their divergent competencies invite the construction of different symbolic worlds, which then struggle for discursive authority.

I would like to discuss one other application of the indexicality of content model having to do with the increasing historical reflexivity that had become important to psychedelic culture by the late 1970s. Signs that had previously signified contemporary struggles and abstract values maintained these associations, but with an added layer of signifying the 1960s themselves. In structural terms, what is being shown in table 1.3 is that the indexicality of content is arrived at through the mediation of an additional stage of signification. This sort of chain is characteristic of Peircean semiotics.

Table 1.1. Two straightforward examples of psychedelic indexicality of content

Musical item		Object/interpretant		Signification
Indian stylistic influences in the Beatles' "Love You To"	Index	Indian spirituality	Index	Consciousness expansion (as part of psychedelic philosophy)
Harmonic oscillation in the Grateful Dead's "Dark Star"	Icon	Suspended time sense	Index	Altered sensory and cognitive states (as part of psychedelic experience)

Table 1.2. Two different readings of the same topical sign

Musical item		Object/interpretant		Signification
Sitar-like guitar solo in the Hollies' "Bus Stop"	Heard as an index	Raga rock as a trend	Index	Psychedelia as a style with which the Hollies display solidarity
	Heard as an icon	Raga rock as a trend	Index	Psychedelia as a style that the Hollies are cynically exploiting

Table 1.3. Historical reflexivity in later psychedelia, analyzed as an instance of indexicality of content with one extra signifying stage

Musical item		Object / interpretant 1		Object / interpretant 2		Signification
Drum loop in the Chemical Brothers' "Setting Sun"	Icon	The Beatles' "Tomorrow Never Knows"	Symbol	The Chemical Brothers asserting their place in a lineage	Index	1960s psychedelic culture both reinscribed and seen as an object of solidarity and tribute

The Shifting Ground:
Topic, Prototopic, and Style Component

Throughout the following chapters, special interest is taken in the shifting line between topics and near topics, and I should clarify certain terms that arise in that connection. When I speak of a *topic* or *topicality* without qualification, I have in mind the sort of fully conventional topic described in this chapter. Such discussions will also involve the theoretical vocabulary of indexicality, along with the terminology I developed related to base styles, donor styles, and different kinds of cognate relationships. When I speak of *style components*, I have in mind features of the music that are like topics in that they are discrete formal types and are sometimes correlated with conventional meanings but are not yet fully topical. This is either because the meanings are too vague, because the style component is not typically associated with a particular meaning at all, or because there is not yet enough conventionalization of either the signifier or the signified. In most cases, when I emphasize a style component it is either because the component is important in supporting one or more existing topics or because it is a *prototopic*. By prototopic I mean a style component that was not fully topical in its original context but that later became topical through further conventionalization.[5] In many cases, when prototopics become fully topical in later time periods, their function is to connote the earlier period in which they were formed. Film scholars have commented on a similar process, where not only do new topics emerge over time but certain topics in film scores come to signify earlier film-scoring practices (Scheurer 2008, 37). So the two points of interest here are, first, the liminal state occupied by such components during the earlier period and, second, their later association with historical reflexivity and how that allows them to make the switch to topicality.

Overall, my analysis will often be focused on topicality as a process more than on fixed topics. And while making an inventory of topics will be part of the work, the emphasis will be on what Hatten would call a *topical field* or *mode*. By saying that psychedelia is a topical field or a topical mode, we are saying that it is a structure that subsumes many related topics and is an overarching force in shaping meanings, but at the same time it is flexible and open to many varying articulations (Hatten 1994, 290, 294–95; 2004, 53). My objectives are to create an inventory and survey of relevant topics but with attention to details that reveal the dialogic and dynamic development of psychedelic topicality. We will examine how earlier topics were taken up and adapted, charting the relationship between psychedelia and various base styles and donor styles, along with the nuances that made these styles sufficiently cognate to fulfill such roles. We will also pay special attention to the shifting boundary between topicality and other forms of signification, with a special interest in how new topics emerged and were subsequently transformed.

Notes

1. Much of the discussion that follows is in the middle ground between common and specialist knowledge. I will not burden the passage with citations, but for those interested to pursue this history in more detail, good starting points (and my most important sources) are Albanese (2007); Bernstein (2008); Boon (2002); Grunenberg and Harris (2005); Heelas (1996); Lattin (2010); Lee and Shlain (1985); Letcher (2007); McKay (1996); Perry (1984); Reynolds (1998); Saldanha (2007); and Stevens (1987).

2. Out of Charles Peirce's trichotomy of icon, index, and symbol, only iconicity does not have a necessary role to play in the definition of the topic. The symbol is implicated because topics are conventional, which by definition means that they are symbols. And in terms of their structure, topics must display indexicality of content. Iconicity, by contrast, can often be implicated in the structure of and motivation for a topic but is not necessary to topicality as such. Although the details of Peirce's semiotics evolved throughout the course of his life and an overview is difficult to obtain, readers interested in more detail might wish to consult volume 2 of *The Essential Peirce* (1998).

3. When citing Tagg throughout this book, I am referring to the PDF versions of his publications accessed at www.tagg.org in April 2013. Interested readers can look into the original publication dates, which are mostly not relevant to my argument, although it is important to know that Tagg was a pioneer in popular music semiotics and that his theoretical approach was first developed in the late 1970s.

4. This tendency in the literature is surveyed by Lowe (2007, 15–18).

5. My use of the term "prototopic" is similar to Monelle's (2000, 17) but also narrower. Monelle raises the concept in relation to the idea of complete standardization, such that a given signifier always and inevitably has the same topical association. By contrast, for the purposes of this book I am only using the term in reference to musical features that we know in retrospect have made the transition from being components of a given style to being topical signifiers of the time, place, and general cultural associations of that style. For example, sitars or sitar-like sounds in a mid-1960s rock context could not yet topically signify "the sixties," but we know they eventually came to do so. Interestingly, a feature can be simultaneously topical in one sense and prototopical in another. The sitar sounds in question would have been topical with respect to existing traditions of Orientalism but prototopical relative to still-emergent traditions of representing the 1960s as such.

2   Developments through 1966

The period 1965–66 was a decisive one for the development of psychedelia. In musical terms, by the end of 1965 the Yardbirds had begun to explore most of the components that would be essential to their later, more obviously psychedelic work. The Beatles had released *Rubber Soul*, the Kinks had released "See My Friends," and a great deal of sonic experimentation had taken place in genres such as instrumental surf rock. During 1966 the psychedelic implications of such material became fully explicit and much more widely distributed. Some key events include early releases by the 13th Floor Elevators, the Beatles' "Rain" and then *Revolver*, the Yardbirds' "Shapes of Things," the Byrds' "Eight Miles High," and early releases by Love. By the end of 1966 most of the key elements of psychedelic topicality had been at least broached, and as a result this chapter stands apart from others in the book in that it is the only one that attempts a full survey of what was taking place in a particular time period. By describing the psychedelic music of 1965 and 1966 in detail, we will be able to establish the main outlines of the whole genre and topical field. In order to present such a survey, I have treated key texts and artists in rapid succession, with an eye toward overview and synthesis. In later chapters the focus will shift toward pinpointing moments of transformation and hybridity relative to the overview presented here.

Since we're about to start looking at particular songs and artists, I should say something about lyrics. While lyrics are clearly important, I will discuss them only occasionally, when they have an especially interesting relationship to musical topicality. For example, some songs will be singled out for lyrical discussion because they exemplify a relationship between music and lyrics that is widespread and noteworthy. Also, lyrics will sometimes be discussed when they add significant layers of meaning different from what the music is suggesting. But for the most part, the focus of this book is on meanings created through musical sound. So in order to avoid making the presentation overly dense, I will not take the space to develop a detailed theory of lyrics or to discuss lyrics in every example.

The Yardbirds

There are many places we could start, but none better than the Yardbirds. As Ann Johnson and Mike Stax put it, "Aside from being among the first to incorporate Eastern elements into a rock sound, the Yardbirds also experimented with Gregorian chants, controlled feedback, and radical tempo and time signature changes. While not as commercially successful as the Beatles or the Rolling Stones, by the middle of 1966 the influence of the Yardbirds on the American garage band movement rivaled that of either of those bands" (2006, 414).

By starting with a detailed look at the Yardbirds, we will make an excellent start in opening up much of the topical and stylistic field of psychedelia in the mid-1960s. I will start with a topical reading of one well-known Yardbirds song, "Heart Full of Soul," and then move on to prominent topical elements in the Yardbirds more generally. The overarching point is that all of the topical moves and style components to be identified in the Yardbirds became widely adopted by other groups of the period. These were not necessarily all pioneered by the Yardbirds, but the Yardbirds were among their earliest and most influential exponents.

"Heart Full of Soul": Concise Song Form with Psychedelic Decoration

Psychedelic music could be broken up into subtypes in many different ways. In terms of historical development, one of the more important distinctions has to do with the difference between psychedelia as a decoration applied to conventional song forms and the slightly later appearance of new formal strategies cognate with psychedelia. According to Johnson and Stax, "Many bands incorporated elements that might be considered psychedelic while maintaining the basic structures of garage rock, i.e., two- to three-minute songs with conventional verse-chorus arrangements usually based around three to five chords. This psychedelic garage-rock hybrid was prevalent in the period 1966–67, with many examples predating the more improvisation-based sound popularized by San Francisco bands" (2006, 414).

The same phenomenon was identified by Steve Waksman during his discussion of the *Nuggets* anthology, an influential 1972 double album compilation of 1960s era garage bands: "This was clearly a species of psychedelia. . . . Yet this was not the more fully formed psychedelic rock of Jimi Hendrix or the Grateful Dead, in which the alteration of the mind was joined with an expansive form of instrumental improvisation. Guitar and organ solos abound on *Nuggets*, but rarely are they the true centerpiece of the songs. Instead, the songs on *Nuggets* stress a more holistic, group-oriented sort of musical freak-out that remains encased within the conventional three-minute pop and rock song format" (2009, 58).

In terms of the relationship between psychedelia and its base styles, we could say that in songs like these the base styles dominate the form, and psychedelic signifiers are used more as decoration. This arrangement foregrounds topical aspects of the psychedelic elements, because it highlights that they have been removed from their original contexts. It also encourages troping of topics by borrowing from diverse sources and highlighting contrasts between materials. However, even though songs like these can have striking topical moments, those moments do not tend to string together into more temporally elaborated topical structures such as narratives or expressive genres. The decorative role of topics in these songs tends to cause the conventional logic of the song to come to the foreground more strongly than subtle transformative or sequential relationships between topics. The main factor here is not just the foregrounding of formal convention, since other conventional forms such as sonata allegro are highly compatible with temporally elaborated meanings. But conventional pop song structure emphasizes the alternation of contrasting sections over continuous development and tends to use topics as a means of highlighting those sectional contrasts. None of this is to say that longer-range structures such as narrative and expressive genre are impossible or completely absent in such cases. But they do not seem to be invited very strongly.

There is also a similarity between this sort of pop song and certain aspects of the visual in psychedelic style. It is often striking how much textural and affective complexity can arise from clustering colorful and topical elements around a conventional song form. The result is not unlike the visual effect of a Persian carpet, mandala, or kaleidoscope, all of which were strongly influential on psychedelic design. These sorts of patterns resemble one another in being simple and bold on higher levels but almost fractal in their richness on smaller scales. Similarly, concise song forms with ornate psychedelic decoration are clean-lined and simple on a higher formal level but reveal considerable complexity on more local scales. By contrast, some of the more structurally protracted later psychedelic forms, such as the group improvisations and early space rock, have an almost opposite structure: quite simple on a moment-to-moment level but formally more extended.

"Heart Full of Soul": Sitar-Like Guitar and the Western Topic

Of all the topical features in "Heart Full of Soul" the one that has been most widely noted by commentators is the introductory guitar figure, in which Jeff Beck employs a fuzz effect to emulate an earlier demo version played on sitar. This figure serves not only as an introduction but also as a transitional figure and an outro (see music example 2.1). This figure is one example of a much broader trend circa 1966 toward guitar figures evocative of Indian motifs used either by themselves or in conjunction with other signifiers of Indian music. Other examples found in this chapter include "See My Friends" (music example 2.13), "Time Has Come Today" (music example 2.6), and "Eight Miles High" (music example 2.22). The significance of the Beatles in this connection is also widely rec-

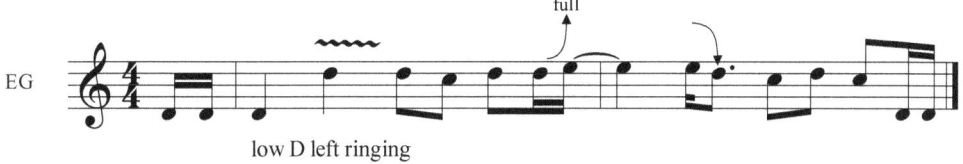

Music example 2.1. The Yardbirds, "Heart Full of Soul," introduction, guitar (0:00–0:04). Written by Graham Keith Gouldman. © Schubert Music Publishing obo Man-Ken Music Ltd.

ognized. Since the subject of Indian classical topicality is covered in depth a little later, we do not need to do more than note its presence here and to remark that "Heart Full of Soul" is frequently cited as a key text in starting the trend.

Given the formal functions of this figure, it stands apart from the rest of the song. This separateness is further underscored by harmony: the sitar-like figure is accompanied by minimal, drone-like harmony, while the rest of the song is harmonically more mobile. On the other hand, there are interesting tropes to be explored. For example, the Orientalist exoticism of the Indian topic resonates with the exoticism and romanticism of the song's western topical features.[1] By *western* I mean the set of features that resemble typical soundtrack elements in Hollywood westerns and western-themed records from the 1930s to the mid-1960s. Some aspects of western music in this sense had become fully standardized by the early 1960s, but at the same time the genre was still evolving, especially due to the influence of spaghetti westerns and the soundtracks of Ennio Morricone. In the case of "Heart Full of Soul," the acoustic guitar is one western signifier. Apart from its distinctive timbre, there is the galloping rhythm in the chorus. These features are admittedly mild in their effect but are strengthened by another western feature: the repeated use of rising background vocals—wordless and reverberant—at the end of phrases in the verses, evocative of a cowboy chorus.

"Heart Full of Soul" is not the only Yardbirds song to deploy the western topic. Another example is the introduction and main rhythm figure of "Still I'm Sad." In this case the western topic is established by the acoustic guitar rhythm, the overall sparse and repetitive texture, and the triangle, which has a dialogic ability to signify both Orientalist exoticism and conventions of suspenseful movie music, which in turn overlap specifically western conventions.

What does it mean to treat conventions of film and TV soundtracks as topical? As you will recall from chapter 1, a topic needs to be indexically founded in a particular historical or geographical context. Hunting horns, for example, can be part of the pastoral topic in part because they were at one time used in a pastoral context. But what about a situation where the original context is at least partly virtual, as with genre-specific soundtrack conventions? These sorts of signs often function topically, and indeed some of them will turn out to be among the most important psychedelic topics. In one sense this is not surprising. Genre soundtrack styles are highly conventionalized, widely imitated, and amenable to being made part of larger structures such as tropes or expressive genres. They also have historical connections to worlds and contexts, both to the real world (albeit often in a highly stylized and imaginative form) and to the virtual worlds of the genres themselves. This last point is the crucial one for topic theory. In order to treat such signifiers as topical, we need to expand our view of topicality far enough to accept the idea of an indexical connection to a virtual world and to allow this virtual indexicality a role in topic formation similar to the role played by real-world indexicality. Given how ubiquitous this sort of topic is in psychedelia—and indeed in all popular culture of the twentieth century—I will adopt this expanded version of topic theory as a working interpretive model.

Given the interaction between different media in popular culture, it is not surprising that we often find topics from prominent film genres being used in mid-1960s psychedelia. For the most part, the topics in question are associated with genres that were reaching their peak of popularity and topical conventionalization in the 1950s and early 1960s, especially spy films, historical epics, westerns, psychological thrillers, and science fiction. A proper history of any of these would require a substantial book of its own, so I am going to take it as given that certain features of such genres were widely recognized, take them as read, and go on to discuss how they were incorporated into a psychedelic context.

Western Spinoff: The Twang Guitar Continuum

One of the most potent signifiers of the western topic is not featured in "Heart Full of Soul": the *twang guitar*. While this signifier can be difficult to pin down with precision, it can clearly be heard in the records of Duane Eddy and many other guitarists of the period. It usually involves a relatively nondistorted electric guitar timbre articulated with a strong attack and a melody played on the lower strings. Reverberation is ubiquitous, and almost equally common were echo, amplifier tremolo, and use of the guitar's vibrato bar. This overall guitar sound is often called a Fender sound, but that is a bit misleading, since Gretsch guitars were equally specialized for the purpose, and many other brands were also used. What makes the twang guitar interesting in topical terms is that it not only signified the western topic but also was key to a linked set of genres that intersect one another in complex ways: western, spy, and surf. Because these were all signified by overlapping musical features and in turn resemble one another in some of their broader connotations, we could speak of a *twang guitar continuum*: a range of topics that coalesced only shortly before psychedelia and were cognate with it in a variety of ways. Philip Tagg and Bob Clarida point out that the twang guitar, often in a minor mode with a flat seventh, was a common factor between spaghetti western and Bond/spy scores in the late 1950s and early 1960s. I would add surf guitar to the list, with its sonic experimentation and general relationship to fun, escape, and exoticism: "[The twang guitar] probably owes some of its immediate success as a spy sound to its similarity with various pre-rock 'Viennese intrigue' sounds like Anton Karas's *Third Man* zither licks (1949). But in the 1962–64 period that produced *The Virginian* (1962), *Dr. No* (1963) and Leone's *A Fistful of Dollars* (1964), steely Fender guitar was well on its way to becoming an all-purpose excitement/adventure timbre" (Tagg and Clarida 2003, 367).

Tagg and Clarida note that this general complex in turn links up with Chuck Berry's distinctive guitar style and with 1950s rock and roll, extending the cluster of connotations to include teenage fun, cars, dancing, and the myth of a rock lifestyle. This created a potent and only partly coherent set of associations—notice especially the adult/teenage divide, as well as the fun/danger one—that was extensively explored by groups like the Shadows (Tagg and Clarida 2003, 368). From the perspective of psychedelia, it is important that many of these connota-

Music example 2.2. The 13th Floor Elevators, "Kingdom of Heaven," introduction, guitar (0:05–0:09). Written by R. P. St. John. © Penny Farthing Music obo Mainspring Watchworks.

tions involved "other times and other places" in addition to adventure and that the contexts in which these devices were used were gendered strongly male, emphasizing heroic images of the individual who stands alone (371, 378). In terms of psychedelia, this is all clearly cognate on multiple levels. At the same time, the case of psychedelia and the twang continuum illustrates the extent to which a new topical area will draw upon whatever is popular or widely distributed at the time of its emergence. These particular genres may well have become widespread in psychedelia even if they were not so cognate simply because of their ubiquity at the time that psychedelia was being formulated. Later, I will make essentially this same argument in connection with the large number of Latin music features to be found in early psychedelia.

There were a few other twang continuum features that became prominent in mid-1960s electric guitar playing and that are displayed by several examples in this chapter. As already noted, one typical component is the use of modes other than the major or raised-seventh minor to convey various degrees of exoticism. Apart from providing melodic material, such pitch choices also led to striking dissonances in the harmonic language (see, e.g., the use of the flat fifth in music example 2.2 and the ninth in music example 2.4). This tendency to highlight unresolved dissonances was often reinforced by a texture of sparse, ringing chords.

A genre such as surf incorporates many distinct signifiers that can, on their own, evoke the topic. But sometimes a musical passage will fall within the topic not because of any single feature but because of how features that in themselves might be ambiguous can collectively create a more focused impression. Consider music example 2.3. None of the individual instruments definitively present a surf topic, but at the same time they are all compatible with one: the drums are driving yet mechanically simplistic, the bass plays a drone with occasional dramatic upward leaps, the guitar riff emphasizes scalar movement over a motoric drone note, and the lead guitar winds through a syncopated melody that gradually explores the pitch space in a stepwise and eventually chromatic manner. Collectively, this illustrates that a certain kind of motoric approach to the rhythm section was typical of the surf topic.[2]

In the broader history of rock style, these genres are also important because they were sites of sonic experimentation in guitar playing in terms of both technique and early signal processing. We have already noted the use of reverberation, tremolo, and vibrato. Other modulations such as volume swells and, in later

Music example 2.3. The 13th Floor Elevators, "Roller Coaster," introduction (excerpt) (0:19–0:27). Written by Tommy Hall, Roky Erickson. © Charly Publishing Ltd. obo Tapier Music.

Music example 2.4. The Yardbirds, "Still I'm Sad," transition (0:36–0:48). Written by Paul Samwell-Smith and Jim McCarty. © EMI April Music Inc. obo B. Feldman & Co. Ltd. / Niji Music / Charly International (APS).

periods, stereo panning were also common. Music example 2.4 shows a transition from a Yardbirds song that could not be narrowly linked to any individual twang guitar topic but that draws on many features typical of the twang continuum overall to evoke a mysterious, liminal mood clearly cognate with psychedelia.

"Heart Full of Soul": The Fuzz Guitar Continuum

With the twang guitar continuum, we named a range of preexisting significations and how they map onto a fairly unified set of timbres, harmonic and melodic resources, and playing techniques. We can also speak of a fuzz guitar continuum, but this is a slightly different sort of grouping. Fuzz was a new effect in the early 1960s and did not have as many preexisting connotations.[3] Fuzz certainly can be discussed in terms of how it links with earlier signifiers and meanings, for example, as one among many techniques for using dissonance and noisy timbres to signify chaos, disorder, and fear. But these connotations had not cohered into full-blown topics to the same extent as we saw with certain twang guitar examples. Fuzz at this time corresponded not to a continuum of topical meanings but rather to a range of textural options. In this connection, Johnson and Stax (2006, 416) have remarked that certain new technological effects available to garage bands—especially fuzz, reverb, tremolo/vibrato, and the Echoplex—became important early signifiers of psychedelia. On one level we have seen how, circa 1966, several of these would already function topically in evoking slightly earlier topics such as surf, western, and spy. The component we are adding at this point is to draw attention to a second topical process, whereby the specific manner in which these elements were combined by psychedelic bands amounted to a new style that would later become a topic of psychedelia.

Fuzz was used in at least three distinct ways in the mid-1960s. First, it could provide a new timbre for musical lines that were not otherwise different from what might have been played without fuzz. Second, due to the way fuzz at more extreme settings can increase the sustain of the guitar, it could allow for a style of playing that explored long-held notes and complex ornamentation. Finally, fuzz at extreme settings could be a source of very noisy sounds and textures outside of anything that would have been considered conventionally musical at the time. In the case of "Heart Full of Soul," fuzz is most relevant in the introductory guitar figure and in the guitar solo. In both cases, the application is borderline between the first and second types. The style of guitar playing is not radically different from what might have been done with a different timbre, but at the same time subtle inflections of vibrato and pitch bending are crucial to these passages and are enhanced by the fuzz effect. These enhanced ornamental resources also allow for the sitar-like qualities of the guitar to be foregrounded.

A different Yardbirds song, "Shapes of Things," shows the full range of fuzz possibilities. There are power chords in the rhythm guitar that are enhanced by the fuzz but not dependent on it. The lead guitar is extremely rich in pitch bends, vibrato, and left-hand articulations that would not translate to nearly this degree without the extra gain and sustain offered by the fuzz. As with "Shapes of Things," this helps the guitar evoke topics of exoticism. Finally, the fuzz is part of a set of arranging techniques that create a densely noisy environment. Apart from fuzz, these techniques include the use of three electric guitars at once (two playing lead) and a very dense drumming style with emphasis on the high end of the frequency spectrum (snare drum in motor sixteenths and constant use of the crash cymbal). Another Yardbirds song that simultaneously explores different points on the fuzz continuum, to be discussed shortly, is "Happenings Ten Years Time Ago" (music examples 2.8–2.11).

This concludes our look at topical elements in "Heart Full of Soul." The song has given us a good start at identifying important elements of mid-1960s psychedelic topicality, and we can now move on to look at other important elements of topicality in the Yardbirds.

The Yardbirds: Gregorian Chant

Textures resembling Gregorian chant are common in mid-1960s psychedelia and were especially associated with the Yardbirds. One of the more striking examples is "Turn into Earth," and others include "See My Friends" by the Kinks (music examples 2.13–2.15), "Happenings Ten Years Time Ago" by the Yardbirds (music example 2.9), and "Eight Miles High" by the Byrds (music example 2.23, with interesting complications to be discussed later). The Gregorian signifier is variable, but typical features include medium-register voices in unison intoning a largely stepwise or static melody with a strongly modal flavor. Heavy reverberation is often present, and the voices are sometimes singing wordlessly. The voices are usually male, but female voices can also evoke a Gregorian topic. In many cases, it is likely that the relevant topical signified is a general medieval character rather than monastic or liturgical contexts in particular. But it is still useful to provide a more specific topical label in order to help distinguish this particular signifier from others related to the medieval topic and also because in some instances the specifically liturgical or monastic reading may be appropriate.

The cognate nature of Gregorian chant relative to psychedelia in terms of both formal affect and intent is clear. But one of the most important nuances is the overlap between Gregorian signifiers and those of folk melodies. This similarity on the level of the signifier is reinforced by parallels in the signifieds of Gregorian and folk topics: mysticism, retreat from modern urban life, collective values, the archaic and ancient. Another overlap worth noting is the one between Gregorian chant and the male chorus as sometimes used in westerns, which in turn opens up onto other cognate areas. For example, Mervyn Cooke (2008, 122), following Christopher Palmer, notes that the male chorus in *Gunfight at the OK Corral* suggests a parallel with the Greek chorus and links the western mythos with the tradition of Greek tragedy. Finally, such vocal textures could connote the "classical" in the sense of a historicized European style associated with prestige, tradition, and institutionalized power. As with the twang guitar, what we have here is a loosely coherent set of signifiers coupled in turn to a widely overlapping set of topics. The affinities are clear, but the variations and nuances are considerable and need to be evaluated on a case-by-case basis.

The Yardbirds: Echo and Reverberation

Some production techniques and timbral effects were new in the mid-1960s and eventually became topics of psychedelia. But some have longer histories and were already topical by the time they were first used by psychedelic artists. One I would like to discuss in detail is reverberation, but I will also address echo insofar as the two are closely related.[4] The use of reverberation in psychedelic recordings is too ubiquitous to require specific examples, and this ubiquity means that it is frequently not best read in topical terms. But in some cases the use of reverberation is extreme enough to be noteworthy, especially when it combines with other topical signifiers (as often happens with the Gregorian and western topics, for example). Peter Doyle has studied how reverberation and echo came to be significant in popular music recording of the twentieth century, and his description shows that the meanings of reverb by the late 1950s were both deeply engrained and cognate with psychedelia:

> Echo and reverberation made it seem as though the music was coming from a somewhere—from inside an enclosed architectural or natural space or "out of" a specific geographical location—and this "somewhere" was often semiotically highly volatile. On reflection it became clear that with the addition of echo and reverb, "place" and "space" had become part of the musical equation.... The spaces ranged from the decidedly concrete to the mythic and/or purely imaginary. Furthermore, some of these sonic spatialities were "pictorial," somehow referring me back to my own learned preconceptions of, say, the American West or the beach at Waikiki.... At other times this musico-sonic spatiality was less explicitly pictorial, even tending towards the hallucinatory, in some way evoking in me a sense of strangeness or disquiet. Yet another type of less pictorial spatiality was to be found in, say, the music of Bo Diddley, Little Walter, or early Elvis Presley recordings, in which everything seems to be vibrating, echoing, reverberating in and out of control, manic, "atomic" kinesis, suggesting movement in space but without any special reference to specific real-world spaces or places. (2005, 5–6)

The importance of spatiality here is twofold. First, it reinforces topics such as the western and the Gregorian that work partly by evoking particular spaces. Also, the construction of virtual spatiality has close ties to psychedelia understood as an exploration of fantastical, otherworldly places. While this takes us into aesthetic and psychological territory beyond the scope of this book, I have written about it elsewhere (Echard 2011). But as Doyle points out, the meanings of reverberation are complex, and he goes on to note other salient features. One has to do with the supernatural and the subconscious: "By the late 1940s performers as unalike as pop singer Vaughn Monroe and blues singer John Lee Hooker were using echo and reverb, albeit in different ways, to signify uncanny presences. Presumably audiences readily understood what was intended by the effect. It is difficult to account for this relatively sudden appearance without reference to the prior semiotic listener training groundwork done by Hollywood movies, in which these same acoustic effects are explicitly linked to stories of terror and the supernatural, and moments of mystical transformations" (Doyle 2005, 8).

Finally, Doyle points out how reverberation came to be associated with certain sorts of architecture and concepts of authority, whether divine or secular: "The temples, mausoleums, palaces, ziggurats, and legislatures of antiquity were highly reverberant spaces, and this quality provides specific acoustic 'framing' of utterances made within them.... It is more than likely that the 'aura' of reverberation in the ancient world was a quality much associated with the pronouncement from on high. . . . There is an integral and enduring connection between what might be called 'reverberancy' and the sacred" (2005, 42–43).

In topical terms, this association of reverberation with natural and architectural spaces is not primarily important because reverberation can be used to simulate real-world environments, although it is often used that way. More interestingly, reverberation in a studio context can be applied differently to different elements of the mix, creating virtual spaces that combine and transform in ways that would be impossible in the real world, even shifting between implications of "inner" and "outer" space. It is striking that the same production technique can be ubiquitous and relatively prosaic—simply a way to provide a bit of extra body and coherence to the sound of a recording—and also one of the richest sources of topical reference during this time period.

The Yardbirds: The Regularly Spaced Chords Texture

Up to this point we have discussed elements that were either clearly topics or were clearly nontopical style components. But there are other aspects of mid-1960s psychedelic style that present more ambiguous cases. One of these I have called the *regularly spaced chords texture*, and while its coherence and conventionality are marginal on the level of both the signifier and the signified, that is precisely what makes it interesting. Textures of this kind arose sufficiently frequently in my sample, and with sufficient similarity of affect and formal function, that I consistently noted them as significant.[5] They have an affinity with certain topics, and especially with the epic topic (soon to be discussed), but without the degree of explicitness or conventionality necessary for full topicality. What I ultimately want to suggest is that the regularly spaced chords texture, as frequently used in mid-1960s psychedelia, is perhaps an example of a topic that began to develop but never quite fully cohered. Or, more simply, it is instructive as an example of the middle ground between general connotation and topicality in the full sense.

In speaking of a regularly spaced chords texture, what I have in mind are cases where one or more instruments play loud, sustained single chords or notes and repeat them with a frequency intermediate between metrical and formal timespans, often at the level of the half-measure or the measure. This is often combined with repeated, or at least very similar, fill figures in other instruments. For instance, in music example 2.5 the regular chords are provided by the guitar, bass, snare, kick drum, and cymbals. The fills are provided by the toms and snare. In music example 2.6 the relevant texture begins in measure 5, with the regular chords provided by the second guitar, bass drum, and snare and the fills provided by the lead guitar and toms. Other examples transcribed in this chapter include Love's "Seven & Seven Is" (music example 2.28) and "Happenings Ten Years Time Ago" (especially music example 2.9, but other examples from that song as well). The clearest examples of this texture usually appear in introductions and transitions, and the association of this texture with particular formal roles helps lend coherence to its semiotic function.

Music example 2.5. The Yardbirds, "Evil Hearted You," introduction (0:01–0:09). Written by Graham Keith Gouldman. © Schubert Music Publishing obo Man-Ken Music Ltd.

This description of the signifier is quite schematic, but I believe that the texture is distinctive and common enough to deserve categorization. Even more important, there is some coherence on the level of the signified in that this device is often associated with an overall mood that could be characterized as epic or portentous. Although these affective and formal consistencies are not perfect, they are frequent enough to suggest a stylistic device that is at least partially formalized. It becomes topical in flavor through one additional factor; such a texture is quite common in orchestral and soundtrack music of an epic nature, especially in the genre of epic films.

Cooke describes topical features of the 1950s era epic film as follows: "expansive overture and entr'acte, regal fanfares, delicate writing for flute and harp serving as 'ancient' diegetic music, mystic triads, . . . exotically colourful dance music, and a heroic and exuberant manner of march-like brass writing" (2008, 193). We can also draw here on Stephen Meyer, who outlines some diegetic music types typically found in postwar epic films: "bacchanalian dances, religious ceremonies, trumpet fanfares, and the like" (2015, 7). Regarding more general topics and moods typical of the genre, Meyer emphasizes the religious, the martial, the pastoral, and various aspects of gender and sexuality (forbidden eroticism at once teased and disavowed, and the pairing of different female stereotypes). The most obvious point of contact between these epic topical signifiers and the regularly spaced chords texture comes in the fanfares and marches, where such a texture is quite common. These links are tenuous in many cases but are strengthened because psychedelic music often draws from the epic topic more generally. The similarity between how these topics cluster in epic film soundtracks and in psychedelia could strengthen the tendency to hear the regularly spaced chords texture, in itself fairly indeterminate, as somehow epic or portentous. Finally, this texture could signify the cinematic in general.

Why was the epic topic attractive in a psychedelic context? One obvious area of overlap is with Orientalism and exoticism more generally. Also, the same af-

Music example 2.6. The Chambers Brothers, "Time Has Come Today," introduction and beginning of first verse (0:00–0:17). Written by William Chambers and Joseph Chambers. © Universal Music-Careers.

fect of adventure and excitement that we saw in spy and western topics would apply here. Indeed, beyond the affective links there are musical ones as well. Meyer discusses many similarities between biblical epic films and the western—themes of power and freedom, landscape, horses, heroism—and points out that these existed in the music as well: "Heroic Jews, of course, have no special claim to rising fifths, turning arabesques, or the Dorian mode" (2015, 135). Finally, Meyer makes another point that raises less obvious but equally important links between the epic topic and psychedelia: "Long and complex underscoring, it can be argued, is most important precisely in those cinematic genres (fantasy, science fiction, historical epic) in which the gap between everyday life and the film's diegetic world is the greatest. In this sense, the scores to the biblical epics helped to bridge the gap between postwar America and the reimagined fantasy of ancient Rome, Israel, or Egypt. But the biblical epic was also beset by other, more generically specific contradictions: between materiality and transcendence; or between the glorification of freedom and the (implicit) celebration of power and control" (2015, 7).

Many of these same themes were also important in psychedelia, and this resonance is likely an important reason why we will find epic topics in several different kinds of psychedelic music.

The Yardbirds: Harmonic Devices

That completes our survey of topical elements in the Yardbirds. But aside from fully formed topics, there are other style components that need to be highlighted. Some of these are important because they supported particular topics and some because they are prototopics. One such area is harmonic language. Certain topics involve harmonic devices as fundamental. Perhaps most obvious is the connection between drone-like harmonies and the Orientalist Indian topic. Also, there are harmonic practices that could be seen as cognate with psychedelia in a general way but that are too widely distributed to be read as psychedelic in any exclusive sense. For example, there was in the mid- to late 1960s a proliferation of chord progressions that do not follow a common-practice teleology and instead are based on processes such as prolonged oscillations, ternary root relationships, and scalar root movements, often in modes that avoid or lack a strong dominant function.[6] This sort of tendency is cognate with psychedelia insofar as it can help create a focus on the present moment.

The use of what could be called *strong color effects* is another harmonic technique of special importance to early psychedelia. These are chords that have some striking effect in a local way but do not confuse the prevailing tonal organization. One example was already mentioned in connection with the twang guitar continuum and its use of an alteration such as the flat fifth or added ninth (see music examples 2.2 and 2.4). Along similar lines, Walter Everett (1999, 48–49) identifies the "jarringly frozen" $I^{\sharp 9}_7$ sonority in the Beatles' "Taxman" as a feature that has a psychedelic aspect. At the same time, this chord voicing can connote blues or jazz and was also important in the personal idiolect of Jimi Hendrix. These sorts of altered-chord color effects are highly local, although the effect can be modified or enhanced by the progression as a whole. Other color effects are more context dependent, for example, modal mixture and major-minor alternation. One good example of major-minor alternation is in the introduction to "For Your Love," where the third chord is A major and immediately reverts in the next measure to A minor. A second example can be seen in Donovan's "Guinevere" (music example 2.24).

Finally, although it is more rare than might be thought, outright tonal ambiguity also sometimes played a role, especially in songs by the Beatles. In some cases, the borderline between modal mixture and tonal ambiguity can be obscure. Consider another example from the Beatles as described by Everett: "'Doctor Robert' prescribes two contrasting tonal areas without organic connections between them and thus uses structural pitch relationships to contrast the normal, workaday world portrayed by dull motives in A major with a supercharged, blissful state in B. Such irregular tonal contrasts will be exercised more often in the psychedelic songs of 1967" (1999, 45–46).

All of these harmonic devices, taken together, play an important role in supporting preexisting topics, creating a pool of affective resources cognate with psychedelia and in later periods providing components of new psychedelic topics.

The Yardbirds: The Structural Pause

Another style component that was used to great effect by the Yardbirds is what I call the *structural pause*. By this I mean a moment where the music suddenly stops and there is an extended silence, often after a multimeasure buildup and often with a strongly contrasting section following. One clear example is "For Your Love" (at 0:57). After a fairly continuous textural buildup through the introduction, first verse, and first chorus everything abruptly comes to a stop; then, after a brief silence, there is a change of tempo and a variation on the chorus different enough to count as new thematic material. Another good example is "Seven & Seven Is" (at 1:55). The second instrumental builds to a peak of volume and density, at which point there is an explosion, a brief silence, and a shift to a completely different texture.

A similar technique is sometimes used to mark or intensify a slightly less sharp formal division, such as a phrase boundary or a change of intensity within a section. One example is the pause and explosive interjection in the A section of the Electric Prunes' "I Had Too Much to Dream Last Night" (music example 2.7, mm. 4–5 and 12–19). And finally, there is at least one mildly topical subcase of the structural pause: in Donovan's "Guinevere" (music example 2.24) and also in "Lady Jane" by the Rolling Stones, structural pauses are used in a way that strongly evokes chorale form, which in turn resonates with the self-consciously archaic, reflective mood of these songs.

As is the case with many style components, the structural pause shades off into a broader family of related devices: a range of effects that are hard to differentiate but that share in common some feeling of the musical texture dissolv-

Music example 2.7. The Electric Prunes, "I Had Too Much to Dream Last Night," from middle of A section (0:32–0:57). Words and Music by Annette Tucker and Nancie Mantz. © 1966 Sony / ATV Acuff Rose Music. Copyright Renewed. This arrangement © 2015 Sony / ATV Acuff Rose Music. All Rights Administered by Sony / ATV Music Publishing LLC, 424 Church Street, Suite 1200, Nashville, TN 37219. International Copyright Secured All Rights Reserved. Reprinted by permission of Hal Leonard Corporation.

ing or being taken apart piece by piece. Some of these—such as stop-time and, in the eventual case of electronic dance music, the breakdown—have already been given names by practitioners and theorists and will be discussed where they arise. But the larger point is that various substyles of psychedelia employ a spectrum of devices for introducing textural disjunctions and diversions.

"Happenings Ten Years Time Ago": Psychosis

Before moving on from the Yardbirds, I want to look in some detail at their relationship to affects of noise and chaos, first in connection with a single song and then through a discussion of the rave-up as a formal strategy. One thing that made the Yardbirds stand out was their ability, on the one hand, to develop the sorts of subtle stylistic and formal techniques discussed above and, on the other hand, to unleash extended passages that for the time came across as near chaotic in their intensity and in their suspension of conventional song form. These moments were not truly chaotic but rather represented a different set of codes that would over time become important topics in their own right. The Yardbirds made a major contribution in helping develop techniques for harnessing noise and signifiers of chaos as part of popular music style.[7] We can link this to a general distinction that has been made between two families of psychedelic songs in the 1960s:

> The musical and technological innovations of the late garage era resulted in the production of two types of psychedelic song. One of these types employs the available technology to create songs emphasizing the mystical and mind-expanding potential of psychedelic experience. This tradition was continued in the more popular psychedelic music of 1968 and beyond. The other type of song employs the available technology to suggest that the psychedelic experience is one of psychosis. This type of song saw less commercial success at the time, though it has received much attention from collectors and garage fans since the 1960s. (Johnson and Stax 2006, 411)

This sort of dichotomy can exist within the work of a single artist and sometimes within a single song. Perhaps the most significant catalyst in this area was the Yardbirds' innovation of the rave-up as a standardized format for inserting chaotic, frantic, perhaps even psychotic affect into a song form. But before discussing the rave-up, I would like to look at a song that features similar devices but no rave-up as such: "Happenings Ten Years Time Ago." The first noteworthy feature of this song is the opening riff, which stands out for its nearly heavy-metal quality based on distorted punctuating chords, a repeated descending chromatic line, and drums with strong accents on every beat (music example 2.8). Then, in a striking trope, the B section introduces tones of the ritualistic, epic, and ancient by using the Gregorian topic and the regularly spaced chords texture (music example 2.9).

"Happenings Ten Years Time Ago" also provides an example of what I call the *siren trill*. This device underscores the ominous, tense mood and is extremely common in psychedelic arrangements of the period. There are many variants, but I use the term for passages where there is an extended alternation between two pitches, often a major or minor second apart, standing out from the rest of the texture and typically imposing an affect of tension or suspense. Siren trills are especially common in transitional passages, as in music example 2.10, where one is present in the bass and strongly suggested in the vocals.

Music example 2.8. The Yardbirds, "Happenings Ten Years Time Ago," introduction, second part, rhythm section (0:08–0:12). Words and Music by Jeff Beck, Jimmy Page, Keith Relf, and Jim McCarty. © 1966 B. Feldman & Co. trading as Yardbirds Music Co. Copyright Renewed. This arrangement © 2015 B. Feldman & Co. trading as Yardbirds Music Co. All Rights Administered by Sony / ATV Music Publishing LLC, 424 Church Street, Suite 1200, Nashville, TN 37219. International Copyright Secured All Rights Reserved. Reprinted by permission of Hal Leonard Corporation.

Music example 2.9. The Yardbirds, "Happenings Ten Years Time Ago," B section (beginning) (0:30–0:38). Words and Music by Jeff Beck, Jimmy Page, Keith Relf, and Jim McCarty. © 1966 B. Feldman & Co. trading as Yardbirds Music Co. Copyright Renewed. This arrangement © 2015 B. Feldman & Co. trading as Yardbirds Music Co. All Rights Administered by Sony / ATV Music Publishing LLC, 424 Church Street, Suite 1200, Nashville, TN 37219. International Copyright Secured All Rights Reserved. Reprinted by permission of Hal Leonard Corporation.

Music example 2.10. The Yardbirds, "Happenings Ten Years Time Ago," C section (beginning) (0:42–0:46). Words and Music by Jeff Beck, Jimmy Page, Keith Relf, and Jim McCarty. © 1966 B. Feldman & Co. trading as Yardbirds Music Co. Copyright Renewed. This arrangement © 2015 B. Feldman & Co. trading as Yardbirds Music Co. All Rights Administered by Sony / ATV Music Publishing LLC, 424 Church Street, Suite 1200, Nashville, TN 37219. International Copyright Secured All Rights Reserved. Reprinted by permission of Hal Leonard Corporation.

As with components such as the structural pause or the regularly spaced chords texture, it is not always easy to tell whether a particular oscillating figure should be singled out as a siren trill. Nonetheless, even with a conservative selection of examples, siren trills are ubiquitous. They sometimes appear as a bass figure or riff, for example, in "Paint It, Black" (music example 2.17) and "I Had Too Much to Dream Last Night" (music example 2.7). They are also common as underlying figures in passages of instability or transition, sometimes in a way that is seamlessly integrated with the texture (as with music example 2.10), and sometimes in a more decorative or call-and-response capacity (as in "Section 43" by Country Joe and the Fish, music example 2.36). Sometimes the iconic evocation of a siren seems intended literally, for example, at the beginning of the instrumental in "Happenings Ten Years Time Ago" (music example 2.11). Although the oscillation in siren trills is generally fairly slow, the word "trill" draws attention to the general affective kinship between siren trills and other foregrounded and drawn-out trills, like those used frequently by Jimi Hendrix or the one in Love's "Stephanie Knows Who" during the buildup to the solo (music example 2.31).

The final thing to note about "Happenings Ten Years Time Ago" is the closing instrumental, which intensifies the chaotic, sinister tone of the song in a number

Music example 2.11. The Yardbirds, "Happenings Ten Years Time Ago," instrumental (beginning) (1:34–1:54). Words and Music by Jeff Beck, Jimmy Page, Keith Relf, and Jim McCarty. © 1966 B. Feldman & Co. trading as Yardbirds Music Co. Copyright Renewed. This arrangement © 2015 B. Feldman & Co. trading as Yardbirds Music Co. All Rights Administered by Sony / ATV Music Publishing LLC, 424 Church Street, Suite 1200, Nashville, TN 37219. International Copyright Secured All Rights Reserved. Reprinted by permission of Hal Leonard Corporation.

of ways, including a regularly spaced chords texture, a siren trill, a bass line that begins with a drone and then suggests repeated figures, harmonically static dissonant guitar accents, and a claustrophobic texture created by the layering of two lead guitars and urgent megaphone voices. Overall, this instrumental provides the song with something like a narrative arc, beginning with a foreboding tension (the introductory riff), which then alternates with a more reflective and mystical yet still suspenseful texture, and ultimately opens out into a chaotic panorama. The end result is that the noisy, chaos-associated elements are allowed to display their full affect while at the same time being incorporated into a clear design.

The Yardbirds: The Rave-Up

The rave-up was a signature device of the Yardbirds and has been described extensively in print (see, e.g., Johnson and Stax 2006, 415; Waksman 2009, 62). Individual components will be discussed below, but very generally the term describes a passage inserted into a conventional song form, generally initiated by suspension of the previous texture, a switch to double time in the drums, and a drone bass. Then, most typically, one or two guitars and harmonica will enter and play overlapping riffs and solos, gradually building to a peak of density and volume. After a dramatic climax, there is a return to conventional song form. The rave-up is like a detour, an opening onto gradually increasing excitement and intensity that stands apart from the song form as such but at the same time intensifies it. All of the relevant features are included in the rave-up from the Yardbirds' "I'm a Man" (music example 2.12). In many ways the rave-up is a summary of psychedelic instrumental techniques slightly before the fact, and it went on to become an important topic of psychedelia.

The rave-up was one of the earliest ways of inserting long instrumental passages into a rock song. And by creating an extended digression from the surrounding form during which intensity is emphasized over structure, it strongly suggests metaphors of travel or exploration. The rave-up functions by taking riffs, melodic motifs, and other materials from a rhythm-and-blues context and redeploying them as the basis for a texture of striking novelty. These sorts of materials are well suited to form the basis for extended improvisation and are in that respect cognate by formal affect with psychedelia. But the exact manner in which they are treated in the rave-up—extremely repetitious, motoric, and noisy—means that their original topical associations are strongly attenuated. The rave-up in this sense shows how forms can become cognate by context. Bands that originally mastered these materials in a rhythm-and-blues application evolved into psychedelic bands through the process of developing forms like the rave-up, such that possible contradictions or tensions in meaning are resolved by virtue of new and old applications of the materials coexisting within the same song, artist, scene, and so forth.

Taking a long view of psychedelic style, one of the most important features of the rave-up is its extreme repetitiveness. Riffs and motifs are reiterated without

Above and facing: Music example 2.12. The Yardbirds, "I'm a Man," rave-up (1:28–2:18). Words and Music by Ellas McDaniel. © 1955 Arc Music Corporation. Copyright renewed. This arrangement © 2015 Arc Music Corporation. All Rights Administered by BMG Rights Management (US) LLC. All Rights Reserved. Used by Permission. Reprinted by permission of Hal Leonard Corporation.

being relegated to an accompanying role, harmony is reduced to a drone, and rhythm is strongly motoric. This kind of *loopiness* became a key feature in many varieties of psychedelia. As Simon Reynolds and Joy Press note, one thing most psychedelic music shares "is a belief that minimal-is-maximal; that simple patterns, repeated, can generate both complexity and immensity" (1995, 181–82). Similarly, when discussing the Beatles' "She Said, She Said" Everett makes a point about the repetitive chord progression that can apply much more generally: it is a "type of repetition that may be related to the timeless quality of both an LSD trip and the mantra-based meditation in Indian practice" (1999, 66). The rave-up is a key site where repetition, as it evolved in rhythm-and-blues dance contexts, is given slight adjustments such that it starts to develop psychedelic aspects.

Music example 2.12 illustrates many of the relevant musical features of a rave-up. The drone bass is evident at the outset. The predominance of motor rhythm is also clear. It can be seen in the hi-hat at the very start and nearly throughout. The drums become more straightforwardly motoric around measure 22, as do the bass and electric guitar in measure 23. One common feature in the rave-up is for the lead instruments to gradually rise in pitch. This can be seen in the general guitar profile from measures 14–22 and again in the following muted passage. It is also evident in the harmonica around measures 14–17, although less dramatically. Extended rises in pitch are an obvious way to build excitement and will also show up in many psychedelic soul and funk examples. This links in a general way to the tendency in psychedelic styles toward long shapes in many parameters (e.g., long dynamic changes), which we will see in several later examples.

Maybe the most striking general feature of the rave-up is how it harnesses and intensifies noise, gradually moving through increasing levels of intensity to a climax. In music example 2.12 this is shown clearly by the hi-hat, which over the course of many measures gradually includes more and more half-open and then fully open strikes along with more accents—a fairly continuous transformation from the beginning through measure 29. The extended muted guitar passage is another example: in it, the guitar transitions from a melodic instrument to a percussive one (mm. 23–38). In fact, all of the instruments tend to move in the direction of noise and toward extended performance techniques. This recalls a general point made by Paul Hegarty, who argues that "surplus sound is a key characteristic of electrified music" (2007, 60). The rave-up is a paradigm case of difficult-to-control surplus sound being foregrounded and allowed to make up a space parallel to conventional musicality: it is divergent from it yet in a symbiotic relationship with it.

This brings us to the close of our Yardbirds discussion. We have seen how within one early psychedelic idiolect there was a range of reference made to established topics (e.g., Indian, Gregorian, western, spy, surf, epic films, classical), some of which existed in families of closely related variants (as in the twang guitar continuum). The signifiers are varied, ranging from conventional melodic, rhythmic, and harmonic devices to production techniques such as reverberation. And in addition to this extensive vocabulary of preexisting topics we have seen many style components that would develop into topics of psychedelia, for example, the structural pause, motor rhythm and loopiness, colorful and surprising harmonies, and the rave-up. This detailed look at one band has given us a good start on sketching the overall topical field of psychedelia circa 1966. But the Yardbirds did not encompass the full range of possibilities, and the rest of this chapter will consider topical areas that were more strongly associated with other artists of the era, such as jazz, folk, the avant-garde, and the early beginnings of space rock.

The Kinks: "See My Friends"

One of the most characteristic ways that early psychedelia borrowed from existing topics was its adaptation of Indian classical music. In the process, it both repeated aspects of European Orientalism and developed its own distinctive modalities of exoticism. The Kinks' "See My Friends," released in July 1965, is a good example to lead us into this area since it is one of the very earliest rock recordings to deploy signifiers of Indian music in a manner that went beyond momentary decoration. The topical area is established immediately in the introduction (music example 2.13), which sets up an accompaniment texture that continues largely unchanged throughout the song: a guitar riff presenting scalar movement over a drone (reminiscent of the sitar), a bass line emphasizing a single chord and nearly a single note, and slide guitar accents that are simultaneously reminiscent of Indian music and of the regularly spaced chords texture. Topical echoes of Indian music can be found throughout the rest of the song as well on many levels. I will first discuss melodic and formal aspects, then move into a detailed discussion of the Indian topic in connection with 1960s countercultural Orientalism, and then return to remark on some other features of "See My Friends."

The formal structure of the vocal line is subtle, creating an overall effect that is mildly articulated into sections but also smoothly and continuously flowing. I divide the A section of the verse into two six-measure phrases, the second of which is a repeat of the first. The first six measures are included at the end of music example 2.13. Notice how the cadential Isus4 chord in measure 10 gives a slight sense of lift and movement while maintaining the overall drone feeling. The B section of the verse is a more continuous section, ten measures long (music example 2.14). The verse B section introduces a strong feeling of lift due to the expanded range, upward movement, and sudden vocal harmony. It also introduces a greater feeling of flow and unpredictability because of the way the second gesture is extended with a $\frac{2}{4}$ measure and because of the increase in harmonic rhythm. The section concludes with a feeling of circularity and closure by returning to the opening material, and the cadence is made ambiguous and less forceful by the harmonic movement: V–Isus4–I.

After the verse is presented twice, there is a vocal bridge (music example 2.15). Since the bridge is a modified version of the verse B section, it adds to the overall feeling that the form is drifting along and gradually exploring somewhat unpredictable variations, rather than following any strong teleology. The end impression left by the whole form taken together could be described as flow and a

Music example 2.13. The Kinks, "See My Friends," introduction and beginning of first section of verse (0:00–0:24). Words and Music by Ray Davies. © 1965 Jayboy Music Corp. Copyright Renewed. This arrangement © 2015 Jayboy Music Corp. All Rights Administered by Sony / ATV Music Publishing LLC, 424 Church Street, Suite 1200, Nashville, TN 37219. International Copyright Secured All Rights Reserved. Reprinted by permission of Hal Leonard Corporation.

Music example 2.14. The Kinks, "See My Friends," second section of verse, vocals (0:34–0:53). Words and Music by Ray Davies. © 1965 Jayboy Music Corp. Copyright Renewed. This arrangement © 2015 Jayboy Music Corp. All Rights Administered by Sony / ATV Music Publishing LLC, 424 Church Street, Suite 1200, Nashville, TN 37219. International Copyright Secured All Rights Reserved. Reprinted by permission of Hal Leonard Corporation.

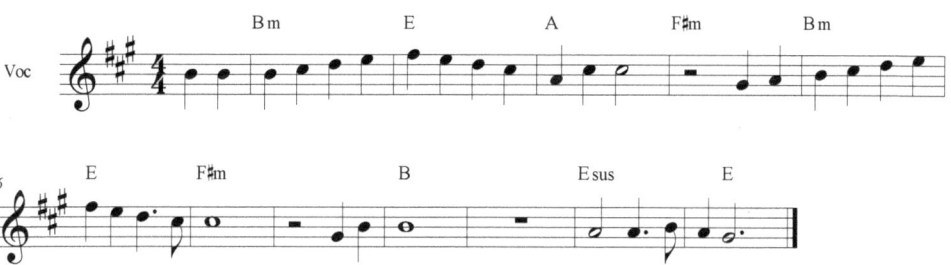

Music example 2.15. The Kinks, "See My Friends," bridge, vocals (1:37–2:01). Words and Music by Ray Davies. © 1965 Jayboy Music Corp. Copyright Renewed. This arrangement © 2015 Jayboy Music Corp. All Rights Administered by Sony / ATV Music Publishing LLC, 424 Church Street, Suite 1200, Nashville, TN 37219. International Copyright Secured All Rights Reserved. Reprinted by permission of Hal Leonard Corporation.

gradual interlocking of similar melodic and harmonic motifs, without a strong feeling of sharply delineated sections.

In topical terms, the overall effect is somewhat dialogical. There are elements of the Gregorian topic, elements of the Indian topic, and also a generally folkloric feeling. Finally, the suspended-fourth cadence is reminiscent of a plagal cadence, which brings evocations of hymn tunes and a general mood of spirituality. All of this is loosely echoed in the lyrics, which are mostly made up of repetitions and variations of two themes: "She is gone" and "see my friends, [laying or playing] 'cross the river." On one level this is just a folky song of love and loss. But who are the mysterious friends who remain? There is a subtle tinge of mysticism and transcendence to the lyrics that is not overtly psychedelic but strongly cognate with psychedelia, just as we find in the topical profile of the music. All of these nuances will be unpacked further, but first we should take an extended look at exoticism and Orientalism as they apply to mid-1960s psychedelia.

Indian Classical Music, Orientalism, and Exoticism

There is considerable slippage and interplay between Indian topics, Orientalism more generally, and exoticism in the broadest sense. This is especially true in the case of mid-1960s psychedelia, which was extremely broad in its cross-cultural appropriations. The discussion that follows centers on the Orientalizing appropriation of practices and concepts from South and East Asian religions in Europe and especially the United States. This history has been extensively surveyed in the existing literature on Orientalism, and a useful summary is offered by Andrea Grace Diem and James Lewis:

> South Asian religion entered the United States in at least three distinct waves. The first wave was almost purely literary: In the latter half of the eighteenth century, a group of scholar-officials working for the British East India Company translated some of the more important Hindu religious scriptures into English. The ideas contained in these texts directly influenced the transcendentalist movement ... and, both directly and indirectly, influenced New Thought. . . . The second wave was set in motion by a handful of Hindu religious teachers who visited the United States in the late nineteenth and early twentieth centuries. . . . In the late sixties and early seventies, a new wave of Indian gurus found a receptive audience among young Americans. . . . While the spiritual subculture of the seventies was composed of Buddhists, Sufis, and other non-Hindu groups, Indian spiritual teachers were the most numerous (as well as, in the long run, the most influential). (1992, 48–49)

Catherine Albanese has coined the term "Metaphysical Asia" to describe the particular synthesis that arose from this protracted encounter. Metaphysical Asia "constructs the process and results as Americans reinvented South and East Asia according to their Americanized metaphysical categories" (Albanese 2007, 17). Albanese sets out four themes that were central to most American metaphysical religions and philosophies: (1) "a preoccupation with mind and its powers"; (2) "a predisposition toward the ancient cosmological theory of correspondence between worlds"; (3) rather than thinking of the mind as static, "metaphysicians have thought in terms of movement and energy"; and (4) the movements formed "in the midst of a yearning for salvation understood as solace, comfort, therapy, and healing" (2007, 13–15). Among the many movements and organizations holding to such a viewpoint, one of the most significant were the Transcendentalists. This is partly because, as Diem and Lewis argue, the Transcendentalists were largely "responsible for introducing certain themes into the American literary tradition which would later contribute to the New Age stereotype of the East," for example, the "materialistic West / spiritual East" dichotomy, the "ancient wisdom of the East" theme, and the idea of the "sensual East" (1992, 54–55). In addition, the psychology of William James, especially his interest in altered states of consciousness, would later provide one inspiration for many in the psychedelic counterculture. As Marcus Boon puts it, "Although it is hardly the core of his philosophy, James's interest in chemical revelation was a natural part of his attempt to synthesize scientific, psychological, and religious points of view, and marked the coming full circle of the departure that Transcendentalist and Idealist philosophy made from empiricism at the end of the eighteenth century" (2002, 111).

Orientalism of the Metaphysical Asia type diverged from much other nineteenth-century Orientalism in that its center of focus was not Islam but rather Hinduism and to a lesser extent Buddhism. This was not only a change of philosophical emphasis relative to other Orientalisms but also an affective and political shift in that it supplemented an Orientalism rooted in military conflict and fear with one more inclined to view the other as a spiritual teacher, although still within a framework of European colonial power. And when we adjust this picture further to address the context of mid-twentieth-century popular culture, additional changes in the geopolitical framework of Orientalism need to be taken into account. For example, Timothy Taylor (2007) argues that when moving from the nineteenth century into the twentieth we need to shift our focus away from frameworks of colonialism and empire and look instead at globalization and capitalism as the new dominant power structures (without losing sight of how these reinscribed power structures of the colonialist period). This is a context where corporate power must be accounted for as closely as state power, where flows and connections are as important as boundaries, and where consumption must be analyzed as a crucial site of self-definition (Taylor 2007, 113–15).

It is against this backdrop that 1960s psychedelic exoticism needs to be read. This period not only is a crucial one for the history of popular music but also has special interest for the study of exoticism more generally. As Gerry Farrell puts it, "Perhaps there is no better illustration in recent history of the dizzying speed with which mass media can absorb, distort, consume, and redefine elements from another music culture than that of Indian music in 1960s pop music" (1997, 168). Again, Diem and Lewis highlight some of the key contextual issues: "Like the Orientalist picture of the golden age, the sixties picture was shaped by a dual projection: (1) Asian culture was imagined (for iconoclastic purposes) to be the reverse image of everything the counterculture disliked in America, and (2) Asian philosophies and religions were made to reflect countercultural (and later New Age) ideas" (1992, 56).

Up to the nineteenth century, European Orientalism was preoccupied with Islamic cultures and tended to emphasize themes of violence and sensuality (Al-Taee 2010, 3). This led to a tendency for Orientalist discourse and artworks to function through two related complexes of representations, one of which centered on concepts of threat, masculinity, and degenerate culture, while the other centered on concepts of inferiority, femininity, and the sensual. By contrast, psychedelia offers very few tokens of exoticized Islamic culture. Instead, psychedelia reworks ideas about South and East Asian cultures that gained prominence in the late nineteenth century. And there are other interesting points of contrast between earlier Orientalisms and the psychedelic varieties. In the course of comparing the Beatles to earlier Orientalisms, David Reck has written:

> Missing . . . are the popular Nineteenth Century stereotypes of the East as a place of unbridled sensuality, brutal violence, exotic but spectacular landscapes, kingly opulence, unspeakable poverty, and a people and environment displaying inscrutability, irrationality, or unbridgeable "otherness." Missing also is the portrayal of the Asian as a comic figure. . . . On the other hand, the stereotype of the East as the font of wisdom and divine knowledge . . . is strong indeed. . . . The musical stereotypes

> common in the West's portrayal of the Orient . . . are usually utilized as normal musical materials, not necessarily as attempts to picture in sound the exoticism of lyrics or theme. . . . However, there is the . . . strong connection between Indian sound as the description of dream states and hallucinogenic experiences, as well as with philosophical or religious lyrics. (1985, 126–27)

Although this was offered as a reflection on the Beatles, it can stand as a summary of Orientalism as it was developed by many mid-1960s artists. One thing I would add is that in 1960s psychedelia there are few depictions of Asian people and places as such. Asian materials are conceived as coming from somewhere else, but that somewhere else is understood not in geographical or temporal terms but rather as an exotic modality of the here and now. Related to this, any exoticism or strangeness ascribed to these others is also ascribed to the self, and, by extension, Anglo-American traditions are exoticized along with Asian ones. Compared to some other exoticisms, psychedelia was often not so much about the other in the sense of an other culture or an other person. Rather, representational practices developed in those sorts of exoticist contexts are redeployed in psychedelia to represent the self and one's own culture as an other. In this sense, Orientalist representations are significant as technologies of defamiliarization and self-othering. This is not entirely different from any other sort of Orientalism, given that Orientalist representations have always been, among other things, a matter of European Americans appropriating signs of the Asian other as a way to explore and expand their own self-images. On the other hand, the intensification of this tendency as it collided with the self-transformative ambitions of the psychedelic counterculture arguably produced a new situation.

By discussing self-othering, we draw close to the broader theme of othering within a single cultural group or geographical context. During a discussion of exoticism and Jewish musical identities in Europe, Philip Bohlman makes some remarks that could also be relevant to psychedelia:

> Western music's others have not all been imagined in the same ways. The other within and the other without are quite different. . . . The other without exists at the "rim of the world," and the great distance between that other and the self generated for Europeans in the Age of Discovery a sense of awe and wonder. . . . The other within exists within the space also occupied by the self, thereby creating a situation of competition rather than awe. Competition for cultural resources and public attention is immediate, which in turn may lead to a sense of being threatened by the other. Rather than the wonder of distance, the other within generates a nervousness of proximity. (2000, 191)

This sort of dynamic is clearly relevant to psychedelic exoticism in a variety of ways. It touches on how counterculturalists were often seen by others. It is also related to the psychedelic agenda of self-othering. And it gives us a chance to consider one of the more prominent indigenous otherings in US psychedelia: the exoticized representation of Native American cultures. Psychedelia of the 1960s and early 1970s presents many examples of Native American exoticism. Most obvious was the idea of the countercultural "tribe," along with visual motifs in graphic design and clothing. But at the same time, Native references were circumscribed in a way that Orientalists ones were not, insofar as there was little discernible Native influence on psychedelic musical style. Another difference is that Native images were usually subsumed within Wild West frontier imagery. They evoke a degree of historical self-reflexivity different from Orientalist imagery, at least in the US context. In terms of Bohlman's distinction between the other within and the other without, Native exoticism in psychedelia is interesting in that it functions both ways. This theme is taken up again in chapter 3 in the discussion of early psychedelic poster art.

Psychedelic exoticism is complex not only because of the signifieds but also because it involves a large number of signifiers that are appropriated and used in a large number of ways. Ralph Locke argues that the primary feature of musical exoticism is that it creates a sense of the music "coming from (or referring to, or evoking) a place other than here" (2009, 1). In a similar vein, for Jonathan Bellman musical exoticism "may be defined as the borrowing or use of musical materials that evoke distant locales or alien frames of reference. . . . Characteristic and easily recognized musical gestures from the alien culture are assimilated into a more familiar style, giving it an exotic color and suggestiveness" (1998b, ix). Tentative as such definitions are, they do point to one of the features that makes most varieties of musical exoticism strongly topical: a vocabulary of highly conventionalized signifiers. Making a catalog of these signifiers is one obvious analytical task and has been pursued by several authors. Before following a little along this path, we should note a warning from Nasser Al-Taee, who argues that the practice of compiling lists of Orientalist and exoticist style features "only reinforces the idea of the timeless and static Orient" (2010, xi). Taylor (2007, 7) also feels that an emphasis on texts and on catalogs of signifiers has obscured broader ideological and historical questions. To a certain extent, taking topic theory as a framework can help mitigate such tendencies because any catalog of musical features would be only half of the analysis (a list of signifiers). On the other hand, topical reading requires such a list as part of the analysis. If the Orientalist discourse was not rooted in clearly deployed conventional signifiers, then it would not be topical. So when working on topicality, we should not take such warnings as a call to abandon lists of signifiers and textual features altogether, but we should certainly keep in mind the need for balance and the importance of situating topical signifiers within the broader cultural negotiations of which they form a part.

So what are the specific Orientalist topical signifiers in mid-1960s psychedelia? Locke provides a list of musical features important in defining exoticism that can get us started. The ones that seem to have most obviously found a place in psychedelia are "non-normative modes and harmonies" (especially gapped pentatonics, chromatic alterations, and symmetrical pitch collections [both octatonic and whole tone]); "bare textures" (unharmonized unisons and octaves, bare and parallel fourths and fifths, drones and pedal points, and static harmony or slow oscillation); "complex and inherently undefined chords (sometimes described as 'magical' or 'mystical')"; "distinctive repeated rhythmic or melodic patterns"; ritualistic and chant-like vocal passages (chanting, monotone, cries, unusual words, and dialect); "instrumental lines that are the presumed equivalent of the melismas common in many traditional vocal styles"; "departures from normative types of continuity"; "foreign musical instruments, or Western ones that are used in ways that make them sound foreign"; "highly distinctive instrumental techniques"; and "distinctive use of vocal range and tessitura . . . [and] unusual styles of vocal production" (Locke 2009, 51–54). Locke also notes that certain features "can carry widely differing associations, depending on which other elements are/were simultaneously present. . . . Many of these features are so malleable in themselves that they only take on exotic coloration when joined to one or several others" (2009, 55). In terms of topicality, it is important to note another variety of dialogism in cases like this. When psychedelic artists in the mid-1960s employed such signifiers, one set of topics being mobilized were those linked to psychedelic representations and understandings of Asia. But at the same time, these could well have been received in some cases as signifiers of nineteenth-century Orientalism as its own topical area.

So what about raga rock in particular and how it overlapped with psychedelia? For a timeline, we can rely on Bellman: "The most recurrent topos in Rock exoticism of the middle 1960s is that of India. Because the heritage of the Raj and London's thriving Indian community made Indian influences more familiar in England than in the United States, this style was predominantly an English phenomenon (though the name 'Raga Rock' was coined by a publicist describing a song by an American group). In fact, our perspective of Raga Rock has been shaped by the Beatles, although the story is more complex" (1998a, 292–93).[8]

According to Bellman, it was in April 1965 that George Harrison first began thinking about learning to play the sitar, and "Norwegian Wood" was the first pop record to feature a real sitar (1998a, 293). But he also notes that Ray Davies wrote "See My Friends" in late January 1965 and the song was released in July, before Harrison's interests were public and before "Norwegian Wood" was recorded. According to Bellman, "historically, ["See My Friends"] may have been even more influential than is generally assumed" (1998a, 294–95). Bellman and others present many more details, but the main point is that the idea of raga rock was in the air around London in 1964–55, and no single artist can be definitively singled out as a point of origin.

Besides marking an important moment in the development of psychedelia, raga rock presented an alternative way of understanding and undertaking Orientalist borrowing of signifiers: "In pop, unlike [earlier eras of transcription and composition], the evidence of experiments with Indian music exists primarily in sound, not in notation. With pop there was no question of 'polishing' or 'cleaning up' Indian musical material to fit the parameters of staff notation and harmony. The Indian sounds arrived on vinyl in their raw state, even if the musical settings were unfamiliar. For this reason alone the pop encounter with Indian music was different from all antecedents" (Farrell 1997, 179). This difference from earlier Orientalist style resonates with Albanese's remarks on Metaphysical Asia and an attitude that, for all its stereotyping, often intended to emulate and learn rather than to correct or regulate. The raga-rock period also displayed its own idiomatic ways of understanding and mobilizing signifiers taken from Indian classical music. It helped that the electric guitar and the sitar are timbrally similar in many respects; there was enough overlap that one could frequently substitute for the other. For example, Farrell argues that Harrison used the sitar in "Norwegian Wood" "as a substitute guitar rather than as an Indian instrument as such. . . . The sitar is employed in a colouristic manner and the sound is very 'European' rather than Indian, reminiscent of a Landler or some similar type of folk-dance in triple time" (1988, 193).

Besides the similarity between sitar and electric guitar, other musical affinities between Indian classical music and 1960s rock included modality and the use of notes outside of twelve-tone equal temperament (e.g., blue notes) (Farrell 1997, 180). The list of relevant signifiers also includes drones; "partial use of specific Indian sounds"; "mimicking of certain types of vocal delivery perceived to be Indian in style—e.g., flat tone, with slides, slurs, etc."; occasional additive rhythm; modal melodies based on Indian scale types; question and answer between instruments; instruments in unison with vocal lines; and "mystical or quasi-religious lyrics" (182). According to Farrell, such borrowings were usually decorative, and he argues that "pop was unable to accommodate the overall form of an instrumental performance of Indian music" (180). At the same time, several authors (including Farrell) have noted that there are Indian formal elements worked into the basic design of Beatles songs such as "Within You Without You" and "Love You To" (Bellman 1998a, 294). "Love You To," in particular, provides a clear example of a rock song based loosely on the *alap-jor-jhala* form of Hindustani classical music, and, probably not coincidentally, Everett reports that it is also the first Beatles composition to change meter (1999, 40, 41).

I would argue that the use of decorative Indian elements rather than formal procedures is one thing that distinguishes earlier psychedelic pop from other kinds of psychedelic music where we will see formal principles from Indian music being adapted. This distinction recalls one made by John Corbett in his discussion of American experimentalist composers. Corbett distinguishes between what he calls "conceptual orientalism" and "contemporary chinoiserie" (2000, 170–73). In the same vein, Locke distinguishes three broad types of musical exoticism: (1) "overt exoticism," which he suggests became less popular among progressive composers around 1900; (2) "submerged exoticisms" such as the arabesque, certain harmonic procedures, and scales such as whole-tone and octatonic; and (3) "transcultural composing . . . the practice of composing for Western contexts . . . a work that incorporates certain stylistic and formal conventions of another culture's music" (2009, 214–28).[9] Psychedelic Orientalism provides examples of all three.

We can now return to "See My Friends" in order to elaborate on a few important Indian topical signifiers. Many of these relate to the discussion of the Indian topic but also cross over into being parts of psychedelic style more generally.

Raga Rock: Scalar-over-Drone Guitar Riffs

This form of guitar riff—combining a drone note with an oblique and often scalar upper line—has already been noted in music example 2.13. There are many other examples in music of the time. These are often Indian in flavor, but they also frequently overlap with spy or surf topics, as in the 13th Floor Elevators' "Roller Coaster" (music example 2.3), or they function as part of a general "jangle guitar" sound, as in "Think for Yourself" by the Beatles. By evoking jangle in this context, I am going a little beyond some uses of the word that limit it to sounds produced by the electric twelve-string guitar to include any texture where an electric guitar plays a mostly arpeggiated texture in a bright and sustaining timbre, often with some drone elements in the chord voicings. The Orientalist implications of such a figure overlap with the twang guitar continuum, since it is likely that the original reason why such figures would have made their way into genres such as spy and surf was because of their association with adventure and the exotic. Such guitar figures also resonate with aspects of blues and folk guitar styles, where open tunings and drone strings are often used to produce similar effects.

Other typical features of raga rock found in "See My Friends" that do not require as much explanation or are covered elsewhere include long melodic rise-fall shapes (which also recall the Gregorian chant topic); extended phrases (which play with expectations and weaken teleology); and harmonic color effects (the hymn-like cadence and drones). The composite effect is that "See My Friends" not only is evocative of the Indian topic but also presents a general mood of religiosity and the sublime. It demonstrates that the borderline between Orientalism and other forms of exoticism is porous.

Raga Rock: Exotic but Not Specifically Indian

Orientalist versions of exoticism were just one branch of a general tendency in psychedelia toward the strange and the unfamiliar. The result was a proliferation of signifiers drawn from various sources, all of which are similar in that they evoke, in addition to their specific associations, a general mood of the exotic. As Farrell puts it, "The sitar was not the only exotic sound to be dragged into the service of pop. By the mid-1960s, bagpipes, harpsichords, Gregorian chant, kotos, tuned glasses of water, and tape-loops could all be heard in mainstream pop" (1997, 169). But to return to Orientalism for one moment, it is worth noting that there are occasional stylistic borrowings that are clearly Asian or Middle Eastern in origin but are not Orientalist in the more developed sense discussed above. One such case can be seen in "Over, Under, Sideways, Down" by the Yardbirds (music example 2.16). In this instance the guitar melody, vocal exclamations, and claps are as much Arabic as Indian. This is also an interesting example of troping: the walking bass is a clear rhythm-and-blues signifier, and the claps and shouts can be heard in this way as well. So the passage overall tropes an Orientalist topic

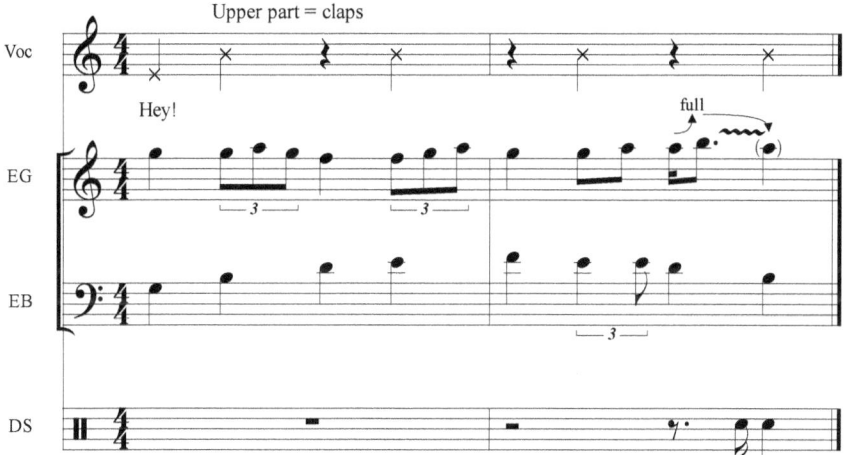

Music example 2.16. The Yardbirds, "Over, Under, Sideways, Down," introduction, mm. 3–4 (0:00–0:03). Written by Jeff Beck, Chris Dreja, Paul Samwell-Smith, Jim McCarty, and Keith Relf. © Glenwood Music Corp. / Wade Circle Ltd.

Music example 2.17. The Rolling Stones, "Paint It, Black," first verse, rhythm section (beginning) (0:15–0:21). Written by Mick Jagger and Keith Richards. © ABKCO Music Inc.

with a rhythm-and-blues one, and in addition the claps/shouts are dialogic in that each one signifies both elements of the trope.

The Rolling Stones' "Paint It, Black" also combines various sorts of nonspecific exoticist borrowing (music example 2.17). The melody is Indian in flavor, but the rhythm section—clearly exotic in its emphatic off-beat emphasis relative to rock and pop norms—could evoke any number of Middle Eastern or Mediterranean musics, and perhaps even ska. Finally, recall that the surf and spy genres explore a broad range of exoticism beyond the Indian. In summary, while it is important to look in depth at how exotic signifiers resonate with a long history of Orientalism, it is also worth bearing in mind that they exist on a continuum with a broader range of exoticizing practices.

Raga Rock: Drones

Drones are key to psychedelic style because of their prominence as a signifier in the Indian topic but also for more general reasons. Drones of many types are found throughout the music, including long passages with minimal chord changes, the use of harmonic pedal tones, and outright drones. Besides being formally cognate with psychedelia and in addition to their Orientalist resonances, drones have connections to European folkloric and pastoral topics. As Philip Tagg notes, it is common "to find plains and other large, empty, motionless rural spaces musically portrayed in terms of static harmony, often furnished with an 'ethnic' or exotic flavour (i.e., distance in time, culture and/or place)" (2000a, 31). Drones, and static harmonies in general, often have a folky quality, especially when used in conjunction with other signifiers of the pastoral. In a similar vein, drones and minimal harmonies can be important signifiers of the blues and related topical areas. In terms of base styles and donor styles, drones are interesting because they are overdetermined. They have a variety of sources—Indian classical music, certain coloristic effects in Western classical music, folk music, and blues among the most significant—all of which are cognate with psychedelia in different ways. This may help explain why drones are so ubiquitous in psychedelic music.

The 13th Floor Elevators

The 13th Floor Elevators, unlike other artists we've looked at so far, were among the first to frankly endorse psychedelic drugs and to be explicit about the psychedelic intent of their music. They were also part of the scene in Austin, Texas, which is a contrasting situation relative to better-known scenes in London and San Francisco. As one of the earliest psychedelic proselytizing groups, the Elevators were regarded as pioneers even by many on the San Francisco scene (Drummond 2007). Since we are looking at the 13th Floor Elevators specifically to say how they contributed to psychedelic topicality, I'll concentrate on three areas. First, I'll examine how they managed to create a darker and more countercultural mood using essentially the same topical resources as the other bands we've studied. This will show how intensive and affective choices made in performance can have topical effects. Second, we need to think about the most idiosyncratic feature of the group: the electric jug. And finally, I want to show that they had an approach to extended instrumentals that differed from the Yardbirds-style rave-up and that anticipated later developments in areas such as space-rock and jam bands.

The 13th Floor Elevators' first single, "You're Gonna Miss Me," demonstrates most of the band's key features. One thing it shows is that while the Elevators are often portrayed as an underground and garage-oriented band, they actually share many features with the Yardbirds. Stylistic components in "You're Gonna Miss Me" that match things we have already discussed include loopiness (e.g., the riff that repeats throughout the introduction and first section; see music example 2.18); minimal drone-like chord changes (as in the transition riff; see music example 2.19); surf characteristics, especially in the transition (see music example 2.19); noise techniques (e.g., the guitar timbres and the vocal tendency toward shouts and screams); and abrupt textural shifts. Also, unlike many other bands often included in the garage-rock category, 13th Floor Elevators arrangements often feature longer forms with a variety of sections and carefully crafted levels of tension and release.

In topical terms, the basic elements in "You're Gonna Miss Me" and in most 13th Floor Elevators recordings are not very different from what we have already seen. However, they demonstrate how the affective result of similar topical choices can be quite varied, depending on performative nuance and contextual factors. In terms of context, the main difference was the band's open endorsement of psychedelic drugs and their reputation for performing under the influence. In sonic terms, some elements that enhance this more underground stance include heavy use of echo and reverberation; a tendency toward distorted guitar tones (not just the use of fuzz but a louder and more saturated sound overall); the constant and bizarre jug; and droning, prophetic inclinations in the lead voice. The overall effect of the 13th Floor Elevators is darker and more countercultural than a band like the Yardbirds, and many topics reveal a different range of nuances in that context. For example, the surf topic can have a dark edge for several reasons. For one, its particular form of timelessness is symbolic not only of an endless summer but also of social alienation. And the ocean itself is sublime in the full sense of the word, both beautiful and dangerous. So when a surf topic is deployed by a band like the 13th Floor Elevators, there is potential for the darker tones to emerge more forcefully than when they are deployed by the Beach Boys or even the Yardbirds. A similar reading could be given for folk topics, especially since the electric jug embodies a defamiliarization of these (discussed further below). The main point is that while a given topic is defined by the way that it consistently refers to a particular set of cultural units, there is still considerable variation in how those cultural units are valued and what affective coloration they take on in any particular instance.

Music example 2.18. The 13th Floor Elevators, "You're Gonna Miss Me," introduction (0:00–0:18). Written by Roky Erickson. © Charly Publishing Ltd. obo Tapier Music.

Aside from their open advocacy of psychedelic drugs, probably the most widely noted aspect of the 13th Floor Elevators is their use of the electric jug. It is described by Paul Drummond:

> In a traditional jug band the player blows into the empty vessel to produce a slow and low percussive bass sound, whereas Tommy [Hall] used his voice and throat to mimic fast, jazz-inspired runs into a microphone, and employed the jug to add resonance and reverb, creating an entirely unexpected new sound.... Tommy's idea was that the jug would embellish the Elevators' sound in the same way that the Byrds employed a twelve-string guitar to create their folk-raga-rock sound, but several of the other band members disliked the jug in general, or at least the way it was applied to every song. (2007, 73–74)

Music example 2.19. The 13th Floor Elevators, "You're Gonna Miss Me," transition (beginning) (1:03–1:10). Written by Roky Erickson. © Charly Publishing Ltd. obo Tapier Music.

Further aspects of the jug's lineage, and Tommy Hall's intentions in adopting it, are explored by Jim DeRogatis: "According to Elevators lore, the jug was filled with Hall's pot stash, and Hall drew inspiration for his playing from John Coltrane. In retrospect, his random noises foreshadow the chaotic synthesizers of Roxy Music, the krautrock bands, and Pere Ubu" (2003, 70). Many commentators, like DeRogatis, characterize the jug as random noise and do not acknowledge any degree of musical sophistication in its use. However, music examples 2.18, 2.20, and 2.21 show that there was a degree of control and nuance in Hall's jug playing. His general approach to phrasing explores expansions and contractions of short motifs. The rhythm is generally a string of sixteenth notes, but they are broken up with silences to create phrases of varying length, not unlike the typical rhythmic profile of a bebop solo. This style of playing also creates timbral effects similar to those achieved through signal-processing techniques such as vibrato, tremolo, and rotating speaker systems. Hall generally starts in a lower register and then very gradually introduces higher pitches, creating a controlled increase of excitement. And there is a variety of texture from song to song. The most typical texture, as described above, creates what could be called a rubber band effect, but at times the jug produces a texture closer to a cooing dove (see music example 2.20) or to a siren with long glissandi ("Kingdom of Heaven," not transcribed).

In terms of topicality, one interesting thing is how weakly this amplified jug connotes its folkloric and 1920s popular culture sources, even though topics related to these sources were, in only slightly different contexts, incorporated into psychedelia in a variety of ways. This jug is closer in effect to the Theremin and

Music example 2.20. The 13th Floor Elevators, "Roller Coaster," A section, voice and jug (beginning) (0:31–0:47). Written by Tommy Hall and Roky Erickson. © Charly Publishing Ltd. obo Tapier Music.

other electronic sounds as used in science fiction and horror soundtracks. Also interestingly, it never became a topic in its own right, since it was never replicated and therefore never standardized. However, it does provide one example of a general textural feature that I call the *garble line*: an instrumental or vocal part that presents pitches in a very fast/dense manner, often with an unpredictable mixture of clearly articulated notes and others that are somehow obscured. A garble line often meanders widely through pitch space, following a rhythmic profile that does not adhere strongly to the prevailing harmonic or melodic logic. We will see garble lines in other contexts. Often they have Orientalist connotations, as with the lead guitar in "Eight Miles High," several of the loops in "Tomorrow Never Knows," and the clavioline in "Baby You're a Rich Man." The Orientalist garble line will also emerge in later periods, for example, in Prince's "Around the World in a Day." But if the garble line is always to some degree exotic, it is not necessarily always Orientalist, and the electric jug in the 13th Floor Elevators provides a good example.

There are two other aspects of the 13th Floor Elevators that require special note. The first has to do with the lead vocals, which are often intoned in a chant-like fashion, with heavy reverberation and with lyrics urging the listener to take up a psychedelic quest. A voice staged in this way can easily be heard as a guide or prophet persona. In the next chapter we are going to consider psychedelic guide figures more fully, but it's important to note that the 13th Floor Elevators were among the very first rock bands to provide a sonic image of one. In topical terms, this raises general themes of religiosity and mysticism, but in a somewhat different manner from the way they have come up in examples already discussed, and so it's another example of a performative variation of a familiar topic.

Music example 2.21. The 13th Floor Elevators, "Roller Coaster," first jam (beginning) (1:26–1:40). Written by Tommy Hall and Roky Erickson. © Charly Publishing Ltd. obo Tapier Music.

Finally, I want to say something about how the 13th Floor Elevators often sounded in their extended instrumental passages, because they tended toward a texture that differed from other available templates like the vamp, or the solo, or the Yardbirds-style rave-up. When we discuss the emergence of space rock, I will describe a form of group improvisation called the *developing variation jam*. Many of the salient features can already be seen in "Roller Coaster" (music example 2.21). An instrumental of this sort shares features with a rave-up and also with a vamp—loopiness, static harmony, digression from conventional song form—but an important difference is that this instrumental does not build to a climax like a rave-up and also does not suggest its own imminent ending like a vamp. Instead, it develops a much more linear, hypnotic affect. There is also an absence of extreme noise techniques and a fairly relaxed tempo, both of which emphasize the relative lack of directedness compared to a rave-up. Some other instrumentals of this type, to be discussed later, do employ more noise and often double-time drums, but again they do so without any feeling of overall directness (see music example 2.11). In the period 1965–66 this sort of instrumental was less common than those that followed a rave-up, vamp, or solo template, but it became more prominent in the later 1960s. So for now, this kind of extended instrumental texture is one of the things that made the 13th Floor Elevators a bit of an anomaly, and in the long run it was one of their contributions to psychedelic style.

"Roller Coaster" is also an important example lyrically. Like many 13th Floor Elevator songs, and unlike a more oblique and only vaguely psychedelic lyric such as "See My Friends," "Roller Coaster" contains the kind of frankly psychedelic lyrics that will become increasingly common in the later 1960s. There is a mysterious guide figure; explicit drug-related language ("after the trip"); exhortations like "come on, and let it happen to you"; and a counterculture us-and-them implication ("you're looking at the world with brand new eyes, and no-one can ever spoil the view"). In all these ways, the lyrics unambiguously advocate psychedelic experience. And while the drug references are technically still somewhat veiled, they could not be more clear. The words have a powerful sense of urgency that is also typical of later psychedelic lyrics. This is created in part through grammatical forms of direct address (which also helps create the prophetic and oracular tone) and with words like "realize" (a word used to great effect in another 13th Floor Elevators song, "You're Gonna Miss Me"). In a way, even seeming indirections—such as calling the trip a roller coaster ride rather than literally saying LSD trip—are a form of directness. Like a Tin Pan Alley pop song, such lyrical devices frame the message in terms that are more likely to be widely understood, thereby perhaps ultimately spreading it more widely rather than hiding it.

Drums

Before continuing with artists and songs, I would like to make a few remarks on topical aspects of drums during this period. Given the importance of the rhythm section in defining many popular music styles, drums are an important site of topical activity. And, as we do in other areas, when we look at the drum set in psychedelia we see an interesting mix of older topics being reinscribed and newer topics emerging, often as transformations of the older ones. What follows is a survey of some of the highlights.

Rhythm Box Drums. By this I mean cases where the drums follow a stereotypical pattern that is repeated for a long time—often an entire formal section or more—without much variation. I call this approach *rhythm box drums* because it is like selecting a rhythm on an early preset drum machine. This was a strong tendency in rock/pop drumming in the early 1960s, and the loosening of drum style was an important marker of a new style period in the later 1960s. In the rhythm box drums style, each pattern is associated with a stereotypical style, and each pattern tends in itself to be a topic. Often these are topics whose presence seems explicable more in terms of general norms of drumming rather than any specifically psychedelic agenda. The use of such stereotyped patterns can produce tropes that sound like the result of a clash, or at least a somewhat disjunctive mixture, between pop trends and the more psychedelic elements. Picture this as a performance situation: the drummer sticks to a rhythm box drums pattern (cha-cha, march, waltz), while some other band members (maybe the lead guitar and organ) go off into an ambient noise exploration. Visualizing it in this way helps make an important point about troping, because it shows how tropes can arise as a side effect of musical interactions and collaborations, not necessarily planned ahead of time as textual features but evolving as musicians with different backgrounds and methods find ways of working together. This is a very general point that could have been made elsewhere, but the prevalence of rhythm box drums in the earlier 1960s gives us a good opportunity to bring it up.

Four-on-the-Floor Drums. By this I mean any drum set pattern where the rhythm is dominated by one or more drums playing relatively even accents in motor rhythm, usually at the level of the quarter note. In the mid-1960s this was most commonly done on the snare drum, although sometimes the kick drum was used for similar purposes. Examples in this chapter include "Paint It, Black" (music example 2.17), "Seven & Seven Is" (music example 2.28), and "Happenings Ten Years Time Ago" (music example 2.8). One preexisting topical association of four-on-the-floor drums is soul music, where it was not a default rhythmic device but was very common. When performed on the kick drum it can also be evocative of parade drums and might also be related to the American Indian topic as a subtopic of the western, along with certain Orientalist depictions of ritualistic drumming.

Military Snare. It is very common for snare drum patterns during this period to reflect the influence of rudiments exercises and of characteristic rhythms from parade and military drumming. To an extent this is simply a side effect of rhythm box drumming and also an outcome of drum pedagogy. But in some cases the militaristic dimension is unmistakably topical, for example, in "Shapes of Things" or the drums near the end of "Paint It, Black" and "White Rabbit" (discussed in chapter 3). To look at one specific rhythmic pattern in this family, Tagg (2000b, 207) points out that "martial triplets" are a well-established signifier and names many instances of pop ballads with military themes that use such snare drum patterns. He also notes the overlap here with bolero-type snare drums. Taken as a whole, such a pattern might be expected "to connote something Hispanic (the *Boléro* connection), something military (like the *Green Beret* snares), something scary (*Running Scared*) and something dramatic, fateful and inexorable" (Tagg 2000a, 42–43). I would add that there are often affective shadings of a lighter, more playful, or mocking nature: toy soldiers, celebratory parade, pomposity. These overlap with general topics of the quaint or nostalgic, discussed later in this chapter.

Toms. Sometimes a single drum within the drum set can display one or more topical potentials. Cymbals can function as Orientalist gongs, for example, and snares can evoke military topics. Similar things can be done with toms, and there are several different varieties of tom topicality that crop up with some frequency during this period. For example, toms are often used to provide regular interjections in a rhythm pattern, as in "See My Friends" (music example 2.13) and "Eight Miles High" (music example 2.22, although the toms in this case switch to a different sort of function by about m. 13). This technique is not always strongly topical, but it does have topical importance, since it was one factor whose increased and flexible use began to pull drummers away from the rhythm box tendency described earlier. Also, because these sorts of tom interjections were generally used to emphasize a rhythmic periodicity intermediate between the beat and larger formal units (e.g., every bar or every two bars), they could help reinforce a trance-like affect or even produce something akin to the regularly spaced chords texture.

Sustained Tom-Centric Textures. Regular tom interjections are also important because they exist on a continuum with more dramatic and topic-rich tom-dominated textures. I have in mind here examples such as "You're Gonna Miss Me" (music example 2.19). These are passages of moderate to fast tempo where the rhythm is carried mostly or exclusively on the toms and the composite rhythm is nearly or literally motoric. This sort of pattern is strongly topical both in the way that it can deploy preexisting topics and the way it developed into a prototopic of psychedelia. Very similar patterns were characteristic of swing drumming since the 1930s, and the texture also evokes rhythm-and-blues and rock-and-roll drumming of the 1940s and 1950s. Apart from connoting these genres, such tom patterns were often understood as "jungle drums," carrying a general hint of the exotic that overlapped with stereotypes of the African diaspora and by extension with trance, adventure, and ritual. In the present day, these associations survive in commonly encountered stereotypes of "tribal" drumming. In any specific example, it may be the case that the more historically specific topical layers will be highlighted or, conversely, that the more generalized trance-like and ritualistic implications of the patterns will be foregrounded. Over time, this more abstracted version of the texture led to an arguably new topic: *space toms*.

Space Toms. I use this term to describe the sustained-tom texture in cases where it is combined with a general space-rock context, such that the earlier exoticist topical elements are sublimated into this new articulation of adventure and frontiers.[10] One example discussed later in this chapter is "Section 43" (music example 2.33). Other examples crop up frequently in Nick Mason's drumming for Pink Floyd. The difference between this sort of tom-centric topic and the earlier jungle toms is more a matter of context than a clear formal distinction, although in some cases space toms have a slower tempo and a more gapped composite rhythm. There is also a tendency to move frequently between several toms rather than sticking with one or two. Once such patterns became widely understood as "spacey," any connotations of swing or other earlier genres may have been further attenuated.

The Byrds: "Eight Miles High"

"Eight Miles High" is one of the most important songs of the early psychedelic era. It contains many of the style components and topical elements we have been discussing, and it achieved widespread notice. I have already made reference to it in several places, and elements already discussed include long instrumental passages, psychedelic decorations on a largely conventional song form, use of twang guitar as a drone, and heavy emphasis on toms for most of the performance. All of these are evident in music example 2.22. We should also note the crucial role played by the Byrds in popularizing a distinctive style of rhythm guitar that is often called *jangly*. This is a texture that has been described extensively by others, so we do not need to go into technical details. But in topical terms it formed an important link between folk music topics and the emerging psychedelic rock. It also later became an important topic of 1960s psychedelia.

In terms of lyrics, "Eight Miles High" sits between two of our earlier examples. "See My Friends" was lyrically only mildly psychedelic. You could easily hear it as nothing but a vaguely mystical love song. Let's call these *obliquely cognate* lyrics. By contrast, "Roller Coaster" was a completely explicit psychedelic advocacy song. Unlike either of these, "Eight Miles High" is an example of what we could call *skewed cognate* lyrics. It would be possible to hear this just as a song about flying in an airplane and then, upon landing, finding yourself in a city where some people are becoming enlightened but others remain alienated and blinkered. And indeed, the Byrds have generally maintained that this was the intended meaning (landing in London). But apart from the obvious use of "high," there are other phrases seemingly chosen to indicate psychedelic experience ("signs in the street," "stranger than now"). And the themes themselves—enlightenment versus spiritual inertia, trying to find like-minded comrades—are strongly if not specifically countercultural. By this point, we have seen an entire continuum of obviousness in terms of psychedelic lyrical intent corresponding to a range of devices that can increase or decrease the specificity of particular lyrical devices. As a generalization, most psychedelic lyrics in the later 1960s tended to be of the skewed cognate type—not completely obvious, but fairly difficult to miss.

Jazz is one thing we haven't talked about yet. While jazz and psychedelia for the most part remain fairly distinct as topical fields, psychedelia did occasionally rely on jazz both as a donor style and, more rarely, as a base genre (e.g., in some

Facing and above: Music example 2.22. The Byrds, "Eight Miles High," opening through first guitar solo (0:00–0:29). Words and Music by Roger McGuinn, David Crosby, and Gene Clark. © 1966 (Renewed) Sixteen Stars Music, Gene Clark Music and Chrysalis One Songs LLC o/b/o BMG Rights Management (Ireland) Ltd. This arrangement © 2015 Sixteen Stars Music, Gene Clark Music and Chrysalis One Songs LLC o/b/o BMG Rights Management (Ireland) Ltd. All Rights for Gene Clark Music and Chrysalis One Songs LLC Administered by BMG Rights Management (US) LLC. International Copyright Secured All Rights Reserved. Reprinted by permission of Hal Leonard Corporation. Additional copyright permission: Words and Music by GENE CLARK, DAVID CROSBY and JIM McGUINN. © 1967 (Renewed) RESERVOIR MEDIA MANAGEMENT, INC., GENE CLARK MUSIC (Administered by BUG) and SIXTEEN STARS MUSIC All Rights for RESERVOIR MEDIA MUSIC Administered by RESERVOIR MEDIA MANAGEMENT, INC. RESERVOIR MEDIA MUSIC Administered by ALFRED MUSIC. All Rights Reserved. Used by Permission of ALFRED MUSIC.

Vox

Music example 2.23. The Byrds, "Eight Miles High," first verse vocals (0:29–0:59). Words and Music by Roger McGuinn, David Crosby, and Gene Clark. © 1966 (Renewed) Sixteen Stars Music, Gene Clark Music and Chrysalis One Songs LLC o/b/o BMG Rights Management (Ireland) Ltd. This arrangement © 2015 Sixteen Stars Music, Gene Clark Music and Chrysalis One Songs LLC o/b/o BMG Rights Management (Ireland) Ltd. All Rights for Gene Clark Music and Chrysalis One Songs LLC Administered by BMG Rights Management (US) LLC. International Copyright Secured All Rights Reserved. Reprinted by permission of Hal Leonard Corporation. Additional copyright permission: Words and Music by GENE CLARK, DAVID CROSBY and JIM McGUINN. © 1967 (Renewed) RESERVOIR MEDIA MANAGEMENT, INC., GENE CLARK MUSIC (Administered by BUG) and SIXTEEN STARS MUSIC All Rights for RESERVOIR MEDIA MUSIC Administered by RESERVOIR MEDIA MANAGEMENT, INC. RESERVOIR MEDIA MUSIC Administered by ALFRED MUSIC. All Rights Reserved. Used by Permission of ALFRED MUSIC.

improvisations by the Grateful Dead, discussed in the next chapter). So we will see several songs in which jazz topics are prominent in a variety of different ways, and this is our first. It has become common knowledge that "Eight Miles High" was influenced in part by Indian classical music (specifically Ravi Shankar) and in part by John Coltrane. Both of these make sense relative to the dense, angular, and often dissonant lead guitar line. The Orientalist aspects of such a texture have already been discussed, but another crucial resonance is with experimental jazz of the early 1960s. And with respect to John Coltrane we need to look not only at the more experimental aspect of the guitar solo but also at the motif that opens the solo and recurs elsewhere in the song in several variations (music example 2.22, mm. 7–8). The triadic emphasis, sparse rhythm, and boldly directed profile of this theme resemble the sorts of themes often explored by Coltrane, especially around 1965 (e.g., on *A Love Supreme*). The theme in turn resonates with a generally epic and perhaps even cinematic topicality that is not incidental, given that Coltrane's work of this period was also self-consciously epic in scope. Overall, I would include this motif in a family along with "Section 43" by Country Joe and the Fish (discussed later in this chapter), Jimi Hendrix's "Third Stone from the Sun" (discussed in the next chapter), and the signature motif in the Beatles' "Love You To" (not transcribed, but see Fujita et al. 1989, 641). In this particular instance, jazz appears in a form overlapping strongly with the Indian topic and also with the epic.

A second significant thing about "Eight Miles High" is the vocal arrangement, as shown in music example 2.23. On one level these vocals stay within norms of the folk-rock style, which the Byrds did much to standardize. But in topical terms, it is striking how many different nuances are hinted at in these sixteen measures. Initially, the texture is reminiscent of the Gregorian topic, although, strictly speaking, it is an organum. In any event, the evocation is of an archaic or medieval topic with a tinge of mysticism. But as the tessitura rises and the intervals of doubling move from fifths, to sixths, to thirds, there is a feeling of uplift that goes beyond these more specific associations. The repeat, beginning in measure 9, opens with contrary motion. This not only is a striking textural contrast from the first part of the phrase, but it also hints at classical music topics. The rest of the phrase is similar to the first time around, except the oblique motion that was only hinted at in measures 6 and 7 is more prominent in the final measures. And then the entire phrase ends with a dense, ambiguous sonority that is strikingly modern relative to the rest and could be heard as evocative of jazz choir voicings. It may be too much to argue for a fully developed narrative or change-of-state schema in these sixteen measures, but it is still striking to see the degree of textural variation and how it affords a range of rapidly changing topical readings. In this respect, the brevity is noteworthy in itself, forming a bridge between the less temporally elaborated approach discussed under pop song form and the sorts of longer-range forms to come.

Voices

Vocal textures are an important source of topical materials, quite apart from their involvement in conveying lyrics. As with the drums, we should take a moment to look at some of the most striking vocal textures and conventions from this period with an eye toward their topical features.

Vocal Doubling. The doubling of a monophonic vocal line is one of the simplest possible arrangement techniques. It was so frequently employed by the Beatles that Abbey Road engineers in the mid-1960s developed a mechanism for its automation. Vocal doubling, especially in its electronically generated form, is part of a family of more or less defamiliarizing doubling effects that also includes flanging and chorusing. According to Walter Everett, the double tracking of lead vocals (as opposed to backing vocals) was "an unusual technique outside of novelty recordings, before the Beatles" (2001, 276). It was especially associated with recordings by Les Paul and Mary Ford, where Peter Doyle suggests that "the multiplying of the voices is an uncanny effect, a kind of double exposure" (2005, 151). Overall, vocal doubling up to the mid-1960s is better viewed as a style component and affective resource than as a topical one (apart from its contribution to the Gregorian and cowboy chorus topics), but once it became a characteristic and heavily used effect it was poised to become a topic in later eras.

Oblique Motion. Another technique that began to be more widely used on rock recordings in the mid-1960s was oblique motion between background and lead vocals or within the background vocals themselves. One famous instance is in the chorus of the Yardbirds' "For Your Love," and another is the Beatles' "Love Me Do" (see Fujita et al. 1989, 636–37). Oblique motion is another simple device, but one with powerful topical potential. By evoking a drone, it can be linked to the Indian topic and also to a generally folkloric set of references. To a very slight extent, oblique motion could also connote classical music insofar as it is a contrapuntal technique.

Choral Texture. In some cases, a variety of the devices described above are deployed to create a choir-like end result. For example, this description could be applied to the vocals in "Eight Miles High," discussed earlier. A choral vocal texture does not immediately open up any new topical areas but does resonate with some existing ones, especially with classical music and spirituality / the church. Also, some variants could be said to evoke musical theater, as in "Blues from an Airplane" by Jefferson Airplane (discussed in the next chapter).

Voice as Sound Effect. In some cases, vocal sound effects serve an important affective and even topical role. By "effects" I mean nonsung sounds that invite attention given their clearly human origin yet also overlap with the wider category of extramusical or exotic sounds. One typical example is the sound of a joking, laughing group, and others include babies, loud whispers, breathing noises with various affect, near laughs, and sexual/scatological noises. In all of these cases we are dealing with fairly clear connotations and a range of different ways these can be cognate with psychedelia. But perhaps the most significant thing is that the tendency to use such effects at all became an important topic in its own right.

Multiple Speaker Blur. Within the broad family of vocal effects, one in particular deserves special notice because it is among the most common and also because it inhabits an interesting middle ground between types of codes. This is the device whereby several nonsinging voices are mixed together, often at a low-enough volume and with a high-enough degree of signal processing that they are on the borderline between intelligible and unintelligible. I have chosen to call it multiple speaker blur, although the informal "word soup" would also be appropriate.[11] One example already discussed were the megaphone voices in "Happenings Ten Years Time Ago." The technique was also frequently used by Frank Zappa and many others, and it became increasingly common in the later 1960s and into the 1970s.

Insofar as multiple speaker blur presents spoken language and invites close listening in an attempt to understand the words, it is an example of verbal code and is therefore outside the specific bounds of musical topicality. On the other hand, the texture asserts itself as a signifier in its own right and comes close to overwhelming the verbal content, which allows it to function as a topic in a more musical sense. The same is true of all the vocal techniques discussed above, insofar as all of them generally coexist with a text on which they are not dependent for their topical significance. The layer of musical topicality in such cases is relatively autonomous, although it can't help but enter into a relationship with the text. But the duality of the codes is especially striking in the case of multiple speaker blur because the tug-of-war between verbal semantics and more music-specific modes of signification is dramatized in the texture itself.

The Folkloric

A few times in this chapter I have remarked on the importance of folk music and ideas of folklore. For example, many Indian topical signifiers overlap with folk music ones, and there is also overlap on the level of the signified. Indeed, by the mid-1960s "Indian music was also widely perceived as a type of folk-music, albeit a folk-music with mystical connotations" (Farrell 1997, 175). As Ralph Locke (2009, 27) has pointed out, the similarities between exoticism and folklorism are general and go far beyond the Indian overlap. This is partly because certain folk-based subcultures were important precursors of psychedelia. Rob Young (2010), for example, gives an overview of how mysticism, nationalism, pastoralism, travel, folklore, and nostalgia intertwined in musical and artistic movements of the nineteenth and early twentieth centuries in the UK. The same was true to a degree in the United States, so it is not surprising, for example, that the 1952 Folkways *Anthology of American Folk Music*, edited by Harry Smith, displayed such a striking mixture of scholarship, nostalgia, and occultism: "Smith's careful shepherding of the material was part of a plan to craft a magical talisman that would engineer social change. This was not necessarily the Marxist humanism of Alan Lomax and Ewan MacColl, but revolution on a more mythopoeic level. He was reading Plato's *Republic* at the time, and noted the Greek philosopher's references to music as a potent agent of challenge to the ruling status quo" (Young 2010, 184).

In both US and UK contexts, folk music explored mythologies and aesthetic resources that were cognate with psychedelia on many levels and also shared a significant social and institutional overlap in their connection to college-based and beatnik subcultures. Stewart Home summarizes: "Until the late sixties folkies were ahead of the curve in terms of using mysticism and world music influences on their records, since they'd emerged from a beatnik scene that was fascinated by India and other non-Christian cultures. . . . Where the folkies led, the new breed of psychedelic bands weren't far behind" (2005, 140). When considering the lyrics and historical contexts of traditional folk songs, it isn't difficult to find themes and features that are cognate with psychedelia. These include political protest, magic and mythical creatures, images of the rural that could reinforce a back-to-the-land pastoralism, a range of powerful and interesting characters who can serve as guide figures or as fellow travelers, childhood references, an anachronistic tone that can serve as a beguiling virtual world, and a sense of whimsy and humor that can be both escapist and subversive. All of these are themes and traits that sit well with psychedelia, and all can be found in folk lyrics. But, interestingly, all of them can also be found to varying degrees in the musical topics that will be our focus.

Folkloric topics were explored in slightly different ways in US and UK contexts. Among the San Francisco and Los Angeles bands, they were a key component of the jangle-rock sound, contributing a range of signifiers: particular guitar textures (clean and arpeggio-oriented while still loud and electric), vocal harmony, and a tendency toward certain harmonic and melodic resources. This has already been discussed in connection with the Byrds, and another good if lesser-known example is Lyme & Cybelle's "Follow Me." The song has an overall feeling that could be called folky but not folkloric, since the folk elements are melded into a generally sunshine-pop effect. This kind of fusion was typical of the California folk-rock sound and its psychedelic offshoots. By contrast, while folk-infused jangle-pop was not unknown to the UK, there was a greater tendency to use folkloric materials in ways that were more overtly mystical and self-consciously historicized. Two good examples of these tendencies are "Lady Jane" by the Rolling Stones and "Guinevere" by Donovan.

The Rolling Stones example is less overtly psychedelic because it does not have the Indian-instrument component found in Donovan, and the Stones overall had far less of a contextual link to the psychedelic. Still, it has many features that resemble those we have already identified as relevant to psychedelia, for example, the repetitive melody with structural pauses and prominent drones. The folkloric dimension comes in part from the use of the dulcimer and in part from the self-consciously archaic overall mood. This is complicated, though, in the way that the more folk-like passages alternate with a contrasting passage that is more classical in many respects.

Overall, the topical effects here are strongly dependent on a point made earlier in connection with the idea of a cinematic topic: whether a particular cultural unit is narrow enough to support topicality depends on how it relates to the overall context. In a Western art music context it would be far too crude to speak of a "classical music" topic, just as it might make little sense to speak of a "cinematic" topic in detailed discussions of film soundtracks. But if our frame of reference is mid-1960s rock music, where style tokens from different subgenres of Western concert music are prominent yet always marked, it does make sense to link all of these together into a broadly "classical" topic. The same can be said of the "folk" topic, although here again the viability of such a reading depends on context. When discussing an artist such as Bob Dylan or the Incredible String Band, it may well be that specific folk topics need to be distinguished from one another. But in a case like "Lady Jane," we can observe on a more general level that there are folk topics and classical topics in the song that are linked through their shared historicism but are also distinct.

In the case of "Guinevere" (music example 2.24), the most significant trope is the one combining the folk and Indian topics. The first is established by the overall melodic and harmonic feeling, the acoustic instrumentation, the lyrics, and the $\frac{3}{4}$ meter, which verges on being a waltz topic but does not quite arrive there due to the frequent pauses. The pauses in themselves hint at a hymn form, not unlike the way the plagal cadence was hinted at in "See My Friends." The Indian topic is mildly raised by the use of Indian instruments (sitar, harmonium, subtle percussion), although these play parts that do not in themselves have many Indian characteristics. Overall, it is illustrative to consider "Lady Jane," "Guinevere," and "See My Friends" together as representing a range of options regarding

Music example 2.24. Donovan, "Guinevere," first verse, vocal and guitar (0:18–0:35, 0:55–1:09). Written by Donovan Leitch. © 1966 by Donovan (Music) Ltd. / peermusic Canada Inc. Used by Permission. All Rights Reserved.

the deployment of folkloric and Indian topics and showing how they had the potential to shade continuously into one another.

Love

While the troping of topics is usually studied within texts, the concept can be extended to describe the overall style of an artist or group where that style displays striking contrasts and dichotomies. This could be done for several of the artists discussed in this chapter, but one of the most suggestive cases is Love. The contradictions and tensions within their image are described by Barney Hoskyns, who also gives hints as to how these produced recurrent tropes within individual songs and albums: "On one level, Love were just one of several garage-style bands playing 'Hey Joe' on the scene that year. But on another level they were a unique phenomenon: an interracial, 'two-tone' group playing an extraordinary hybrid of R&B, folk-rock and psychedelic pop" (1996, 120). Hoskyns goes on to quote contemporaries who felt that Love's image was threatening and dark, with adjectives including demonic, manipulative, destructive, punk, gangster, and intimidating. Similar antisocial tendencies were sometimes attributed to other garage rockers, for example, the Seeds, but in the case of Love it seems likely that racial bias was a factor. Nonetheless, the essential dualism stands, because however these garage elements are described, Love's music at the same time contains a great deal of pop sweetness: "If Love were hoods, they were psychedelicized hoods, and the tension within the band between punk and flower power was part of what made their songs so compelling" (Hoskyns 1996, 121–22). In the mid-1960s, such a combination of elements was perceived as dichotomous, whereas in the long run, tropes along these lines would come to symbolize Los Angeles as a unique scene. Hoskyns (1996, 124) notes that LA had a long-standing tradition of orchestral pop along with early garage rock. He also argues that the underlying tone of menace and darkness is in line with established themes of film noir. While Love sometimes combines such elements into a single song, the trope is more obviously active on the level of idiolect, in the contrast between individual songs. With that in mind, I will compare topical features of a few different songs that illustrate the full range of affect. The first is "Softly to Me."

The song opens with an extended guitar introduction that seems influenced by flamenco and is strongly rhythmic but at the same time lacks a clear sense of meter. After that, the second part of the introduction adds several other psychedelic style components that we have not yet seen in other examples (music example 2.25).

Jazz Pop. Love frequently evokes jazz topics. In "Softly to Me" these are most strongly presented in the guitar (chord voicings, timbre, and rhythm) and in the relaxed drums (ride cymbal emphasis and a rolling figure based on both snare and toms). The organ line is also crucial in setting up a jazz topic. Unlike "Eight Miles High," and also unlike the more nostalgic/old-time jazz to be discussed later, this jazz topic is reminiscent of jazz-pop in a West Coast, cool jazz vein. It is just as modern as the Coltrane-inspired jazz topic in "Eight Miles High" but is also more aligned with the show-business side of LA. When Love evoked jazz, it was usually in this mood, and this is one thing that gave them topical distinctiveness at the time, causing their style to itself later become a topic not just of psychedelia but specifically of mid-1960s Los Angeles.

Latin. The cool jazz topic is also important in the way it overlaps with Latin topics. In "Softly to Me" that overlap is evident throughout the rhythm section. And there is more than one Latin topic at play, since the flamenco coloring of the first part of the introduction evokes a more folkloristic, exoticized Latin topic in advance of the more modern, jazz-related one that follows. It is extremely common to find Latin features in rhythm sections of the mid-1960s, psychedelic ones included. And as Tagg and Clarida have remarked, there was significant overlap between what I have called the twang guitar continuum and various 1960s Latin crossover genres (Tagg and Clarida 2003, 395). Latin topics are also relevant to what I called rhythm box drums, since many of the popular rhythm patterns used in this way were Latin in origin. However, despite their prevalence in early psychedelia, Latin-style features are not often foregrounded or exploited in a way that would suggest any particular psychedelic importance. They are more often blended in and relatively unmarked, present as part of the period pop style.

Organ. The organ in this case is crucial to the jazz topic, and we will have more and more cause to look at organ timbres in later chapters. The organ can evoke a wide range of topics because it is so variable in timbre and texture and also because it has been associated with so many different styles and contexts since Roman times. The situation with organ in these respects is similar to the twang guitar continuum. However, unlike guitar-based topics, the organ will not form a

Music example 2.25. Love, "Softly to Me," introduction (0:16–0:30). Words and Music by Bryan Maclean. © 1966 Trio Music Company. Copyright Renewed. This arrangement © 2015 Trio Music Company. All Rights Administered by BMG Rights Management (US) LLC. All Rights Reserved Used by Permission. Reprinted by permission of Hal Leonard Corporation.

central strand in my analysis because while it is complex and often important, it is not a central instrument in the rock tradition to the same degree as guitar, bass, and drums. Nonetheless, it will be worthwhile to keep in sight the extraordinary range of topical resources associated with this instrument and how they have helped define a range of psychedelia-related topics (e.g., garage rock, various jazz subgenres, different eras of classical music, gospel, and space rock, among others).

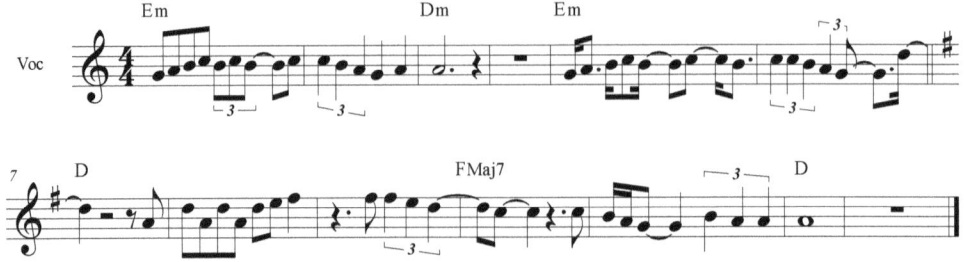

Music example 2.26. Love, "Softly to Me," A section, vocals (0:30–0:53). Words and Music by Bryan Maclean. © 1966 Trio Music Company. Copyright Renewed. This arrangement © 2015 Trio Music Company. All Rights Administered by BMG Rights Management (US) LLC. All Rights Reserved Used by Permission. Reprinted by permission of Hal Leonard Corporation.

Music example 2.27. Love, "Softly to Me," C section and return to A section, vocals and lead guitar (1:22–1:36). Words and Music by Bryan Maclean. © 1966 Trio Music Company. Copyright Renewed. This arrangement © 2015 Trio Music Company. All Rights Administered by BMG Rights Management (US) LLC. All Rights Reserved Used by Permission. Reprinted by permission of Hal Leonard Corporation.

Through-Composed Form. "Softly to Me" also gives us a chance to mention a formal device that is often found in psychedelic music but has not yet been raised: through-composition. True examples of through-composition in this period are quite rare, but psychedelic compositions often approximate it by blurring formal divisions through unexpected phrase extensions, elisions, digressions, and so forth. Something along these lines was already seen in "See My Friends," and "Softly to Me" is arguably even more through-composed in effect. As with

"See My Friends," the through-composed effect can be illustrated through consideration of the vocal melody and of the general underlying harmonies. In the first part of the vocals (music example 2.26), there is a loose and discursive approach to rhythm that is enhanced by a dramatic leap upward in the middle of the phrase corresponding to change of key and by colorful harmonies in the new key, especially an F-major seventh chord in the context of D Mixolydian. Also, the phrase overall is thirteen measures long, subverting normal expectations of phrase length.

A little later (music example 2.27) there is another change of key and a dramatically different melodic profile. Then there is an abrupt return to the original key and also a major-minor transformation with respect to the preceding A-major chord, with a change of rhythmic emphasis to quarter-note triplets. There is also a classical or fanfare topic evoked by the guitar in this passage, with its ornamented doubling of the melody.

The end result of all this melodic variation, modulation, and unexpected chord color is that the song feels as if it flows continuously from point to point in an exploratory way. It is nowhere near as bound to conventional formal expectations as most of our examples up to this point have been. "Softly to Me" also presents something like a narrative in the way topics in different sections of the song flow into one another. In most of our other examples, different topics were either juxtaposed directly or alternated in ways that seemed largely determined by conventional song forms. But in this case, partly due to the through-composed feeling and partly because different topics appear in different sections, something more like a narrative reading may be possible: flamenco-inflected opening, followed by jazz-pop, followed by a flowingly discursive vocal, followed by Baroque fanfare flourishes. At this point I will not pursue such a reading but simply note the sorts of formal characteristics that suggest the viability of one. The most important point is that "Softly to Me" stays within something like a conventional pop song form and so is closely related to the other examples we've discussed, but at the same time it displays a formal looseness and a topical fluidity that hint at the more open-ended styles to come in the later 1960s.

"Softly to Me" appeared on Love's debut album, released in March 1966, and on the album its jazz-pop mood, relaxed and exploratory, is contrasted by more aggressive garage-rock songs such as "My Little Red Book" and "Hey Joe." Any such song would do as a point of comparison, so I will contrast "Softly to Me" with "Seven & Seven Is," which first appeared as a single in July 1966.

Most of the topical highlights of this song are established in the introduction, which employs a frantic motoric drum pattern related to four-on-the-floor drums but is also evocative of noise techniques from the rave-up (music example 2.28). In the introduction there is also a regularly spaced chords texture, which adds an epic dimension, and bass glisses strongly evocative of a revving motorcycle, especially when combined with the motoric drums.[12] Later in the song an explosion sound effect is framed by a structural pause, and another important feature is the way a radically new textural space is introduced right at the end of the song, something like a waltz or $\frac{12}{8}$ rhythm-and-blues ballad, with maybe a hint

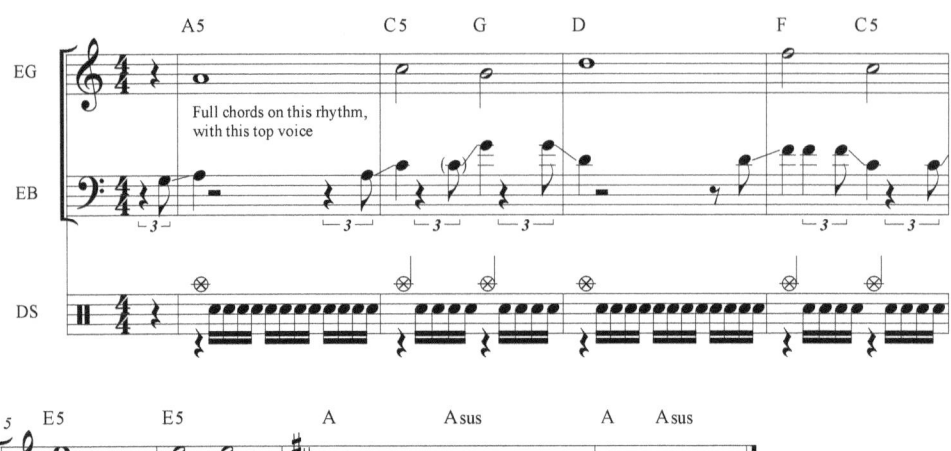

Music example 2.28. Love, "Seven & Seven Is," introduction (0:00–0:13). Written by Arthur Lee. © Trio Music Company, Inc.

of surf/spy topicality as well. One reading would be to suggest that this sudden change creates a trope relative to all of the epic and chaotic connotations of the earlier parts of the song. But there is also an opportunity here to notice how troping can look different when considered at different levels of generality. Looking just at local regions, for most of the song we have a chaotic, restless affect that connotes an epic topic in a particularly psychotic and apocalyptic mood. Then we suddenly have a different set of topics at the end marked by a much more relaxed and contemplative feel. On the local level, this strong contrast separates the regions of the song. However, a moment of disjunction is not affectively inconsistent with the earlier apocalyptic mood. This means that, viewed at a higher level of generality, the last section is consistent with the earlier part of the song precisely because it is inconsistent with it. In any event, the overarching point is that when we consider that songs of this sort existed side by side in the Love repertoire with songs like "Softly to Me," we can start to see the higher-level troping that made their idiolect distinctive for the time.

The last Love song I want to look at is "Stephanie Knows Who." This song presents the strongest examples yet of certain important topics and style compo-

Music example 2.29. Love, "Stephanie Knows Who," introduction (0:00–0:09). Words and Music by Arthur Lee. © 1966 Grass Roots Productions. Copyright Renewed. This arrangement © 2015 Grass Roots Productions. All Rights Administered by BMG Rights Management (US) LLC. All Rights Reserved Used by Permission. Reprinted by permission of Hal Leonard Corporation.

Music example 2.30. Love, "Stephanie Knows Who," first transition, drums and bass (0:43–0:54). Words and Music by Arthur Lee. © 1966 Grass Roots Productions. Copyright Renewed. This arrangement © 2015 Grass Roots Productions. All Rights Administered by BMG Rights Management (US) LLC. All Rights Reserved Used by Permission. Reprinted by permission of Hal Leonard Corporation.

nents and also displays a narrative potential even more pronounced than "Softly to Me."

The introduction (music example 2.29) is already rich in topical suggestion. The fast ¾ tempo evokes a waltz but, more specifically, circus music in waltz time. The arpeggiated line played on harpsichord supports the circus aspect with its clanging, metallic timbre, but it also creates classical music associations. In measure 7, with the entry of bass and drum set, the rhythm brings all the associations already discussed for motor rhythm and four-on-the-floor drums. The circling chromatic riff also adds to the swirling carnival atmosphere. Taken together, the introduction fits in with earlier evocations of classical music but also evokes the circus topic, which was widespread in psychedelic music of this period. The specific nuance of this circus music seems to be somewhat manic and maybe even deranged. This in turn connects this song to the kind of psychotic affect discussed earlier.

When the vocals enter, all of these features are continued, along with a vocal style that verges on shouting and is highly discursive in rhythmic structure and phrasing. The next major element in topical terms is introduced with the first transition (music example 2.30). Affectively, the rhythm and melody of the first transition closely mirror the swirling, somewhat agitated tone already established. But the transition is also evocative of bebop in its unpredictable unison stop-start texture. That association becomes even more clear in the second transition, which segues into the saxophone solo (music example 2.31). The second transition shows how motor rhythm can provide a powerful basis for building tension and also (in the saxophone part) how a fast trill can serve a function

Music example 2.31. Love, "Stephanie Knows Who," second transition and beginning of saxophone solo (0:54–1:05). Words and Music by Arthur Lee. © 1966 Grass Roots Productions. Copyright Renewed. This arrangement © 2015 Grass Roots Productions. All Rights Administered by BMG Rights Management (US) LLC. All Rights Reserved Used by Permission. Reprinted by permission of Hal Leonard Corporation.

similar to the siren trill. Then the tension erupts into an instrumental in $^5_4$, with the saxophone blowing quite freely and other instruments playing figures that are somewhat reminiscent of jazz accompaniment but are a bit more literally repetitive, also therefore evoking rhythm and blues or surf music. These bebop evocations, like Love's use of jazz-pop elsewhere, show how various subgenres of jazz found application in psychedelic music of the period in ways that underscored different affects—edgy and perhaps psychotic in this case, mellow and contemplative in the case of "Softly to Me," and epic or nostalgic in examples discussed elsewhere in the chapter.

Taken as a whole, the music of Love is extraordinary in its emotional and textural range and in the way it evoked various facts of the band's home city of Los Angeles.

The Beatles, Part 1

Given the survey format of this chapter, the Beatles present a special challenge. As one of the most important groups in the development of early psychedelia, they could sustain a detailed study on their own. But by this point, certain important aspects of the Beatles have already been covered. And given that the Beatles also play a key role in chapter 3, they will here be discussed mainly with an eye toward showing how they participated in major trends already surveyed, along with a few observations on topical features that were more distinct to their idiolect. An in-depth analysis of some key works ("Strawberry Fields Forever" and *Sgt. Pepper*) will come in the next chapter.[13]

The line between features that should be read as psychedelic versus those that should be seen as merely cognate is especially fluid in the Beatles. This is partly because they, like the Yardbirds, were pioneers in many style components that would become typical of psychedelia. The Beatles had not yet entered their psychedelic phase when they first explored many of these resources. For example, their interest in signal processing and unusual instruments goes back far before their psychedelic period and had reached a notable state of development by the time of *Help!* (Everett 2001, 281). And even into their psychedelic period, the Beatles explored topics and affects that could be read not only as cognate with psychedelia but also separately from it. One especially rich example is "I'm Only Sleeping." The song uses vari-speed techniques similar to those in the more clearly psychedelic "Rain" (Everett 1999, 50). The harmony is languorous, and the melody tends to avoid strong gestures and closures: "From the melodic and harmonic devices to the unreal colors, [the song contains] particularly expressive text painting" (51). All of this could be read as psychedelic, but on the other hand it could be taken as evidence of how prepsychedelic signifiers of sleepiness and reflective states of mind were available for redeployment in psychedelia while also persisting alongside it.

When considering style components that later became topics, there are a few already mentioned where the Beatles' contributions need to be acknowledged. One is rhythmic originality and unpredictability. As Everett notes, "Originality in rhythmic structures, especially involving changing meters and free phrase lengths and phrase rhythm, marks the mature music of the Beatles as vastly different from that of their contemporaries" (2001, 62–64). Similarly, with respect to harmonic language, the Beatles provide some of the clearest examples of true tonal ambiguity as opposed to the milder forms of mixture and harmonic color already discussed (see, e.g., Everett 2001, 331). And the Beatles were also leaders in the incorporation of Indian music elements and the use of a wide variety of studio techniques, including tape loops, vari-speed, and reversed tape, the latter two being likely first heard as part of a rock release on "Rain" (Reising and LeBlanc 2009, 95). Further details of Beatles songs during the 1965–66 era will find their place in the discussion in chapter 3, so for now I want to focus on one area that was of special importance to other bands in 1965–66 and that has not yet been explored: the relationship between the Beatles and the avant-garde and how it relates to their self-consciously reflexive form of psychedelia. In order to pursue this theme, it can be instructive to compare the Beatles to Frank Zappa, who was also experimenting with tape music and who also foregrounded psychedelic topics, although in his case by way of parody and even derision rather than advocacy or sympathy.

There were clear areas of overlap in the 1960s between various countercultures and avant-gardes. Robert Adlington has argued that this was possible because of revolutionary and political resonances in avant-gardes more generally. He traces "the alliance of political and artistic radicalism" to late nineteenth-century France and shows how the trend was intensified by several prominent movements in the early twentieth century. Adlington (2009, 3) contrasts this interpretation with another, perhaps more common view that avant-garde artists were elitist and disconnected from public engagement. He argues that earlier avant-gardes were not nearly as uniformly elitist nor as uniformly depoliticized as is sometimes asserted and that as a consequence they were available as natural allies of 1960s radical movements. Some such overlaps were especially relevant to psychedelia, for example, the scene around the San Francisco Tape Music Center and the work of individuals such as Ramon Sender, Don Buchla, Terry Riley, and Morton Subotnick, all of whom were either active participants in or at least influences on the growing hippie counterculture (Bernstein 2008; Pinch and Trocco 2002). In New York, similar overlaps could be found in the work of LaMonte Young and Andy Warhol / the Velvet Underground, among others. And within both San Francisco and New York the connection extended back into the earlier 1960s and 1950s through institutions such as the San Francisco Mime Troupe and the early light shows that predated, but were deeply influential on, psychedelic theatricality.[14]

Aside from the obviously cognate relationship between avant-garde formal experimentation and psychedelia, there is a complicated history at play regarding the relationship of earlier avant-gardes to psychedelic drugs. Marcus Boon (2002, 233–42) offers an extended study of how mescaline and peyote were assessed by interwar modernists such as Sartre, Michaux, Benjamin, and Witkiewicz. These experiences were almost all administered under clinical conditions, and none seem to have been uniformly positive or spiritually oriented. Boon speculates that this was partly because the psychedelic experience tested the modernist commitment to a materialist, objective consciousness. The descriptions written by such people tended to emphasize the visual, along with themes of excess, instability, and loss of control (242). But affect aside, it is significant that there were varieties of psychedelia already under development within avant-garde communities. As a result, later 1960s encounters between popular culture psychedelia and the avant-garde would be a complicated negotiation rather than a simple case of borrowing in either direction. Within this earlier avant-garde context, some of the social and political resonances were strikingly different from many stereotypes regarding 1960s countercultures. Most importantly, as Boon notes, interest in psychedelics can be consistent with a markedly right-wing viewpoint. It is not difficult to cast psychedelic experience, especially before the mid-1960s, as "the experience of an elite, the few who believe they have been privileged to go beyond the laws of everyday life" (257). This group would include, a little more broadly, "aristocrats, bankers, German right-wing ex-military men, not to mention the CIA and the Nazis.... Psychedelic drugs evoked several themes that were dear to the hearts of intellectuals on the right. They were associated with the primitive, the irrational, and the mythological, and put the intrepid latter-day gentleman explorer back in touch with his 'origins.'... The 'sacramental' aspect of many of the accounts of psychedelic use by this group in the 1950s often devolves down to a fetishization of exotic or expensive locales, and the privilege of being invited into them" (258–59).

Taking this complex history into account, it is no surprise that the Beatles and Frank Zappa could share many characteristics—an interest in tape music and other formal experiments, self-consciousness about the high-culture origin of such techniques, and an interest in how they interact with psychedelia—while at the same time differing profoundly in their basic attitudes and agendas. For example, Zappa treated tape music on a continuum that included cognate experiments in orchestration. On the other hand, while the Beatles were aware of this broader lineage and were influenced by Cage and Stockhausen, among others, their own releases of this period tended to explore tape effects in a more decorative or self-enclosed manner. Even in a song like "Tomorrow Never Knows," the result is more like a deeply transformed pop/rock song than like musique concrète. And when the Beatles did employ orchestral instruments, they were almost always used in a conventional manner (except, of course, for "A Day in the Life"). An even more profound difference lies in their basic attitude toward psychedelia. While much in Zappa's work was formally cognate with psychedelia, he pointedly rejected and satirized the style and subculture. In this he is closer to the somewhat dark and skeptical view typical of earlier avant-gardes. By contrast, for the Beatles during this period one major attraction of avant-garde techniques was their cognate nature relative to all aspects of psychedelia, intent included. Their phase of open psychedelic advocacy did not last long, but it also corresponded with many of their most striking appropriations from the avant-garde.

Both Frank Zappa and the Beatles were self-reflexive in their use of psychedelic styles and topics. And in both cases there was little doubt about the underlying stance and intent: advocacy in the case of the Beatles (at least for most of 1966–67) and derision in the case of Zappa. Interestingly, around mid- to late 1966 there was a proliferation of songs that are intermediate in tone, featuring a density of psychedelic signifiers that could only have been self-conscious, but with an overall affect that cannot be easily pinned down as either serious or joking. Examples include the Magic Mushrooms' "It's a Happening," the Electric Prunes' "I Had Too Much to Dream Last Night," and the Deep's entire *Psychedelic Moods* album. As Johnson and Stax put it, "Just as in the case of over-the-top bad trip songs, the message of these psychedelic sermons may at times be tongue-in-cheek. Not all garage bands who made songs about mystical, psychedelic journeys did so seriously, they may at times have been joking/satirizing, or making something unusual and interesting without any deeper intent" (2006, 422).

In the case of both avant-garde experiments and possibly tongue-in-cheek sonic extremism, we see the crucial role of studio practices and electronic signal processing in establishing the midperiod psychedelic rock sound. As with many style components, this family of techniques includes elements that are not particularly topical and a smaller number that refer to existing topics. Also, the overall practice of exploring such material serves as an important topic of psychedelia. One of the more important practices in this connection is the inclusion in an otherwise conventional song form of what could be called *unmeasured sound effects passages*: extended passages without a clear meter, often without even a clear pulse, made up either of noninstrumental sounds or of instruments defamiliarized through signal processing and extended performance techniques. By 1966 such passages were especially common as introductions. Many early introductions of this sort presented only a single "strange" noise, often with a swell, that segued into the rhythm section entrance (e.g., the 13th Floor Elevators' "Reverberation (Doubt)" and the Electric Prunes' "I Had Too Much to Dream Last Night"). In other cases, the introduction would present a wider range of sounds but would still be mostly ambient in structure (e.g., the Deep's "It's All a Part of Me"). Finally, some sound-effect introductions resembled musique concrète in being "composed noise," as with Zappa's "Who Are the Brain Police?"

While these sorts of passages were especially common as introductions, they also appeared as outros and as internal digressions from song form. Equally important was the proliferation of sound effects and overtly electronic sounds layered on top of regular song forms. Some common choices included animal and nature sounds (insects, roosters, birds, frogs, etc.), explosions, and vocal noises (already discussed). Most of these have connotations too clear to require elaboration, although subtleties are often possible. For example, the rooster can connote a rural or pastoral context but also connotes temporality and awakening. Such sound effects are often not properly considered topical and function more like lyrics in the way they interact with musical topicality, although several of them

Percussion staff, top to bottom: shaker+tambourine, small cowbell or woodblock, wooden ratchet

Music example 2.32. Lyme & Cybelle, "Follow Me," transition, rhythm section (0:48–0:53). Written by Warren Zevon and Violet Santangelo. © EMI Longitude Music Co.

did become psychedelic prototopics. However, one sound effect in particular deserves more comment because of its ubiquity and the subtlety of its variations. This is the clockwork effect.

While discussing Timothy Leary and the general call to "wake up," Reising and LeBlanc note that "both before and since *Sgt. Pepper*, psychedelic rock has used alarm clocks, chimes, bells, effects of clocks ticking and other effects to signal such psychedelic awakenings" (2008, 111). A wide range of different signifiers can achieve this effect. The most obvious are recorded clockwork sounds or percussive noises strongly reminiscent of them (see, e.g., "Time Has Come Today" by the Chambers Brothers, music example 2.6). But consider a case such as "Follow Me" (music example 2.32). Here the effect is not just a clock but clockwork in the broader sense of a machine-like texture made up from the rhythmically regular drone in the guitar and bass, and the drum and percussion parts, which are regular yet polyrhythmic and timbrally multilayered. In terms of both signifiers and signifieds, the lines between a clock, other machinery, and the machinic in more abstract terms can be porous. In some cases this is deliberately exploited, for example, in a category of sound effect that could be described as "mechanical laughter." This sort of sound combines elements of clockwork with elements of the vocal, as, for example, at the end of Pink Floyd's "Bike," where the overlaps between mechanical laughter, carnival, and a psychotic affect are in full evidence. This flexibility of "the machinic" in terms of both signifiers and signifieds will also be crucial to our discussion of space rock.

Although I am generally deferring discussion of individual Beatle songs to the next chapter, we'll make an exception for "Yellow Submarine." This song provides an especially rich example of how sound effects can function topically, and also introduces a few important new areas for discussion. To start, "Yellow Submarine" is not alone in being both psychedelic and nautical. For example, the oceanic is a component of the surf topic and so can be present to some degree anytime surf topicality is evoked. Also, oceanic and naval topicality are found in psychedelia more generally, for example, in Jimi Hendrix's "1983 . . . (a Merman I Should Turn to Be)," in Donovan's "Atlantis," and in certain metaphors common in space rock (space ships, etc.). Oceanic imagery continued to be an attractive framework for neopsychedelic artists into the 1980s and 1990s, as in "Strangers Die Every Day" by the Butthole Surfers (1986) and *The Mollusk* by Ween (1997). It was also occasionally a prominent theme in works that straddled the line between psychedelic and progressive rock, such as *Tales from Topographic Oceans* and the cover art of *Fragile* (both by Yes). The range of these examples illustrates the rich variety of cognate themes offered to psychedelia by nautical topics: adventure and exploration; mysticism and magic; varied historical contexts; and intense representations of the natural world, from the sublime to the highly intimate.

Apart from their nautical specificity, the sound effects in "Yellow Submarine" are interesting both because of how they signify individually and because of their narrative quality. They contribute to the naval and oceanic mood and evoke a feeling of nostalgia or distance largely due to their timbre, recalling radio broadcasts not only as a contemporary experience but also as an emblem of the near-distant past. The idea of a general cinematic topic is clearly relevant here not only because the sound effects reinforce the storytelling aspect of the song but also because they are assembled into a coherent sonic scenario, one that could be diegetic to an imagined series of filmic events. This would be true even if the song had not in fact been the basis for a film.

Perhaps the most prominent aspect of "Yellow Submarine" is the way it evokes childhood and nostalgia as general areas of signification. Many commentators have argued that a seeming desire to return to childhood is typical of 1960s British psychedelia, arguably more so than in the United States (Lovesey 2011, 136; Young 2010, 453–55). That desire certainly became a key theme for the Beatles, and "Yellow Submarine" is one of the more obvious examples. The childhood lyrical themes in "Yellow Submarine" also link up with a more general mood of nostalgia deriving from the sing-along texture and the use of a marching band. This is an area requiring a discussion of its own.

The Nostalgic and Quaint

Many common topics in mid-1960s psychedelia refer to the near-distant past (the nineteenth century through the 1940s or so). These topics are often used in ways that seem deliberately nostalgic or quaint. One of the most common is the brass band, heard, for example, on Bob Dylan's "Rainy Day Women #12 & 35," the Beach Boys' "Good Vibrations," the Deep's "It's All a Part of Me,"

Donovan's "Mellow Yellow," and many Beatles tracks, including "Yellow Submarine." In a related discussion, Tagg and Clarida (2003, 409) report that major-key $^6_8$ march music such as Sousa's "Liberty Bell" march tends to elicit responses with a noteworthy degree of consistency. Connotations of the style include social activities, the circus, celebrations, humor, ceremonies, public institutions, provincialism, the military, public occasions, marching/parades, and old times. The scope of the old-times connotation is often from the late nineteenth century into the early twentieth, a period I'll generally refer to as belle époque.

One striking point of complexity is that while the militaristic connections are very pronounced, this sort of music also connotes happiness and childhood and is not generally associated with aggression: "It seems that we are dealing with a process in which members of the listening public are able to detach their perception of the festive, presentational and celebratory aspects of the same sort of music—its *fun-and-power potential*, so to speak—and apply that perception to any context in which *either* fun *or* power is the more essential social characteristic" (Tagg and Clarida 2003, 412). This internal tension can also be worked for its absurdist potential in a way that links to political issues and oppositional stances of 1960s countercultures (418). I would also add that in the case of psychedelia the elements of safe childhood, celebration, and humor were especially important, as was the satirical potential of such materials. Also significant is how *human* many of these associations are, compared to the more cosmic connotations of some other psychedelic materials. This is another reason such topics could have been comforting, apart from their evocation of childhood.

Apart from brass and marching bands, other topics generally evocative of the near-distant past include circus music, the waltz, ragtime (especially piano-based), early Tin Pan Alley pop, and music hall. There is a range of ways in which these topics interact with the surrounding context. For a listener whose own heritage overlaps significantly with such topics, a mixture of association and disassociation is possible. The topics are strongly separated from the present identity of the listener in temporal terms and often as well by social and institutional distinctions, but at the same time they constitute a part of that listener's heritage and identity. There are also simpler dynamics at work. Such topics are often strange or novel in a straightforward way, being non sequiturs relative to the prevailing stylistic frame. There is also the nostalgic comfort of familiarity and of the mythological past. Not all of these elements will be relevant in each case, but, taken together, they describe much of the way such topics are framed and function affectively.

Such topics enact a structure similar to what Roland Barthes (1972, 114–15) found in his analysis of the mythological sign as a second-order semiological system. For such topics in a psychedelic context, the original meanings and contexts are not absent but are somewhat attenuated and put into parentheses, sublimated to an overriding affect and mythologization. This is likely true of every case in which a preexisting topic or cognate style is mobilized, but it is especially clear in such nostalgic and pointedly anachronistic examples. This being

Music example 2.33. Country Joe and the Fish, "Section 43," introduction (0:00–0:17). Written by Joe McDonald. © Joyful Wisdom Music / Alkatraz Korner Music Co. Used by Permission. All Rights Reserved.

Music example 2.34. Country Joe and the Fish, "Section 43," first guitar solo (beginning) (0:17–0:34). Written by Joe McDonald. © Joyful Wisdom Music / Alkatraz Korner Music Co. Used by Permission. All Rights Reserved.

Above and facing: Music example 2.35. Country Joe and the Fish, "Section 43," B section (1:17–1:54). Written by Joe McDonald. © Joyful Wisdom Music / Alkatraz Korner Music Co. Used by Permission. All Rights Reserved.

said, there is also a level of interpretation where it seems important to deal with the specificity of the topics rather than their general mythological application, as with the waltz-as-carnival-psychosis reading of "Stephanie Knows Who," or the links between a specifically British nostalgia and particular periods of history in "Yellow Submarine," or the links between countercultural rebellion and Wild West topics discussed earlier.

Country Joe and the Fish: "Section 43"

There is one more song to discuss before summarizing our findings. "Section 43" by Country Joe and the Fish is striking in the way it presents several of the topics we have already discussed but in novel versions and combinations that collectively suggest a whole new topical area: the space topic. In chapter 4 we will look in detail at how space rock became a relatively freestanding genre in the late 1960s after first emerging as a subgenre of psychedelic rock. "Section 43" is one of the earliest and clearest examples of this earlier phase, and it is even more interesting given that little else in the group's repertoire hints at a similar direction. The mood is set immediately in the introduction (music example 2.33). The bass enters alone, setting up a looping near-repetition texture that will later be key to our analysis of space rock. The organ is intermediate in timbre between a church pipe organ and a garage-rock organ, and the figure it plays resembles the sort of epic/cinematic theme discussed in connection with "Eight Miles High," although with a more relaxed overall feel. The drums and percussion also provide a superb example of space toms.

The start of the guitar solo (music example 2.34) is interesting in that while certain features might recall the Indian topic, the overall effect is not particularly Orientalist. Neither is it strongly surf. Instead, it represents a type of meandering, diatonic, moderately ornamented lead guitar that will become more and more typical of space rock. In this sort of context, specific exotic topical references become increasingly attenuated, but a generalized affect of exoticism and otherworldliness remains. I would say the same about the organ solo, although there, explicit Orientalist tendencies are a bit stronger.

One crucial feature of "Section 43" is that it is not a song but an instrumental, the first entirely instrumental piece we have studied. Space rock was marked by an increasing amount of time spent on instrumental passages over vocal ones, and this is an early example. The importance of instrumental passages to psy-

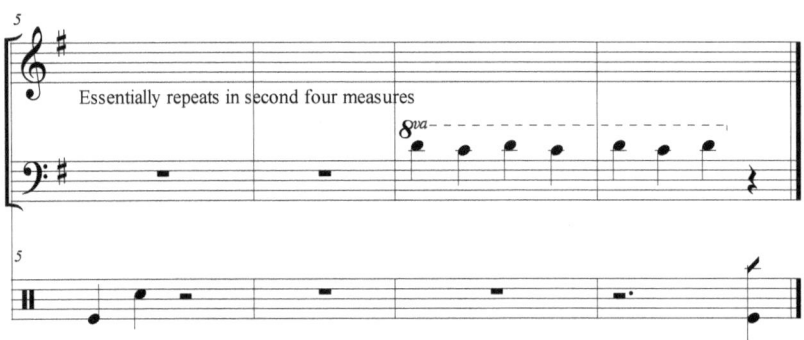

Music example 2.36. Country Joe and the Fish, "Section 43," transition following harmonica solo (4:01–4:19). Written by Joe McDonald. © Joyful Wisdom Music / Alkatraz Korner Music Co. Used by Permission. All Rights Reserved.

chedelia has been discussed several times already, especially in connection with the rave-up. There is another connection to the rave-up in "Section 43," when the rhythm section goes to double time at measure 18 of the first guitar solo, although the linearity of the rave-up is entirely absent.

Up to this point, the connections to space rock and space topics have been a matter of small nuances and adjustments to topics we have seen in other contexts. However, in the protracted B section there are structural and topical features that more directly evoke outer space (music example 2.35). Regarding early science fiction film scores, Timothy Scheurer has written: "Space is not often the subject of program music, opera, or even musical comedy. Popular music provides no topics, primarily because it borrows from film or the limited serious music examples cited above. . . . It is in science fiction films, then, that we observe some of the greatest innovations in film scoring" (2008, 56). One thing we can take from this is that the situation had changed by the time of late 1960s space rock. In that genre, popular music did develop and extend topics related to outer space. But also, with respect to earlier science fiction film scoring practices, Scheurer notes two particular topical signifiers of space, both of which are found in "Section 43." One is the use of ostinati and extended arpeggios to evoke a feeling of long undulating waves, which in turn evoke the vastness of space. Scheurer (2008, 57, 69) calls this the "weightless" gesture, and the examples he chooses suggest that it also employs voice leading that moves from one chord to another mostly by stepwise and often chromatic increments, with many common tones, such that the gestural affect of drifting overtakes functional harmony. This texture is clearly dominant throughout the B section of "Section 43" (music example 2.35). The second topical signifier identified by Scheurer (2008, 57) is the use of high-pitched metallic percussion to evoke twinkling stars. That signifier is also evident throughout this passage in the use of vibraphone and in the clean electric guitar timbre. All of these components combine to create a topical evocation of outer space and science fiction. Without this passage, it would be much more difficult to make the case for "Section 43" as an early space rock song.

From a topical point of view, the most striking thing about the sections that follow is how they present tropes that could seem like non sequiturs but on another level point out interesting parallels and overlaps between the newly emerging space rock topics and some other topics we have already seen. For instance, the harmonica solo is evocative of the western topic. The nostalgic, low-tech, and rural connotations of this topic are at odds with concepts of outer space, but, on the other hand, there are parallels in the vast expanses of the plains and in the macho heroism of exploration. Perhaps more difficult to directly integrate is the transition following the harmonica solo (music example 2.36). This section begins with an abrupt shift to a circus topic (calliope-like dissonances, alternating bass, and clown-like interjected bends), but the passage also evokes clockwork and the siren trill. Rather than searching for subtle semantic connections between topics, it may be more pertinent to note that the circus topic is frequently used to create a disjunctive and disorienting effect, and this is a prime example. Also, while specific hearings will vary, it is not difficult to hear the clockwork and siren trill topics as subservient or secondary to the circus topic in this case, showing how within tropes one or more topics may be present largely to elaborate on another that forms the dominant point of reference.

Conclusion: The Big Picture through 1966

We have seen that by the end of 1966 there was an extremely rich topical field taking shape around psychedelia. Many preexisting topics were given psychedelic inflections, including topics such as the Indian, Gregorian, folkloric, belle époque (waltz, marching bands, music hall, etc.), circus, space, and jazz in many incarnations (1960s experimental, bebop, swing, cool jazz, and jazz-pop). While sources for these topics were diverse, there was an especially important influence from film genres such as westerns, spy films, epics, and science fiction. In some cases we had cause to evoke topics that would not cohere as such in other contexts (e.g., the classical, folk, and cinematic topics), illustrating the sensitive relationship between topic formation and the overall expectations, scope, and norms of a particular style. We identified areas in which topics clustered into particular formations, such as the twang guitar and fuzz continua, and also certain productive overlaps between the signifiers and signifieds of otherwise quite different topics, forming loosely affiliated groupings such as western/Gregorian, western/space, folk/Indian, and so forth. Finally, we had occasion to show how certain of these topics are embedded in rich historical lineages, which in turn allowed us to further situate psychedelia in a broader history of cultural practices. One example of special importance was the place of psychedelia in Western exoticism and Orientalism, where an especially subtle relationship was explored between self-othering and the othering of non-European cultures. Also important was the way in which psychedelia can be placed in the longer history of European American avant-gardes.

With respect to the borderline between clear-cut topicality and more marginal cases, we elaborated a vocabulary of musical resources, again representing a mixture of novel features, literal borrowings, and transformations of earlier styles. Highlights in this category included the place of concise song forms versus more formally extended structures; the rave-up as a strategy for formalizing signifiers of noise and chaos; strategies for weakening teleology, such as through-composition and the structural pause; characteristic harmonic devices; the special role of drums and of vocal textures; the semiotic richness of simple production techniques such as echo and reverberation; and prototopics that would eventually become quite well-defined topics of psychedelia, such as the siren trill and the use of certain production techniques (especially backward tape, vari-speed, and unmeasured sound effects passages). Finally, above the level of particular topics and style components, we considered some of the large-scale processes that allow the psychedelic style to function as a topical field. Highlights included the way in which the same topic can produce extremely different affective results; the sublation of earlier topical associations to allow new significance for a topical signifier (as with space toms vs. jungle toms, or the electric jug vs. the folkloric jug); the manner in which tropes can emerge not through any central planning but rather through the ongoing interaction of musicians (e.g., the default use of certain rhythm box drums patterns); the extension of the concept of troping to apply at the level of an individual or group idiolect; and the shifting boundary between topics that signify in isolation and those that cluster into temporally elaborated structures, along with observations about how differences in this regard can help mark off different subgenres of psychedelia. The rest of this book will largely be a matter of exploring how the possibilities of this topical field, already well in place by 1966, fueled a family of related psychedelic musics and imaginaries that continue to ramify into the present day.

Notes

1. Capitalization of topic names presents an interesting problem. In some cases, a topic is based on a style or genre that is usually capitalized, for example, Indian classical music or Gregorian chant. In other cases, capitalization is not appropriate, for example, as in the western topic, which is named after the western film genre. I have opted

to avoid capitalizing topic names except in cases where the capitalization is called for by a preexisting practice.

2. I use the word "motoric" in two related ways. At times it simply refers to the presence of motor rhythm. I also sometimes use the word in a more affective sense to describe textures that evoke a feeling of machinic consistency and repetition.

3. "Fuzz" refers to a family of signal-processing circuits, usually housed as outboard units patched between the instrument and the amplifier. Fuzz circuits differ in their specifics, but all serve to clip the input wave so that it more closely resembles a square wave. The audible effect varies from mild compression and distortion, to a sustaining kazoo-like or bee-like timbre, to very extreme forms of distortion and modulation, which leave little of the input signal intact. Commercial fuzz boxes first became available around 1962.

4. The line between echo and reverb is flexible. Reverberation is itself a very close overlapping of a large number of echoes. And within any reverberant texture there will be certain discrete repeats that are audible as such. In many cases, we can speak of echo and reverb as unified in their signifiers and signifieds. On the other hand, certain kinds of echo are semiotically distinct from reverberation, especially in later, more electronic musical textures.

5. I use the word "affect" in a Deleuzian sense to connote the general ability to effect and be effected. Its overlap with areas such as Baroque theories of affect and modern psychological theories of emotion is deliberate, but that is beyond the theoretical scope of this book to explore in depth (Echard 2006b, 2008, 2011).

6. Elsewhere I have given more details of my approach to the harmonic language of rock music during this period, along with a more detailed discussion of bibliography (Echard 1999, 2005).

7. Elsewhere I have presented an analysis of the semiotics of noise in rock contexts (Echard 2005). Further development of these theoretical aspects is beyond the scope of this book, but if I were to present such a discussion it would take as a starting point the work of Hegarty (2007).

8. Gerry Farrell also presents some useful perspectives on this complicated and rapidly changing period of popular music history (1997, 172–74).

9. A similar distinction was made by Steve Reich (2002, loc. 915–25/3298) as early as 1973.

10. By evoking a space topic here in connection with drums, I mean something more general than the drums/space linkage that emerged in the music and fan discourse of the Grateful Dead. Variants of the space topic specific to the Dead are discussed later.

11. I mean this in the sense of multiple speaking voices rather than multiple loudspeakers, although in many cases the effect arises in the context of a stereo mix, where panning between loudspeakers can emphasize the multiplicity of voices and can also enhance the depth of the resulting virtual space.

12. Thanks to Walter Everett for pointing out the motorcycle aspect.

13. For the most part I will refer to the album *Sgt. Pepper's Lonely Hearts Club Band* by the abbreviation *Sgt. Pepper*.

14. For an historical overview of light shows, see Pouncey (2005a, 2005b), Riley (2008), Martin (2008), and Bernstein and Payne (2008).

3 The Later 1960s

By the end of 1966, most of the musical topics central to psychedelia had been introduced in one form or another. In chapter 2 we gained an overview of this emergent topical field, surveying its major areas. With that perspective available, the rest of the book will be more thematic, focusing on selected important developments of later periods. This chapter, for example, centers on two main areas related to the later 1960s. First, we will look in depth at psychedelic soul and funk and their dramatic implications for the overall direction of psychedelic topicality. Second, we will consider how the topics we've already studied can function in larger contexts and in larger texts. In terms of larger contexts, we will consider the San Francisco scene, with special attention to visual culture and improvisation. And in terms of larger texts, we will explore the topical structure of an entire album by closely analyzing the Beatles' *Sgt. Pepper's Lonely Hearts Club Band*.

Early Psychedelic Soul and Funk

Psychedelic soul and funk have topical features that are extremely complex and suggestive. They also underwent a dramatic evolution in style and lyrical content from the late 1960s to the mid-1970s. In order to keep these various strands clear, I'm going to cover psychedelic soul and funk in two phases. For now we will look at the earlier period, up to around 1970. The next chapter considers the more explicitly Afrofuturist psychedelia of the mid-1970s. We will begin with some critical theory in order to situate African American culture more generally relative to mid-1960s psychedelia. This is potentially a very deep and wide-ranging subject, so I'm going to focus on a few selected concepts that can help with three particular topical questions: (1) Which specific preexisting African American musical styles and topics were incorporated into psychedelia? (2) In what ways were they resonant with other psychedelic styles and with 1960s psychedelic imaginaries? (3) In what ways might the markedness of race have conditioned these relationships?

Foregrounding race in this way is not without its problems. Some theorists have made a compelling case that categories like "black music" and "white music" suffer from such serious logical and ethical problems that we should avoid them altogether (perhaps the most pointed and most musicologically complete argument of this sort is Tagg [1989]). While I sympathize with these arguments, there are several reasons why we need to engage with some of these racialized musical categories, albeit cautiously. The approach I take is to start from the historical fact of racial markedness in late 1960s rock culture. By that time, rock artists and audiences had become predominantly white, and the overtly African American roots of rock music had generally been obscured. Black artist and black-associated styles such as soul and funk were important participants in late 1960s rock culture but were also marked as unusual, perhaps especially in psychedelia. This markedness is something that needs to be taken into account, especially since markedness relations are of crucial importance in structuring topical fields. So in moving forward, I will engage with race and racial categories in three main guises: (1) with respect to the discursive and stylistic categories of the time; (2) as an orienting axis within the topical field; and (3) as an important family of myths and stories that help structure the cultural practices and ideologies that framed psychedelia.

This last point deserves special attention, because racially reflexive myth making becomes increasingly important over the history of psychedelic funk. Ronald Radano has shown how the concept of myth can provide a path out of simple essentialisms without minimizing the role played by racial categories in cultural life. He challenges "the view, still common to our time and culture, of an immutable black musical essence that survives apart from the contingencies of social and cultural change" while still acknowledging the important and specific ways in which "the commitment to a viable essence of black music that still occupies the popular imagination remains an important ideological component of national memory that emerges historically as one of the many coherence systems binding people musically. Rather than a falsity it suggests what Roland Barthes called 'myth': the stories we tell in giving texture and meaning in the making of our worlds" (Radano 2003, 3).

One thing about deep-seated cultural myths and stories is that they are not without complication. They keep things separate but also mix them up, and Radano reminds us that in order to remain attentive to the lived experience and history of racial difference, we must keep all these aspects in play. In both theoretical and practical terms, "situating black music within the texture of American life means no longer easily separating 'black music' from 'white music,' nor, indeed, black music from the rest of the social experience" (Radano 2003, 4). This is how I will approach the role of African American styles and features in the psychedelic topical field. Insofar as they were foundational to rock music, they were also foundational to psychedelia. They also formed the basis for crucial additions to psychedelia during its ongoing development. Yet at the same time, African American styles remained marked as other within psychedelia, which was broadly understood as a style dominated by white audiences and artists. These are the dynamics I would like to unpack in more detail before moving on to the musical specifics. My argument is going to be that black contributions to psychedelia were generally racially marked, but at the same time there was a profound affinity between certain features of African American expressive culture and psychedelia more generally, which is why styles like psychedelic funk and soul have had such longevity and have gone on to produce so many influential variants.

The sociological trend toward whiteness in psychedelia has been stressed most strongly by Arun Saldanha:

> Insofar as whites use the pleasures of drugs, art, ritual, travel, the risky, and the exotic to alter their minds and position in the world as whites, I call them psychedelic. ... What is significant is that these bodies are most *probably* white. Hence psychedelics isn't antithetical to white modernity. On the contrary, to argue for the creativity of whiteness is to show to what extent it can reinvent and reinforce itself.... Psychedelics is the commitment certain whites have to transforming themselves through drugs, music, travel, and spiritualism borrowed from other populations. Psychedelics is less an organized, antagonistic kind of politics than an "unraveling from within" of the "moral cement" that defines the privileged position of the white bourgeoisie ... which seeks not to destroy the culture from which it sprang but to explore its fringe possibilities to the advantage of one's individuality. (2007, 6, 12)

Saldanha's formulation is useful in several respects. It draws attention to the markedness and importance of race and engages the histories of exoticism and colonialism. It also makes the link to broader cultural formations, especially to modernity, that will become increasingly important when we consider space rock, Afrofuturism, and eventually electronic dance musics. On the other hand, by virtually defining psychedelia as a white cultural practice, Saldanha begs the question of what to say about all of the other participants and all of the stylistic hybrids drawing upon styles such as soul and funk. We will come back to these questions, but for now we can leave the strong version of Saldanha's definition in play to help dramatize the role of racial specificity and markedness within psychedelia.

Saldanha's remarks on race and modernity allow us to bring in certain formulations that have relevance to the earliest stages of psychedelia and whose importance will become only more obvious with the later Afrofuturist psychedelias. For example, Alexander Weheliye has elaborated on the relationship between racial markedness and modernity: "How does blackness operate paradoxically as both central to and outside of Western modernity? ... The very category 'black' is an invention of Western modernity, which does not mean that it can be reduced to a mere colonialist imposition on empirically verifiable black beings that preexist this classification" (2005, 5). This formulation works in harmony with that of Saldanha and puts it in a slightly broader frame.[1] To the extent that psychedelic cultures were linked to modernist projects, this racial logic conditioned them directly. And there are other theorists besides Saldanha who have explored how this plays out in terms of specific psychedelic ideas and practices. A great deal of that work was developed in connection with the criticism of cyber cultures, as, for example, when Alondra Nelson points out that many prophets of psychedelia, such as Timothy Leary, and the later cyber theorists who drew upon 1960s thought shared the view that the body would become increasingly unimportant to human identity—that technology would grant the freedom of unlimited self-definition. This lays several sorts of traps for racialized subjects, who remain marked by their embodiment (Nelson 2002, 1–2). The ideology of bodily irrelevance can create othering and exclusion not only by perpetuating markedness but also by suggesting that subjects who might wish to retain and claim racialized aspects in their subjectivity are doing something wrong.

Potential black participants would also on occasion self-exclude from psychedelia by choosing to think of their identities as incompatible with it. Although the following quote from Joseph Jarman is drawn from a slightly different context, Jarman being a key figure in African American experimental jazz from the 1960s onward, it still gets at the essential point: "Some of my peers would never admit that they were into the hippie culture—the flower children, free living, the awareness of LSD and what it did to people's consciousness. That's not a part of the illusionary black history orientation that they want to be identified with" (quoted in Lewis 2008, 211). So there are many ways we can formulate the markedness of black subjects and black-associated styles in psychedelia. However, there is a flip side. Jarman continues: "I knew all the Beatles songs at that time. The Art Ensemble in Europe would perform opposite very famous rock stars from that era. We used to go to the Detroit Artists Workshop, which was the home of the MC5. We used to rehearse in the same place in Chicago as Mike Bloomfield. We had the Black Panther Party, the hippies had the White Panther Party. . . . We were able to participate in a whole universal kind of world, rather than just be motivated by an isolated one" (quoted in Lewis 2008, 211–12, 213).

My argument has two parts. We have now looked in detail at the first part: black subjects and music were marked and often excluded within psychedelia. But at the same time, there were profound compatibilities that led to many Afrodiasporically inflected psychedelic styles. We have already seen some initial arguments for overlap and resonance, which can be made more specific. But rather than simply outlining institutional, personal, or stylistic continuities, I want to argue that certain general aspects of African American expressive culture were broadly compatible with certain aspects of 1960s psychedelia. The discussion is going to be focused on African American culture in particular rather than on broader contexts such as the black Atlantic or Afrodiasporic cultures overall, because so far as psychedelia of the 1960s through the mid-1970s is concerned, it was specifically in the United States where the major developments took place. This simplification would be less acceptable for later periods, for example, the early 1990s, once styles such as trip hop had emerged in the UK and psytrance had begun to develop as a more global phenomenon.

Alondra Nelson's work on cyber cultures can again be a useful starting point. Following Kali Tal, Nelson argues that substantially prior to the appearance of cyber theory, African American thought had developed theories and practices that "provide political and theoretical precedents for articulating and understanding 'multiple identities, fragmented personae and liminality'—most notably W. E. B. Dubois's concept of double consciousness" (2002, 3). Nelson's comments are directed toward showing how African American thought prefigured certain aspects of posthumanism, but the point extends to compatibility with psychedelia. And where psychedelic-friendly traits of African American thought and practice are concerned, we can add the tradition of linguistic subtlety and playfulness, founded in a deep-seated sensitivity to the relationship between language and other ways of knowing—a relationship where language, at least in its more rationalist modes, does not always have the upper hand. One specific formulation in this area is Henry Louis Gates's (1988) description of signifyin(g), and I would also add what Paul Gilroy has called the topos of unsayability: "The topos of unsayability produced from the slaves' experiences of racial terror and figured repeatedly in nineteenth-century evaluations of slave music has other important implications. It can be used to challenge the privileged conceptions of both language and writing as preeminent expressions of human consciousness. The power and significance of music within the black Atlantic have grown in inverse proportion to the limited expressive power of language" (1993, 74). Taken together, these remarks sketch out a picture of African American culture that shows it to be highly cognate with certain aspects of psychedelia. It contained expressive forms and sensibilities well tuned to express the fluidity of identity (in its aspects of both freedom and danger), the limits of language (along with the rich field this opens up for linguistic experimentation), and the value of direct personal experience as a basis for knowledge. And it is also important to note that African American communities participated in some of the same movements and institutions that would become influential in early psychedelic culture.

In the previous chapter, we saw how Catherine Albanese (2007) developed the concepts of Metaphysical Asia and American metaphysical religion in order to look at specifically American variants of Orientalist mysticism and occultism. One key feature of her work we didn't consider at the time is that she shows how early African American spirituality overlapped considerably with metaphysical religion. Some of the key elements here include the idea that a supreme God will be both immanent and transcendent (linked closely to animism and pantheism); ancestor veneration; respect for nature; attention to the balance of individual and collective identities; magic and spirits (and the theme of controlling dangerous or irrational forces); an interest in death and immortality; and practices focused on communication with spirits (revelation and relationship as a force for practical action) (Albanese 2007, 85–89). Many African American religious leaders and institutions were participants in the general development of American metaphysical religion, which in turn was influential on the aesthetics, mysticism, and exoticism of psychedelia.

In chapter 1 I suggested three different ways that an existing musical style or genre might be cognate with psychedelia: by intent, by formal affect, or by context. The material I just presented on African American cultural traits has largely to do with cognate intent. It demonstrates that African American culture contained many themes and practices that resonate with core concerns of 1960s psychedelic subcultures. In terms of context, there were also many areas of practical overlap between institutions, styles, and communities associated with psychedelia and those associated with more traditional African American styles. But at the same time, the context and history of racism meant that these overlaps were often not explored. And when they were, the issue of race was often foregrounded above other factors.

Having sketched out this background, we can now turn to the question of formal affect. Among those musical styles and features generally marked at the time as African American, which were most compatible with psychedelia in general and vice versa? Raising this question allows us to return to specific musical examples.

I'll start with a brief description of two recordings from 1967 to introduce some of the general features and themes that will be of interest. But first, a note about presentation. For the rest of the book, when song-length examples are to be discussed I will usually start with a bulleted list. That list identifies musical features that are of special topical interest, but it generally presents those features in more analytic language and doesn't explore the topical aspect. The bulleted list is followed by a summary of the main topical points in less analytic language. Readers less interested in the technicalities can still get the main points by skipping the bulleted lists and simply reading the summaries that follow.

Since we've already briefly considered one psychedelic soul recording in chapter 2, we can start by filling out some more details about that track.

THE CHAMBERS BROTHERS, "TIME HAS COME TODAY" (LP VERSION, 1967)

- As described in chapter 2, the introduction is a good example of the epic topic (see example 2.6).
- There are very few clear soul music reference points in the sung parts of the song. While the vocal timbre and ornamentation have something of a soul sound, the overall effect is much more along the lines of garage rock psychedelia.
- From the perspective of psychedelic topicality, apart from the introduction, the main feature is the very long instrumental/montage section (2:28–9:08).
- The instrumental starts with a clockwork-like tick and voices sparsely chanting "time," along with a dramatic slowing down of the tempo. Then, starting at 2:55, the tempo begins to gradually increase, and deep echo is added to the entire mix. The speedup takes many measures and is accompanied by a crescendo. The texture gradually changes into a one-chord jam with fuzz lead guitar, starting at 3:30, very much like the sorts of instrumentals we will later discuss as typical of space rock.
- When voices reenter after several minutes (at 6:50), they are of the layered, uncanny type (shrieking, laughing, muttering, etc., and heavily echoed).
- Throughout, the instrumental develops incrementally through intensive and textural changes or slight modifications to the groove. All of these gradual events feel like inflections or variations rather than pronounced structural shifts.

This track is of importance to psychedelia not only because of the epic opening but also because of the extremely long and experimental instrumental passage. It is also important as one of the earliest psychedelic soul recordings.[2] But in that connection, maybe the most noteworthy feature is that it sounds as much like Dylan-inspired garage rock as it does like soul or early funk, in fact, arguably more so. More significant for the long-term development of a psychedelic topical field were those pieces and artists that mined the psychedelic potential of more specifically African American styles and topics. To gain some perspective on that, we could look at different Chambers Brothers songs. But instead we will move on to Sly and the Family Stone, whose work in this area became widely known and highly influential.

SLY AND THE FAMILY STONE, "TRIP TO YOUR HEART" (1967)

- There is a fairly substantial (fifteen seconds) unmeasured sound effects introduction that layers near-screaming vocalizations, seemingly random drum fills, and glissandi on guitar.
- The song follows an ABC structure. Each of these formal sections becomes increasingly dense with signifiers of the psychedelic and the uncanny.
- The A section is not particularly psychedelic, except insofar as many typical elements of soul and funk are cognate with psychedelia: an emphasis on repetition, on texture and immediacy over form and harmony, and on the layering of vocals and a less focal mix. In terms of conventional signs of the uncanny and exotic, the horn riff and backing vocals trace out a diminished triad. The horn riff also emphasizes the flattened second scale degree at one spot, and the bass riff alternates between 1 and ♭2. All of this can be seen in music example 3.1.
- In the B sections there is a more jazz-influenced harmonic language and a freer shaping of lines in the rhythm guitar. The backing vocals become more frequent, intensifying the gospel feel but also creating a somewhat epic mood. In general, there is a feeling of increasing density in this section.
- A psychedelic reading of the previous two sections would be less tenable were it not for the clearly "strange" staging of the C section. In this section all parts are vamping on a diminished triad. There are dense backing vocals that are somewhat Theremin-like and that also carry other signifiers of the uncanny: sliding, ululating, and dense layering. There are slide effects from the guitar, and in the drums there are two distinct layers of ride cymbal, creating a somewhat unstable and polyrhythmic feel. All of this can be seen in music example 3.2.

This sort of example differs from "Time Has Come Today" in that it sounds less like a soul band playing a version of psychedelic garage rock and more like an exploration from within of the psychedelic potentials present in soul music and in the emergent funk genre. These potentials are so numerous and topically complex that I will immediately move on to a general discussion, drawing on a range of Sly and the Family Stone songs as examples. We'll start with some more nar-

Facing top: Music example 3.1. Sly and the Family Stone, "Trip to Your Heart," A section (beginning) (0:16–0:26). Written by Sylvester Stewart. © Sony / ATV Songs LLC obo Mijac Music.

Facing bottom: Music example 3.2. Sly and the Family Stone, "Trip to Your Heart," C section (beginning) (0:59–1:09). Written by Sylvester Stewart. © Sony / ATV Songs LLC obo Mijac Music.

rowly formal aspects, especially those that are both normal features of soul music and amenable to psychedelic interpretation.

Psychedelic Soul: Layering of Voices and the Less Focal Mix

One general feature of soul music borrowed largely from gospel is the layering of multiple voices, often in call-and-response format. Along with this often comes a less focal mix than was common in pop music of the time. There is less emphasis on a fixed separation of foreground and background and greater freedom for elements to blend and to temporarily move forward and backward in the mix. This often creates a kind of pointillistic or swimming-in-and-out effect. It has become a commonplace to remark on how these features can encode values of democracy and communal music making, and the link to countercultural tribal values should be clear. It should also be clear how this resonates with many psychedelic mix techniques we have already discussed, especially multiple speaker blur. We'll return to this layered and less focal approach to sonic space frequently in later discussions, for example, when considering groove and form.

There are other general features of soul music that are also cognate with psychedelia. One of these is the tendency to arrange transitional passages, such as bridges, with what I call a textural *dissolve*. This is especially clear in the C section from "Trip to Your Heart," described above. By dissolve I mean a passage where the regular course of the song seems to gradually fall away to be replaced by transitional or nondirected material. This could involve a range of factors, such as thinning or dropping out of the rhythm section; disappearance of core instrumental timbres (often alongside the introduction of more coloristically oriented or pointillistic ones); disappearance of the main melody line and of other strong formal markers; a change to more ambiguous or less directed harmonic materials; production techniques that imply entry into a large and less articulated virtual space (echo, reverb, modulations of timbre or volume); and others. What I am here calling a dissolve is not unlike what later comes to be called a breakdown in electronic dance music, although the meaning there is more narrow (and discussed later). Another good example from Sly and the Family Stone is the B section from "I'm an Animal" (0:58–1:18), which features highly repetitive toms; a repeated octave rise figure in the bass; a repetitive organ riff/pad in fourths;[3] a guitar meandering around a major seventh chord with an added ninth (jazzy and spacey); and an unusual timbre that sounds like reiterated horn squeaks.

Overall, the dissolve was an established arranging device that also provided a good opportunity for the sort of formal diversion and textural experimentation so characteristic of psychedelia. One other common soul music device worth noting is the constantly rising sequence, where a melodic idea and harmony continue to ascend step by step to a climax. Two good examples by Sly and the Family Stone are the B section of "Higher" (e.g., 0:26–0:44) and the A section of "I'm an Animal" (e.g., 0:06–0:32). These kinds of preexisting devices created many opportunities for arrangements to be both distinctively soul music while at the same time creating effects similar to those being explored in psychedelic rock.

But perhaps the most important areas of formal overlap have to do with time and the overall approach to form.

Psychedelic Soul: Approach to Time and Form

When considering the influence of soul and funk on popular music, one of the most important features is their approach to time and form. Soul, and especially funk, altered the typical balance between tightly structured song forms and more open-ended groove and jamming passages. We have already seen some tendencies of this kind in psychedelic rock as well, for example, in the Yardbirds-style rave-up and in some of the more open-ended jamming of the 13th Floor Elevators. But compared to either of these, funk grooves provide an even more immersive and open-ended environment, and they did so with a dramatically different rhythmic sensibility. While it is difficult to trace exact lines of influence, it is interesting to note that psychedelic soul and funk came to prominence at roughly the same time as more open-ended rock forms, such as space rock and jam bands, began to supplant the more pop-oriented earlier psychedelia. Collectively, these all stand as important influences on later psychedelic electronic dance musics, where again the specific formal aesthetics and rhythmic approach of funk are crucial. Examining this long series of changes will occupy us for much of the rest of this book, and we can start by considering some highlights of time and form in early psychedelic soul and funk. At this point, most of my remarks are going to bear more on funk than on soul, although the boundary is extremely porous.

The emphasis on groove and on extended passages dominated by groove has three major effects that I want to highlight. First, there is a formal effect: a shift toward extended passages based on texture and away from song form. There is also an effect in terms of the relationship between the music and embodiment: while there is no lack of dancing or exploration of embodied experience in psychedelic rock, these are even more foregrounded in funk. Finally, there are important effects on the nature of musical temporality. Funk temporality is in some respects nonteleological and circular, perhaps even suspending time in favor of duration. Anne Danielsen (2006, 154–55) has offered a detailed analysis of this aspect of funk temporality. She critiques earlier work on musical temporality insofar as it tends to describe all nonlinear temporalities largely by negation—marked by what they are not rather than by what they are—and also because it tends to lump all kinds of stasis together without distinction. There is a tendency to describe all nonteleological music as standing still, being timeless: "However, a groove does not stand still. Even though it is unchanging, consistent, and of a potentially infinite duration; even though the principles comprising it are supplied in advance . . . and even though the groove is not proceeding toward a definite goal, it is—to the last second—in motion" (155). On this basis, Danielsen posits at least two distinct kinds of nonteleological musical time:

> Both forms of musical time—the one potentially characterizing contemporary music's sculptures of sound and the other potentially present in repetitive rhyth-

mic music—may be described as states of equilibrium.... In each case the passing of time is no longer noticed [but for different reasons]: either we do not notice the passing of time because no time passes—that is, because the work manages to convey the impression that no time passes—or we do not notice the passing of time because we move together with time. For what is time when one is being in time? (Danielsen 2006, 156)

One fundamental contribution of funk to psychedelia is a rich musical language for crafting experiences of moving together with time. And besides developing temporalities of this sort around groove, psychedelic funk also helped further develop the technique of mixing song forms and rhythmic passages together with long unmeasured sound effects passages in which the nongroove form of stasis is dominant. As we will see in more detail below, some of the most extreme passages of this type are found not only in space rock but also in psychedelic funk. So we can see that funk is deeply engaged with both forms of nonlinear temporality. Danielsen also expands on the formal consequences of such a temporal effect, arguing that funk music is subject to a dual requirement: it must function both as pop song (therefore short, highly structured, more teleological) and as groove. In terms of reception, this duality doesn't just produce different audience segments with different tastes and practices but "can also be present in one and the same person, who might, for example, experience the song when listening and the groove when dancing. In fact, these two approaches can be present in the same *act* of listening-participating" (Danielsen 2006, 178).

All of the stylistic features we've discussed so far occupy a middle ground between topical meaning proper and other features of musical meaning such as affect. Soon we will consider other aspects of soul and funk that have a more clearly indexical aspect and are therefore more clearly topical. But even the features we've discussed so far have an important role in topicality for several reasons. First, they are cognate with various aspects of psychedelia, and so they smooth the way for soul and funk to become part of that topical field. Second, they are important prototopics that in later periods help especially to link psychedelic electronic dance musics to earlier psychedelia. Finally, more discrete and clearly topical features such as soul vocal ornamentation and funk wah guitar timbres came along with these more large-scale features as part of a total stylistic package.

Psychedelic Soul: Humor and Wit

The humor and wit often associated with psychedelic soul is another area that occupies the borderline between affect and topicality. Other forms of psychedelia are not uniformly humorless, but there is often a kind of levity in the soul material that is not so common elsewhere. This might come about partly through the long history of signifyin(g) and also partly because soul music retained close ties to R&B party music, a connection that tended to be minimized in the more self-important psychedelic rock. Especially in the case of Sly and the Family Stone, many of the self-aware psychedelic references seem carnivalesque and witty, for example, the rapid-fire changes of texture throughout "Dance to the Medley." This is not unlike the sorts of sectional forms found in psychedelic rock, except there's arguably a different sort of realism involved. A song like "Dance to the Medley" feels more like a pastiche of the urban environment than a trip to an entirely different fantastic world.

"Higher" is another song that could easily be heard as containing a few sonic jokes. In the introduction, the vamp seems almost absurdly generic in the extreme squareness of the drums, the strictly oompah bass, and the deep organ modulation (mostly tremolo, although perhaps some vibrato as well). Against this is a very country-sounding electric guitar. So the humor is twofold: there's the excessive cliché of the vamp, and there's the way this is troped with a completely different and unlikely style. Then later, after the B section rising sequence, there is a big structural pause that makes way for a cheeky country/vaudeville turnaround fill standing completely out on its own (0:45–0:48). This sort of parodic mood is even more evident in another Sly and the Family Stone song, "I Hate to Love Her." In that case some of the performative choices strongly resemble Frank Zappa. There are wah horns, an overblown lounge aspect to some of the vocals, and doo-wop elements that may or may not be parodic.

To the extent that these lighter moods are often linked to explicit or implicit party references, they are also often accompanied by at least one vocal part that could be construed as an MC or a DJ. This leads us to one of the most interesting topical aspects of gospel and soul music to be imported into psychedelia: the preacher or guide persona.

Psychedelic Soul: The Preacher and Guide

Guide figures were important archetypes in psychedelic culture. They were a staple of the psychedelic guidebook literature, and it is tempting to hear certain vocal performances as enacting this sort of figure. One example from rock would be much of Jim Morrison's singing, especially "The End," where the voice is staged as a prophetic narrator and commentator: a guide to the unfolding psychodrama. Two other examples, which we'll look at later in this chapter, are Grace Slick, whose voice is frequently staged in a commanding oracular mode, and the ringmaster/bandleader personas in *Sgt. Pepper*. But in cases like these, although details of vocal production and performance might be deployed to make the voice seem mystical, commanding, enticing, or otherwise appropriate as a guide, outright musical topicality specific to the guide aspect is rare. A circus ringmaster persona, for example, can be reinforced by various circus topics but does not in itself have a strong musical dimension. The same is true for the generically shamanic personas sometimes associated with Grace Slick and Jim Morrison. There are musical topics that can help stage them as guide personas, but no available guide topics as such (or at least none that were employed).

Gospel and soul are different in this regard, insofar as the preacher is a topical persona with its own musical vocabulary and performative style, as is the soul singer who is closely modeled on the preacher. So psychedelic guide figures based on preacher or soul personas are topical in a way that the rock guide figures are not. Similarly, the celebrity DJ persona had also become topical by this point and was also a performative model for some guide figures. Funkadelic's "Eulogy and Light" is one example of psychedelic funk drawing on a preacher persona. And a good example of a DJ-based guide persona is Sly and the Family Stone's "Dance to the Medley," for example, in the spot where Sly Stone introduces Larry Graham on bass (0:51).

The distinction between rock guide figures and soul/funk guide figures also has an affective dimension. The templates for most rock guide figures are generally otherworldly and as a result are somewhat severe (like the spooky prophet guide) or ridiculous (like the circus barker guide). By contrast, the preacher and DJ/MC guide figures draw on soul music's mobilization of both sacred and sexual charisma. In this context, the guide figure can also be a lover, greatly extending the richness of topical resources. This more intimate kind of guide can also be related to something I noted in connection with humor: the different degree of realism in psychedelic soul and funk when compared to much of psychedelic rock. Psychedelic soul and funk guide figures are highly charged in topical terms because they are both congruent with psychedelia more generally and at the same time tightly coupled to topical features of black musical culture in particular. Adopting a guide or prophetic persona of this sort does not require weakening the indexical side of topicality (the real-world historical and community connections). This is unlike some other psychedelic styles, where the available guide figures are more remote and fictional.

Psychedelic Soul: The Urban

As I hinted at earlier, one source of the relative realism is psychedelic soul and funk is their association with contemporary urban environments. For example, in a slightly different context Philip Tagg argues that an electric bass playing funk-style lines might introduce "a character of modernity . . . and possibly, even more particularly . . . an atmosphere of a large North American city" due to the relatively recent advent of electric bass and the way it transformed bass playing in the 1960s, along with geographical and sociological associations of the genres. "It will therefore be of little surprise to find similar bass lines used elsewhere in connection with media situations where modernity, action and urban life are important ingredients" (Tagg 2000b, 153–54). The bass is just one of the signifiers of funk style that by the late 1960s had acquired this set of associations. This stands as a major contribution to the psychedelic topical field, which was otherwise relatively poor in resources for signifying the urban.

It is fairly clear how an association of soul and funk with the urban rests in part on broader racial stereotypes. And to the extent that the urban also came to represent forms of abjection connected to crime, social decay, and drug addiction, this association could be seen as part of the markedness that at times made soul and funk outsiders to psychedelic culture. However, there is an interesting reversal that also sometimes takes place. Consider the lyrics and production in earlier psychedelic recordings by the Temptations produced by Norman Whitfield, like "Cloud 9" and "Runaway Child, Running Wild." In those songs, taken together with Whitfield's initial reluctance to produce in a psychedelic style, there's a feeling that it is the psychedelic elements that represent the abject juvenile delinquency and all the social problems referenced in the lyrics. The psychedelic theme of freedom comes up frequently, but as a form of irresponsibility or waywardness. This tone both reinforces the association of psychedelic soul with realism and resists some of the racial biases implicit in that association, since it is the psychedelic elements rather than the more traditional soul or funk elements that are linked to social delinquency and abjection.

Psychedelic Soul:
Temporal Sedimentation, Markedness, and Dialogism

I'd like to step back from specific topics for a moment and say a few things about the general structure of topicality. Because psychedelic soul and funk were at the same time highly modern and deeply rooted in traditional styles, they give us a good opportunity to distinguish between a few different layers of historical reference. Up to this point, one of our fundamental concepts has been the difference between prototopics and topics proper. We have also noted that topics vary in their historical and social distance from the moment of interpretation. In order to discuss these kinds of historical dynamics in more detail, we can make a further distinction. Rather than simply speaking in terms of prototopics and topics, we can expand the second term by speaking of *near topics* and *distant topics*. The basic distinction is still between topicality and a phase that precedes it, but we can also indicate something about the relative temporal distance of topics themselves. What's being captured here is not necessarily absolute time span but rather the process through which topics come to seem more or less archaic. This process can go at different speeds in different contexts, and one of the characteristics of the 1960s is that the process went very quickly, with many styles becoming dated relatively suddenly. In terms of the layering of such historical nearness and distance in early psychedelic soul, we can note the following progression:

- In the 1940s, contemporary gospel and R&B could both be described as *prototopics*.
- From the mid-1950s to the mid-1960s, both gospel and R&B became *near topics* and are among the topics subsumed into early soul, which itself would have been a *prototopic* at that time.
- From the late 1960s to the early 1970s, gospel and R&B were carried into early psychedelic soul. But there is a shift of perceived distance, with psychedelic soul as the *prototopic* and early soul as a *near topic*. Gospel and R&B had by then largely become *distant topics*, present only as sedimented layers of meaning within the near topic of soul.

The Later 1960s 117

This is only an outline argument, skipping over many nuances and assuming much about the way people would have heard and interpreted these genres. However, it gives us a glimpse into the temporal dynamics at play and how topics are enfolded into one another. This sort of temporal layering is another way to think about the cultural tensions we've discussed in psychedelic soul and funk, and it also has broader applicability. We will see similar things in other cases, for example, with the Grateful Dead and their appropriation of US roots musics, with the Incredible String Band and their relationship to British folk idioms, and with the Beatles in terms of their widely varied frames of historical reference.

The phenomenon of historical sedimentation in topicality is closely related to two other concepts that we've already worked with: dialogism and indexicality. I'd like to expand a bit on the role these play in early psychedelic soul and funk by returning to a question we left open earlier: Was Saldanha simply wrong when he defined psychedelia as essentially a white practice? My earlier response was to say "yes and no" and then to bracket the issue. At this point I am going to stick with "yes and no," but I want to make it more nuanced, taking into account the details we've accumulated about topicality in early psychedelic funk and soul. The best defense of Saldanha's position rests in arguments about markedness. Even though there were many black participants in early psychedelic culture, various cultural factors conspired to render them marked and to resist their full integration into the psychedelic imaginary. So it is interesting to note that some have argued the same thing about funk, but in the opposite direction. For example, Danielsen claims that "funk is commonly regarded as black rhythm music par excellence. As such, funk has served as a consummate example of the blackness of black music" (2006, 35). From this perspective, it is interesting that funk is also the black-associated music that has had the most profound long-term effect on psychedelia. Whatever is going on with the markedness relationships, it is undoubtedly complex and multilayered. And that is the sort of situation that invites further remarks about the dialogism of topics. What I would like to do is to take my earlier theoretical argument—that African American culture was both highly cognate with psychedelia and marked as other to it—and describe a similar dynamic in terms of the divergent dialogic connotations of some particular soul/funk topics.

This argument will hinge on the claim that while psychedelic imaginaries are otherworldly, that does not mean they rely only (or even primarily) on references to the abstract or to the unreal. Often psychedelia is imagined and expressed topically through signs that evoke indexical connections to real-world contexts. So in order to create, through topics, an otherworldly or abstract imaginary, some kind of strategy is needed for dealing with the indexical aspect. We have seen two main ways that this happens in psychedelia: first, through being very selective about which indexical relationships to highlight and which to suppress, and second, through revisionist or partial understandings of the specific histories and contexts involved. In less theoretical terms, psychedelia will fit more comfortably with some historical and social contexts and less comfortably with others. Dialogism is important because it means that this isn't just a matter of picking some topics that are altogether comfortable and suppressing others that are completely uncomfortable. Dialogism means that many topics will point in both directions at once and that to use them forces an ongoing negotiation.

Let's consider various areas of reference that made up the near and distant topical components of early psychedelic soul and funk. Many of the histories and contexts indexed by these topics were cognate with psychedelia, for example, early metaphysical religion or signifyin(g). But at the same time, many evoked aspects of history and social reality of the sort that psychedelic imaginaries tended to ignore or avoid, such as slavery and urban decay. We can group these sorts of references into categories that highlight the particularly dialogic areas as follows:

- *Fluidity and multiplicity of self*: can evoke freedom and transcendence but also radical disempowerment and loss of control over one's own identity.
- *Linguistic experimentation*: can be playful, evoking discovery and the uncovering of new meanings, but can also be linked to a lack of freedom to speak directly and to stereotypes of incoherence or inarticulateness.
- *Foregrounded sexuality*: can resonate with the 1960s free-love ideology, with sex as spirituality, and with constructive resistance to hegemonic values, but can also recollect histories of intersex conflict and violence and stereotypes of amorality.
- *Transformative spiritual experiences*: can overlap with psychedelia's interest in the magical and the mystical, but in specifically Christian versions the fit is less comfortable due to the frequent (although not exclusive) association of the church with social conservatism.
- *The rural*: resonates with ideals of pastoral living and ecologically based spirituality, but the specific history of plantations, sharecropping, and underdevelopment fits less well.

Parliament-Funkadelic

To round out our overview of early psychedelic funk and soul, we need to consider the two interlinked projects spearheaded by George Clinton: Parliament and Funkadelic (P-Funk). This is for two reasons. First, they provide a strong stylistic contrast to the artists we've already discussed. Second, Parliament eventually evolved into the most important Afrofuturist psychedelic outfit of the mid-1970s. That later phase is discussed in the next chapter, but even by 1970, substantially before the science fiction story line developed, Parliament-Funkadelic were sketching out new potentials for psychedelic funk. We can start by describing one of the most stylistically layered songs on the debut Parliament album, *Osmium*.

PARLIAMENT, "THERE IS NOTHING BEFORE ME BUT THANG" (1970)

- The first thing we hear in the preintroduction (0:00–0:10) is a semimeasured figure on two guitars. Timbrally, and in terms of pitch choice and melodic/rhythmic profile, this line has aspects of Orientalist East Asian pentatonic clichés and also aspects of sitar imitation.

- The introduction highlights a galloping and repetitive fuzz guitar riff (music example 3.3, m. 1). The introduction also features a siren-like figure on a cleaner guitar (music example 3.3, m. 3) and a galloping snare-centric drum pattern. All of these are used frequently throughout the song.
- The final noteworthy topical feature of the introduction is the lead guitar interjection, somewhat reminiscent of a sitar (see music example 3.3, mm. 8–11). As with the other features of the introduction, this fill returns frequently and helps set the overall feeling of the entire song.
- In the A section, the rhythm section adds an off-beat guitar part not unlike the one in "Paint It, Black" (music example 2.17), which could be heard as evocative of ska, among other things (music example 3.3, m. 11).
- As with the examples from Sly and the Family Stone, a key feature of this entire arrangement is the ongoing interplay between multiple voices, first in a fairly strict call-and-response format but later a bit looser (see music example 3.3, mm. 11–14 and also the vocals throughout music example 3.4).
- Also as seen in several Sly and the Family Stone examples, there is a passage in this song that features an extended sequential stepwise rise, this time in the B section (0:59–1:17).
- Starting at 2:20, the arrangement shifts into something like a rave-up, crossed with a soul testifying feel. Many of the key features can be seen in music example 3.4. The general form in this section is one of increasing density, rising register, and constant exploration of variations on short, repeated ideas. The voices are repeating basic cells in several layers, the bass and drums are loopy and repetitive, and the organ is droning and rising. The lead guitar first presents a long rise and then repeats a simple rhythmic cell based on the earlier galloping riff (which also persists in another guitar).

Like "Time Has Come Today," much in this song is interesting for its similarity to garage rock. The links to the Yardbirds are also clear, especially in the raga-rock touches, in the concluding rave-up, and in the way the whole thing stays fairly close to a conventional pop song format. However, like the Temptations or Sly and the Family Stone, there are a large number of specifically soul and gospel reference points, especially in the multiple layered voices. In some ways, this song is the most thorough fusion we've yet seen of elements of psychedelic rock and pop with elements of funk and soul. Neither side dominates in either structural or decorative terms. So one message to take from this recording, even more than from "Time Has Come Today," is the wide zone of compatibility between soul, funk, and psychedelia. On the other hand, I also hear an inter-

Facing: Music example 3.3. Parliament, "There Is Nothing before Me but Thang," introduction, part 2 (0:10–0:34). Words and Music by George Clinton, Eddie Harris, and Edward Hazel. © 1969 GOLD FOREVER MUSIC, INC. and EDWARD HAZEL. Copyright Renewed. This arrangement © 2015 GOLD FOREVER MUSIC, INC. and EDWARD HAZEL. All Rights for GOLD FOREVER MUSIC, INC. Administered by SONGS OF UNIVERSAL, INC. All Rights Reserved Used by Permission. Reprinted by permission of Hal Leonard Corporation. Additional copyright permission: © Southfield Music Inc. (ASCAP). Reprinted by permission of Southfield Music Inc.

esting reciprocal markedness. To the extent that neither the soul nor the garage rock elements dominate, each set of elements seems somewhat out of place relative to the other. The effect is not unlike early rockabilly, in which a demonstration of compatibility between differently racialized styles also served as a demonstration of estrangement, not in the sense of mutual alienation but in the sense of a mutual making-strange. Which is to say that out of all the examples we've considered, this track might do the best job of dramatizing the dialogic tensions introduced into the topical field of psychedelia by soul and funk (and vice versa).

While *Osmium* is a fascinating album, in the early 1970s it was arguably Funkadelic rather than Parliament that presented the sharpest contrast to other branches of psychedelic soul and funk. We can see many of the highlights in "Mommy, What's a Funkadelic?"

FUNKADELIC, "MOMMY, WHAT'S A FUNKADELIC?" (1970)

- There is an unmeasured sound effects opening—rhythmically panned speaking voices, moist mouth noises with heavy sexual overtones, and other sexually suggestive sounds (gasps, etc.) coming and going throughout.
- Many sound effects elements continue throughout the song, especially echo, rapid rhythmic panning, and the general feeling that there are many densely layered voices. Unlike most earlier psychedelic recordings with sound effects openings, in this case there is never a feeling of leaving the sound effects behind and moving on to the song proper. Rather, the song emerges as one component in a persistent sonic space established during the opening.
- The main riff first enters at 0:35. It has acid rock features (doubled by bass and guitar, framed around a minor pentatonic scale) but also aspects of funk (quite syncopated, gaps in the rhythm, but constantly returning to emphasize the first beat, some chromaticism). Over time it becomes evident that the riff doesn't belong to any one instrument but is passed around between them.

In some ways the relevant differences between this song and those we've already discussed, though striking, are more affective and stylistic than topical. But that only really applies if the main topical question we want to ask is simply which topics are present. If we are interested instead in how they are nuanced, then the topical dimension of this newer style is easier to tease out. In discussing "Time Has Come Today," we noted the extremely long and experimental nature of the instrumental sound effects passages. And we also found similar

Facing: Music example 3.4. Parliament, "There Is Nothing before Me but Thang," concluding jam (excerpt) (2:42–2:56). Words and Music by George Clinton, Eddie Harris, and Edward Hazel. © 1969 GOLD FOREVER MUSIC, INC. and EDWARD HAZEL. Copyright Renewed. This arrangement © 2015 GOLD FOREVER MUSIC, INC. and EDWARD HAZEL. All Rights for GOLD FOREVER MUSIC, INC. Administered by SONGS OF UNIVERSAL, INC. All Rights Reserved Used by Permission. Reprinted by permission of Hal Leonard Corporation. Additional copyright permission: © Southfield Music Inc. (ASCAP). Reprinted by permission of Southfield Music Inc.

noteworthy passages in Sly and the Family Stone. But overall, it was arguably Funkadelic who stood out in this area, for several reasons. First, they provided more such passages than anyone else. Second, they melded them into the overall formal structure in a distinctive way. Finally, their sound effects passages had a unique affective tone, one that was still psychedelic but that was also darker, more sexual, and often more politicized. Another noteworthy example from this period is "Free Your Mind and Your Ass Will Follow," which includes a sound effects introduction that is particularly long (about 1:44 in duration) and again features several voices coming and going sporadically, one of which is notably preacher-like ("free your mind," "the kingdom of heaven is within"). The voices are layered with fuzz lead guitar and various other sound effects: sonar- or Morse code–like bleeps, UFO-like chirps, occasional wind, and delay feedback. The dominant trope is multiple speaker blur plus psychedelic fuzz plus space in a mode that is simultaneously spiritual and political. As in most Funkadelic passages of this kind, one consistent feature is the large number of voices: various male speakers, male soul singing, wordless female singing, gasps and laughs, and other passing noises. All of these are further multiplied by echo, the intensity of which ebbs and flows throughout.

Funkadelic's sound effects passages, in their frequency and extremity, more than kept up with and in many ways exceeded what was happening in other branches of psychedelic music at the time. The most immediate comparison would be with space rock, which was the psychedelic rock substyle most concerned with exploring the formal implications of these kinds of textures. This being the case, there are at least two reasons to expect that in Funkadelic the space topic would be prominent: first, the band was texturally akin to space rock, and second, their sibling act, Parliament, would soon become the predominant Afrofuturist funk outfit. Yet what's interesting is that these sound effects passages in Funkadelic were generally not spun particularly in a science fiction or a cosmic direction. And what's doubly interesting is that by the mid-1970s, when psychedelic funk does become preoccupied with space topics, the unmeasured sound effects passages were largely absent, having given way to more narrative passages and extended funk jams. We will think about this more in the next chapter.

In formal terms, one thing that made Funkadelic distinctive was that there was no longer a strict dividing line between the unmeasured sound effects passages and the song proper. These tended to blur together, with rhythmic and melodic elements coming and going relative to a more continuous wash of ambient noises. Elements that would previously have been used to create strong formal divisions, such as riffs and vocal motifs, are similarly chopped up and cycled in a seemingly free manner. For example, we saw that the main riff in "Mommy, What's a Funkadelic?" is fluid in its location, continually passed around between instruments, never quite fixed in place but never quite vanishing. Another good example is the riff/theme of "Free Your Mind and Your Ass Will Follow" (which first enters at 1:49). The other important feature of riffs in Funkadelic, especially the guitar riffs, is that they are often sites of troping. For example, the riff from

"Mommy, What's a Funkadelic?" has acid rock characteristics but is also funky. Another good example of troping in a guitar riff is "Music for My Mother," which strongly resembles gris-gris era Dr. John (swampy psychedelic funk jam). This particular trope (funk plus heavy acid guitar) was not limited to Funkadelic. For example, the work of Jimi Hendrix provides many similar examples. But nowhere was it more noteworthy or dramatic than in Funkadelic, given the extent of their commitment to the funk style.

So to sum up Funkadelic's contribution to psychedelic funk, the main features include a shift in the balance toward groove and texture and away from song form; a darker tone that includes a more raw sexuality and more obvious politics; and more pointed humor. This suggests a comparison with what we observed earlier about the Temptations and psychedelic abjection. Under one view, that somewhat negative spin on the psychedelic contrasts with the P-Funk attitude, which was generally one of full commitment. But then again, consider Kodwo Eshun's take on Funkadelic. He characterizes their music, lyrics, and visual style almost entirely in terms of fear, abjection, and anger: "Funkadelia impeaches the universe, confronts reality, sets out to destroy an insane world over and over. . . . Funkadelia isn't an escape into other worlds, but a deathtrip into the hallucinogenres of LSD and the superpsychedelic STP. . . . The formal structure of time collapses into swill. Space loses its dignity, falls kneedeep into the shit of the world. Funkadelia intensifies the osmosis of funk, amplifies its imperceptible aroma. . . . You breathe in the putrefaction of the universe" (1998, 53–54).

In terms of specific imagery, you might say the same of a scatological satirist like Frank Zappa. But the difference is that Zappa stood apart from and rejected the psychedelic culture, whereas Funkadelic explored the abject side of psychedelia from within. The appropriateness of this reading is most strongly felt during the relatively brief association between Funkadelic and the Process Church, circa 1971–72. But if it was most literally appropriate at that point, it also captures a general atmosphere of darkness, death, and oppositional politics that strongly contrasts with work along the lines of early Sly and the Family Stone. This is not to say that the humor and transcendence of other psychedelic soul and funk are absent in Funkadelic. But in topical terms, the structure and inflections are different. Sex is more physical. Humor is more barbed and political. The underlying theology, riding in with the gospel element, includes more damnation but also a more sublime transcendence. And the psychedelic and space reference points are perhaps more psychotic. In structural terms, the nature of tropes and dialogism changes in a setting like this. Everything is more continuous, not as much about flashes and moments as about field structures, and centered on topical moods more often than distinct topical moments.

And with that, we have finished our survey of early psychedelic soul and funk. In terms of complexity and long-term influence, the emergence of these styles is one of the most significant events in the development of the psychedelic topical field. We will return to soul and funk in the next chapter, but now it is time to move back toward rock and folk musics for a while.

San Francisco

In the public imagination, San Francisco is ground zero of psychedelia. Even compared to the London scene, San Francisco's Haight-Ashbury district in the mid-1960s has been elevated to iconic status. The special importance generally accorded to this scene suggests many possible lines of inquiry, and so our challenge is to decide what to say about it specifically with reference to musical topicality. Rather than attempt another broad survey, my approach will be selective, identifying a few highlights that both typify events in San Francisco and also advance our overall understanding of how the topical field of psychedelic music was changing in the mid- to late 1960s. Many of the candidate areas have already been touched on or will be touched on in other parts of the book. For example, everything just said about psychedelic soul and funk has a San Francisco connection. Other areas in which San Francisco had important involvement but that are discussed elsewhere in the book include garage rock, jangle pop, folk music and folk pop, avant-garde crossovers with classical electronic music, psychedelic blues, and space rock. With all of that left for elsewhere, what will be the focus of this present discussion? There are four areas I have chosen to isolate, each of which highlights a different aspect of what was special about the San Francisco scene around 1967, and each of which invites us to discuss something different in psychedelic topicality.

The first of these four areas is the visual culture of San Francisco, especially early poster art. Visual elements are of special importance because of the multimedia aspect of subcultures and because of the specifically spectacular nature of the San Francisco hippie subculture. Early San Francisco psychedelic concert posters are a convenient corpus for structuring a survey of visual topicality of the time. Second, I'll consider the claim that the San Francisco subcultures were especially invested in forms of grassroots participatory theater and look at this from a topical point of view through selected recordings by Jefferson Airplane. Third and fourth, I'll offer some remarks about topical aspects of improvisational jam bands and about some distinctive features of countercultural relationships to American imaginaries, both with special emphasis on the Grateful Dead.

Early San Francisco Poster Art

It makes sense that the visual culture of psychedelia should be considered somewhere in this book. One reason is that topics are defined partly by their distribution across multiple media and practices. We would expect that anything worthy of being considered a musical topic would also have a presence in visual forms and that by comparing the musical and visual manifestations we can learn more about the topic in question, as well as gaining a greater appreciation for how its musical versions differ from its versions in other media. Also, psychedelic culture was especially productive in visual terms, and it would be a shame to leave the rich and influential design style completely unaddressed. Visual culture could have been introduced to the book in various ways, but it is especially appropriate in connection with San Francisco because the intermediality of topics is of special importance in subcultural scenes, and San Francisco was not only one of the first localized psychedelic scenes but also one of the first such scenes in rock culture overall. As Steve Waksman puts it: "San Francisco produced one of the first functioning rock scenes in the contemporary sense of the term, in which local performers were supported by an infrastructure of radio stations and performance venues. In this setting the notion that a rock concert was a potent reflection of, and even a means of producing, a more broadly felt sense of community took hold with distinctive force" (2009, 29).

One way to describe the scene is by contrast, through its difference from other contemporary scenes. For example, Barney Hoskyns (1996, 142–44), among others, has discussed the rivalry between the San Francisco and Los Angeles scenes in the mid-1960s. Although such narratives of rivalry depend a great deal on generalization, they can still get at crucial distinctions. For example, it is often remarked that the San Francisco bands were part of a subversive grassroots scene, whereas those in LA were more show business oriented, more centered on studio recordings, and more skillful in a traditional sense. Compared to the professionalism of LA, San Francisco bands had a reputation for being more powerful in live performance, more experimental, but also more inconsistent. It is also sometimes asserted that the LA freaks were more abject and socially marginal, whereas San Francisco hippies were conforming to a scene norm. Finally, Hoskyns notes that the New York scene, centered on Andy Warhol and the Velvet Underground, also failed to resonate with San Francisco, whereas Warhol admired LA for obvious (if ironic) reasons, and the Velvet Underground members admired the Byrds and Brian Wilson, among other LA figures (143–44).

Another way to characterize a scene is by enumerating its influences and artifacts. For example, Charles Perry (1984, 257–58, 269) lists some of the main intellectual influences on the early Haight-Ashbury: the Beats; yoga; Gurdjieff; Immanuel Velikovsky's book *Worlds in Collision* (1950); Herbert Marcuse; Aldous Huxley; Alan Watts; Zen; the I Ching; American Indian mysticism (especially the 1932 book by John G. Neihardt, *Black Elk Speaks*, and William Willoya and Vinson Brown's *Warriors of the Rainbow* [1962]); Hinduism; occultism; astrology; Perls, Hefferline, and Goodman's *Gestalt Therapy: Excitement and Growth in the Human Personality* (1951); *Summerhill: A Radical Approach to Child Rearing* by A. S. Neill (1960); Jung (not so much Freud); Tolkien; and conspiracy theories based around the CIA and the Mafia. These kinds of lists are always subjective, but they can also suggest windows into topicality. Without putting too much weight on any single list, note that for some of these reference points we've already seen substantial musical overlap (e.g., the Orientalist elements, fantasy, science fiction, and spy paranoia) and for others not so much (e.g., the specific authors and concepts from psychology and critical sociology). The more general point is that by situating musical topicality relative to a specific scene, we can more readily observe how the topicality of parallel contemporary media does or does not align with the music. We will draw similar comparisons through an examination of San Francisco visual culture in the form of poster art.

Some of the major zones of visual topicality on the San Francisco scene included fashion, album cover art, handicrafts, light shows, concert posters, and handbills. To focus on any one of these would provide a slightly different perspective, and to survey them all would take us too far afield. The posters are a convenient way to get at some highlights. Also, the posters are important because they were a medium for spreading the San Francisco visual style internationally. Bill Graham, for example, not only printed posters for local use but also made them available for sale through the mail. As early as December 1966, Graham reported monthly poster sales of 59,000 and ultimately up to 150,000 per week, shipped globally (Tomlinson 2001, 21). Because of this broad influence beyond the local scene, I will view the posters as encapsulating general features of psychedelic visual culture, rather than reading them in narrower terms specific to what was happening in San Francisco. Similarly, when making comparisons to musical topicality I will draw upon all the psychedelic music up to and contemporary with these posters, not just San Francisco bands. This is because while exact proportions vary, the San Francisco bands made at least some use of all the musical topics we have discussed up to this point.

I'll be considering mostly posters within the Bill Graham numbering system up to the end of 1967. This time span includes the first two years of Bill Graham productions and gets us through the Summer of Love. It is also stylistically convenient, stopping just before a second wave of design associated with artists like Rick Griffin and Lee Conklin. I will also discuss a few key posters from other venues, mostly Family Dog events at the Avalon Ballroom. The full list of posters under discussion is in appendix B, and beyond these specific reference points my comments are shaped by all the other Bill Graham Productions and Avalon Ballroom posters produced during this period. Since it wouldn't be practical to reproduce a sample of posters in this book large enough to support the discussion, I've developed a reference system that should allow readers to easily find the relevant posters on the Internet or elsewhere. In the text, I'll use a notation of the form PstN (e.g., Pst15, Pst3), which points to full references given in appendix B.

Among general influences on San Francisco psychedelic poster art, maybe the most consistently evident is Art Nouveau. On the one hand, this style by the 1960s would have been nostalgic and archaic. But at the same time, it would have had continuing connotations of antiestablishment experimentation, the desire to treat art as part of a total life, and the pursuit of the new.[4] Another aspect of the Art Nouveau and of belle époque visual styles in general is the way it resonated with the built environment of San Francisco, especially the Haight-Ashbury neighborhood, with its Victorian houses and ballrooms (Medeiros 2005, 330). Other movements temporally and stylistically close to Art Nouveau that also had an influence on the posters include the Pre-Raphaelites, Art Deco, and surrealism. Aside from these older reference points, poster artists also drew upon contemporary popular culture, including comics, films, science, corporate logos, current events, and hot rod art. Light shows were another important contemporary influence.[5] These highly varied materials were mixed together in a dense visual style. There was an emphasis on ornamentation and on decorative motifs, in some cases to the point that borders and similar functional elements became main design features. Perhaps the most influential example of this was the psychedelic lettering style. Overall, the visual field was often crammed with many small embedded details, sometimes as elaborations on the main features but sometimes as visual non sequiturs. This was on occasion achieved through the use of collage, which again resonates with early twentieth-century styles and techniques (especially dada and surrealism). However, in the case of artists like Stanley Mouse and Alton Kelley, collage also helped create a popular cultural visual sampling aesthetic that was more blatantly intertextual than many other psychedelic visual techniques because of the more literal borrowing of familiar images.

This sort of visual language is effective in producing tropes, and it is also rich in dialogism. The dialogism arises partly because many of the elements, both the figures and the decorative features, are sufficiently abstract as to suggest multiple interpretations. Just a few examples:

- Pst3: The main figure could be Joan of Arc, or a knight, or a witch/priestess.
- Pst11: The monolithic, downcast, text-covered head could variously be seen as a phrenology head, a Greco-Roman god, or an alien.
- Pst14: The central shape could be a tree (perhaps a tree of life), or an atomic mushroom cloud, or a psychedelic mushroom.
- Pst29: The androgyny of the central figure could be seen as a kind of dialogism. Also, the specifics of the figure could be seen variously as a sorcerer/ess, or an actor, or a craftsperson of some sort.
- Pst31: The monolithic figures could be aliens or Greco-Roman mythical figures (maybe Titans).
- Pst40: The central figure could be East Indian, but it is unclear whether indigenously so or a colonist. The hair and face could also be seen as Greco-Roman.

And a few striking visual tropes:

- Pst12: Native American troped with hippie troped with a textual reference to "baby Jesus."
- Pst22a: Indian guru troped with Masonic pyramid and eye. The eye is also dialogic, both a Masonic eye and a Hindu third eye. All of this is troped in turn with the border motifs, which are reminiscent of Art Nouveau.
- Pst32: On the largest level this design tropes outer space panorama motifs with a figure that could be African or Aboriginal (because of the large earring and the face covered by patterns). The many smaller details trope these with the medieval Gothic (a skull), the belle époque (an old-fashioned umbrella), the nautical (a seashell), yoga mysticism (a mandala-like figure where the third eye would be), Chinese culture (the circular motif on the jaw, very much like a shou symbol), among other more vague associations suggested by other figures embedded in the design.

Further analysis of these aspects would be fascinating to pursue, but for now the main thing is to emphasize is that troping and dialogism are key to the visual style. While the bulk of my comments will have to do with individual visual topics, it should be remembered that the visual language overall, like the musical one, strikes a balance between the more isolated and pointillistic effect of the individual elements and the way these can be made to transform into one another and refer to one another. With that in mind, we can move on to an examination of some individual topical elements.

We can start by asking after musical equivalents of the general belle époque ambience. The musical parallels have mostly to do with the frequent use of anachronistic style elements such as brass bands, ragtime, old-time, and bluegrass music. One crucial difference is that in the case of music these nearly always function as donor styles. Rarely do they sound like the principal or normative stylistic identity or formal framework, and they are often disjunctive in effect. By contrast, in the poster style these nostalgic elements more often function as base styles. They provide an overall framework that feels foundational rather than disjunctive. Also, the belle époque references are part of a broader family of visual references to particular historical periods that includes:

- medieval Europe: a knight or Joan of Arc (Pst3), skeletons and skulls (Pst17), and castle interiors (Pst42)
- the Catholic Church: cruciform figures and halos (Pst6, Pst20), textual reference to "the baby Jesus" (Pst12), and ornate carved wood panel motifs (Pst27)
- the Old West and other Americana: lettering styles (Pst18), Native American faces and figures (Pst23), Civil War–era costumes and ornamental styles (Pst35)
- Greco-Roman iconography: heroic human faces and figures (Pst2, Pst40), god-like faces and figures (Pst11, Pst31, Pst35, Pst39), faces like classical theatrical masks (Pst28)

Musical parallels for many of these references are clear and frequent enough to be considered in depth elsewhere. But there are a few differences to notice. For example, while Gregorian chant does have a generally medieval flavor, the musical references do not feel as temporally particular as do the visual ones, and they lack entirely the nineteenth-century dimension found in some of the visual topics (e.g., the carved wood motif of Pst27). Maybe the most interesting variation has to do with Greco-Roman iconography.[6] Interest in Greco-Roman culture was widespread in the 1950s and 1960s. Musically, it comes through most clearly in the epic topic and in general aesthetic concepts like the Doors' stated interest in classical theater as a model of performance. But that said, there's nothing musically equivalent to the frequent, clear, and specific visual topicality in this area. Also, the Greco-Roman imagery has pagan and sometimes pastoral elements generally missing from the musical equivalents. These elements in turn often shade into Western occultism and other exoticized historical mythologies, often Orientalist ones. Some specific examples of visual topics in this area include:

- the Oriental in general: belly dancers (Pst1), gurus (Pst22a), cobras (Pst30), Nehru jackets, and paisley (Pst40)
- the *taijitu* (Pst4, Pst18)

- eye motifs (Pst4)
- Egypt (Pst18, Pst22a)
- Masonic symbolism (note that this overlaps with eyes, Egypt, and Americana) (Pst4, Pst22a, Pst35)

Again, the musical parallels are clear, but interesting differences exist. With respect to the Oriental, the visual topics have a degree of specificity generally lacking in the musical ones. Sometimes this produces interesting juxtapositions. For example, the 13th Floor Elevators often used the eye-and-pyramid motif in their artwork, which is an Egyptian/Masonic topic. However, there is nothing in their music that specifically picks up on this connection. The music is often mystical and oracular in a more general way, evoking these topics indirectly. But the specifically Egyptian and Masonic overlays are contributed only by the visuals. More generally, many of the visual signifiers in the posters are East Asian in tone (Chinese, Japanese, etc.), which is perhaps to be expected from the American West Coast. However, the musical signifiers of Orientalism, even in San Francisco bands, are much more like those in the UK, focused on Indian topics and, to a lesser degree, Middle Eastern ones.

Just as the historical references shade off into various sorts of exoticism, they also shade off into science by way of archaic science:

- the old airplane, which was the Jefferson Airplane logo but also part of a category (Pst9, Pst38)
- modern or slightly archaic science (Pst7, Pst11, Pst13, Pst14, Pst30, Pst44, Pst47)

The combined field of archaic science and technology is one area that was prevalent in the visual style but that has almost no equivalent in the music. Music does signify the general era in various ways, but the clockwork topic is the only clear-cut and common sonic signifier of old technology in particular. Things like brass instruments and calliopes also signify themselves as technologies (this is part of their generally nostalgic tone), but they do not signify technology as such. As we've already seen and will discuss further, musical evocations of technology in the later 1960s tended to be more otherworldly and futuristic. In the poster art as well, science shades off into space, but to a surprisingly small degree. The examples of clear space topicality in the early posters are few and far between but include:

- solar or planetary coronas that also could be microscopic biological structures (Pst8, Pst44)
- figures that could be aliens (Pst31)
- outer space panoramas with planets, stars, etc. (Pst32, Pst38, Pst44, Pst47)

Space topics in the visual style occupy a position that is similar to their position in the musical style. By 1967 most of the key elements of what would be called space rock were in place, but they represented a relatively small part of the overall landscape, not yet having separated out into a distinct genre either musically or visually.

Moving on to other topics, the nature-based magic and the pastoral topics are already implicit in many of the areas already discussed, but sometimes these show up in even more distilled forms. For example:

- the tree of life (Pst1, Pst14)
- Eve (Pst1, Pst5)
- the pastoral (Pst5, Pst16, Pst17, Pst38, Pst46)
- Native American: the Southwest and Great Plains (Pst12, Pst22b)
- Native American: the Pacific Northwest (Pst12, Pst24, Pst25, Pst33)
- magic and magicians (Pst17, Pst22a, Pst28, Pst29, Pst36, Pst43, Pst46)

Musical evocations of the pastoral have already been discussed, but again we can notice some nuances or variations that are common in the visual material but not so easily conveyed musically. For example, there are the biblical and pagan images, with their specific evocations of mythologies, literatures, times, and places. Also, in the poster art there is a frequent troping of magic and pagan spirituality with the pastoral, a trope that is much less often explored in the music. Artists like Pink Floyd and the Incredible String Band, as we will see, did explore a kind of pastoral mysticism, but with nothing so specific as a tree of life, or Eve, or the wizards and white witches who populate the posters. There *were* ways to say "serpent" in music at the time, but typically in an Orientalist mode more than a pastoral or neopagan one.

There are also a few topics that I want to consider more abstractly in terms of affect and mode of signification. For example, eroticism comes across differently in the posters and in the music. I would suggest that in the visuals it comes across more topically, since the posters can draw upon specifically visual topical formulations of the erotic, such as belly dancers and the Western fine art nude. Consider, for example, the Wes Wilson Woman, a figure who was frequently included in designs by Wes Wilson with many variations.[7] Taken together, her appearances cover a range of specific erotic and sensual moods and topics, appearing variously as:

- Eve (Pst1, Pst5)
- "nude" in a general Western fine art way (Pst1, Pst4)
- Oriental (Pst1)
- pastoral (Pst1, Pst5)
- mythically heroic (Greco-Roman, Egyptian, Central American) (Pst2)
- medieval knight (Joan of Arc) (Pst3)
- witch/sorceress (Pst3, Pst4)
- Christ (Pst6)

Like the visuals, music can also be highly sensual, but there are differences. While visual images can quite easily create sexual references that are at the same time specific and graceful, music has a more difficult time in this regard. It tends either to be vaguely sensual rather than specifically sexual or to make the leap directly to the fully explicit. In any event, overt and subtle eroticism is nearly absent from the music we've been considering, but it is quite common in the poster art.

Before switching to a different topic, we should also note the Wes Wilson Woman's importance as a repeated figure with variations—a kind of metatrope or metadialogic presence appearing in multiple posters but always different. I believe that this allows her to function as the visual equivalent of a psychedelic guide figure. Her effectiveness in this regard relies partly on her power of constant return melded with constant transformation. She is a presence that lends continuity across moments and contexts but at the same time mirrors the mutability of the psychedelic experience. This effect of a single character recurring in different guises is something that music can also evoke, but with more difficulty. And it's arguably a potential that was not generally explored in psychedelic music of the time, being more common in art music contexts (e.g., in the way themes are treated in sonata allegro form or in the idea of a leitmotif).

I'd like to conclude our survey of poster art by saying a bit more about Native American imagery by way of another image that was often repeated in the posters: the Family Dog logo. Overall, Native imagery was extremely important to the visual culture, but it was almost completely absent from the music. The contrast here is not just distributional but also ethical. We've already seen a few cases in which the specificity of visual images differs from musical evocations of the same topics. This ability of the visual to evoke particular individuals and histories can highlight interpersonal and intercommunity politics and ethics. One of the better-known posters featuring the Family Dog logo is Wes Wilson's design for the Blues Project and the Great Society at the Avalon Ballroom (Pst12). The logo, repeated and varied in other posters, is a photo of a Native American in a top hat, smoking a large cigarette or joint. The photo was reportedly borrowed by Chet Helms from *The American Heritage Book of Indians*, with the joint/cigarette added by him (Tomlinson 2001, 22). The background is stars and stripes, and the poster also includes a caption: "May the baby Jesus shut your mouth and open your mind." The phrase was reportedly seen by Helms on a bathroom wall (22). From the perspective of topic theory, one interesting thing is the degree of borrowing in this design, not just the collage of found and familiar images but also the textual layer. But let's focus instead on the complexity of the identity politics. Helms is said to have chosen this photo because of its affinity with tribalism and its outsider status with respect to authority (Medeiros 2001, 62). From that perspective, the choice can be read as affectionate or even respectful. It involves a self-othering of the hippie position through association with the Native other, who is in turn assimilated into the countercultural tribe. On the other hand, this is also a blatant and one-sided appropriation. And "logo" in this case is disturbingly close to "mascot." Seen from that perspective, the logo underscores a degree of violence inherent in topicality, since the formation of topics relies on a removal from context and a redeployment of meaning that can involve ethical questions of respect and control. In this case, the ethical issues are intensified through repetition. The logo was used frequently and almost every time with new tropes designed to be provocative and satirical. Each repetition deepens and renews the shift of control and the removal from context.

When comparing this sort of visual exoticism to musical exoticism, there are three differences that should be stressed. First, there is specificity. Exoticist musical borrowings tended in that era to be of general style traits rather than of anything that could be traced to specific individuals or even to specific communities. So the musical representations seem less personal. Second, there is the repetition of essentially the same image in multiple posters. Although broadly similar types of musical signs could be found in multiple recordings and performances, they were almost never repeated exactly and did not have strict canonical forms. So again, the sense of appropriation seems less focused in a specific direction. Finally, there is the nature of the visual as a channel of identity and control. Because we are so accustomed to the visual being used as a tool of authority, visual appropriations often feel more direct and pointed than sonic ones. None of this is to say that musical appropriations are less problematic than visual ones in any absolute sense, only that they are potentially less blatant.

I can offer two broad conclusions from our brief discussion of San Francisco poster art. First, the music and the posters drew upon mostly the same topics. Second, they did so with greatly differing emphasis and sometimes drawing upon quite different modes and affects of signification. This is to be expected from two such different signifying systems, and that is one reason that the study of topics benefits from cross-media comparisons.

Jefferson Airplane and the Theatrical

Another aspect of visual culture that overlaps with musical topicality is theatricality. Charles Perry notes that participatory theater was a constant interest and tool among many otherwise distinct San Francisco groups and that this extended to grassroots performativity becoming a key part of the psychedelic subculture: "The theater motif was one thing that distinguished the hippie use of psychedelics from that of the Beats a few years earlier. The Beats had understood the world in terms of spontaneity, religion, psychiatry and so on, and had even envisioned a world freed from greed and war by psychedelics. But the theater motif proved a particularly effective handle for assimilating the psychedelic experience, otherwise so vast and formless, into everyday life" (1984, 253).

This raises the question: Which musical topics in San Francisco rock music of the time might have shown traces of a theatrical sensibility? We will pursue the answer by looking at Jefferson Airplane. However, theatricality can be understood and approached in many ways, and we need to be careful about eliding differences on the scene. For example, much of the theatrical tendency in San Francisco was developed through politicized groups such as the San Francisco Mime Troupe and the Diggers. Whatever we may say about psychedelic musical theatricality, it will not necessarily overlap substantially with these areas (although if we were to look into psychedelic theatricality in Detroit just a few years later, we would see that the activist political dimension had become much stronger). We also need to consider a contrary viewpoint from Philip Auslander, who argues that the counterculture was suspicious of theatricality because it valued "a seamless unity between rock performers and their audiences," whereas theater always presumes some separation between performer and audience. "Because the hippie counterculture sought to resist this separation of performer and audience in favor of an imagined social collective, rock musicians were constrained to perform in ways that stressed their identity with their audiences. The ideology of authenticity mandated that musicians appear on stage as themselves, not as any other persona or character" (2006, 13).

On a related note, Auslander (2006, 15–18) also argues that psychedelic rock culture had a strongly antiocular bias. On one level, this seems like a strange claim, given the importance of poster art, fashion, light shows, and other visual elements to the scene. However, Auslander is thinking here of occularity not in the general sense of an interest in visual experience but in the more specific sense of a mode of authority and control centered on the visual. For example, we saw how representational and historically referential elements in the poster art were, through abstraction and troping and dialogism, turned in directions that celebrated visual experience but did not encourage occularity in the sense of a mode of control or discipline. Similarly, Auslander's claims about theatricality might at first blush seem to contradict the otherworldly flamboyance of performers such as Jimi Hendrix and Arthur Brown (neither of whom were San Francisco figures, but both of whom were emblematic of psychedelic performance styles). But rather than seeing a contradiction between the perspectives of Auslander and Perry, we can put them together by noting that the San Francisco subcultures were invested in a form of participatory theater but that this was often understood as a mode of self-expression and as an exploration of self-actualization rather than as role play.

The ways in which theatricality can be expressed in music vary widely and were not restricted to the San Francisco bands. We have already looked in detail at several cinematic topics that also could be seen as theatrical (especially the epic). And theatricality will be an important theme in our discussion of *Sgt. Pepper* as well. That being said, at least one San Francisco band—Jefferson Airplane—explored theatrical moods and topics in a musically distinctive way, and one that resonates with the particular sort of theatricality I have associated with the San Francisco hippie subculture. In order to sketch out some of the possibilities and topical features in this area of psychedelia, we will discuss two Jefferson Airplane songs in depth. One area where Jefferson Airplane had considerable success was in crafting short songs that had appeal as pop singles but at the same time expressed a fundamentally psychedelic aesthetic. The first song I'd like to look at is one of these: "White Rabbit."

JEFFERSON AIRPLANE, "WHITE RABBIT" (1967)

- The introduction (0:00–0:10) is just drums and bass. The rhythm is like a *bolero-son* (it is in $\frac{2}{4}$, with a similar accent pattern), but the snare drum timbre and triplets evoke a more Spanish bolero via Ravel and at the same time are militaristic. The

introduction also sets up the main chord progression: two bars of F♯ and two bars of G, repeated. There is a great deal of reverberation, which persists throughout the song.
- The connotations of the guitar solo (0:10–0:28) are exoticist but fairly nonspecific, equal parts flamenco and Orientalist. The guitar uses both the major and minor third of F♯ (A and A♯) at various points, which is part of the generally exoticist effect.
- The vocal entry at "One pill" (0:28) resonates with the exoticist/bolero mood but also intensifies the specifically Orientalist aspect through many slides and arabesques, along with unusual volume modulations. The voice is commanding: the lyrics have a guide-like or prophetic instructional tone, there is relatively little vibrato, the diction is very clear, and the Orientalist features already noted tend to underscore this oracular mode of address.
- The overall buildup is moved forward with the entrance of louder rhythm electric guitar and the introduction of a new harmonic progression that resolves the long-standing F♯–G alternation through the changes A–C–D–A (starting at "Alice" [0:46]). Compared to the major-minor ambiguity of the earlier oscillating progression, this cadence creates a much more grounded harmonic feeling while still relating back to the F♯.
- At "You go" (0:55) there is a return to the previous verse in all respects, although with greater density and volume (e.g., the rhythm guitar has now more clearly taken up the bolero rhythm).
- At "When men" (1:22–) the whole band switches to a more rock-oriented groove, as does the voice, and the overall volume and density increase yet again. There is another new set of chord changes: E–E–A–A, repeated. On the one hand, these chords are solid and fairly static, a prolongation of the V–I cadence in A. But this definiteness is somewhat undermined by the song's ultimate return to the F♯ area. For a while the rhythm section largely abandons the bolero material, but then it returns and is fused more strongly with rock features in conjunction with a static F♯ harmony on "Alice" (1:40). The overall effect is of a return to the earlier, harmonically ambiguous bolero framework but with more heaviness. This passage also features the loudest and longest vocal notes so far, on "Alice" and "know." The vocal intensity here is sufficient to suggest an operatic topic briefly troped with the others.
- The motor rhythms that start at "Remember" (2:07) and that had previously decorated the bolero rhythm and helped mark formal transitions now take over the texture and rhythmic feel and remain dominant for the rest of the song. This is also the start of the vocal climax, which continues to the end. The bolero and the less marked "rock" topics are both canceled from here to the end; or, rather, certain of their affective properties spill over and obscure all other details. This section also provides a final resolution to the ongoing harmonic ambiguity: a rising A-based progression (A–C–D–A) moves directly to a clear V–I alternation ending solidly on A.

Many things in this song could be heard as theatrical. First, there are the lyrics. These present a compelling dramatic situation: a kind of crisis, a suggested solution, and a range of supporting and opposing characters. The sense of theatricality and adventure is enhanced by the familiarity of the specific characters from *Alice in Wonderland*. Also, the element of self-dramatization comes in partly by way of the barely veiled drug references. These make the singer and band into outlaws of a sort and suggest that the drama is at least partly their own.

The music supports these dramatic themes in several respects. Most obviously there is the formal structure, which builds incessantly to a peak. More topically there is the exotic setting, equal parts fantasy Latin and Orientalist. These two forms of the exotic continually interact and take turns coming to the forefront. The result is not exactly a narrative, because there is no definitive change-of-state schema in place, but it resembles narrative in juxtaposing and circulating between two related but distinct topics. Another important dramatic element is the vocal staging, commanding and oracular. In topical terms, the voice evokes the epic, the operatic, and also the prototopical guide figure, all of which support the sense of drama. Finally, is all of this consistent with the specific sort of theatricality that I've suggested is typical of the San Francisco counterculture? It can certainly be heard that way, since the guide figure, the nature of the crisis, and the proposed solution are all consistent with an element of autobiography. While the figure of Alice is powerfully dramatized and is clearly fictional, there is still no impression of artifice or role play.

It is striking to see such a clear dramatic and theatrical structure in a relatively simple song form. By contrast, many Jefferson Airplane songs have more exploratory forms that often go even farther in creating an overtly theatrical atmosphere. One good example is "Blues from an Airplane."

JEFFERSON AIRPLANE, "BLUES FROM AN AIRPLANE" (1967)

- In the introduction (0:00–0:10), the guitars, bass, and a small bell play a chime-like repeated pattern. There is also a dramatic buildup created by a tom pulse plus cymbal roll.
- In the A section at measures 1–8 (0:10–0:25) the drum groove is largely standard rock, but the repeated open-close hi-hat pattern evokes clockwork. The bass and guitars are a bit more active than in the introduction but are still essentially holding down the chimes effect. The vocals feature a lead voice in call and response with fairly dense sustained chords from the backing vocals. At measure 8 the vocals move to a dominant seventh harmony, which is striking after all of the triadic vocal material. This jazz choir or Broadway chorus sort of gesture becomes more frequent and pronounced throughout the arrangement, but this is the first moment it crops up. The melody throughout the A section and in the whole song has a slightly Gregorian flavor.
- At measures 9–12 in the A section (0:10–0:36) the voices move to a block-chord texture on motor quarter notes, harmonizing a repeated scalar descent. The band sound starts to be dominated by repeated heavy cymbal crashes. The overall density and volume then fall back gradually over two measures to set up the repeat.
- The A section repeat (0:36–1:03) is quite similar to the first A section, but right away the guitars introduce a twangy riff based around the notes A–C–B–C–B–A, adding a surf/spy flavor. Overall, the texture is a bit denser and heavier than the first time around. This time when the voices begin the quarter-note block-chord

texture the bass, guitar, and drums move to a similar texture so that the whole band is emphasizing it.
- During the tag to the A section repeat (1:03–1:08) the guitar, bass, and drums play three full measures of just quarter-note block-harmonized C–B–A–G (four times in total).
- In the B section at measures 1–6 (1:08–1:21) the voices become even more harmonically dense and theatrical, building to a ninth chord at the end of the first phrase. The guitar emphasizes single-bar sustained chords for much of the phrase, building to a fanfare-like high major triad on quarter triplets for the last measure.
- In measures 7–12 of the B section (1:21–1:35) everything repeats, but the phrase ending is more dramatic, since the voices this time finish with a quarter-note triplet pattern leading into the final thirdless ninth chord (E + A + B + E in the voices over an A in the bass), and the guitar this time plays an even more fanfare-like figure on ascending octaves G–A. Throughout the whole B section, the rest of the band sometimes maintains a rhythm section function but frequently deviates to provide rhythmic doubling of the voices and also crescendo effects (motor eighth notes on climaxes, cymbal rolls, etc.).

In terms of topical materials, the dominant impression here is epic rather than narrowly or specifically theatrical. But the spectacle of a rock band portraying epic topics on so many levels could itself be seen as a theatrical gesture. Also, many of these features undermine the more expected rock elements, which become decorative to the epic framework rather than the other way around. Although there is a prominent spy/surf riff in the A sections, the band overall stays close to more orchestral sorts of textures and materials rather than grooves and riffs. The formal structure, too, follows a through-composed framework (albeit one that is repeated) rather than a typical blues or pop form. There is a constant sense of meandering into surprising harmonic areas, of breaking up the rhythmic flow with grand gestures such as the preponderance of quarter-note block chords, with triplet versions for climactic moments. Even where the drums play a more regular and propulsive rhythm pattern in the A section, the lopsided open-closed hi-hat pattern sounds strongly mechanical, like a variation on the clockwork topic more than a groove as such. This also serves to make the chimes sound dialogic, suggesting at the same time epic chimes, bells in a ritual context, and the chimes of a clock.

The role of the vocals in setting up this epic mood is especially subtle and important. The vocals are often choral in effect, almost like a Broadway chorus due to some of the jazz-related harmonies. The vocals are also a bit Gregorian in their frequently scalewise movement, adding to the mystical tone. Like many Jefferson Airplane performances, these vocals reflect the nascent state of rock opera, which would soon produce full-blown expressions such *S.F. Sorrow* by the Pretty Things (1968) and *Tommy* by the Who (1969). The directness of the rock opera connection is also evident in *Blows against the Empire* (1970), a rock opera album project spearheaded by Paul Kantner and Grace Slick and featuring guest appearances by prominent San Francisco and Los Angeles rock artists. In one respect, the Broadway-like aspect of these vocals resembles other nostalgic and theatrical topics common in psychedelia such as music hall and ragtime. But there is an affective difference in that Jefferson Airplane seemingly lacks the sense of irony and playfulness that often accompanies such topics. Here the elements of musical theater are deployed in a way that boosts the epic topicality and by extension the representation of subcultural solidarity.

The only aspect of "Blues from an Airplane" that does not match this single-minded epic quality is duration: the song is relatively short at 2:10. But then again, in a cinematic context the most strident epic topics are often relatively brief in duration, setting a scene rather than underscoring a longer narrative arc. Like "White Rabbit," "Blues from an Airplane" largely stages a single dramatic gesture. And although the form is much less linear than "White Rabbit," the overall trajectory of the gesture is the same. Both begin with quieter material that topically resembles an exotic dance and that contains a strong affect of potential energy and portent. "Blues from an Airplane" is more epic in its initial chimes motif, but the beginning of the A section more closely resembles the beginning of "White Rabbit." Then both build to a climax where the more oracular, heroic, and sublime topical elements implicit in the beginning are pushed to their extreme. "White Rabbit" does this just once, whereas the gesture is repeated a few times in "Blues from an Airplane." But the short duration of "Blues from an Airplane" means that the whole thing still retains a certain sense of singularity: the repeated gesture is like one gesture seen from multiple angles, rather than a more elaborated narrative.

The lyrics are also interesting in this context of epic theatricality. They are extremely simple and everyday, presenting the first-person emotional reflections of a man. Roughly the first half is dedicated to the man telling us that he is lonely because the woman he loves is not around and he doesn't know where she is. In the second half, nothing circumstantial changes, and yet the man expresses a burst of reassurance because he suddenly knows that her love is real and that he can achieve his desired identity: "I can be the man I feel." What's striking is how these everyday lyrics and sentiments are married to such portentous and epic music. If we were feeling ungenerous, the result could be called self-obsessed. But coming back to my earlier suggestion that we read San Francisco hippie theatricality as a meeting ground between larger-than-life gestures, on the one hand, and values of self-exploration and self-expression, on the other, we could suggest that this song provides a strong example of the aesthetic. Through the use of epic and theatrical topicality, the everyday feelings of an individual are portrayed as momentous, and the shift of mood is a revelation.

The Grateful Dead: Improvisation and Topicality

Like any kind of musical material, topics can be a resource for improvisation. And since the San Francisco scene did much to nurture group improvisation as a new area of rock practice, it makes sense to discuss improvisation at this point in the book. Several of the San Francisco bands explored group improvisation as a part of their styles, but none more so than the Grateful Dead. Through a discussion of the Dead, we can explore one example of how a collective improvisational style drew upon topicality. This will not produce an overall theory of topical improvisation, but it will allow us to highlight some of the possibilities in that area. The other feature of the Grateful Dead I would like to consider, one closely connected to their improvisational practice, is their distinctive relationship to roots music genres. Up to this point I've been using the terms "folk music" and "folkloric" to refer to some of the genres in question. In the case of the Grateful Dead, I will switch to saying "roots music" in order to highlight that they draw upon a wide range of folk and folk-related sources, some of which are very traditional but others of which, like bluegrass and zydeco and Bakersfield country music, are more contemporary but still closely connected to traditional musics. I am using the word "roots" in the sense it came to acquire in the 1990s, when it was one of several genre names such as Americana and alt-country that emerged to describe a new wave of traditional/contemporary fusion musics. So by applying the roots label to the Grateful Dead I am back-dating the term a little, but this works because the band was in many ways a model for that later fusion. We will be looking at the role played by roots music topics (among others) in Grateful Dead improvisations, and we will also be considering how the band's relationship to roots music helps situate them in a particular way with respect to American imaginaries.

Before looking at improvisation, we should consider a few general features of topicality in the Grateful Dead. The first point has to do with their use of superficially nonpsychedelic roots music genres and the role played by context in framing these as psychedelic. Apart from their importance as an improvisational unit, the Grateful Dead are significant for the extent to which they worked folk, country, and other roots materials into their music. Often, and especially on studio recordings, they played these styles fairly straight. And yet by all accounts the band was perceived as uniformly psychedelic, rather than as careening between unrelated styles. On one level this isn't surprising, since we've already seen many areas of overlap and resonance between psychedelic aesthetics and various kinds of roots music. But in another way something seems unusual, given the conservatism of some of the specific material the Dead drew upon. Some roots genres, such as folk ballads and hymns, wear their psychedelically cognate potential fairly openly. But the Grateful Dead would just as often draw on genres that did not, such as bluegrass and honky tonk. And they would often perform this sort of material in a manner that was, topically speaking, fairly homogeneous. In their earlier years that homogeneity was most common in the extended blues performances, for example, the album version of "Good Morning Little School Girl." Slightly later it was also typical on country and folk ballad material, for example, much of *Workingman's Dead*. One key Grateful Dead feature, then, is how certain performances or long passages in a performance can be read as psychedelic through context without many or even any psychedelic features in the music as such.

Relative to what we saw in the visual language of psychedelia, there are both parallels and differences here. In many of the visual media, troping of historical Americana images with more immediately psychedelic elements is common, just as it is in the Grateful Dead's music. The difference is one of time scale. In the visual imagery the entire trope is accessible at once, with all elements visible. Sometimes, as we will see, the Dead would create similar tropes in sound, simultaneously layering more traditional elements against more psychedelic ones. But on other occasions they would present these elements sequentially, sometimes with the traditional material lasting an entire song or longer before the psychedelic elements appear in force. Even here, the composite effect could often be psychedelic because the contexts in which this traditional music was produced and received would frame it with psychedelic elements. In a fluid situation of this sort, where much of the production and reception is embedded in a multimedia scene, it is often not appropriate to draw sharp distinctions between text and context. This is a point that can often be lost in topic theory, sometimes justifiably so, since looking at topics involves finding those elements that have fairly stable meanings of the sort that are less context dependent. On the other hand, conventional signs are only truly topics when they participate in much broader contexts. The Grateful Dead are a good example to remind us that the text-context distinction is very porous, especially where topicality is concerned. More than for many bands of the time, a single recording or performance by the Dead is likely to reveal only a small portion of their overall stylistic and topical range. But that full topical range will still be an active factor in how the more isolated moments are heard and valued.

Pushing the point a little further, we can think in terms of a different sort of troping in cases like this. The troping of topics is generally treated as something that happens within single texts, and for the majority of this book I will follow that practice. However, in some cases a topically homogeneous text can be heard as troped with other elements not present in that text because those elements are present in the immediate surroundings or because they are generally understood as relevant. So it can often be reasonable to read a homogeneous blues or country performance by the Grateful Dead, for example, as troped with space topics or psychedelic prototopics. In one sense this is simply the commonplace observation that contextual information always conditions interpretations. The decision to evoke the extra concept of troping in many cases would simply confuse the issue. But at the same time, there is some kind of topical framing effect at work here that requires attention. A weaker formulation would be to say that such a text could be heard *as if* there were troping elements in the text itself, even though there are not. This effect is similar to one I discuss elsewhere: the ability of a trope to permeate our hearing of a large passage of music, even when the signifiers for that trope literally occupy a much shorter span. The main point, whether you prefer the weaker or stronger formulation, is to note that contextual factors and troping can be very closely related and that the Grateful Dead provide an especially rich test case in this regard since, among rock bands of this period, they were both one of the most committed to psychedelic experimentation and one of the most committed to roots music forms.

I've been stressing the case of topically homogeneous performances and how these could have been heard as psychedelic due to contextual effects. Another way that psychedelic features can be troped into roots music is through performative choices. For example, in an extended blues jam like "Good Morning Little School Girl" there is the same potential for exploration of intensive variation and hypnotic repetition as we discussed earlier in connection with the Yardbirds. One such intensive variation, used on occasion by both the Grateful Dead and the Yardbirds, is to speed up and build density over the course of a long jam. While this technique is not inherently alien to the blues, it is also cognate with psychedelia and even indirectly evokes an Orientalist topic, since it resembles a Hindustani *alap-jor-jhala* form. By emphasizing these sorts of features in "Good Morning Little School Girl" and in other examples such as "Viola Lee Blues," even a stylistically homogeneous blues performance can gain psychedelic resonances. And besides the blues, other traditional source genres such as country, folk, and ragtime were also sometimes used by the Grateful Dead as vehicles for intensive variation. When these performative variations become sufficiently intense or idiosyncratic, they can in their extremity be consistent with a psychedelic reading without necessarily changing their generic or topical identities in any other way. Examples here might include the extreme energy and volume swells in "Cold Rain and Snow," "Sitting on Top of the World," and "Beat It On Down the Line" or the drawn-out and spacious phrasing of "Morning Dew," which is only hinted at in the album version but was often quite extreme in live performances.

Having spent some time considering more traditional roots musics and how they can be inflected in a psychedelic direction, we also need to consider ways in which the Grateful Dead drew upon more obviously psychedelic resources. On their earlier studio recordings the Dead did use psychedelic prototopics that even at that time were clichés. Sometimes these would be added into an otherwise less psychedelic framework. For example, "The Golden Road (to Unlimited Devotion)" features an introduction based on the siren trill along with a highly ambiguous metrical structure. Also, at the very end of the song there is an organ cue on an F♯ diminished seventh chord that seems melodramatic and theatrical in a self-consciously old-fashioned way. But apart from that, the song is straightforward sunshine pop. On other occasions they would make more thoroughly psychedelic statements in a studio context. For example, the "Dark Star" single is nearly a catalog of psychedelic topics and prototopics.

THE GRATEFUL DEAD, "DARK STAR" (SINGLE, 1968)

- Part 1 of the introduction (0:00–0:05) begins a little like a fanfare, with bass and electric guitar doubled on a repeated and decorated rising interval (albeit a minor third). The phrase finishes with a figure more like a jazz or blues turnaround lick.
- Part 2 of the introduction (0:05–0:15) introduces the main oscillating chord pattern (from A to an E-minor seventh chord). As discussed in detail by Graeme Boone

(1997, 176–77, 205), this oscillation is tonally ambiguous, and the song tends to play around the ambiguity rather than resolve it. There is also a tambura drone. The bass could almost be said to play a riff, but its figures are a little too varied and florid to fully qualify. The electric piano enters with a motif based around three descending, slightly separated blips (D–A, B–F#–G, A–E).

- At the beginning of the A section (0:15–0:45), the tambura fades out, and an organ enters with occasional quiet stabs. The first vocal theme enters. None of this is particularly topical, although the vocals are like a combination of blues (descending melodic shape, largely minor pentatonic, three times through the phrase) and Gregorian styles. On the second time through the theme (starting at 0:25), the organ is louder and more sustained, having switched from an electric organ timbre to a more pipe organ timbre. There is also a single gong strike (0:26). In general, during this repetition the rhythm section elements all get quieter. On the third time through the theme (0:35), the texture thins again to just guitars and bass, although with slightly more rhythmic intensity in how they are played. A pitch-shifted voice (higher) enters and doubles the vocals for most of this phrase, but it fades in slowly so as to become more obvious as it goes along. The tambura reenters near the very end of the section.
- At the start of the B section (0:45–1:06) there is a noteworthy pointillistic cluster of textural events: an increase in the loudness of the voices; a big swell on a single chord with pipe organ timbre; and a few very loud strums on an acoustic guitar. There is a total abandonment of the groove as instruments are used to follow the vocals or to introduce disjunct splashes of color. Also, the rhythm of the voices is based largely on half-note triplets. This is something like the dissolve texture I discussed under Sly and the Family Stone.
- At the instrumental break (1:06–1:20) the whole band eases back into the original groove, with some prominent lead guitar.
- There is then essentially a repetition of A, B, and the instrumental break. The vocal harmony is notably denser on "the transitive nightfall of diamonds" (2:04–2:12), and this phrase is extended relative to what might be expected based on the form up to now, much more evocative of a hymn or choral music in general. Also, the instrumental break this time starts with an ascending harmonized line on guitar that is somewhat reminiscent of mariachi trumpets.
- The coda (2:24–2:42) is a typical sound effects ending, featuring a tambura drone, half-note motor rhythm chords in guitar and bass, whispery voices, with other quiet, indistinct electronic drone effects. A quiet but disruptive banjo suddenly enters at the very end and finishes the song with a short solo fade-out (2:38–2:45).

The "Dark Star" single contains many overtly psychedelic signifiers: tambura, pitch-shifted voices, oscillating and ambiguous chord changes, and a delicate and somewhat unstable sense of time (in part because there are no drums on the track). This pointedly psychedelic mood is made more intense by frequent textural and rhythmic shifts and by the mix, which features many moments where clearly topical signifiers come and go pointillistically. Some examples include the tambura drone, the pipe organ timbre, the gong, the loud acoustic guitar, the quiet spoken voices, and the banjo.

One of the most important topics in "Dark Star" is the space topic. There are some specifically space-oriented signifiers, but beyond that the title and lyrics make it likely that even the more general psychedelic features would have been interpreted as spacey. Some of the song's elements are especially close to features that became typical of space rock proper, for example, the reiterated organ figure (which sounds like Morse code, or a satellite, or an alien message), the cymbal washes and gong, the pipe organ pads, and the overall delicacy and floating quality. A full discussion of space rock will need to wait until the next chapter, but since we will have occasion to frequently evoke the space topic when analyzing live performances by the Grateful Dead, a few preliminary remarks are in order. First, to a certain extent I am applying the term "space" retroactively, since it was not as commonly applied to the Dead in the late 1960s as it came to be later. It is appropriate in hindsight because of how certain Grateful Dead traits of the time resemble certain later space-rock features, and also because in the 1970s "space" became an increasingly common word in Grateful Dead reception. For example, the Drums > Space concert segment became standardized sometime in the late 1970s.[8] But even during the 1960s there were space reference points in the Grateful Dead. Besides "Dark Star" there were also "Mountains of the Moon" and "Cosmic Charlie." The band had links, largely through Phil Lesh and for a while Tom Constanten, to the San Francisco Tape Music Center, to Don Buchla, and to electronic experimental music more generally, all of which, while never foregrounded, fed into the space topic aspect of their profile.

In terms of signifiers and formal features, some elements of the space topic as found in the Grateful Dead are the same as what later became typical of space rock more generally: long pad sounds (especially with echo and reverberation or other modulation), combined with a suspension of the groove in favor of an ambient swimming-in-and-out texture. But in the case of the Grateful Dead, there is much more interplay and troping with roots music elements. In their music, space is frequently evoked as a movement away from the traditional through the technique of starting with less spacey textures and gradually introducing other noises and extended techniques, pulling the traditional style in a more experimental direction. Because of this, I will speak of a space/noise topic in cases where a major feature of space is that it represents a loss of constraint and an increase of noise relative to what went before. Finally, in later space rock we will see that the typical relationship between metrical elements and ambient elements is for a very strict, even motoric groove to be maintained and for these noisy and ambient elements to be layered on top of it. By contrast, in spacey Grateful Dead passages there is often a more liminal situation in the rhythm section, where grooves will be present but unstable, constantly changing, almost as if the layers of regular groove themselves are being treated as ambient sounds that fade in and out and transform into one another. There are specific examples of all these features in the analyses that follow, but the main point is that the space topic in the Grateful Dead has a great deal in common with how it was manifested in later space rock but is also quite distinctive.

In the particular case of the "Dark Star" single, the space topic doesn't particularly represent noisy excursion from a traditional baseline. Rather, the space topic is troped more continuously with roots topics. Specific roots signifiers include the nature of the melody line, the acoustic guitar, the hymn-like group vocals on "transitive nightfall of diamonds," and the banjo. This particular trope (space/roots) is not one we have yet seen, apart from the harmonica in "Section 43." It is not unlike the space/pastoral trope we will discuss later in Pink Floyd, but it is also different. One difference is that the Grateful Dead's version of folk and roots topicality includes considerable African American influence. As we will see in the upcoming analysis of "Alligator" and "Caution (Do Not Stop on Tracks)," the Dead created a space/blues trope quite different from the African American space tropes explored in psychedelic soul and funk. Apart from the specifically black aspect, the Grateful Dead were also unique for a psychedelic band in the extent to which they identified with American imaginaries, and it is worth taking a moment to consider some aspects of this.

Space is a kind of frontier, and many commentators have noted the central importance of frontiers, open spaces, and mobility in US history. These can easily be linked to elements of the rock counterculture. For example, Dominick Cavallo (1999, 78–86) has shown that rhetorics of the psychedelic trip engage concepts of the frontier. But he goes on to note that another crucial concept in US history is settlement, and that settlement and the frontier are locked in a creative relationship (86–89). By frequently troping experimental space and psychedelic elements with roots music, the Grateful Dead in a way enact a synthesis between the models of settlement and frontier. Along similar lines, consider how Richard Moser (2003) makes a distinction between an apocalyptic strain and a prophetic strain in American history. Both are relevant to psychedelia because both involve understandings of radical change, and both raise questions about the ultimate meaning and purpose of ongoing events. The apocalyptic outlook insists on a dramatic break from the past, leading to either dystopia or utopia, while the prophetic strain adopts a more workerly attitude, trying to build a better future out of the existing order. From a prophetic perspective, the shape of the future is clear, whereas the future is obscured under an apocalyptic perspective. Like the frontier mentality, the apocalyptic strain can encourage a mixture of activity and fatalism, whereas the prophetic strain encourages a gradual and careful accumulation of effort, albeit one marked by a spiritual aura. Connections between the apocalyptic strain and psychedelia seem fairly straightforward. Less obvious is whether we can find a prophetic aspect. One possibility is in the respectful and sometimes traditional use of roots materials—especially those that in other contexts would even be culturally conservative—as part of an experimental psychedelic style. Also fitting the prophetic strain is an interest in building communities (even countercultural ones) and pursuing aesthetic interests with a near-spiritual zeal. In all of these respects, while the Grateful Dead occasionally displayed an interest in chaos consistent with the apocalyptic strain, they also had prophetic aspects. So, as with the relationship between frontier and settlement, the Dead encompass a wide range of philosophical and practical possibilities within American imaginaries, and as a result their deployment of roots topics often carries a sense of gravity and purpose.

Now that we've considered some highlights of the Grateful Dead's topical universe on the broadest scale, we can start to move toward a detailed discussion of live group improvisation. We have not yet considered the question of how topicality can be an improvisational resource, and the Grateful Dead provide an ideal opportunity. The result will not be a complete survey of the question, but it will serve to demonstrate the sorts of new perspectives that improvisation can open up.

One common practice in Grateful Dead concerts was for certain songs to be chained together. For example, a frequently encountered sequence during the late 1960s was "Dark Star > China Cat Sunflower > The Eleven." Another common sequence at that time was "Alligator > Caution (Do Not Stop on Tracks) > Feedback." I will frame my discussion of Grateful Dead improvisational style around a reading of three different performances of this second sequence. The "Alligator > Caution > Feedback" sequence is of special interest because of the way it tropes roots music elements with space and psychedelic ones. Two of the three versions I will describe are live concert recordings: one from February 24, 1968, and one from August 23 of that same year. The other is nominally a studio version, released on *Anthem of the Sun* in July 1968.[9] However, edited into this version is a substantial amount of previous live material, and the overall structure of the album version is very similar to that of the live recordings. I will discuss the album version first and use it as the basis for comparison with the other two versions because its status on the album makes it marginally more canonical. But really, the broader point about this sequence is that it dramatizes the fluid relationship between studio and stage in the band's work.

First, I'll describe and compare the three performances in some detail and then move on to say how they illustrate general topical procedures and features in Grateful Dead live improvisations. But before doing that, I should explain what I mean by the *typical percolating jam sound*. This is the baseline sound that the band tends to fall into when they are not playing something more specific. The exact texture and topical mix varies widely, but it usually contains simultaneous elements of country, bluegrass, blues, bebop, R&B, space rock, raga rock, gospel, garage rock, Latin jazz, and New Orleans parade music. A detailed analysis could easily take up a chapter of its own, but the main point to note is that the band's default live groove hints at all of these topics without being primarily defined by any of them. This leaves a great deal of scope for exploring various tropes and changes of state. The typical percolating jam can variously be an engine for short-range troping, troping as a sustained mood or texture, narrative or other changes of state, veering off into new directions, or returning to something that has been gone for a while. Whenever I use the phrase *typical percolating jam sound*, I am indicating not only that the band has converged on its baseline sound but also that it has entered into a topical region where these sorts of potentials are likely to be explored.

So let's begin the detailed discussion by looking at the album version of "Alligator > Caution (Do Not Stop on Tracks) > Feedback." This description is especially dense so that it can serve as a point of comparison. I've divided the performance into eleven zones during which different topics or topical procedures are dominant. The material in italics names each zone and highlights its main topical features, and the plain text identifies some particular musical features that support the topicality of that zone.

THE GRATEFUL DEAD, "ALLIGATOR > CAUTION (DO NOT STOP ON TRACKS)," VERSION A (ALBUM VERSION)

- *Song form zone: While specific elements come and go, the main feature of this section is that it is dominated by a soul music style briefly troped in spots with psychedelic kazoos and with space and classical topics. The topical implications of the kazoos are similar to other psychedelic kazoos: circus, mock parade, mock military fanfare, jug bands, and skiffle. In this song, it is striking how the kazoo is used not as a quick novelty color but rather for more extended passages and on multiple occasions. Unlike many other Grateful Dead songs in live performance, the method here is to play the song straight through and then move on to the more improvisational sections, never returning to this initial song form.* The song begins with relaxed $\frac{4}{4}$ drums, leading to a straightforward blues-rock riff. At 0:17 a long descending kazoo line enters. The kazoos come and go at points throughout the song. When the lead voice comes in, it is very much in a soul music vein. The kazoos drop out at that point, but some of the electric guitar lines are very kazoo-like. The bridge after the second verse has a striking tinkling piano texture, the drums drop out, and the backing vocals go to long held notes (1:39–1:50). In this way the space topic is suggested on multiple levels and very suddenly, although the soul and carnivalesque elements are maintained in the kazoo-like guitar, the lead voice, and the ragged aspect of the backing vocals. In the third verse there are some very classical single-line countermelodies from the piano.
- *New Orleans drum solo zone: This is a second line style drum solo (in the sense that only drums are playing, not in the sense of just one drummer being heard), with the Latin elements emphasized.* At 3:14 there is an abrupt shift away from the traditional song form, and a long drum solo starts. It includes a persistent 3–2 clave.
- *New Orleans / acid / blues trope zone: The second line drums are troped first with blues vocals and then with acid rock guitar.* The drums remain solo until 4:20, when a voice comes in repeating "alligator runnin' 'round my door" in a blues style. This vocal motif continues to be extemporized over the continuing drums, sometimes joined by other voices either singing or shouting in the background. The band is absent, apart from very occasional single bass notes. At 5:29 an acid rock lead guitar enters, replacing the voices, playing alone with the drums.
- *Percolating jam zone: This is the typical Grateful Dead jam texture, with extra emphasis on the New Orleans and jazz-gospel aspects (in the drums and organ, respectively). This passage is an interesting example of how the typical percolating jam sound can gradually emerge out of something more narrowly topical, with no feeling of disjunction.* At 6:09, the entire band suddenly enters to accompany the continuing lead guitar. The organ is especially active: in timbre and figuration it sounds like peppy gospel organ or Jimmy Smith–style jazz. At 9:55 group harmony voices come in, riffing on the word "alligator," which reinforces the soul and R&B dimensions.

- *First noise breakdown zone: An extended noise finale.* At 10:30 the groove suddenly breaks down, and the overall texture becomes a cacophonous noise finale that tapers down to a quieter unmeasured noise passage.
- *Runaway train zone:* The sound is continuous, but the clock resets to 0:00 as the album moves on to "Caution (Do Not Stop on Tracks)." The new song begins with a very fast shuffle rhythm on the drum kit: a runaway train motif. The band keeps up a typical fast blues vamp, quiet and sparse.
- *Extended narrative blues zone, centered on the lead voice:* A blues lead voice enters at 0:19. The voice develops a story line that is very much the focal feature and in a traditional blues style. There is lead electric guitar in a call-and-response relationship to the voice, which reinforces the blues dominance.
- *Blues/space trope zone: A passage in which additional voices and other elements begin to layer in explicitly psychedelic elements. Neither the blues nor the space topic dominates in this zone, although the overall movement is toward space.* At 1:48 the lead voice starts to repeat "all you need," with variations. Several other voices join at this point, doing the same thing. The other voices do not sound like blues singers. They sound conversational—strangely so. The texture develops into a sung call-and-response tapestry. At 2:00 the sparse multivoice texture is joined by a lead guitar with volume swells on each note. The timbre and spaciousness of this guitar are not particularly blues-like, but the part still serves the same function as another call-and-response voice would do. The whole passage is a little space-like in its sparseness and in the volume-swell guitar, but it is still heavily rooted in blues interplay.
- *Space/noise zone: A passage that deepens the psychedelic elements toward a space/noise jam texture, nearly unmeasured but never fully without groove.* Gradually, starting around 3:01, other more space-like sounds start to fade in—long swelling bass notes, repeated motor-rhythm guitar notes, various extended-technique guitar sounds. The topical balance continues to shift gradually away from blues and toward space/noise. By about 3:35 the groove is becoming noticeably unstable. It sounds like a tape music pastiche made with Grateful Dead source materials, and it stays that way to about 4:17. In this case, being the album version, it literally is a tape pastiche. But as we will see, a similar effect is also created in some live performances through other means. At 4:17 the overall texture again sounds like the band playing in a normal context, but the groove is still unstable. The drums mostly present typical groove patterns, but these constantly change, so nothing settles in. The effect is like strands of groove woven into a more chaotic overall texture, almost succeeding in fulfilling their normal stabilizing function, but not quite.
- *Temporary reconsolidation zone: A short return to the typical percolating jam texture.* At 5:04 the groove solidifies back into the runaway train motif, and there is a guitar solo. There are also foregrounded long held notes from the bass that in this context sound like a rumbling, thunderous component of the train motif.
- *Final dissolve zone: Transition into an extremely long, unmeasured noise/feedback exploration.* At 5:23 there is a very sudden transition to an unmeasured noise finale clearly created by a tape edit. The overall texture transitions into "Feedback" starting around 5:48 and continues that way with greatly varying intensity and texture to the end, at about 9:30.

Taking this album version (version A) as a baseline, we can start to describe similarities and differences in how these zones and materials are handled in the other two performances. It isn't until we have these comparisons in place that we can start to answer the question of what sorts of things the Grateful Dead would do as a matter of course with topics in their improvisations. So we need to stay with close reading for a while longer in order to set up the eventual overview.

This next version stands out because of an interesting paradigmatic substitution of songs and a strikingly different mixture of space and roots elements.

VERSION B: "ALLIGATOR > CAUTION (DO NOT STOP ON TRACKS) > FEEDBACK" (FEBRUARY 24, 1968, KINGS BEACH BOWL, LAKE TAHOE)

- *Song form zone:* As noted earlier, two of the most common song sequences in Grateful Dead concerts of this time were "Dark Star > China Cat Sunflower > The Eleven" and "Alligator > Caution (Do Not Stop on Tracks) > Feedback." But at this particular show, the band made a substitution of "Alligator" for "Dark Star" by performing "Alligator > China Cat Sunflower > The Eleven" and then returned to "Alligator" in progress for the sequence described below. The first "Alligator" was very close to the song form as described in version A. The two noteworthy topical differences are, first, that the piano is absent (so the space and classical tropes do not appear in this section) and, second, that the kazoo lines are replaced with voices singing a similar part, which creates a different topical effect. Some of the same carnivalesque elements are present as in the kazoo version, but these kazoo-substitute voices serve even more to reinforce the soul music elements. Overall, though, this section is topically the same as the other versions. The only difference is how its usual continuation has been interrupted, or perhaps prolonged, by a detour through "China Cat Sunflower" and "The Eleven."
- *New Orleans drum solo zone:* "The Eleven" ends by thinning the texture out to just drums, followed by a very slight shift of groove that leads into the long drum solo part of "Alligator" (right where it left off about twelve minutes and two songs earlier). This passage is topically the same as version A, although the clave and other non-drum-set percussion are a bit more prominent. Texturally, none of this is particularly dramatic. But topically and thematically it would have been striking to anyone in attendance who knew the repertoire and would have recognized that at this moment a very long digression had been concluded.
- *New Orleans / acid / blues trope zone > percolating jam zone > first noise breakdown zone:* For a long time the performance proceeds essentially as in version A: the voice enters at 1:37, the acid rock lead guitar at 2:42, the full band at 3:44.
- *Runaway train zone:* After 6:38 the clock resets to 0:00, but the groove is continuous for the transition into "Caution (Do Not Stop on Tracks)." So unlike version A, there is no breakdown of the rhythm section or noise passage at this transition. Rather than suddenly change grooves, the drums gradually shift gears, creating some rhythmic ambiguity in the process. After about ten seconds of this transition, the rhythm section converges on the runaway train motif. The topical transition is the same as in version A, but it is even more striking when we hear it as a continuous transformation.
- *Extended narrative blues zone > blues/space trope zone:* This is where things begin to diverge more from version A, with the space/noise topic asserting itself much

The Later 1960s 149

earlier. The guitar goes into highly distorted tremolo chords at 1:37. For a little while the bass reinforces this with long held notes. These are very similar to the long loud bass notes in version A, but here they sound much more like an epic topic or a space/noise topic, whereas on the album they sound more like simple reinforcement of the train topic. The bass then starts a peppy walking R&B pattern at 1:52. The guitar does repeated pings for a bit, evoking the space topic (2:04–2:10). Then the whole band settles into a light Latin/R&B groove. Soon the bass resumes the epic noise aspect with long, portentous fuzz notes starting at 2:22. At 2:35 the vocals enter over all of this. As on the album, they are blues-like, but the effect is very different given that the space and noise elements were established so much earlier. Rather than a gradual adding of tropes to a fairly pure blues foundation, there has been a complex series of implied topics all within one groove over a short period of time. If version A comes across more like a narrative, this present version is set up more as a complex trope from the outset, and the rest of the performance explores various combinations and ratios within it.

- *Space/noise zone:* For the most part the performance proceeds as in version A, although the space/noise elements are more varied and more consistently foregrounded. And unlike the album, there isn't the same instability in the groove.
- *Temporary reconsolidation zone:* At 5:20, when things in some ways reach their most chaotic, everyone switches to a much faster riff (still an R&B/boogie walking riff) and a much more conventional boogie jam. Once this gets going it's another typical percolating jam, but with more consistently blues-like elements worked in on all levels. Portentous/epic long bass notes return at 7:05–7:24 before a major drop-back in overall intensity and a vocal reentry. Around 8:54 everything thins to a slightly more space texture (although gradually, and still percolating). At 9:09 cymbal rolls start to creep in that introduce another space flavor and an Orientalist epic flavor as well. Harmonica makes its first clear entry at 9:45. This gives a strong boost to the traditional blues topic, but it does so at a point where things overall are becoming very spacey and transitional. So interestingly, both the blues topic and the space/noise topic intensify together.
- *Final dissolve zone:* The band builds to a sudden climax, with the same distorted tremolo guitar chords as before, but now with a typical "big ending" function, and then segues into "Feedback," which lasts for nearly five minutes.

Already we can see some of the possible topical variations in group improvisation. But before summarizing the main points, we need to consider a third performance. Compared to the previous two versions, the first thing to stand out in version C is the extension of the second and third zones into a long bebop-flavored passage. There are also noteworthy new topical elements in the form of a variation on the epic regularly spaced chords texture and a riff with an almost proto-doom-metal quality.

VERSION C: "ALLIGATOR > CAUTION (DO NOT STOP ON TRACKS) > FEEDBACK" (AUGUST 23, 1968, SHRINE EXPOSITION CENTRE, LOS ANGELES)

- *Song form zone:* Like version A and unlike version B, this performance starts with the song form.

- *New Orleans drum solo zone:* This begins at 3:40 and is initially very similar to the other performances. However, the drums soon move in a more exploratory, jazz direction. There are more snare/militaristic moments than in the other versions. This drum solo is extended both in length (the lead guitar does not enter until 7:40) and in the number of textures explored.
- *New Orleans / acid / blues trope zone:* The next basic move is the same as in the other performances: lead guitar comes in for a while to play with drums before other elements enter. The guitar resembles a bebop solo more than in the other versions, with many fast lines, long note groupings, and syncopated accents. This continues until 10:10, substantially longer than in the other performances. Overall, once the song form ends, this performance immediately creates a progressive jazz mood that is not found in the other versions. At 10:22 the texture briefly becomes sparse and spacier, with repeated guitar notes and a thin and repetitive drum pattern.
- *Percolating jam zone:* At 10:38 the full band finally enters, very much the same as in the other versions both topically and texturally. The whole performance of "Alligator" is almost nineteen minutes, much longer than the others. And it's almost all made up of the typical percolating jam, with no other strong topicality. Overall, this version provides a nice example of how the Grateful Dead will occasionally abandon the reference points of a song altogether for extended periods before returning to them.
- *First noise breakdown zone:* At 17:40 the bass starts in with the long, low, held notes. As in the other versions, these have something of an epic/portentous topical flavor, but in this context they seem to function primarily as a structural cue for the transition to "Caution (Do Not Stop on Tracks)." The texture thins, and other "Caution" material gradually starts to creep in (muted motor note guitar rhythm, walking bass, etc.).
- *Runaway train zone:* After 18:44 the clock resets to 0:00. There is the same feeling of rhythmic ambiguity and continual transformation as in version B, settling into a blues-rock shuffle as before, although this groove is faster. In the other versions the sense of chaos and noise in this zone were confined largely to the distorted guitar chords, but in this version the whole band supports a sense of edgy noisiness before settling into a more stable groove and timbral space around 1:10. After this, the performance is very much like the others.
- *Extended narrative blues zone > blues/space trope zone:* At 2:41 the performance becomes very much like version A. At first a traditional blues vocal dominates and is then gradually troped with space/noise elements.
- *Space/noise zone:* Most of what follows is very similar to version A. This includes the unstable sense of groove. As in version B, there is the switch to a faster walking bass groove (this time at 7:51). But unlike either of the other performances, this peppy walking bass motif is combined with an epic regularly spaced chords texture, with bouts of the walking bass riff and various noise elements stuck in between longer held chords.
- *Temporary reconsolidation zone:* By about 8:23 the overall texture has shifted into a more stable groove, although a notably fast and ramshackle one. It falls apart back into a noisier, less metrically stable texture by about 9:03. By about 9:20 the sound is dominated by cymbal rolls plus noise. Grooves keep trying to assert themselves but never catch on. At 9:54 there's a sudden change to a new riff: a doom-rock

A-minor–G–F chord progression doubled in rhythm guitar and bass and supported in the drums with a straightforward rock groove. This riff is not heard in the other versions and is quite unusual for the Dead. It quickly starts to evaporate back into a typical slow percolation, still with a pronounced refusal to find a single groove.
- *Final dissolve zone:* Around 11:00 everything starts building to the big finale, which fairly rapidly arrives at the noise ending and then on to "Feedback."

Now we are in a good position to make some generalizations about the way that musical topics are typically treated in Grateful Dead group improvisations. The first thing to note is that the sung portions of a song are generally treated as fairly fixed. Improvisational passages are interspersed between the more composed-sounding sung passages, and the improvisation is rarely a matter of extemporizing on or extensively varying these materials. Closely related to this formal point is a topical one: the sung portions, and the composed instrumental material that accompanies them, generally contain all the topics that are subsequently explored in the improvisations. It is rare for an improvisation to introduce a radically new topical area, other than the general tendency to trope whatever is in the song with a space/noise topic. The improvisations also do not tend to leave topics out relative to whatever is core to the sung passages, although these topics are often presented in strikingly different versions. This is especially evident in comparing studio versions to live versions, since the instrumentation was often quite different between the two during this period. Also, since the improvisations range widely through various combinations of topics and variations on topics, not all of the topics central to the song will be present in any given passage.

One definitive feature of Grateful Dead improvisations is that they tend to emphasize topical zones over topical moments. They stay in one place for quite a while, exploring various possibilities within a single set of topics—intensive variations, permutations for moving from one to another, and tropes—before changing to a new combination. This is evident within single songs and in the practice of continuously chaining one song into another. The importance of the topical zone as a unit and of the transition from one topical zone to another can also be seen in how certain sequences of songs became standardized, which in turn standardized certain topical changes of state (like the *carnival > blues > space > noise* schema that governs the sequence of "Alligator > Caution > Feedback"). Whether any of these change of state schemas became widespread enough to be considered expressive genres would be an interesting subject for further research.

From this perspective, the typical percolating jam sound could also be considered a topical zone, one that is marked primarily by its rich stylistic mix and flexibility. There are three ways in particular that we saw this flexibility being exploited in "Alligator > Caution > Feedback." First, version C greatly amplified the jazz implications of the song by emphasizing jazz components of the percolating jam sound. This change in topical balance went along with a formal change, inserting a very long jazz-inflected jam that wasn't in the other versions. So one available procedure is to selectively amplify one or more of the song's topical aspects by selectively emphasizing just a few of the many topical implications always percolating in the jam sound. Second, there was a striking and singular topical addition to the song in the doomy riff inserted briefly near the end of version C. So another available procedure is to exploit the formal and affective open-endedness of the percolating jam sound in order to temporarily move into a topical area foreign to the song's other versions. Third, there is the way that the transition from the "Alligator" groove to the "Caution" groove was managed in versions B and C as a gradual rhythmic cross-fade. So another available procedure is to exploit the ability of the percolating jam sound to create fine-grained intensive variations in order to make certain topical transitions gradual or otherwise subtle. Collectively, these are a few examples of the sorts of topical effects that can be generated when you start from a baseline with a rich set of topical implications, combined with few binding relationships to any particular formal structure.

We can also generalize about things that are typically done to single topics in Grateful Dead improvisations. The three most common procedures are trope a topic with something else (often something more psychedelic), dissolve it into the percolation, or distill it out of the percolation. Also key to the treatment of individual topics is that performative intensive changes can enact topical changes. For example, all three of our examples featured low, sustained, and often distorted bass notes. But these function in different ways, variously as a topically nonindependent layer in the runaway train motif, a more freestanding portentous space/noise/epic topic, and a structural marker that is relatively neutral in topical terms. The differences are largely intensive, but they can greatly shift the topical effect from performance to performance or moment to moment. Also, recall how in version C the peppy walking bass riffs emerge as a strong R&B topic in ways they didn't in earlier versions, because in those other versions they were played a little less forcefully. In version C this slight variation in performance style tips the bass part toward presenting a fully formed R&B topic that then allows for a new R&B/epic trope unique to that particular performance. Finally, another kind of intensive variation is simply to spend differing amounts of time in particular topical zones or on the exploration of a particular potential within a single zone. This is one area explored frequently by the Grateful Dead, who were especially unpredictable in the length of their performances. One thing related to the issue of duration is that some topics require more time than others to become fully established. Some jazz topics, for example, often require that a solo extend for a long time, and the same is true of some funk topics. Another effect of duration is that it can affect whether topical elements are more likely to be perceived as coming one after another, perhaps as a narrative or as an expressive genre, or if they are more likely to be perceived as nearly simultaneous and therefore as a trope or as a dialogic elaboration.

This brings us to the end of our Grateful Dead discussion and also our discussion of the San Francisco scene. By focusing on some larger frameworks suggested by the nature of the scene itself, we have been able to expand our understanding of topicality in psychedelic group improvisation and in the creation of a certain kind of countercultural theatricality, as well as exploring similarities and differences between the way that topics were articulated in musical and visual contexts. Methodologically, we have taken the opportunity to expand beyond a focus on relatively bounded texts and have considered a little of how topicality functions across media and across different improvised versions of a particular song. This focus on units larger than a single text will continue to be a theme as we switch our focus to late 1960s events in the UK.

The Incredible String Band

So far we have only considered folk music and folkloric topics as components taken up occasionally by bands that are largely defined by other styles such as rock, pop, and soul/funk. Even in the case of the Grateful Dead, the overall impression is usually of a rock band deeply immersed in roots music, rather than of a folk group as such. On the one hand, I do not want to suggest that there's anything absolute in these sorts of categories. One of the most interesting things about such distinctions is how they can always be contested. For example, Philip Auslander argues that while the Incredible String Band was often compared to Tyrannosaurus Rex, presumably because both were acoustic duos performing on the circuit of psychedelic music clubs, the comparison is not substantial. And the reason for questioning this comparison hinges on a distinction between folk music proper and folk-influenced rock music: Auslander cites Marc Bolan of T. Rex as having said, "The difference is that they're folk musicians. I come from rock and roll" (2006, 76). But even without uncritically subscribing to any particular categories, the Incredible String Band stand out for the extent to which they developed a music that is rooted in traditional genres, and is based on acoustic rather than electric instruments, but at the same time fundamentally psychedelic in much of its attitude and topicality. Looking at their work will allow us to expand on observations we've already made about the nature of folkloric and traditional materials in the topical field of psychedelia. Even more than the Grateful Dead, the Incredible String Band found ways to combine and extemporize on folk materials in order to render them cognate with psychedelia, rather than simply layering them with more contemporary psychedelic elements. We'll look at some details of how this was accomplished and also consider their particular formulation of exoticism.

I'll begin by highlighting some key features of their style through brief discussions of three contrasting songs, starting with "Chinese White":

THE INCREDIBLE STRING BAND, "CHINESE WHITE" (1967)

- The introduction (0:00–0:25) is ten measures long (2 + 2 + 2 + 2 + 2). Essentially, it is a decorated drone around an F-major triad, using just gimbri (a three-stringed African lute, also known as the sintir) and acoustic guitar.
- The A section (0:25–0:44) is nine measures long (4 + [4 + 1]). The acoustic guitar texture is conventional for folk, but the gimbri is extremely free rhythmically.

Both the chord changes and the melody emphasize a major-minor alternation: F–F minor–C–F, repeated.
- The B section (0:44–1:07) is eleven measures long (3 + 3 + 5). The vocal tessitura goes up, and the voice is slightly louder. The first vocal statement lasts for three bars, with the third feeling something like a tag but at the same time like a cadence that came early. There are then three instrumental measures, with chord changes F^7–B♭–B♭–F. By now the overall sense of metrical and formal orientation is quite fluid. In the second part of this section (starting at 0:57), both voices sing together for the first time in oblique motion (the higher voice sings F against each note of the lower melody). So there is a strong textural tension in the voices, somewhat reinforced by the chords that present both major-minor alternation and a suspension: F–F minor–C–Csus4–C.
- The C section (1:07–1:29) is ten measures long (4 + 2+ [2 + 2]). This section is essentially a repeat of the B section in harmony and overall texture, but with a different and slightly more active melody. There is a notable feeling of relaxation after the peak of the preceding B section. On the last "lay me down" there's a fermata that sets up the word "dream" to be sustained for three measures over a simple F–C harmonic alternation. So on several levels the end of this section feels like a point of arrival.
- The length of the D section (1:29–1:44) is difficult to specify in measures because of the extreme fermata and rubato. It starts with four measures of a cappella vocal duet, still in rhythmic unison, but now with both voices mobile. This creates a more choral effect in contrast to the earlier oblique motion, but it also has a very open sound since the longer notes rest on less dissonant intervals (a fifth, unison, and fourth, respectively). After one long fermata, the guitar and gimbri reenter for a I–V–I cadence stretched out via a second fermata.
- After this, the entire form essentially repeats to complete the song.
- Note: In this analysis what I'm calling A, B, C, and D sections can also be heard as subparts of a single large section. They are long enough, and distinct enough, to be somewhat independent, but on the other hand, they elide into one another and can be heard as forming a single long arc.

Unpredictability is a core feature of the Incredible String Band style. In "Chinese White," neither the chord progression nor the melody settles into an easy pattern of repetition, creating a through-composed feeling. There are several devices frequently used by the band that enhance such a restless, always-changing quality, and most of them can be found in this song: tempo shifts, no clear adherence to foursquare phrase structure, colorful harmonic devices (which draw attention to momentary sensation over long-term function), and the dropping out of some or all core instruments during moments of heightened metrical ambiguity. This kind of approach to composition and arranging could easily sound incoherent, or at least anxious, whereas in the case of the Incredible String Band it more often creates affects of ease, playfulness, and gentle propulsion. This is largely because of the way lyrics are privileged: the music is built up in a prosodic manner in order to enhance rhythmic implications of the text, rather than fitting the text itself to a strict meter or formal scheme. As a topical feature, this sort of structure is dialogic. It enacts a psychedelic prototopic and also evokes folk music topics by resembling the text-centered rhythmic extemporization in genres like traditional ballad singing, folk blues, and lining hymns. Affectively, it can produce moments of freedom in the voice that feel like an overflowing of boundaries, an outpouring of intensity. Note the similarity to the vocal phrasing in "Dark Star," on the lyric line "transient nightfall of diamonds." We could also draw a comparison to Bob Dylan's rhythmic extemporization in a song like "Mr. Tambourine Man." In all of these cases, the technique is shown to be cognate with psychedelic suspension of time and exploration of unexpected formal digressions while also being rooted in more traditional features of folk singing.

This freedom of phrasing and rhythm is extended to some of the instrumental parts. For example, in "Chinese White" the gimbri provides many examples of simple patterns made complex through unpredictable and sometimes irregular (in the sense of asymmetrical) ornamentation. A comparison with the lead guitar in "Eight Miles High" is useful not only because it supports the point I just made about psychedelic/traditional dialogism but also because there's something else shared by that lead guitar and the gimbri in "Chinese White": they are both closely tied to psychedelic exoticism. In the case of "Eight Miles High," the exoticized referents are Orientalist (by way of the raga-rock aspect), which makes it entirely typical of psychedelia at that time. In the case of "Chinese White," the exact exoticized referent is less clear. The gimbri has a specific origin in North Africa, but it is not played by the Incredible String Band in a traditional manner; instead, it is played by them in a manner that vaguely resembles many Arabic and North African musics but is specific to none. This Arabic and African inflection introduces a distinctive element compared to the ubiquitous Indian-derived exoticism of most other psychedelic artists. Indeed, it is a clue to one of the more complicated and important aspects of the Incredible String Band, and so we should take a moment to consider the exact geographical extent of their exoticism.

When borrowing musical materials from sources outside of Western Europe, the Incredible String Band show an unusual degree of scope. The signifiers in question involve folk and classical traditions of Eastern Europe, the Mediterranean, Central and Southern Asia, the Middle East, and North Africa. Although some of the band's borrowings are specific to one of these regions, they more often emphasize elements that can be found in many or all of them. So the cumulative reference is vague and yet hangs together loosely around some very broad mythologies and cultural/geographical groupings. For example, the regions of borrowing are roughly coterminous with a union of the Indo-European and Afro-Asiatic language families. The resulting topical reference is very broadly "traditional" and "non-Western," but in a way that sits somewhat outside of the typical Orientalist clichés discussed to this point. Also, I suggest that an implicit message of the Incredible String Band's stylistic approach is that the British folk elements are not meant to be heard as separate from these other influences but on a continuum with them. So one challenge in finding an overarching name for this topicality is the geographical scope. The other challenge is that the complex trope of the band's overall style is best understood not solely as the result of unfocused tourism or exoticism (although there is some of that, to be discussed soon) but more as a panspiritualist perennialism. It is not only about including elements from outside the usual scope of British folk music but also about finding ways to highlight features of British folk music that could be seen as cognate with this broader region. To be clear, I'm not suggesting that there actually is any geographical or cultural region that provides a referent for this high-level trope. Instead, I am trying to draw attention to a certain faith in common roots that is often held within psychedelic subcultures and that seems to be reflected in this particular mode of musical exoticism. Further implications of this will be discussed in later chapters when we consider new psychedelic imaginaries after the late 1970s. For now, I will just propose an umbrella term that can expedite references to this complex set of signifiers and referents, understood as enacting a certain kind of perennialist ideology and drawing upon the wide range of geographical and traditional signifiers just described: the *universal roots topic*.

While "Chinese White" achieves rhythmic and formal flexibility by suspending or blurring the underlying sense of time, in other songs the Incredible String Band achieve rhythmic fluidity within the context of a regular pulse. For example, "Little Cloud" shows how these sorts of metrical complexities work with what sounds on the surface like a very simple and catchy folk song:

THE INCREDIBLE STRING BAND, "LITTLE CLOUD" (1967)

- There is an unmeasured introduction with voices in oblique motion.
- The meter of the A section (0:25–0:54) is based on a repeated cycle of three $\frac{4}{4}$ bars and one $\frac{5}{4}$ bar (i.e., a simple four-measure unit with one added beat). It is sixteen measures long.
- The meter of the B section (0:54–1:04) is based on two times through a cycle of $\frac{3}{4}$, $\frac{4}{4}$, $\frac{3}{4}$, $\frac{2}{4}$.
- In the C section (1:04–1:15) analysis in terms of a measure-centric meter would be a stretch. The passage sounds more additive, based on variable-length beat groupings that could be heard as 2, 4, 3, 2 / 2, 4, 3, 3 / 3, 2 (the slash shows the melodic repetition structure rather than measures).
- The ABC structure makes up a single strophe, which is then repeated three times.

Metrical structures with this sort of additive flavor tap strongly into the universal roots topic. Indeed, this sort of rhythmic approach is the other most significant source of universal roots topicality in the Incredible String Band, along with their vocal style and frequent use of the gimbri. It's also interesting that the internal ABC structure of each strophe traces a continuous line to greater and greater metrical complexity, gradually deepening the feeling of exoticism.

"Little Cloud" is significant partly because it incorporates a challenging metrical structure into such a simple, strophic folk song form. The last song I want to consider goes in the other direction and brings us back to meandering, open-sounding forms more akin to "Chinese White." "The Mad Hatter's Song" is a much more extreme example of through-composition and rhythmic freedom. It doesn't even really have the same "one song" feeling as "Chinese White." And like a Grateful Dead improvisation, the effect is one of moving through distinct but loosely related topical zones. Here is a description of the first eight zones, which takes us just past halfway through the song:

THE INCREDIBLE STRING BAND, "THE MAD HATTER'S SONG" (1967)

- The introduction and section A (0:00–0:51) are based on British Isles folk with universal roots inflections.
- Section B (0:51–1:05) is the same as the A section, but with the introduction of handclaps and a more regular melody. After the preceding fluidity, this section introduces a more dance-like quality and also a hint of gospel music.
- Section C (1:05–1:18) is a relatively unmeasured transition on a rising sequence, followed by a long melismatic trill. Overall, this section adds a slightly orchestral feeling and also evokes the more narrative aspects of musical theater (like recitative, or a more contemporary equivalent).
- This B section (1:18–1:36) begins like the first but then moves to a more extreme version of the C section transition texture.
- The D section (1:36–1:58) is narrative/recitative, with the instruments doubling the voice and the overall rhythm being highly prosodic.
- The E section (1:58–2:45) presents a sudden switch to blues/barrelhouse style, complete with the sudden entrance of piano. This section is very long relative to what went before (sixteen measures) and so becomes a sudden island of rhythmic and textural stability.
- In the transition, part 1 (2:45–2:51), the meter is again suspended, with heavy rubato. The transitional, prosodic texture resembles some earlier sections, but this time based on blues material.
- In the transition, part 2, through the F section (2:51–3:40) there is a return to a folk style, but now with more of a folk-rock inflection and with all new melodic material.
- This pattern of extreme variability continues, with a few more sections of substantially new material (songs within the song) appearing before a recap of B and C minimally ties it all together.

While there is no specific evidence that this song was improvised or has roots in improvisation, it certainly sounds like it could have been. It is very much like a Grateful Dead improvisation in the topical zone approach, but it differs in that this structure is more lumpy than what would be typical of the Dead, for three reasons: (1) the topical zones are more strongly contrasting; (2) they are separated by sharp transitions or material clearly intended as transitional; and (3) there is less exploration of performative and intensive variation within each topical zone. Because of the clarity and frequency of these transitions, one could be tempted to read this as a narrative. But the predominant effect, at least to my hearing, is of constant unpredictable drifting from one thing to another, rather than any kind of directed change-of-state schema. This is another reason that the cumulative effect is improvisational.

Although this kind of form lacks the directedness necessary to be considered narrative, we do at this point need to give it a name. By 1967, and even more by the later 1960s, there were many examples of psychedelic songs featuring long sectional forms, each section of which often defines a clear topical zone but in which the overall formal effect is one of wandering aimlessly. Although it is stretching the term a little, we could consider this to be an expressive genre, because it is a high-level schema for organizing the relationship between contrasting topical zones. I will call it the *strange trip* expressive genre.

Having summarized the main features of Incredible String Band musical style, we need to return to the question of exoticism, because more can be said about what made them distinctive in that area. As we saw in chapter 2, authors on musical exoticism usually distinguish between tokenism and more thorough immersion in a style. Early debates about the Beatles' Indian songs hinged on this point, and it is relevant to the Incredible String Band as well, because, as Oliver Lovesey has demonstrated, they foreshadow 1980s world music, presenting a very early "synthesis of Arab and Celtic traditions" (2011, 130). Their connection to the Hippie Trail (a network of routes between Europe and Asia commonly used by countercultural travelers in the 1960s and 1970s) makes them an important link between nineteenth-century touristic Orientalism and later traveler culture of the 1970s and onward. One place to see the topical effect of this orientation is in their choice of instrumentation. Rob Young (2010, 349–50) points out that throughout the 1960s the Incredible String Band made unconventional sounds almost exclusively with acoustic instruments, rather than through electronics or electrification.[10] In a psychedelic context, this strict limitation to acoustic instruments was a marked feature, made more so by the exotic nature of the instruments themselves and by the way their manner of combination evoked the universal roots topic. Given just the sounds, this association with a universal roots topic and in turn with perennialist religious philosophy would perhaps be a stretch. But the perennialist viewpoint was common in early psychedelic literature and also among participants in the Hippie Trail. Moreover, it became central to many later understandings of the world music genre and also to some of the new psychedelic imaginaries of the later 1970s considered in the next chapter. The Incredible String Band are the most striking early example of how such a worldview can be expressed through topical features in an artist's style.

Another aspect of the topical and affective world of the Incredible String Band, and one closely related to exoticism, is a persistent sense of unreality or dream: "What connects the pastoralism, the cult-of-childhood, and the pantheism is a profound nostalgia. . . . In the present, this wonderland can only be reached in dreams. The Incredible String Band took psychedelia's cult of slumber further than most" (Reynolds and Press 1995, 163). This confluence of exoticism, pastoralism, and dream touches on the kind of psychedelic self-othering I've discussed a few times already. But it also returns us to ethical issues. If we are going to view the Incredible String Band as world music avant la lettre, it is especially important to think further about their particular mode of cross-cultural appropriation. As often happens in such situations, the band tended to reduce complex cultural practices to the status of "found objects," removed from their original cultural networks and significance (Lovesey 2011, 131, 134). In the case of the Incredible String Band, the metaphor of finding can be extended to one of exploring and discovering, because their performance style didn't just symbolize the unfamiliarity of these instruments and styles but rather enacted it. As Lovesey reports, "Williamson embraced what he called 'inspired amateurism . . . having a go at playing instruments that one couldn't play at all, to try and create a sort of naive music or an innocent music, like naive painting'" (134). The ethics of this inspired amateurism are complex, because while it was often applied to elements borrowed from other cultures, it was also used to create a new relationship to their home cultures:

> Many of the ISB's songs, and especially their lyrics . . . have a self-consciously or at least unapologetically unstudied, unedited or uncorrected quality. This quality may be partly an attempt to forestall expertise or virtuosity, or to put a psychedelic spin on the moon-in-June, boy-loves-girl lyrical conventions of the popular song and the polish of hit-making recording, but it is more likely the result of haste of composition and recording, their youth and, of course, as with anything related to the 1960s, their consumption of psychedelics. What results is a musical and lyrical text with gaps and erasures that virtually demands the listener's participation. (132)

This not only relates to psychedelic self-othering but also creates an interesting relationship to garage rock and even more to later punk rock, where amateurism was often elevated to an aesthetic goal. All of this can and should be critiqued as cultural appropriation. But in order to notice the topical procedures at play, we also need to emphasize the nuances. The Incredible String Band do as much to exoticize their own immediate heritage as they do to exoticize any other, in a manner similar to what artists like the Grateful Dead did with American roots musics. For psychedelia, Orientalist exoticism is often wrapped up in a self-exoticizing and self-deterritorializing impulse that complicates the cultural dynamics, although it does not negate the troubling colonialist resonances.

The Beatles: Part 2

One major theme of this chapter is to see how psychedelic topicality has functioned in contexts larger than a single song. Somewhere in that discussion it would make sense to develop a topical analysis of an entire album, and no candidate makes more sense than *Sgt. Pepper's Lonely Hearts Club Band*. So a detailed topical analysis of that LP is the main focus of this second Beatles discussion. A secondary purpose is to reflect on what the Beatles represented in the topical field of psychedelia overall. Specifically, I will ask to what extent *classicism* could be used as a concept for tying together features that made the Beatles distinctive relative to other psychedelic artists in 1967. I mean classicism not just in the narrow sense of drawing from classical music topics but also as a certain kind of psychedelic rock aesthetic: tightly arranged, nonimprovisatory, with a clear and concise approach to form. I also mean for the term to resonate on a sociological level. Classicism in this sense can mean an emphasis on topics that would have been associated with tradition and social order. This would apply not only to classical music but also, for example, to brass bands, music hall, and the way that George Harrison channeled Orientalism and raga rock into a traditional guru-disciple situation through his studies with Ravi Shankar. I am not suggesting classicism as a final conclusion or categorization of the Beatles, but we will keep it in mind as an orienting theme.

Also, please recall that I have decided to include transcriptions in this book for the most part only when adequate transcriptions are not available elsewhere. In the case of the Beatles, sufficiently reliable and complete transcriptions have been collected in *The Beatles: The Complete Scores* (Fujita et al. 1989). My analysis is going to focus on fairly high-level features, ones that can be summarized in words, so transcriptions are not necessary to follow the argument. But readers wishing to consult some can find them in that collection.

"Strawberry Fields Forever": Detailed Reading

As a warm-up for the full album analysis, and to demonstrate some typical Beatles topical procedures in a smaller framework, let's develop a detailed topical analysis of a song originally intended for *Sgt. Pepper* but ultimately released separately and in advance: "Strawberry Fields Forever."

For this analysis and the full album analysis that follows, there is unfortunately no way to make the presentation entirely smooth and natural for the reader. This is because the overall analysis needs to be based on a description of many moment-to-moment details, but at the same time the importance and even sometimes the identity of those details don't become clear without reference to the overall analysis. I've decided to proceed by first discussing the small details, and I will divide that discussion up by instrument, since most of the important topics are centered on one particular instrument. After that, I will discuss the overall form and the larger topical features. This order of presentation demands a bit of patience from the reader because it starts with much detail that isn't fully explained until later. But it has the advantage of keeping similar kinds of material close together for future reference. To keep your bearings while following the detailed analysis, you may wish to refer to the form chart below and perhaps also glance ahead as needed to table 3.1. Or you may prefer to read the overview first and then return to the point-by-point analysis later.

Introduction	0:00–0:09
A	0:10–0:33
B	0:34–0:54
A	0:55–1:20
B	1:21–1:41
A	1:42–2:06
B	2:07–2:26
A	2:27–2:45
Tag	2:46–2:59
Instrumental	3:00–4:04

Note: the instrumental contains a false ending made up of a long fade-out to an extremely brief silence, from about 3:20 to 3:34, and then a fade-in that subjectively returns to full volume at about 3:45.

One interesting feature of "Strawberry Fields Forever" is that instruments vary in their topical richness. Some are restricted to conveying a single topic or prototopic, while others are more involved in tropes, dialogism, and topical changes of state. I will look at the simpler cases first and then move on to the more elaborate ones.

Mellotron. The Mellotron appears three times. The first time it is the central feature of the introduction, and it continues through the first A and B sections (0:00–0:54). This appearance is both foregrounded and strongly topical. The dominant topics are pastoral and classical, largely because of the timbre and the smooth voice leading. On two later occasions, the Mellotron appears more briefly as a pad color on the return of A-section material (1:47–1:50 and 2:32–2:36). This likely wouldn't be topical at all, except that the Mellotron's topicality was so well established earlier that even a brief timbral flash later is evocative. It is also noteworthy that the Mellotron introduction figure and the brass choir in the second and third B sections are extremely similar in harmonic, melodic, and rhythmic material, but their respective topical effects are quite different (more pastoral and classical in the case of the Mellotron, and more belle époque in the case of the brass). This is a good example of the role played by timbre in shaping topical implications.

Reverse Mellotron Flutes. These appear twice in the closing instrumental: first at the quietest point of the false ending and subsequent crescendo (3:34–3:42), and then again near the very end (3:50–3:55). This texture combines the earlier Mellotron pastoral topic with a more avant-garde and psychedelic set of associations. Also, the looping and reversing of a flute timbre could be heard as evoking an exoticist "ethnic" atmosphere.

Morse Code. There is a single brief appearance of Morse code near the beginning of the first A section (0:16–0:20). The syncopated brass figure at 1:54–1:55 could also be heard as resembling Morse code. This would be an unlikely reading for that brass figure, except for the way it is primed by an earlier, more obvious Morse code snippet. The complex topical profile of Morse code is discussed in the next chapter. In this case, it would have likely evoked at minimum the war years as an element of the recent British past, along with affects of distance (both temporal and spatial), mystery, and adventure.

Military Snare. This appears in the closing instrumental, largely as part of the fade-in following the false ending (3:39–4:04). The snare is military in some of its patterns and basic timbral association, but the way it is combined with the lower drums, along with other aspects of the snare rhythm, make it also sound something like New Orleans parade drums as well.

Obscure Speaking Voices. These are primarily important as a prototopic. They carry affects of mystery, inner space, and the uncanny and also pick up on the radiophonic implications of the earlier Morse code snippet. They first enter very quietly (3:27–3:33), but since this occurs well into the fade-out, the effect is still striking. Because close listening has been encouraged by the fade-out, quiet elements such as these can seem magnified. Speaking voices sneak in again after the loud siren guitar figure, almost inaudible at first (3:49–3:50). Just a few words can be clearly heard, and then the flutes reenter loudly, and it is difficult to tell if the voices continue. After that there are two points where speaking voices are unmistakably present: 3:56–3:59 and 4:02–4:04. But, as is so often the case with this sort of production technique, their effect pervades the entire instrumental following their first appearance. Because they are so often obscure and half-heard, one can never be entirely sure that they are not present, and there is a tendency to feel the mood they create permeating the music even when they are not literally audible.

Piano: Time-Passing Motif. At this point I need to explain a term that will be ubiquitous in my Beatles analysis: the *time-passing motif.* This is an extremely common figure characterized by repeated or alternating pitches or chords at slow or moderate motor rhythm, usually medium to high register, usually with a fairly percussive timbre such as piano or clean guitar. By emphasizing periodic pulsation while at the same time minimizing metrical markers, such a figure can evoke the passage of time and/or clockwork. Paradoxically, it can also evoke a feeling of pure duration: an experience of temporality in which the usual standards of measurement and relationship to real-world events are attenuated or absent. The time-passing motif will arise frequently in my later Beatles analyses and also as a major style feature of space rock. In this particular song, it appears mostly in the piano and as a composite timbre between various combinations of piano, swarmandal, and guitar. Because motor rhythm is such a common feature in rock accompaniment patterns, it is always a judgment call as to whether a particular instance should be given extra interpretive weight. But the time-passing motif is clearly present throughout much of the "Strawberry Fields Forever" closing instrumental, and its entrance right at the start of that passage is one of the strongest and earliest cues that we are entering into a freer and more experimental part of the song.

While looking at elements that are fairly singular in their topical implications, we should also consider a few noteworthy production techniques.

Vari-Speed. The beginning and the end of the song were both altered in speed, but in opposite directions—part 1 was sped up, and part 2 was slowed down—in order to splice together two takes in different keys and tempos. Walter Everett (1999, 78–79) provides a detailed description of the procedure. The result is that many timbres in the song, especially the voices, are slightly unusual and dreamlike. This technique is topical insofar as vari-speed effects, and tape editing effects in general, are an important psychedelic prototopic. We could also include the reversed drum sounds in this general category.

False Ending. It may be a stretch to call this effect topical, but it has at least three connections to topicality: (1) it is a psychedelic prototopic insofar as it toys with norms of production and reception; (2) it could be taken to reference extreme dynamic shapes common in European orchestral music; and (3) several other clearly topical events cluster around this point in the form.

All of the elements we've considered up to now generally signify single topics in a straightforward way. But there are other elements that are slightly more dialogic or that suggest different topics at different times. So let's move on to consider some of these.

Swarmandal. Contrary to what is often reported, this instrument is not a sitar. Its identity as swarmandal is confirmed by Everett (1999, 80), but it is also clear on close listening. This difference is not trivial, because the ability of the swarmandal to produce sounds similar to both a sitar and a European dulcimer or zither allows it to assume a dual topical identity in this song, evoking various topics of the Indian, the European folkloric, and a generally spooky affect. Because it evokes both Indian and European reference points, fusing them in the same instrument, we could link this use of swarmandal with the universal roots topic discussed in connection with the Incredible String Band. The sitar-like aspect is highlighted in two prominent downward gestures at the end of the second and third A sections (1:18–1:20 and 2:04–2:06). These are very clear and well-known examples of psychedelic Orientalism. Later, throughout the closing instrumental, the swarmandal appears in its more dulcimer-like guise, which can be heard as retaining the Indian topical flavor but troped with a more European folkloric one. At 3:06 this new dulcimer-like swarmandal texture is heard for the first time as just a single note that stands out strongly not because of volume but because of its difference relative to everything else. From 3:15 to 3:33 there is a longer line that continues to the near-silent point of the false ending.

Apart from this troping of Indian and European elements, there are two other important topical aspects to the swarmandal. First, it sometimes appears in the time-passing motif as part of a composite timbre with piano and/or guitar. Second, at the very end of the song (3:55–4:04), there is a simple major-chord arpeggio figure (quarter-note triplet, B♭ up to D and down to F) quite different from what has appeared previously.[11] Everett (1999, 83) points out that this could be heard as a reveille figure, and I would add that as such it also evokes pastoral topicality more generally.

Lead Guitar. The lead electric guitar is only topical in a few spots, but in all of these it provides interesting nuances. At the very opening there is a brief decorative slide guitar ornament that evokes both Indian and country music topics (0:14–0:15). But the guitar doesn't become a forceful topical presence until the loud contemporary psychedelic fill that ushers in the closing instrumental (2:57–3:00), appearing where a third swarmandal descent might have been expected. A similar psychedelic guitar fill appears at 3:10–3:12. And finally, from 3:42 to 3:47 there are repeated loud single guitar notes that could be heard as a siren (a single-note variation on the siren trill) or as a version of the time-passing motif.

To conclude the moment-to-moment, instrument-based part of this song analysis we need to pay special attention to the strings and the brass. These are noteworthy for three reasons: (1) they are present throughout much of the song; (2) at certain points they illustrate how subtle changes of arrangement can suggest dialogism or evoke different nuances within a single topic; and (3) at other points they clearly present different well-defined topics.

Strings. From 0:59 to 1:19 the strings are low and ominous, atmospheric. They evoke the classical orchestra and are also reminiscent of cinematic topics of horror, doom, and action/adventure. The phrase from 1:30 to 2:06 begins similarly but is more strident, ornate, and contrapuntal. This tips the balance toward the classical and away from cinematic action/adventure to some degree. From 1:42 to 2:06, the strings returns to something more similar to the first string phrase, both texturally and topically. The next major string phrase, from 2:15 to 2:31, is similar again, although the extended quarter-note triplet figure is new and striking in the way it combines motor rhythm with a bit of temporal disorientation. From 2:32 to 2:57 the strings continue, but now as part of a much more insistent overall motor rhythm. This movement toward overall motor rhythm could be heard as an exploration of varying affects within the classical and cinematic topics, but it could also be heard as troping those topics with the time-passing motif and with psychedelic prototopics (motor rhythm as central to the rave-up and to the emerging space-rock genre). From 2:41 to 2:57 the strings return to a more melodic contrapuntal texture. While all of these variations in the strings have only subtle topical nuances, there is a much more dramatic shift in the phrase from 2:59 to 3:08, where prominent glisses and the general nature of the line suddenly shift the strings into Indian territory. But that's just for half of the phrase, and the concluding half presents a new marcato Western classical motif. From 3:12 to 3:14 there is a strong reiteration of the Indian topic with a glissed alternating minor second, but this too quickly fades.

Brass. The brass enters with a rising line from 1:10 to 1:19 to emphasize the high point of the section and then becomes more of a pad. In timbre and chord voicing it suggests something of a belle époque brass choir. This association sounds even stronger from 1:21 to 1:40. From 1:46 to 2:05 the brass reenters sparsely but strongly with occasional shots and changes to a pad texture by the end of the section. The brass throughout this passage sounds strikingly contemporary, given the more nostalgic tone of the earlier brass choir, and could be taken as adding a layer of film or TV score reference. This dialogic quality is maintained throughout the solo brass section from 2:06 to 2:15, which presents block chords on motor quarter notes. For the rest of the song the brass continues to move between the more nostalgic sound (e.g., in the pad texture from 2:22 to 2:31) and a more contemporary one (notably from 2:32 to 2:50). Finally, we must note the striking fanfare/bells motif from 2:34 to 2:36, which stands out from the prevailing texture as a free-standing topical signifier in its own right.

And with that we've reached the end of the more particularistic phase of the analysis. We can move on to a bird's-eye view of the song's overall organization, based on the presentation in table 3.1. In reading table 3.1, you may find it useful to refer back to the overall form diagram given earlier. In order to fit everything onto one page, events in table 3.1 are quantized to a five-second grid. Variations in shading show different topical references within each instrument but not relationships between instruments (i.e., I am not using a consistent fill for similar topics everywhere in the song, just within single instruments). So the table shows the number of topics stated or implied by each instrument and how the instru-

Table 3.1. Distribution of main topics in "Strawberry Fields Forever"

	I								Tag	Instrument
	A	B	A	B	A	B	A			
Mellotron		▨	▨							
Strings			▨	▥	▨	▥	▥		▥	
Brass				▥	▥	▥	▨▥	▦		
Morse code	▨									
Swarmandal				▨		▨				
Guitar		▨							▥	
Fade-out/fade-in									▨	▨
Mel. flutes										▨
Voices									▨	▨
Snare drum										▨

ments are distributed in the song, but the detailed point-by-point analysis above is where you will find descriptions of each particular topic.

The overall formal design is in two large sections: a straight pop song form (albeit one with much color and overlay) and a more free-form instrumental. The moment of transformation is evident on table 3.1, where a cluster of new instruments and sounds appears in the lower right. The difference between these two large parts of the form is considerable, but there are points of continuity. One such link comes about through the psychedelic touches to the earlier pop song section, such as the vari-speed and other production effects, the Indian topics, and belle époque nostalgia. Also, even within the more conventional song section the chord changes are ambiguous and contain very few referents to common progressions, which adds to the generally dreamlike feeling (Everett 1999, 83). So while the form is clearly divided into two sections, the second is an intensification of implications from the first, rather than a complete break. The other most noteworthy overall feature is the gradual thickening, both texturally and topically. From the beginning of the song to the first B section, there is a relative paucity of topical elements. This is followed by a much richer, although still highly structured, topical landscape for the rest of the conventional song section. During this middle section, several different topics are explored individually and also troped. Finally, the concluding instrumental is topically fairly uniform insofar as almost everything in it is a psychedelic prototopic but is texturally very dense and pointillistic.

Overall, there is a fairly even balance between more singular topics, often treated as local color, and more elaborated tropes and changes of state. The distinction between these two approaches can be seen on table 3.1 as the difference between short isolated patches and longer bands. In the strings and brass, the longer bands are notable for the way they present a range of topics and variations of shading within single topics. This contrasts with the other longest band, the opening Mellotron, which is dedicated to just one topical area. That consistency, along with the Mellotron's placement in the song and its timbral novelty, helps explain why the instrument exerts such a strong impact even though it does not persist. Taken together, this is a wide range of topical techniques to include in one song. Yet there is no loss of clarity, and there is a strong overarching feel of compositional intent. In part, this feeling of clarity and intent can be related to the extreme economy of some gestures. For example, Morse code appears just once (and very briefly), the swarmandal descent appears just twice, loud lead guitar appears just three times (and only twice guitaristically), and several of the most distinctive sound effects are saved for the very end. Because of this economy in the way resources are deployed, "Strawberry Fields Forever" provides many good examples of how a brief topical reference can color one's perception and memory of an entire passage or piece. In other words, the degree to which a topic might shape the meaning of a piece is not directly proportional to its literal duration.

When discussing the Incredible String Band, I took the opportunity to name a psychedelic expressive genre: the *strange trip*. That could have been done earlier in the book, but it made sense to wait until a critical mass of examples had been accumulated. Similarly, with "Strawberry Fields Forever" we have another example of something that had become standard by this time: for a larger form such as a song to progress from relative conventionality, through successive stages, to something very obviously psychedelic. In the case of "Strawberry Fields Forever" the specific trajectory is from a lightly topical conventional song form, to a more densely topical and psychedelic version of that same song form, into the experimental instrumental. This can be seen as an example of the more general psychedelic tendency of deepening estrangement. Other examples we have seen include the widespread strategy of introducing an entirely new texture at the very end of a song; the gradual estrangement we noticed in "Trip to Your Heart" and "Little Cloud"; and the continual crescendo of "White Rabbit." I suggest we designate this strategy as another psychedelic expressive genre and call it the *outward journey* expressive genre, defined as a large-scale movement from fairly conventional materials toward more radically psychedelic ones. Sometimes the change is more gradual, and sometimes it is more abrupt, with the four common variants being (1) a single formal section that follows a linear path of change (sometimes repeated); (2) several successive formal sections, each more psychedelic than the last (again, sometimes with the entire formal sequence repeated); (3) the sudden opening up of a new textural space at the end of a performance; and (4) an entire performance that follows a fairly continual transformation (the only clear example we've seen of this is "White Rabbit").

Up to now we have focused on general topical processes and strategies in "Strawberry Fields Forever." We also need to map out the distribution of particular topics with an eye toward the main tropes and transformations. To do this, I have described the main topical contents of each formal section below.

- The introduction through the first B section is focused on the pastoral/classical Mellotron, with a brief troping of Morse code.
- In the second A section the low strings in some respects continue aspects of the Mellotron (classical, atmospheric) but are more cinematic, darker, and tense. These are then troped with the brighter and more nostalgic brass, and at the very end of the section all of this briefly gives way to a quick transformation into Indian and raga rock topicality with the swarmandal fill.
- By the time we have reached the remainder of the conventional song section, two elaborate topical structures have come to the foreground and continue to unfold over the rest of the song form. The first of these is the string part, with its exploration of classical, cinematic, and Indian topics. The second is the brass, which echoes the pastoral Mellotron and also moves between belle époque and contemporary styles. The overall effect is to evoke a shifting affect of reflection on the relationship between the present and the medium-distant past and also between darker and more uplifting moods. Continuity and stability are suggested by the transformations that occur within single instrumental strands and by the web of connections between the specific topics, but at the same time discontinuity and instability are suggested by the constant transformations and by the way topical materials are split between two instrument families. The brass and strings are like individual streams of consciousness, exploring shades of related topics. The other

major topical effect that dominates the conventional song section is the repeated interjection of Indian and raga-rock topicality by the swarmandal. This stands out strongly not only because of its topical distance from everything else and because of its role in punctuating a crucial point in the form but also because its briefness and singularity are so different from the protracted, multilayered topical structure of the strings and brass.
- In most formal respects the closing instrumental section strongly contrasts with what came before. It is also topically distinct in that almost everything here is a psychedelic prototopic. The one other topic that continues from the conventional song section is the Indian topic, now presented mostly in the strings as the swarmandal assumes a more ambiguous topical profile. Also, the technique of contrasting two parallel streams of consciousness against brief interjections is abandoned in favor of a more pointillistic approach. In every way, this closing section could be read as iconic with an intensifying acid trip, or a general sense of estrangement.

It is worth noting that while "Strawberry Fields Forever" has a distinct identity, there's nothing here in terms of individual topics or production devices that can't be found on earlier Beatles recordings, especially "Rain" and *Revolver*. "Strawberry Fields Forever" stands out not because its material is unprecedented but because it concisely sums up a wide range of the psychedelic topical field and because it is experimental while at the same time displaying a high degree of organization and attention to detail. Also noteworthy is the way that a range of different topics and different shades of single topics are mobilized to create a multilayered treatment of one complex theme: nostalgic reminiscence of childhood, and how such reminiscence relates to the complexities of adult identity formation and to the shifting line between fantasy and objective reality. All of this does tend to also suggest the broad property of classicism, discussed earlier. By looking in depth at *Sgt. Pepper*, we will be able to show how similar approaches were scaled up to the scope of an entire album.

Sgt. Pepper's Lonely Hearts Club Band: Detailed Reading

While the iconic status of *Sgt. Pepper* is beyond doubt, the exact nature of its contribution to psychedelic style is a matter of debate. For example, Russell Reising and Jim LeBlanc (2008, 104–106) have suggested that *Sgt. Pepper* came quite late in the psychedelic timeline and that its main contributions were ones of consolidation and popularization. I would revise that slightly to say that it was late in the timeline for a certain kind of pop psychedelia but not of psychedelia more generally, since it stood at the transition into genres such as psychedelic funk, space rock, and the jam band era (none of which it reflects to any great extent). This being said, the album was unquestionably groundbreaking in treating the LP rather than the single as a basic unit of rock creativity. Everett has argued that "the most fundamental conversion [in rock music compositional style] in the late 1960s is seen in the phenomenal growth of the LP market and its effect on musical content" (1999, 91), and *Sgt. Pepper* was a seminal event in this regard.

In presenting a topical reading of the entire album, I have three interlinked objectives. First, I want to demonstrate the usefulness of topical analysis for interpreting larger rock texts. Second, I want to identify the particular topics and topical procedures that were (and were not) present on the album in order to situate it within the broader development of psychedelic topicality. Finally, I want to address the question of how far *Sgt. Pepper* actually does cohere as a total statement. This last objective could be a very conservative one, but I do not intend it that way. My interest is not in definitively answering the question, and I do not want to suggest that coherence is an inherently important issue. But in this particular case, the idea of coherence was a core theme in the album's presentation and reception. So the question suggests itself for historical reasons. It is also a convenient question because coherence is a subject that must be explored by looking at the album as a whole, and so it fits with the other objectives of my analysis.

As with my analysis of "Strawberry Fields Forever," presentation of results is difficult because the relationship between detail and overview is unavoidably circular. I have decided to start by presenting an overarching framework and vocabulary, then move on to a detailed song-by-song analysis, and then conclude with the more general features and overview. This means that the presentation is divided into three large sections: (1) summary tables of all topics on the album, (2) a song-by-song analysis, and (3) higher-level summary and commentary on major topical features for the album as a whole. All of these levels of analysis reciprocally depend on one another. Some readers may prefer to look at the overview material first and read the more particularistic sections afterward. Or readers who prefer to see the trees in advance of the forest might wish to read the song-by-song section first and then the others. In any event, please be aware that no individual section will be fully satisfying until all have been read at least once. Also, please be aware that in order to closely follow the analysis you will need to refer to two different naming systems. *Topic types* are identified by numerical labels, which are provided in the first section (the summary tables). *Particular topical moments* are identified with alphanumeric labels, which are provided in the song-by-song analysis section. These two different sets of labels often work in tandem.

Sgt. Pepper: Summary of Topic Types

I begin with an overview of all the types of topics appearing on *Sgt. Pepper*, along with a map of where they occur. Tables 3.2 through 3.4 summarize all of the major topic types (column 1 in each table), along with a brief description of signifiers that are used to evoke these topics (column 2) and a key to which particular moments in the songs provide examples (column 3). The song title abbreviations will hopefully be clear without explanation, but they can also be decoded by looking at the song-by-song analysis. These particular topics and the ways I've grouped them are rooted in all of the discussion and analysis up to this point, but

Table 3.2. Main types of topic appearing on *Sgt. Pepper* (styles and genres)

1 Classical music	1.1 Orchestra (simple presence of)		DIL5, DIL11
	1.2 Harpsichord (or sufficiently similar timbre)		LSD1, FAH1
	1.3 Characteristic piano figures or timbres		DIL2
	1.4 Entire compositional/performance approach based on classical strings		SLH1
	1.5 Waltz time		LSD1
	1.6 Active contrapuntal bass line		LSD7
	1.7 Smooth voice leading		LSD1, FAH1
2 Indian music	2.1 Tambura		LSD3, GB1, GB2, GB3
	2.2 Other drones		GB4
	2.3 Hand drums and other percussion		GB2, GB3, GB4
	2.4 Melodic shape and phrasing		GB3
	2.5 Entirely Indian ensemble and compositional/performance approach		WY1
3 R+B (sometimes overlaps with jazz)	3.1 Motown-like "big beat" drum timbre		LSD6
	3.2 Characteristic bass figures or timbres		LSD7, GM7
	3.3 Characteristic saxophone figures or timbres		GM3, GM5, GM6, GM7
4 Country music / the rural	4.1 Characteristic guitar figures or timbres		FAH4
	4.2 Animal noises		GM2, GM12
5 Ragtime	5.0 Characteristic piano figures or timbres		LR1, LR6
6 Earlier 1960s rock styles	6.1 Characteristic organ figures or timbres		LSD8
	6.2 Characteristic drum-set figures or timbres		REP3
	6.3 Extreme fuzz guitar		REP3

they should still be seen as one possible interpretive framework rather than an absolute taxonomy. I haven't offered extremely detailed analysis of the topics or signifiers, because most of them are either discussed in detail elsewhere in this book or are relatively self-explanatory. In other words, for this reading I'm sacrificing justification of detail in order to get us quickly to larger-scale features. In the same spirit, the way I've divided topics up into subgroups is based on earlier arguments. For example, throughout the book I've accorded special topical importance to styles and genres, which suggests that these should have their own chart in this analysis. And the somewhat liminal status of prototopics provides the general reason for giving them their own category here. But there is one topic type that immediately derives from the nature of *Sgt. Pepper* itself: contexts of performance and reception. The album contains a striking number of moments that evoke specific performance contexts, such as the circus, the British music

Table 3.3. Main types of topic appearing on *Sgt. Pepper* (topical contexts of performance and reception)

7 British music hall and dance bands of earlier eras	7.1 Crowd sounds	SP3
	7.2 Alternating brass bass	FAH2
	7.3 Swing-like rhythm section	FAH1
	7.4 Characteristic melodic and harmonic material	FAH1, WSF1, REP5, DIL7, DIL8
	7.5 Fanfare	SP2, SP4, SP7, WLH2, LSD9, GM3
	7.6 Brass band	SP4, SP5, SP6
8 Circus	8.1 Waltz time	LSD1, MK6
	8.2 Calliope	MK1, MK3, MK4, MK6, MK7
	8.3 Drum and/or cymbal shots and rolls	MK2, MK5, GM4
	8.4 Other characteristic rhythmic, harmonic, melodic, and timbral features	MK6, MK7
	8.5 Animal noises	GM12
9 Church	9.1 Amen cadence	LSD9
	9.2 Bells	GB4
10 The military	10.1 Characteristic snare drum	GM9
	10.2 Bugle calls	SP7, GM13
	10.3 Fanfare	SP2, LR4
11 Live musical performance in general (two subtypes follow)	11.0 Count-in	REP2
12 (11.i) Beatlemania	12.0 Audience scream	SP8
13 (11.ii) Classical concert hall	13.1 Crowd sounds	SP1
	13.2 Orchestra tuning up	SP1

hall, the rock concert, and others. This in turn reflects how deeply *Sgt. Pepper* is concerned with the nature of performance, persona, and the way that British identity is mediated through musical performance.

There is, however, one topic in this summary that might require advance explanation: the one called *dream voices*. What I mean by this is the use of vocal textures (often backing vocals, but not always) that are sweet and dreamy in a conventional pop sense but made so extreme as to seem psychedelically otherworldly. There are several elements commonly used to create this effect: lush yet simple harmonies, gentle timbre, long notes, scalewise motion or stasis, a spatial location far back in the mix, heavy reverberation, and the use of vocables. This sort of vocal texture, prior to becoming a psychedelic prototopic, is a good ex-

Table 3.4. Main types of topic appearing on *Sgt. Pepper* (signs that are weakly topical but highly conventional [14–16] and psychedelic prototopics [17–29])

14 Time-passing motif	**14.0** Repeated or alternating pitches/chords at slow or moderate motor rhythm, usually medium-to-high register, usually a fairly percussive timbre such as piano or clean guitar	LSD5, GB1, GB4, DIL4, DIL7, DIL11, ROG
15 Theatrical/cinematic melodrama/suspense	**15.0** Characteristic organ figures and timbres	MK3
16 Classical/cinematic portent and epic	**16.0** Characteristic orchestral figures and timbres	LSD6, LSD9, DIL5, DIL10, DIL11
17 Sound effects intro/outro and other extended SFX passages	SP1, MK7, LR7, GM12, DIL5, ROG	
18 Dream voices	WLH3, LSD4, LSD9, FAH3, SLH2, WSF2, LR2, LR5, DIL3, DIL9	
19 Heavy signal processing	LSD1, LSD2, MK6, MK7, LR7	
20 Extreme textural change at ending	LR7, DIL11, ROG	
21 Jamming	LR7	
22 Nonsung vocal sounds and interjections	LR7, DIL8	
23 Mix effects (e.g., sudden changes of focus, pointillistic)	MK6, MK7, LR7, GM1	
24 Dramatic formal shifts	MK6, MK7, LR7, GM1, DIL5	
25 Fuzz lead guitar (highlighted)	FAH5, GM8, GM10	
26 Clockwork	DIL6, also implied by time-passing topic (**14.0**)	
27 Kazoo (or similar), usually as cheeky subversion	SP2, LR3, LR4	
28 Sustained and emphasized motor rhythm on drums	GM9	
29 Siren trill	GM11, DIL3	

ample of a musical feature that was a conventional sign but not a topic insofar as it lacked the specific indexicality necessary for topicality. However, by the second half of the 1960s the frequent and pointed use of such vocals in a psychedelic context made them prototopical.

The Later 1960s 173

Sgt. Pepper: Song-by-Song Analysis

The analysis of each song is intended to accomplish two things. First, it will identify and uniquely label each significant appearance of each topic type—the *topical moments*.[12] Second, the analysis will comment on how those topical moments are distributed relative to the overall form of the song. In cases where a song's topicality is straightforward, an analysis is presented in the main body of the text. In other cases, the full analysis is laid out as a table. In the tables, the columns are formal section, verbal description of topical moments, schematic analysis of topical moments, and time cues. Times are all rounded to the nearest second. When a time isn't indicated next to a topical moment, then that moment is in force for the entire formal section.

The most dense part of the presentation is the schematic analysis of topical moments. The core of this analysis lies in the topical moment labels. For example, LR4 names the fourth topical moment in "Lovely Rita." Such labels pair a song name abbreviation with a number indicating the order in which specific topical moments first appear in that song. Following each topical moment label there is a schematic analysis of that moment. This analysis shows which topic types are mobilized in each topical moment. The numbers in that analysis therefore refer back to the topic type labels of tables 3.2 through 3.4. For example, WLH3 [18] is the third topical moment in "With a Little Help from My Friends," and the only signifier making this moment topical is the presence of dream voices. Some topical moments, like WLH3, only mobilize one topic type and one topical signifier. However, some moments mobilize several signifiers at once. Sometimes these act together to reinforce the same topic. For example, GB2 [2.1, 2.3]$_C$ is the second topical moment in "Getting Better." It mobilizes tambura [2.1] and percussion [2.3], both of which in this case support the Indian topic. However, in other cases multiple simultaneous signifiers might point in different directions, creating a trope or a dialogic moment. So whenever multiple signifiers are present in the same topical moment, a subscript letter (like the C in GB2 above) is used to clarify what kind of moment they collectively create:

- C = Cluster. Used where the same topic is mobilized by several different signifiers simultaneously.
- D = Dialogic. Used where one signifier expresses more than one topic.
- T = Trope. Used where several different topics are mobilized simultaneously through different signifiers.
- WD = Weakly dialogic.

There is only one other bit of formalism left to explain before we can dive into the song-by-song analysis. Sometimes a topical moment will clearly be a transformation of an earlier moment. It can often be interesting to track the resulting relationships. This is done with curly braces and arrows, which are given whenever a new element is added to a chain of transformations. For example, if the fifth topical moment in a given song is a transformation of the first, then the notation {T1 → 5} would be given at the first appearance of T5. Similarly, if the sixth topical moment in this same song is a transformation of the fifth, then at the first appearance of T6 there would be the notation {T1 → 5 → 6}.

So now, at last, the preliminaries are out of the way. We can move on to a detailed song-by-song description, which will in turn pave the way for an overview of topicality in *Sgt. Pepper*. The goal of this section is to concisely lay out the major topical contents of each song with minimal extra commentary. A fuller discussion of what these details mean and how they fit together in a broader sense is saved for the final part of my analysis.

"SGT. PEPPER'S LONELY HEARTS CLUB BAND"

For detailed analysis, see table 3.5.

This song sets the persona of the Sgt. Pepper band. This persona is complex, containing elements of belle époque brass bands, a name based on flamboyant San Francisco band names, aspects of the Beatles themselves, and possibly some mockery of US militarism (Moore 1997, 21). The shifting boundaries and allegiances within this complex persona are indicated through a fair bit of dialogism, with certain sonic elements being inflected differently at different points. For example, there are several variations on the brass, suggesting at various times belle

Table 3.5. Topical analysis of "Sgt. Pepper's Lonely Hearts Club Band"

Crowd	Crowd sounds and orchestra tuning	SP1 [(13.1, 13.2)$_C$, 17]$_D$	0:00–0:12
Introduction	Lead guitar is like a fanfare, evokes the music hall and the military; the kazoo-like timbre could be heard as adding a layer of irony	SP2 [(7.5, 10.3)$_{WD}$, 27]$_D$	0:12–0:22
A	Audience noise fades in and bridges into the next section, now not so much associated with classical context as with music hall	SP3 [7.1] {SP1 → 3}	0:40–0:48
Brass	Jovial belle époque fanfare brass	SP4 [7.5, 7.6]$_C$	0:43–0:56
B	Sudden brass interjection, not a fanfare, more of an accent to a joke or other stage event	SP5 [7.6] {SP4 → 5}	1:14–1:16
C	Brass reenters as a pad this time	SP6 [7.6] {SP4 → 5 → 6}	1:26–1:33
	Figure at the end sounds like a bugle call or fanfare	SP7 [7.5, 10.2]$_{WD}$ {SP4 → 5 → 6 → 7}	1:33–1:37
		SP3 [7.1]	1:36–2:01
D	Audience sound changes again, this time to a Beatlemania-type scream	SP8 [12.0] {SP1 → 3 → 8}	2:01–2:02
Transition	Continuation	SP8 [12.0]	
		SP6 [7.6]	1:58–2:02

époque reverie, the music hall, bugle calls, and fanfares both military and theatrical. The crowd noises are also extremely interesting in this regard, since they appear in several different variations suggesting different performance contexts: first a classical orchestral concert, then the music hall or vaudeville, and finally Beatlemania {SP1 → 3 → 8}. Overall, the song is marked by multiple identities and shifts of historical reference, many of which are expressed through topics related to modes of address and to particular performance contexts.

"WITH A LITTLE HELP FROM MY FRIENDS"

After the "Billy Shears" vocal fanfare (WLH2 [7.5], 0:00–0:09), there is very little topical in this song.[13] The only other clearly topical element are the vocals in the tag, which could be heard as dream voices (WLH3 [18], 2:35–2:44). Given the lyrics, it's noteworthy that both of these topical elements are used as framing devices to set up and support the lead vocal, which is in itself straightforward and nontopical.

"LUCY IN THE SKY WITH DIAMONDS"

For detailed analysis, see table 3.6.

A great deal of the topical flavor in this song is contained in two complex moments: the keyboard part from the very opening (LSD1) and the cluster of elements at the end of the chorus (LSD9). The first of these moments combines a harpsichord timbre, smooth voice leading, and waltz time, all of which evoke classical music. The signal processing tropes this with a psychedelic prototopic, and the combination of signal processing with waltz time also suggests a further troping with the circus. The other complex moment is LSD9, which concludes the chorus. In this moment, the alternating bass figure resembles variously a bugle call, a fanfare, and epic tympani. This is in turn troped with vocals that evoke the church (a IV–I amen cadence) and dream voices. Overall, both of these complex moments suggest an affect that is dreamy and somewhat nostalgic but also leaning toward the epic and the spiritual. The dreamy affect is further supported by general signal processing (LSD2), the tambura (LSD3), dream voices (LSD4), and the time-passing motif (LSD5). The epic aspect is supported by the dramatic drum shots (LSD6) and to a degree the chorus bass line (LSD7).

"GETTING BETTER"

The first element I've chosen to call topical in this song is borderline, but if we choose to regard it as topical then some interesting subtleties arise. I am thinking here of the high G drone that persists in the rhythm section for much of the song (GB1 [2.2, 14.0]$_T$). In the refrains, B sections, and C section it is like the time-passing motif. In the A sections it is more sporadic. Overall, it lends a general atmosphere of time passing and Indian drone to the entire song, but in a very understated way. It also undergoes an interesting transformation (discussed below).

Table 3.6. Topical analysis of "Lucy in the Sky with Diamonds"

Intro	Opening keyboard (see text for discussion)	LSD1 [(1.2, 1.5, 1.7)$_C$, 8.1, 19]$_D$	0:00–0:33
Verse A	Modulation on keyboard continues, signal processing on voices	LSD2 [19]	Passim (song)
	Continuation	LSD1 [(1.2, 1.5, 1.7)$_C$, 8.1, 19]$_D$	
	Tambura	LSD3 [2.1]	0:18–0:33
Verse B	Dream voices	LSD4 [18]	0:33–0:51
	Straight motor quarter emphasis in bass and drums	LSD5 [14.0]	0:33–0:51
	Drum shots evoke Motown, and epic film scores	LSD6 [3.1, 16.0]$_D$	0:48–0:50
Chorus	Active contrapuntal bass line suggests both classical and R+B	LSD7 [1.6, 3.2]$_D$	0:51–1:09
	Surf/garage organ	LSD8 [6.1]	0:51–1:09
	Final cadence (see text for discussion)	LSD9 [(7.5, 16.0)$_D$, (9.1, 18)$_D$]$_T$	1:06–1:11
Verse A	Same as first verse A, except the tambura is louder and lasts for entire passage	LSD1 [(1.2, 1.5, 1.7)$_C$, 8.1, 19]$_D$	1:09–1:34
		LSD3 [2.1]	1:09–1:34
Verse B	Same as first verse B	LSD4 [18]; LSD5 [14.0]	1:34–1:51
		LSD6 [3.1, 16.0]$_D$	1:49–1:50
Chorus	Same as first chorus	LSD7 [1.6, 3.2]$_D$; LSD8 [6.1]	1:51–2:09
		LSD9 [(7.5, 16.0)$_D$, (9.1, 18)$_D$]$_T$	2:06–2:11
Verse A	Same as second verse A, except the drum shots from the end of verse B are appended	LSD1 [(1.2, 1.5, 1.7)$_C$, 8.1, 19]$_D$	2:09–2:34
		LSD3 [2.1]	2:09–2:34
		LSD6 [3.1, 16.0]$_D$	2:32–2:33
Chorus	Same as first chorus, but drawn out	LSD7 [1.6, 3.2]$_D$; LSD8 [6.1]	2:34–3:28
		LSD9 [(7.5, 16.0)$_D$, (9.1, 18)$_D$]$_T$	2:49–2:53
		LSD9 [(7.5, 16.0)$_D$, (9.1, 18)$_D$]$_T$	3:08–3:13

More obvious topical elements don't appear until about halfway through the song. Most dramatically, in the transition into the third A section (1:36–1:40) there are sudden clear Indian references from tambura, claps, and hand drums (GB2 [2.1, 2.3]$_C$). These Indian elements continue and are expanded into the third A section (1:40–1:58), where the vocal approach is now notably Indian inflected as well (GB3 [2.1, 2.3, 2.4]$_C$). Note how the Indian vocal aspect of GB3 arises as a transformation of material that wasn't particularly topical in its earlier form. In that respect there's a clear narrative aspect (change of state) that relates to the song's theme of personal transformation and in turn to some kinds of psychedelic ideologies. But if change and transformation are important themes, then are the drones ironic? Some implications of the high G drone seem that way: it could be heard as tense, suspenseful, indicating doubt or anticipation rather than completed transformation. But then again, the transformative spiritual aspect of drones is also evoked, most strongly in the tambura.

The return to the B section at 1:58 feels like a sharp retreat from topicality back to a fairly topic-free passage after the strong interjection of Indian elements. This is itself a topical gesture—highlighting the withdrawal of topicality—and we will see the same device used to even greater effect in the "Sgt. Pepper's Lonely Hearts Club Band" reprise. But then near the end of this B section (at 2:15) there is a transformed version of GB1 that continues to the end of the song and becomes a solo element in the tag (GB4 [(2.2, 9.2, 14.0)$_D$, 2.3]$_T$). The alteration is subtle—GB1 gains another timbral layer and starts to sound a bit more like bells—but the slight change has topical implications. This particular bell timbre could be heard as Indian or as a Western mystical/church bell. It is also a little like Christmas sleigh bells.

"FIXING A HOLE"

For detailed analysis, see table 3.7.

Although there are enough topical moments in this song to justify an analytical table, on another level it is extremely straightforward. The song essentially tropes nostalgic elements (music hall, brass band, classical music) with dream voices. Against these are contrasted a fuzz guitar solo, which serves as a contemporary psychedelic reference point, and electric country rhythm guitar, which is intermediate in historical reference between the dreamy nostalgic elements and the contemporary lead guitar.

"SHE'S LEAVING HOME"

This is the first of several tracks on the album that essentially sustain one topical area over an entire song. In this case, it is the strictly classical nature of the accompaniment that dominates everything else (SLH1 [1.4]). As with all of the single-topic songs, finer nuances could be identified. For example, Everett (1999, 107–109) discusses the elaborate text setting in this arrangement, where details of texture, chord voicing, and voice leading underscore a general theme of distance between generations. But even given such subtleties, what stands out most strongly in topical terms is the extreme focus on a single style, and one that is not typical of rock music of the time. As Allan Moore (1997, 37) points out, this is the first song on the LP not to be guitar/drum based (or indeed to use them at all). That being said, aside from the classical strings there are also interesting textural variations on dream voices at several points (SLH2 [18], which appears at 0:51–1:18, 2:04–2:31, and 2:54–3:35). These dramatize a dialogue between several perspectives: the inner voice of the protagonist, the voices of her parents, and

Table 3.7. Topical analysis of "Fixing a Hole"

Intro	Chord changes suggest a music-hall intro; the harpsichord timbre and voice leading lean more classical; also something swing-like in the whole rhythm section arrangement	FAH1 [(1.2, 1.7)$_C$, 7.3, 7.4]$_T$	Passim (song)
A	Alternating brass bass	FAH2 [7.2]	0:07–0:25
	Vocals on "where it will go" evoke dream voices	FAH3 [18]	0:15–0:19
A	Same as first A	FAH2 [7.2]	0:25–0:42
		FAH3 [18]	0:33–0:37
B	Electric country guitar	FAH4 [4.1]	0:49–1:00
A	Same as first A	FAH2 [7.2]	1:00–1:17
		FAH3 [18]	1:08–1:11
Inst	Fuzz guitar solo	FAH5 [25]	1:17–1:33
B	Same as first B	FAH4 [4.1]	1:40–1:50
A	Same as first A, except now the dream voices persist throughout	FAH2 [7.2]; FAH3 [18]	1:50–2:37
A'/Coda	Continuation	FAH2 [7.2]	
		FAH3 [18]	

the voice of the narrator. These dream voices are not exactly psychedelic in tone but are related to psychedelia in that they dramatize inwardness, reflection, and transformation.

"BEING FOR THE BENEFIT OF MR. KITE!"

For detailed analysis, see table 3.8 (*following page*).

Like some others on the album, this is largely a single-topic song. The title and most of the lyrics were taken from an 1843 circus poster (Everett 1999, 110), and the music is largely devoted to troping circus topics with psychedelic prototopics. But unlike a song such as "She's Leaving Home" or the other single-topic songs still to be discussed, this song presents its topic at different intensities in different formal sections. The most striking contrasts of this sort are between the sung portions, which are more mildly circus-like and psychedelic, and the instrumentals, which are extremely so. The song also presents a good example of how underlying harmonic features, not topical in themselves, can reinforce topics suggested more blatantly by other features. As Everett describes it: "The track's superficial effects do not account for all of the musical fantasy; larger-scale swirling is created by novel harmonic relationships. Tonalities of C minor, D minor, and E minor . . . are each supported by traditional tonal means but do not relate

Table 3.8. Topical analysis of "Being for the Benefit of Mr. Kite!"

Intro	Calliope-like high line, and the squeeze-box timbre	MK1 [8.2, 8.4]$_C$	0:00–0:07
A	Bass drum and hi-hat are parade-like	MK2 [8.3]	0:07–0:22
	Right hand on organ is calliope-like; left hand is based around repeated and mostly chromatic scalar descents, adds a touch of melodrama/suspense	MK3 [8.2, 15.0]$_D$	0:07–0:22
B	Calliope-like organ continues, but not so much the suspense element	MK4 [8.2] {MK3 → 4}	0:22–0:37
	Snare roll	MK5 [8.3]	0:36–0:37
A	Same as first A	MK2 [8.3]; MK3 [8.2, 15.0]$_D$	0:37–0:52
B	Same as first B, but without snare roll	MK4 [8.2]	0:52–1:01
Waltz	Very dense cluster of circus elements, in turn troped with a cluster of psychedelic prototopics	MK6 [(all 8)$_C$, (19, 23, 24)$_C$]$_T$	1:01–1:29
A	Same as first A	MK2 [8.3]; MK3 [8.2, 15.0]$_D$	1:29–1:44
B	Same as second B	MK4 [8.2]	1:44–1:53
Instrumental	Starts as a recap of the waltz but quickly shifts to nonwaltz circus music; now also functions as a long sound effects end section	MK7 [(most 8)$_C$, (17, 19, 23, 24)$_C$]$_T$ {MK6 → 7}	1:53–2:37

to each other in a coherent way.... Rather, the three centers can be heard as the rings of a circus, with action taking place in all arenas and no particular object of attention the 'correct' one" (110–11).

The other important feature of this song is its position at the end of side 1, which Moore suggests "is considered important by most commentators" (1997, 40). Although the various interpretations cited by Moore do not strongly converge on a consensus reading, common themes cluster around dualities of alienation versus solidarity, and witty nostalgia versus an unsettling freakishness.

"WITHIN YOU WITHOUT YOU"

This is the third of the songs that essentially presents a single topic in all aspects of the writing, arranging, and performance (WY1 [2.5]). The length of the instrumental passage also stands out. This is a feature afforded by the Indian context but is noteworthy aside from that since long instrumentals are extremely unusual in the Beatles' work up to this point. It should also be noted that George Harrison is the only band member performing on this track—a point to which we will return. Although this song is perhaps the most singular one on the album in that it has the least in common with the others, it was also selected to open side 2, suggesting to interpreters that it should be granted special importance. But there has been little consensus on what this importance should be:

> Responses to this track have been extremely varied.... Goldstein found the lyrics dull and dismal, and Riley is unable to see how it fits within the album. Other writers may be called upon to answer him: for Peyser it summarizes the entire first side in focusing on "the space between us all..."; for Middleton it is the key song on the album, destroying the alienation of side one through its detachment and serenity in an attitude of acceptance. MacDonald, too, insists on its rightness, calling it the album's conscience, the necessary sermon within the community singing. (Moore 1997, 45–46)

"WHEN I'M SIXTY-FOUR"

This is the fourth and last of the fairly straightforward single-topic songs (WSF1 [7.4]). Like "She's Leaving Home," the only notable secondary topical feature is the use of dream voices (WSF2 [18] at 0:40–0:54 and 1:41–1:50).

"LOVELY RITA"

For detailed analysis, see table 3.9.

For most of this song, the major feature is a troping of nostalgic elements—such as ragtime (LR1, LR6) and kazoo-like timbres (LR3, LR4)—with dream

Table 3.9. Topical analysis of "Lovely Rita"

Intro	Hint of ragtime in the piano introduction	LR1 [5.0]	0:00–0:11
Refrain	Dream voices	LR2 [18]	0:11–0:22
A	A very brief kazoo-like gliss	LR3 [27]	0:27
B	A more extended kazoo break (or hokum kazoo brass), following "military man" lyric	LR4 [10.3, 27]$_D$	0:49–0:51
A	Nothing topical of note		
Transition	Dream voices	LR5 [18]	1:01–1:12
Instrumental	The whole instrumental is based around a ragtime-like piano	LR6 [5.0]	1:12–1:23
B	Nothing topical of note		
A	Nothing topical of note		
Refrain	Same as first refrain	LR2 [18]	1:50–2:12
Instrumental	Cluster of psychedelic prototopics: the fact of slipping into a jam and a new space at the end, loud reverberated exhales, several layered and echoed strange voices	LR7 [17, 19, 20, 21, 22, 23, 24]$_C$	2:12–2:42

voices (LR2 and LR5). This kind of trope has been seen several times already on the album, especially in the songs more associated with McCartney. Probably the song's most striking feature is the sudden shift to an extended instrumental at the end that is full of psychedelic prototopics. This is another example of the outward journey expressive genre.

"GOOD MORNING GOOD MORNING"

For detailed analysis, see table 3.10.

Metrically and texturally this is perhaps the most consistently challenging song on the album, a challenge summarized in the pervasive moment GM1. One way to read this dense and always-changing texture is as a psychedelic prototopic. That hearing is reinforced by other such prototopics in the song, like the overwhelming motoric pulse in the second B section (GM9) and the occasional eruptions of fuzz guitar (GM8 and GM10).

Aside from the general affect of noise and confusion, the main topical feature of "Good Morning Good Morning" is that there are two especially multilayered topical elements, both of which recur with transformations: the animal noises and the horns. The animal noises are found in moments GM2 and GM12. The first of these is fairly simple, being made up simply of a rooster. But the rooster is surprisingly nuanced in topical terms. It is associated with the rural but also with awakening and therefore indirectly with clockwork and the time-passing motif. Then at the end of the song, in GM12, the multiplication of animal sounds restates these earlier associations but tropes them with a circus parade. In this context, the badly played bugle moment (GM13) is rendered especially complex. It links with the reveille of the rooster and also has some resonances of the rural (outdoor rural battlefields, or maybe an old bugler playing down on the farm). Finally, the troping of bugle with circus, along with the tentative and nonprofessional nature of the bugle playing itself, introduces a tone of mockery. The circus association of these closing animal noises was already anticipated in the song's overall mood of noise and confusion and in the drum/cymbal shots (GM4).

The horns at first could be heard as an R&B topic in terms of timbre, although their melodic and rhythmic material here is more like a fanfare or a TV bumper (GM3). I am categorizing this fanfare under British music hall because that association catches the campy and show-business aspect. The reported origins of the refrain in a Kellogg's Corn Flakes TV commercial would also introduce another sort of show-business reference for those listeners who recognized it (Everett 1999, 114). Subsequent variations on the horns tend not only to be texturally distinct but also to hone in on various of these implied topics: GM5 is more on the big-band side of R&B, GM6 is more contemporary, and GM7 is transparently on the R&R side of R&B.

Overall, "Good Morning Good Morning" could be heard as exploring how a single affect—noisy daily-life confusion on the verge of spinning out of control—suggests a variety of interlinked topical associations: circus, brash TV, and psychedelic or psychotic breaks with reality.

Table 3.10. Topical analysis of "Good Morning Good Morning"

Throughout the entire song there are repeated devices that create rhythmic disorientation and constant shifts of focus in the mix		GM1 [23, 24]$_C$	Passim (song)
Rooster	Rooster	GM2 [4.2]	0:00–0:04
Refrain	Saxophone opening (see text for discussion)	GM3 [3.3, 7.5]$_D$	0:04–0:12
A	Drum/cymbal shot	GM4 [8.3]	0:16
		GM3 [3.3, 7.5]$_D$	0:20–0:23
A'	Horns are now more continuous, more R&B or big band; at the same time, their material is based on GM3	GM5 [3.3] {GM3 → 5}	0:23–0:34
Refrain	Horns continue same (timing accounted for above); material is related to what will be GM7 (described below)	GM5 [3.3]	
A	Horns still continuous, but now in a pad-and-shots version	GM6 [3.3] {GM3 → 5 → 6}	0:34–0:45
		GM4 [8.3]	0:38
	Horns and bass change to an R&B walking/riffing feel	GM7 [3.2, 3.3]$_C$ {GM3 → 5 → 6 → 7}	0:43–0:55
B	Continuation	GM7 [3.2, 3.3]$_C$	
A		GM6 [3.3]	0:55–1:03
		GM4 [8.3]	0:59
		GM3 [3.3, 7.5]$_D$	1:03–1:06
A'	Same as first A'	GM5 [3.3]	1:06–1:26
Refrain	Same as first refrain (continuation)	GM5 [3.3]	
Guitar Solo	Solo is very acid fuzz	GM8 [25]	1:17–1:28
	Horns initially continue the same (timing accounted for above), then horns and bass change	GM7 [3.2, 3.3]$_C$	1:26–1:38
B	Like first B, but washed over by a constant motor-rhythm snare	GM9 [10.1, 28]$_{WD}$	1:28–1:38
	Fuzz guitar fill	GM10 [25]	1:36–1:38
A	Same as second A	GM6 [3.3]	1:38–1:46
		GM4 [8.3]	1:42
		GM3 [3.3, 7.5]$_D$	1:46–1:49
	Fuzz guitar fill	GM10 [25]	1:47–1:48
A'	Same as first A'	GM5 [3.3]	1:49–1:56
Refrain/ barnyard	A new R&B horn riff, troped with a siren trill flute	GM11 [3.3, 29]$_T$ {GM3 → 5 → 6 → 7 → 11}	1:56–2:35
	Dense layered animal sounds (including an elephant); links to the earlier rooster, and also evokes the circus parade	GM12 [4.2, 8.5, 17]$_D$ {GM2 → 12}	1:56–2:41
	Bugle	GM13 [10.2]	2:26–2:38

"SGT. PEPPER'S LONELY HEARTS CLUB BAND (REPRISE)"

The most interesting topical feature of this track is in something that it doesn't do. It returns us to the Sgt. Pepper band persona, but this time without the nostalgic brass trappings. At the same time, there are features that strengthen the connection of the Sgt. Pepper band to the recent past of Beatlemania. The count-in, for example, could refer to a variety of eras of performance but would fit fine with an early beat group (REP2 [11.0], 0:03–0:05). When compared to the count-in on "Taxman," for example, it is notably crisp and precise—almost militaristic. The vamp and fuzz guitar are reminiscent of earlier 1960s rock styles, which might have already seemed retro by 1967 (REP3 [6.2, 6.3]$_C$, present throughout the entire song). And the crowd noises are now all consistent with Beatlemania-era crowds, without the earlier classical concert or music-hall variations (REP4 = SP8, 0:26–0:36 and 1:12–1:19). The only other topical feature, and the only one that perhaps clearly points to an earlier era of style and performance, is the modulation up by step at around 0:43–0:45, which could be heard as reminiscent of earlier musical theater or variety show arrangement practices (REP5 [7.4]).

"A DAY IN THE LIFE"

For detailed analysis, see table 3.11.

In terms of song sequencing it is significant that this song comes after the reprise, which makes it seem like we are stepping outside or beyond the rest of the album. In that connection, it's also interesting that "A Day in the Life" juxtaposes fairly topic-free and conventionally song-like passages with more experimental and topic-laden ones. Does this track create something like an outward journey expressive genre for the album as a whole? Perhaps to an extent. But the sense of closure created by the reprise means that "A Day in the Life" is just as likely to be heard as entirely separate from everything else, rather than as part of a larger unity.

In the conventional song passages, the only really topical detail is in the piano part, whose block chords occasionally evoke nineteenth-century concert music (DIL2). The transition out of this straightforward mode is the slow vocal trill on "turn you on" (DIL3), which is an instance both of a siren trill and of dream voices. This leads into a time-passing motif on the piano (DIL4) and then the first long orchestral buildup (DIL5). According to George Martin, McCartney saw this orchestral passage as a "freak out," whereas Lennon saw it as a "tremendous build-up, from nothing up to something absolutely like the end of the world" (quoted in Everett 1999, 118). So overall, this passage dialogically evokes two clusters: one of classical epic portent (perhaps with biblical inflections) and one of psychedelic prototopics. While these orchestral passages are unlike anything else on the album, the song's middle section is based on a now-familiar trope: upbeat archaic pop against assorted psychedelic prototopics. This trope is then briefly taken one level further with the addition of orchestral lines evoking classical music and dramatic film music.

Table 3.11. Topical analysis of "A Day in the Life"

Sound effects continued	Trailing-off of audience noise	DIL1 = REP4 continued	0:00–0:02
Introduction	Nothing topical of note		
A	Nothing topical of note		
A	Ascending piano block chords evoke Romantic-era concert music (and follow the "House of Lords" lyric)	DIL2 [1.3]	1:09–1:11
A		DIL2 [1.3]	1:36
Orchestra	"Turn you on" is both a siren trill and dream voices	DIL3 [18, 29]$_C$	1:41–1:46
	Time-passing piano	DIL4 [14.0]	1:41–1:58
	Orchestral buildup (see text for discussion)	DIL5 [(1.1, 16.0)$_C$, (17, 24)$_C$]$_D$	1:41–2:16
B	Alarm clock	DIL6 [26]	2:18
	Pop/swing texture in piano/bass/drums (transforms the earlier time-passing piano DIL4)	DIL7 [7.4, 14.0]$_D$ {DIL4 → 7}	Passim (section)
	Piano fills evoke Romantic-era concert music	DIL2 [1.3]	2:26–2:29
		DIL2 [1.3]	2:40–2:43
	Heavy breathing is both theatrical and a psychedelic prototopic	DIL8 [7.4, 22]$_D$	2:35–2:36
C/transition	Dream voices	DIL9 [18]	2:49–3:19
	Orchestra is low, ominous, portentous	DIL10 [16.0]	2:55–3:18
A	Same as first A	DIL2 [1.3]	3:42–3:44
Orchestra	Same as first orchestral section	DIL3 [18, 29]$_C$	3:46–3:50
		DIL4 [14.0]	3:47–4:21
		DIL5 [(1.1, 16.0)$_C$ (17, 24)$_C$]$_D$	3:47–4:21
Long chord	See text for discussion	DIL11 [(1.1, 16.0)$_C$, 14.0, 20]$_D$	4:21–5:04

Perhaps the most distinctive feature of the song is the immensely protracted closing chord (DIL11). Topically, this chord evokes Romantic-era concert music and cinematic/theatrical codes of portentousness, as well as the outward journey expressive genre. It also indirectly evokes the time-passing motif by suggesting a suspension or ending of time.

RUNOUT GROOVE

The locked runout groove is also topically interesting (ROG [14, 17, 20]$_C$, duration open). In terms of psychedelic prototopics, it is both a sound effects ending and an example of introducing a strikingly new texture at the end (this time the end of an album rather than a song ending). Earlier, I questioned whether "A Day in the Life" creates an outward journey expressive genre within the album as a whole. However we view that question, there is no doubt that the combination of "A Day in the Life" plus the runout groove succeeds in doing so. In addition, the runout groove evokes the time-passing motif in its repetitive, cyclical structure and in the way it presents temporal infinity, this time an actual infinity, or at least as close as is technically feasible on an LP. And aside from formal implications, there are various ways to hear the runout groove in terms of specific topical content, since it has aspects of a hare krishna chant, a pop or theatrical vocal snippet, and an anthropological field recording.

Sgt. Pepper: Overview and Summary

Now we can return to our overarching questions about *Sgt. Pepper* and bring considerable topical detail into the discussion. Let's begin with the question of coherence. I will circulate between three types of coherence in particular, always with the goal of pointing out their topical aspects: (1) formal coherence, (2) thematic coherence, and (3) coherence of authorial personas.

On the face of it, the album is not particularly coherent, at least in musical terms. As Moore points out, "The sheer versatility and stylistic diversity of the material on the album was, and remains, astonishing" (1997, 57). While this sort of diversity does not preclude coherence, it does mean that the coherence would have to be of a particularly inclusive kind. The challenge is increased because the album remains within a model of psychedelia based on concise song forms, rather than creating coherence through longer tracks. But in this respect it does, at least in its stated intention, represent a kind of intermediate strategy. It is very much unlike the emergent psychedelic funk and space rock in that concise pop songs are the major structural unit, and this division into shorter songs is intensified by the large number of single-topic tracks. But at the same time, the Beatles explicitly invited listeners to hear these individual songs as linked into a suite, and this invitation carried a great deal of weight, since it was a new gesture from a rock band. That being said, there is considerable debate as to how far we can achieve the goal of a unified hearing. According to Everett, "Both Lennon and Starr feel that the 'Pepper' concept embraces only the LP's first two songs and the reprise" (1999, 99), although I think we could at least add "Being for the Benefit of Mr. Kite!" to the belle époque family of the basic concept.

I will use topical features of the album to suggest that its coherence goes further than is sometimes acknowledged. But this conclusion is not in itself new, since there are other, nontopical factors that suggest a deeper connectedness between the various songs. For example, the importance of packaging should not be discounted: "The 'package' concept, clichéd now, was brilliantly original. Not only did we have the gatefold sleeve and printed lyrics (inviting us into what was portrayed as a closed coterie), but the badges, the false moustache and Sgt. Pepper stripes that were supplied as cutouts suggested we could all the more easily pretend to be in the band" (Moore 1997, 57). Additionally, the lack of track band-ing was taken by some as both a sign and a source of coherence. But perhaps the most important axis of coherence is thematic. Do the songs hang together in exploring the same theme, or related themes, from multiple angles? Moore (1997, 60–64) presents a detailed summary of common themes in *Sgt. Pepper* reception. Some of the most commonly raised include the tension between alienation and belonging, the question of irony (how much is sincere, how much tongue-in-cheek), drug references and endorsements of countercultural values, a survey of British culture and life, and the tension between illusions in which we may be tempted to live versus harsh realities. These sorts of consideration are more obviously topical, and if we were to reframe some of the main questions of coherence in topical terms, we might ask things like: Is there a relatively small set of core topics that recur throughout the album? Is there some compelling pattern in the way the topics are distributed?

Let's take the question of core topics first. Considering the topical field of psychedelia as we have seen it to this point, are particular areas given special emphasis on *Sgt. Pepper*? Are others particularly avoided? And do these patterns reflect any kind of thematic unity? The answer to all of these questions is yes. Major topical clusters on the album, several of which overlap, include Indian music, Western classical music, nostalgic older styles (British music hall, ragtime, brass bands, older pop), and psychedelic prototopics liberally applied but almost exclusively in decorative roles. As most commentators have noted, this all centers on a few core themes: Britishness, nostalgia, identity and persona. There are also important omissions that help show how *Sgt. Pepper* occupies a specific area of the topical field. For example, there are strikingly few topical references to space; twang guitar (spy, surf, western); the blues, soul, and funk; or folk music. So despite the stylistic range of the album, it centers squarely on topics concerned with Britishness, nostalgia, and psychedelia primarily in its role as a mediator of British nostalgia. This only stands out slightly if you compare the Beatles mostly to other British bands or to earlier psychedelia. But if you compare them instead to a group like the Grateful Dead or to psychedelic soul, the narrowness of focus on this album is more striking.

So what about the question of whether these topics are patterned or distributed in any coherent way. We can start with an observation about the density of topics in particular songs. Consider a rough scale to characterize each song as follows: 1 = just a few passing decorative topics; 2 = a larger number of strong and/or interesting topics; 3 = a single-topic song where that single topic is explored on multiple levels. If we assign a value to each track, we get the following (the first group is side 1 and the second is side 2, excluding the runout groove).

2, 1, 2, 2, 1, 3, 3
3, 3, 1, 1, 1, 2

This distribution does not at all look random. It follows a marked progression from moderate mixed topicality to single-topic songs on the first side, with the same pattern roughly repeated on the second side but reversed. So overall, whatever the intention might have been, the higher-level selection and distribution of topics on the album follow certain patterns and therefore suggest a certain kind of coherence. Having noted these points, we can move on to the second and third kinds of coherence that I've proposed to address in topical terms: thematic coherence and coherence of authorial persona. Since this particular album is already concerned with the nature of persona as one of its main themes, we can consider these two aspects together to a large degree.

At this point we should recall a basic property of topicality, which is that all topics embody a history of displacement. This general feature of topicality resonates with one of the core themes of the album: the question of what it means for celebrities like the Beatles to write and perform from the position of alternative personas. The most obvious instance is the Sgt. Pepper band itself, but from this point of view many other songs from the album can be read in terms of the common theme. With that in mind, consider the following remark from Naphtali Wagner, who suggests that we can classify the various songs on *Sgt. Pepper* "in terms of their proximity to or distance from the here and now. . . . The distance from the 'here' was manifested most prominently in the turn to a foreign (Indian) musical culture. The distance from the 'now' is more complex, as it includes musico-poetic journeys along the time axis. . . . From this perspective, the classical and the psychedelic are both aimed at creating distance from the conventional rock 'n' roll of the late 1950s and early 1960s" (2008, 90).

Similar points are made by Reising and LeBlanc (2008, 109–10), who emphasize the album's interest in metaphors of within/without. So here is a theme that is key to the album and that also resonates strongly with the basic nature of topicality. As I've noted at several other points in the book, psychedelic artists often treat themes of distance and othering from the perspective of self-othering, blurring the lines between themselves and the distant others or highlighting conflicting tendencies within their own personas. From this perspective, we can return to the hybridity of the Sgt. Pepper band persona, beginning with these observations from Sheila Whiteley:

> What was the significance of this Edwardian figure and his Lonely Hearts Club Band? [McCartney submerges] himself in the persona of a bandmaster playing to the lonely, the alienated, in that imaginary (and most English of settings) music hall Palace of Varieties. The use of sound collage—crowd noises, an orchestra tuning up—functions both as a narrative source and as a psychological trigger, creating for the listening audience (both imagined and real) a mood of shared festivity. . . . For the more perceptive, the colourful uniforms and vaudeville-style banter also evoked the cultural politics of the drop-out hippies and student and graduate activists. . . . The intense high-volume guitar and active syncopated bass . . . add their own connotations as they invade the superficial mood of old-time camaraderie; by wearing the uniforms of the past within the context of a psychedelically charged rock album, *Sgt. Pepper* undercuts traditional values and its "military" aspect, as producer George Martin confirms, is shown to be a "send up of the US in Vietnam." (2008, 14)

If we are looking for coherence in the album, then what to make of this hybridity? Under one reading, the old-time and orchestral elements frame the Sgt. Pepper band as entirely archaic, and the electric rock elements would be seen as the Beatles commenting on and framing the fictitious band more than identifying with it. But under another reading, the two bands are one and the same, such that certain aspects of the Beatles' hybrid identity frame and comment on other aspects of that same identity, which would mean that they were both archaic and contemporary relative to the time of the album. This reading is strongly suggested not only by the album's artwork but also by the specific device of mobilizing different sorts of crowd noises throughout the title track, each of which relates the band to a different era of performance but which collectively suggest a single history of transformation. Finally, if we choose to go with this reading, how should we interpret the reprise, which is more topically homogeneous and more Beatlemania oriented in its sonic choices? Should we hear this as a return to selfhood after all the genre and identity experiments in the rest of the album? That reading would lend narrative coherence to the record but is ultimately unsatisfying insofar as it ignores a crucial nuance: the version of the Beatles referenced in the reprise is one with which they had already broken, albeit recently. So the reprise is something of a return to a more contemporary or public layer of their collective persona, but in a subtle way. It might be read as another case of psychedelic self-othering (this time being othered relative to your own recent past) or as an existential reflection on how one becomes trapped by the expectations of others and by one's own earlier selves.

Going beyond the title track but staying with the relationship between topic and persona, it's important to recognize that while topics can be a mask for an artist, allowing for a kind of artifice, they can also serve as an emblem, highlighting personal traits and priorities. Maybe the most pointed example of this is "Within You Without You," where the Indian topicality associated with George Harrison receives its most sustained presentation and where he is literally the only Beatle on the track. Slightly less extreme but in a similar direction are the McCartney-related single-topic songs "She's Leaving Home" and "When I'm Sixty-Four," where the focused genre exercises relate to facets of McCartney's own musical personality and history. By contrast, Lennon on this album is most associated with complex tropes and with moments of dialogism, many of which are ambiguous or even perhaps critical and sarcastic in tone. Summarizing major instances of troping and dialogism on the album, we find that they tend to occur most often in the songs associated with Lennon. While there are a few dialogic moments and tropes in the title track (SP1, SP2, SP7), in "Fixing a Hole" (FAH1), and in "Lovely Rita" (LR4), the more Lennon-associated tropes and dialogic moments include those on "Lucy in the Sky with Diamonds" (LSD1, LSD6, LSD7, LSD9), "Getting Better" (GB1, GB4), "Being for the Benefit of Mr. Kite!" (MK3, MK6, MK7), "Good Morning Good Morning" (GM3, GM11, GM12), and "A Day in the Life" (DIL5, DIL7, DIL8, DIL11). Also, as can be seen in the song-by-song analysis, these dialogic moments and tropes tend to be multilayered and complex, offering a wide range of interpretive options and often seeming either ambiguous, ironic, or both. Finally, at the opposite end of the spectrum but also using a highly focused topical technique to reflect a personal image, Ringo Starr's straightforward Everyman persona is encapsulated in the least topical song on the entire album. The only clearly topical element in "With a Little Help from my Friends," the dream voices, is associated with the supportive friends and not with Ringo himself.

In summary, by putting emphasis on the personal associations of particular topical experiments I have tried to provide some counterbalance to a common criticism of *Sgt. Pepper*: that the album is so engrossed in genre experimentation as to seem inauthentic, or disconnected from the Beatles' core identity. By contrast, I argue that these sorts of topical exercises enhance both the thematic coherence of the album (concerned as it is with the nature of persona) and the impression of authorship by underscoring aspects of the personas of band members.

Finally, I want to return to a question raised at the very beginning of this Beatles discussion: To what degree can classicism stand as a description of the Beatles' work during the later 1960s and of their general position in psychedelia? I argued at that time for an expanded view of classicism as an aesthetic orientation, and some authors have made the same suggestion specifically with respect to *Sgt. Pepper*: "Ostensibly, there is no symmetry: psychedelia is spread over the entire album whereas the classical influence is just one of many stylistic influences in it. ... [But] we have to distinguish between the Beatles' 'classicism' as a range of [stylistic] influences originating in Western art music and its more abstract meaning as an aesthetic ideal" (Wagner 2008, 76). Relative to the overall psychedelic field of 1967, *Sgt. Pepper* stands as a summing up of earlier stylistic moments, one framed around grand ambitions and realized with a high degree of craft and a novelistic level of detail in the exploration of its core themes. It did not add any significant new topics to psychedelia, but it did exploit many of the existing ones to a very high level of sophistication. In all of these ways, classicism works as a summary description and as a key to the position occupied by the Beatles in the field of psychedelia relative to established and emergent possibilities.

Early Pink Floyd

Along with the Beatles and the Incredible String Band, Pink Floyd were arguably one of the most characteristic British psychedelic bands of the period 1967–68. But as with Parliament-Funkadelic, their work of the late 1960s points stylistically both forward and backward. Some aspects of early Pink Floyd are best explored as another inflection of topics we've already discussed. However, other aspects of Pink Floyd are best explored as seeds of later developments. So as with Parliament-Funkadelic I have decided to discuss Pink Floyd in two phases. To conclude the present chapter, my aim will be to highlight a few selected sonic features of early Pink Floyd that marked them as distinct from other bands of the time but are still rooted in topics we have already discussed. These will be the role of the electric organ, their approach to the pastoral and the rural, their distinctive use of clockwork and other mechanical sounds, their tendency toward repetitive and improvisational textures, and their occasional emphasis on dark affects. These elements are all distinctive but are also best understood relative to a somewhat retrospective view of earlier 1960s psychedelia. The more forward-looking space-rock aspects of Pink Floyd will be covered in the next chapter.

Pink Floyd: Electric Organ

The electric organ is especially important in early Pink Floyd. In chapter 2 I briefly discussed the topical richness of the organ, which derives from the instrument's sonic flexibility, as well as its long and varied history. The organ can evoke a wide range of topics, including various genres of classical music, several different church traditions (pipe organ versus pump organ versus gospel electric organ), and several different styles of jazz. It can also be a source of drone and woodwind sounds, often in an Orientalist context, and by the late 1960s it had additionally become evocative of an earlier era of 1960s garage rock. Because of its textural, timbral, and dynamic malleability, the organ is well suited to experimental electronic music contexts, where it was often subjected to various signal-processing techniques. This is especially true of styles and artists where the tempos tend to be slow, emphasizing long lines, drawn-out ambient sounds, and gradually evolving timbres. We have already discussed one example in depth ("Section 43"), and early Pink Floyd is especially rich in other examples.

In some cases, the organ can evoke pop styles of the earlier 1960s, especially spy and surf. A good example is the extended solo in "Lucifer Sam" (2:25–2:41). It also easily evokes classical and religious topics, for example, the pipe organ–like ambience and fairy-tale topical flavor in "Matilda Mother." And it is sometimes used for its clearly electronic character. For example, "Pow R. Toc H." provides an example of a markedly electronic organ timbre (2:17–2:49), with deep tremolo accentuated by its application to long, extended scalar shapes. It is also noteworthy that we are led out of an especially nightmarish passage in this song with the appearance of an expansive pipe organ–like organ pad (starting at 3:06). The variety of organ timbres in "Pow R. Toc H." resembles procedures in other songs, where the topically multifaceted potential of the organ is explored even more widely. For example, the first verse of "Flaming" is shaped in large part through changes in organ timbre and texture. There is a foregrounded siren trill (0:17–0:20), then a slower countermelody (0:21–0:31), then a swelling pad with a more pipe organ timbre (0:32–0:35). Subsequent verses are similar. The organ switches again to a pipe organ timbre and becomes more continuous just before the extended "ever so high" sound effects ascent (1:29–1:41), during which an ascending organ line is layered with several other elements, including a kind of mechanical ratchet timbre, what sounds like a dulcimer, and perhaps harp as well. There is then a segue into an extended jam, during which these sound effects persist and the overall texture is dominated by slow organ lines, organ pads, and space toms, with a very exploratory and extemporized-sounding lead guitar (1:41–2:16).

Even when used as a monophonic solo instrument, the organ in early Pink Floyd is often strikingly dialogic. For example, in "Scarecrow" the organ is in timbre and melody very much like a pastoral oboe or other woodwind (starting at 0:10). However, because it continues to solo in relative disregard for the other musical elements and does so for such an extended period of time, it also takes on something of an Orientalist or space aspect but without adopting any of the more obvious clichés of raga rock. A similar approach is taken throughout "Chapter 24," where the organ resembles more Orientalist extended solos in a general way, but with an overall effect that is less exoticist and more rooted in pastoralism. Although I've decided to reserve my discussion of space rock for the next chapter, in early Pink Floyd the line between space topics and other topics is very porous. A key reason for this is that the organ functioned as a bridge between these topics, at times evoking them in sequence and at other times simultaneously.[14]

Pink Floyd: The Pastoral and Clockwork

Early Pink Floyd had a distinctive approach to the pastoral topic. As it was by the Incredible String Band, the pastoral was often treated by Pink Floyd in a mystical vein. But unlike the Incredible String Band, and more like the Grateful Dead, Pink Floyd's pastoral mysticism was often created by troping the pastoral topic with the space topic. Also, and maybe most distinctively, Pink Floyd on several occasions chose to trope the pastoral topic with clockwork elements, creating a variety of unusual results. One example of a pastoral/space trope in early Pink Floyd is the mostly instrumental passage at the end of "Chapter 24." Aside from the "sunset, sunrise" element in the lyrics, the pastoral tone is enhanced by the layering of voices and the way they rise and thicken through doubling. At the same time, there are many elements of space topics and of mysticism, such as the meandering organ lines, the echo and reverberation, the mystical associations of the I Ching, and those of the voices (if heard as resembling church polyphony). Overall, this passage evokes a landscape at sunrise, but one with a markedly spacey and mystical quality. And the troping of such elements is not limited to "Chapter 24." For example, in the third verse of "Flaming" the lyric line "watching buttercups cup the light" is followed by small tinkling bells, an ascending harp, and an electronic sound effect gliss (0:55–1:01). With "sitting on a dandelion" there is a sudden interjection of loud acoustic guitar, and then in the next verse there are slow trilling dream voices layered with a space wind noise on "starlit skies" (1:17–1:20). In cases like these, the magical associations of pastoralism are troped with those of space, and this space-landscape relationship will be discussed further in the next chapter.

In other cases, the pastoral is troped with magical or mystical elements but without the aspect of space. For example, in "The Gnome" there is a doubling of the lead voice with loud whispering for the lyric line "look at the sky, look at the river, isn't it good?" (1:14–1:30). A related but somewhat different trope is created by the sound that opens "Scarecrow"—a wooden-sounding clockwork ticking that continues throughout the song. There are various ways to read this sound.

It could be seen as forming a pair (by means of reference to technology) with the space jam at the end of the song. Or perhaps it is the sound of the scarecrow dancing or walking about, which would raise a more general, and slightly unsettling, sort of pastoral mysticism. And the troping of the pastoral with clockwork is not limited to "Scarecrow." For example, "The Gnome" also opens with a mechanical ticking motif. The rest of "The Gnome" is typically goofy gnome topicality and therefore by extension pastoral. In this case the ticking doesn't just signify clockwork but is also a conventional sign of marching and of busy hands in a workshop. This is an aspect of the clockwork motif not noted elsewhere in the book—its connotation of diminutive fantasy business.

One more straightforward reason for the troping of the pastoral with clockwork in early Pink Floyd is that clockwork tends to be troped with nearly everything in this music. Simply as a stylistic feature, the band shows a strong tendency toward repetitive, mechanical noises often of a clockwork nature. For example, "Flaming" opens with a single cuckoo clock (0:38–0:39) and foregrounds a ratchet sound in the extended "ever so high" sound effects rise. But the song that stands as the most striking example of clockwork in early Pink Floyd is "Bike." In this song the clockwork appears not only in literal forms but also in a general tendency toward motor rhythm and crashing sounds throughout the song. And when the closing montage of literal clockwork arrives, it is very long relative to the rest of the recording. This passage is noteworthy for how it incorporates other sounds that modify the affective implications of the clockwork: footsteps; a crash/explosion; ratchets; bells/chimes/vibraphone; hard-to-identify melodic sounds (perhaps a squeaky, glissing violin); gong; cymbal rolls; and a creepy loop combining a clownish laugh, a duck-like quack, and some other kind of quasi-vocal chatter.

Overall, clockwork and mechanical noises in early Pink Floyd have a striking range of topical and affective associations. They signify not only the expected ideas of passing time and of technology from the recent past but also a range of psychological states. They participate in surprising tropes with the pastoral and also have a complicated relationship with a range of concepts contained within the space topic: exploration, mapping, suspense, abstract theorization, and the mechanical. In this way, clockwork in Pink Floyd can sound simultaneously futuristic and old-fashioned, clinical and emotional, human and inhuman.

Pink Floyd: Typical Instrumental Jam Texture and Dark Affect

While a detailed discussion of space rock will have to wait until the next chapter, there are certain features of early Pink Floyd that will be central to that discussion but that are also more general aspects of the band. Their use of mechanical and clockwork sounds is one example. Another is their tendency toward extended instrumentals based on layering ambient sound effects and exploratory lead lines over a highly repetitive and simple rhythm section. These passages often seem improvised, and while they are most obvious in the space-rock songs, they are found elsewhere as well. Each instrument in these passages tends to stay close to a particular template. The drums are typically space toms, often so sparse as to resemble tympani and frequently using cymbals and gongs to mark important formal divisions. The bass is often restricted to very short, strictly repeated riffs. The organ and other electronic sounds emphasize pads and ambient noises. And there is an overall tendency toward long shapes and slow harmonic rhythm, often with slowly moving scalewise chord progressions. One example of such an instrumental is the relatively brief jam in "Flaming" (1:41–2:16). But the importance of this texture for Pink Floyd is especially evident in the one song entirely based on it: "Pow R. Toc H." Also striking in this regard is "Scarecrow." It is a fairly short song (2:11), but the entire last thirty-five seconds are taken up with this kind of instrumental texture.

This typical texture of extended Pink Floyd instrumentals is important not only because it is a template for space rock but also because it underscores the band's tendency to sometimes focus on heavier, darker affects. Sometimes this dark tone manifests itself in passages resembling garage rock, as, for example, in much of "Lucifer Sam." At other times it appears in passages of disturbing sound effects, like the clockwork montage at the end of "Bike" and the opening of "Flaming." At other times, it involves elements that in retrospect anticipate heavy metal, for example, the long, descending vocal lines in "Astronomy Domine," the long descent of the main theme in "Interstellar Overdrive," and the relentless motor rhythms of "Bike." These moments of darker affect are important not only for their ubiquity but also because of how in the band's overall style they are troped with moments of childlike wonder and gentle pastoralism. Pink Floyd was unparalleled in their ability to juxtapose the psychotic and the bucolic sides of psychedelia and would often do so in the same song. Especially striking examples include "Matilda Mother," "The Gnome," and "Bike." In order to conclude our discussion of early Pink Floyd, I will present an extended topical reading of one of these multilayered songs: "Matilda Mother."

Pink Floyd: "Matilda Mother" Detailed Reading

- The introduction (0:00–0:09) is based around a single downward scale (B–A–G–F♯) over a drone. The organ sounds somewhat like a pipe organ. The bass and high guitar notes are somewhat like chimes.
- In the A section (0:09–0:26) the accompaniment and lead vocal are still based on the scale and drone from the introduction, now repeated. The guitar arpeggios are a bit like harps and a bit like twinkling stars. The lyrics are like a scene setting at the start of a fairy tale. Overall, the A section is a narrative introduction not only in the lyrics but also in the mood and vamping structure.
- In the B section / vocal transition (0:26–0:36) backing vocals in block harmony are introduced, supporting the modulation and sounding a little like dream voices. Also, the full drum kit enters for the first time. The modulation itself is ambiguous: this section builds up to an E triad, but then the next section is more in F♯ minor than in A. Overall there is quite a bit more motion than before and a generally theatrical feeling. These changes come alongside a lyrical change of perspective—

from an omniscient narrator to a child who is hearing the story told by his or her mother.
- The C section (0:36–0:52) opens with an "Erlkönig"-like riff in both the vocals and guitar (F♯–G–A–B–A–G–F♯, played twice), followed by a high B major triad in the backing vocals. The riff is also evocative of spy/surf styles. The splashy vocal chord is bright and dramatic, especially with the sudden registral height it introduces. The same could be said for the high G in the vocals at the end of the section, which serves as part of the modulation back to B minor and is a semitone above the previously prevailing F♯. There is then a different spy-like guitar riff to introduce a modulation at the end of the section (twangy, emphasizing a decorated F♯–F–E motion with a power chord E + B + E at the end). Lyrically, the tone shifts considerably in this section, with images of uncertainty and abandonment ("Why'd you have to leave me there / hanging in my infant air / waiting?").
- At 0:52–1:08 there is basically a repetition of the first A section but with more density and drive (e.g., there is now a full drum kit groove that was not present in the first A section).
- This B section / vocal transition (1:08–1:24) is also essentially a repeat, except this time it builds to a structural pause on the last held vocal chord to set up the organ solo.
- The organ solo (1:24–1:55) is a good example of the Pink Floyd jam style described earlier. Features fitting that profile include the repeated whispery vocal cell (chhh-poww); the bass and rhythm guitar, which are quite strict in their repetition of short, simple riffs based on an F♯ + C♯ dyad; and the drums, which use only toms and cymbals. The organ solo is very Orientalist. It meanders up and down a scale whose exact gamut seems ambiguous or shifting but is consistently major with a flat second and frequent chromatic inflections. There are many arabesques, grace notes, and trills at varying speeds.
- Not much new happens as the song form is repeated, except that it keeps getting louder and denser.
- The outro (2:26–3:01) moves the song into a whole new textural and thematic area. The drums are limited to ride cymbal, mostly motor eighths with occasional sixteenth-triplet decorations. This persistent cymbal is not unlike the time-passing motif and is also evocative of a $^6_8$ pop ballad. The guitar is understated, extemporizing surf-like licks far back in the mix. The bass plays nothing but whole-bar drone notes on E. The vocals are based on a scalar up-down cell, at first G♯–A–B–A–G♯, then transposed up a third and thickened with thirds (B + D to C♯ + E to D + F♯ to C♯ + E to B + D). These are dream voices in terms of timbre and staging. The organ meanders in a manner similar to its earlier solo but does not sound nearly as Oriental, since the mode is now Mixolydian (without chromaticism), and the ornamentation is much more limited. The overall time feel is both regular—because of the bass, drums, and vocals—and a little unmoored—because of the impromptu sound of the organ and guitar, and because the bass and drums are so regular as to emphasize pulse over meter.

The introduction and the A section clearly evoke topics of childhood and fairy tales. But how much of this is the result of musical signifiers, and how much is lyrical? Certainly there are a number of sounds that could be heard as diegetic to childhood stories, such as pipe organ, tinkling bells, a general affect of drifting, and clockwork-like elements. Many of these elements overlap with signifiers of the space topic, although in this particular case there isn't enough to suggest a full trope.

The transitional B section creates a strong feeling of increased movement, but there is nothing topically specific about it. It does, however, indirectly create a topical effect by dissolving the earlier fairy-tale and space reference points, preparing the way for something else to happen. This potential is realized in the C section, with the Gothic and adventure associations of the main riff and the theatrical and operatic associations of the backing vocals. This is a very clear topical change of state from the opening. By juxtaposing the more comforting, dreamlike fairy tale of the opening with this more Gothic moment, the song depicts varying psychological states within its protagonist. This is an especially narrative way to enact the typical Pink Floyd juxtaposition of contrasting moods.

With this topical narrative in mind, the organ solo has some interesting implications. I've emphasized in several places how, in space-rock solos, it is common to find styles of performance that are clearly related to Orientalist clichés but are not exactly Orientalist. However, in the case of this organ solo there is clear Orientalism. This solo shows how the space and Orientalist topics can overlap in terms of both typical signifiers and affect. As part of the broader topical structure of the song, this Oriental/space trope moves the narrative forward. First there was a magical fairy tale, then there was a darker depiction of childhood psychology, and now the Oriental/space trope takes the song into a dark and spacious landscape that might signify the inner world (a move deeper into the mind) or a more frightening region of the fairy-tale world. The organ solo also, by being the richest section in prototopics of psychedelia and space rock, serves to intensify the feeling that the narrative overall can be heard as an allegory of psychedelic experience.

Finally, the outro adds even more layers both affectively and topically. On one level, it resolves the narrative by moving to a space of relaxation as the tension and negative affect are dissipated into a feeling of stasis and calm. But at the same time, it suggests an openness or a question about the outcome. And like "Chapter 24," this passage tropes space topics with pastoral ones. Overall, "Matilda Mother" is a microcosm of everything that made Pink Floyd stand out in this era. It mobilizes a wide swath of the existing topical field, deploying strongly contrasting elements to enact a psychologically complex narrative. And it pioneers elements that will be central to space rock but in a way that complements rather than abandons earlier styles.

If one metaphor could sum up the wide range of subjects covered in this chapter, it might be *critical mass*. By the period 1967–68, with the advent of psychedelic soul and funk, all of the major elements of the psychedelic topical field were in place. What I mean by this is not that new forms of psychedelia wouldn't arise nor that there wouldn't perhaps be new topics brought into the fold. But as I will argue in the final two chapters, there is a sense in which later developments are best understood relative to psychedelia of the 1960s, as explorations of potentials put in place during that decade. So one thing suggested by the metaphor of critical mass is a certain kind of completeness or self-contained quality. Another implication is that the topical field of psychedelia became somehow unstable due to its own size and high degree of energy. Indeed, one thing this chapter demonstrates is that the metaphor of a single topical field can only be taken so far. By the late 1960s it starts to make more sense to think in terms of overlaps and interconnections between closely related topical fields, all of which are psychedelic in one sense or another.

By applying the metaphor of critical mass in these two different ways, we can become aware of a creative tension in the late 1960s psychedelic situation. On the one hand, the psychedelic field was old enough and rich enough that some musical works began to seem like summations or overviews, with *Sgt. Pepper* being the prime example. It became possible to enact a kind of classicism within psychedelia, a sort of settled comprehensiveness. But at the same time, psychedelia was on the verge of producing new variants like space rock, ambient music, kosmische, Afrofuturist psychedelic funk, and eventually psychedelic electronic dance musics. At the moment of achieving critical mass, one thing you can look at is how dense and developed everything has become. Another thing you can look at is the rapid change that's about to take place.

Notes

1. The idea of blackness being both foundational to and outside of modernity was also broached by others before Weheliye, especially by Paul Gilroy (1993).

2. While the best-known version was the extended single, not released until 1968, the LP version was released in November 1967, and there was an earlier single release in 1966.

3. By "pad" I mean a component of the musical texture dedicated to sustaining background harmonies and ambient textures.

4. Ted Owen and Denise Dickson (1999, 22–26) provide a detailed comparison of selected early San Francisco rock concert posters with similar designs and motifs from Art Nouveau sources.

5. The light shows are especially interesting since they have their origins in multimedia experiments from the earlier 1960s and were subsequently adapted to the rock concert environment. Histories of this process, along with topically suggestive discussions of influences and style, can be found in Bernstein (2008), Martin (2008), Riley (2008), and Pouncey (2005a, 2005b).

6. Almost all of the Greco-Roman iconography in these posters came from one artist, Bonnie MacLean. But that does not lessen its impact as a topical element in the visual environment.

7. Note that many of these images are dialogic, which is why the same poster number is sometimes repeated for different interpretations.

8. This segment is commonly referred to both as "drums" and as "drumz." I have chosen to go with the less idiosyncratic spelling, although the other spelling does have the virtue of specificity.

9. This album track has circulated in various versions over the years. See appendix A for specific information about the version used here and also about the other recordings analyzed in this discussion.

10. This point is also made by Oliver Lovesey (2011, 128).

11. It is difficult to hear definitively if this figure is played by the swarmandal, the piano, or both.

12. I call these *moments* rather than *signifiers* because many of them mobilize more than one signifier at a time. The relevant signifiers collectively make a moment.

13. WLH1 is simply a continuation of the crowd noises from the end of the previous track.

14. The Mellotron and closely related instruments like the Chamberlin had similar potentials as the organ and were used in similar ways, for example, in "2000 Light Years from Home" by the Rolling Stones (1967), where classical and space topics are troped in the Mellotron part.

4 The 1970s

At the end of the last chapter, I used the metaphor of critical mass to sum up psychedelia in the late 1960s. One attractive thing about that metaphor is that it highlighted the transitional nature of the period, signaling that profound changes were about to take place. But the metaphor is also potentially misleading in at least two ways. First, it implies that the changes were going to happen very suddenly, when in fact most of the crucial transformations unfolded over the first half of the 1970s. Second, it implies that the changes were going to be cataclysmic, with the old order suddenly swept aside. But in fact, new forms of psychedelia were increasingly marked by historical reflexivity and by incremental changes to existing styles. So on balance, in this chapter I am going to treat the 1970s as a transitional decade, well past the first phase of psychedelia but before the appearance of self-consciously revivalist rock bands and new electronic dance musics of the 1980s. And unlike the extremely wide scope of the last two chapters, this one will focus on only two styles, both offshoots of those we have already discussed but also both distinctive enough to have moved psychedelic topicality in new directions: space rock and Afrofuturist psychedelic funk.

Space Rock

We have already made extensive reference to space topicality in the previous chapters, so much so that if space rock had never evolved as a distinct genre, we would not need to go into any more detail on this topical area. However, by the late 1960s space rock had emerged as a distinct category, suggesting that the space topic is of special importance and could use some further unpacking both in order to understand space rock itself and in order to add further layers to our reading of space as a topical subfield of psychedelia. In the late 1960s and early 1970s it was common for psychedelic countercultures to be portrayed as hostile to technology and to science. From this perspective, space rock would need to be seen as only superficially connected to actual space exploration and to its associated scientific and engineering communities.

However, this Luddite narrative greatly oversimplifies the links between the counterculture and broader applications of technology. As Charles Perry notes, "[In the Haight] there was widespread interest in the nature and meaning of technology. This was a new subject without clear antecedents in former bohemias, and the most distinctive non-drug concern of the Haight" (1984, 261). This interest derived in part from the idea that technology would free us from work and would usher in a new stage of social and spiritual evolution. But Perry (261–62) also feels that there was a more general interest in design stemming from continuing influence of the Bauhaus school and also from a heightened awareness of environment fostered by psychedelics. For example, Buckminster Fuller had a considerable degree of influence on the hippie worldview, as did Marshall McLuhan. All these perspectives engaged questions of environment and human potential, but with a positive or at least curious attitude toward the possibilities of technology. So it is not surprising, for example, that 1960s countercultural thought intersected strongly with computer culture in the 1970s and afterward, especially with the vision of computers as a framework for the augmentation of human intellect (see Markoff 2005; Turner 2008; Kirk 2002). These developments are also closely related to a general interest in tools for alternative living, as spearheaded by Stewart Brand. None of this is to deny that hippie ideology sometimes also played host to a Luddite strain. However, when thinking about concepts of space that would have gained relevance within rock culture, it is important to recognize that they would have been rooted not only in popular culture (comics and science fiction) but also in more pragmatic and technical articulations of science. If we see these connections from the outset, it will help us understand continuities with cybercultural variants of space rock and psychedelic funk that arose in the 1980s and 1990s.

The space topic in rock overlaps with many other topical areas and style traits. One of the most significant is its overlap with electronic music. This comes about partly because of how electronic sound was already used in science fiction soundtracks, radiophonics, and novelty singles of the 1950s and early 1960s and also more generally because space topics and electronic music share a common connection to technology. So in a broad sense, we could view early electronic-rock crossovers as precursors to space rock. This crossover became prevalent at least as early as 1966, with music from Frank Zappa and the Beatles, but has roots much earlier in experimental pop records such as Joe Meek's production of "Telstar" for the Tornados (1962) and even earlier pop music featuring instruments such as the Theremin and the Chamberlin. But in the case of mid-1960s rock artists such as the Beatles and Frank Zappa, a crucial new element was the way their electronic experiments were framed by an awareness of the classical avant-garde. This three-way meeting between psychedelic rock, electronic music, and classical avant-garde sensibilities was perhaps most fully explored by the United States of America (Holm-Hudson 2002). In the case of all these artists, there was a notable stance of intellectualism in place. However, and significantly for the development of space rock, there were also artists who combined electronic sound with a more raw garage-psychedelic aesthetic. The most notable of these was the *Cauldron* album by Fifty Foot Hose, released at the very end of 1967.

Aside from overtly electronic precursors, there were other traits in early psychedelic music that would emerge as cornerstones of space rock. These include the cultivation of long instrumentals and structures in which a static approach to harmony is combined with an emphasis on short, simple, repeated cells in the rhythm section. These kinds of textures were often used by psychedelic bands to create long, intensive arcs and a mood of dramatic portent, for example, in "White Rabbit." Apart from individual songs, there were certain bands that became associated with these sorts of extended sonic journeys, showing many traits of space rock without much or any overt interest in space topicality as such. Examples would include the Doors and the Velvet Underground. In the case of the Velvet Underground, it is also significant that they combined their avant-garde leanings with a protopunk roughness and minimalism.

I am calling all of these "precursors to space rock," rather than "early space rock proper," because none of them generally made overt reference to space topicality. But it could also be fruitful to read them as enacting space topics in a more covert way—as a kind of subliminal trope beneath the more obvious characteristics. And this would have the advantage of creating a continuum: from early and very subtle space topicality, to individual songs that clearly mobilize a space topic but that predate space rock as a genre, to the establishment of space rock as a relatively autonomous genre. With that continuum in mind, we can recall "Section 43," discussed in chapter 2, as maybe the earliest example of a recording with clear space topicality made by a band that was otherwise not particularly space oriented. To dig further into that important transitional phase, let's look closely at some songs from 1967 that are space-rock songs in advance of the space-rock genre.[1]

Space Rock: Pink Floyd, "Astronomy Domine"

We can now complete our picture of early Pink Floyd by considering them as one of the most important early space-rock bands. The two songs that most strongly linked early Pink Floyd to space topicality were "Astronomy Domine" and "Interstellar Overdrive." I'll give a detailed description of the first and shorter remarks about the second. As usual for major examples, a detailed description comes first, and then there is a topical overview.

PINK FLOYD, "ASTRONOMY DOMINE" (1967)

- Part 1 of the introduction (0:00–0:11) includes overlapping radio/megaphone voices.
- Part 2 of the introduction (0:11–0:31) includes a guitar drone/pulse, but with no clear meter. Morse code also enters (0:23 to the beginning of the A section). The section ends with a long, languid drum fill.
- In part 3 of the introduction (0:31–0:44) the guitar is spy-like in timbre and voicings: a low G–G♯ single-note bend leading to a sting featuring an E-major triad quickly transitioning to E minor with a major seventh and sharp 11 (in tablature, with the lowest string first, that would just be the move 0221xx to 011000, with the simple first-position fingering adding greatly to the percussive ringing quality).
- In the A section (0:44–1:19) the vocals are chant-like but with slightly changing harmonic and timbral colors. At first they are harmonized in thirds, but then they change to fourths for "Jupiter and Saturn, Oberon Miranda and Titania." The

change to fourths in the voices is achieved by moving the higher voice up stepwise, which creates greater harmonic tension (since the upper voice is now an added sixth, rather than a fifth, relative to the prevailing harmony) and also creates a subtle lift in the tessitura. The drums, here and throughout, are a good example of space-toms: constant, slightly varied pulsing and rolls, with continuous motor eighth notes as the basic grid, plus occasional cymbal crashes. The chord changes are largely stepwise and chromatic: E–E♭–G–G♯–A. Overall, there is nothing to strongly establish either E or A as the tonic.

- The B section (1:19–1:31) introduces one of the most characteristic figures of the piece: a long, descending scale (chromatic from E to A on dotted quarters) with falsetto vocals and doubled by guitar and bass.
- The transition takes place between 1:31 and 1:55. There is a dramatic structural pause at the end of the transition (1:37–1:40), preceded by a brief burst of white noise, evoking wind or a spaceship. This same effect comes in much more strongly during the vocal reprise after the instrumental (3:22–3:24). There is a prominent organ cue after the structural pause, heading into the solo (1:40–1:42). This cue evokes conventional signs of mystery, melodrama, and B movies because of its timbre and its ambiguous quartal voicing (A + D♯ + G♯ in the context of E-oriented material). The transition into the instrumental (1:43–1:55) is marked by an unmeasured and only loosely pitched electronic pad and an electronic ping followed by a regular but nonmetric pulse, initially created with a tape delay and joined by guitar and bass from 1:48.
- Perhaps the most important feature of the instrumental (1:55–3:15) is its length, combined with the way it is clearly staged on multiple levels as a space trip. The basic metrical and rhythmic feeling is a continuous stream of motor eighth pulses, which are passed around between instruments. These motor eighths are especially regular in the bass and are punctuated with frequent tom fills. There is a constant and always-changing backdrop of pads and electronic effects, dominated by long chords from the organ. The first lead guitar figure glisses up and down an open fifth, strongly evoking topics of the epic, but this is soon troped with blues-surf elements (1:55–2:01). These opening gestures are the only ones in which the guitar has a clear lead or solo function. For the rest of the instrumental, the guitar explores a shifting ground between relatively nondirected lead-guitar figures and elaborated riffs. Gradually throughout the instrumental the dense background sound effects get louder and begin to dominate the texture. Highlights here include a return of the overlapping radio voices (from 2:43) and a very complex wind or spaceship sound that might be the result of heavy modulation of one or more other components of the mix. This sound fades in gradually but is very clearly audible from 3:00.
- During the vocal transition (3:15–3:30) the vocals return, with a highlight being the loud whisper on "pow" (3:21). There is also a return of the white noise burst from the first transition (3:22–3:24), now louder and more like steam.
- This B section (3:30–3:41) is essentially the same as the first time.
- In this A' section (3:41–4:12) the most striking change from the earlier A section is the vocals, which are now entirely in repeated notes: drone A for the first four measures, then dyad A + D for the final four measures. The vocals are also rhythmically simplified relative to the first A section, abandoning the earlier lilting rhythm for motor rhythm on the fundamental pulse (dotted quarter notes). Note how the vocal pitch rise this time is achieved through thickening rather than

any sense of melodic or harmonic movement. The overall effect of these vocals is something like the time-passing motif and even more like epic tympani. The thickening/rising effect is also not unlike a pastoral sunrise topic.

In the narrowest sense, space topicality in this song is established by the lyrics and by some musical features we have already identified with space: motor rhythm (sometimes so extensive as to replace meter with a sense of pure duration); highly repetitive and simple rhythm section figures; a tendency toward either static harmony or linear stepwise chord progressions; and many ambient sound effects, often of an electronic nature. This space topicality is troped with various other topics, including spy and surf, melodramatic theater organ, and especially the epic. These tropes instill a sense of adventure and journeying, as well as tension and danger. Many of the specific signifiers not only evoke space but are also conventional signs for precarious or heightened psychological states, for example, the long, descending scale figure; the variously distorted voices; and the epic fanfare elements. Returning to our earlier association of Pink Floyd with darker affects, this song is dark like both inner and outer space. It is also notably electronic without being particularly avant-garde. And, as we will see, all of these features are typical of early space rock.

There are a few particular signifiers that deserve special attention because of their interesting nuances in this song, which anticipate their general place in space rock overall. First, we should consider the drone-like features. In chapter 2 we saw that drones traditionally signify not only spiritual and Orientalist topics but also folkloric and pastoral ones. In space rock we generally find a break from the folkloric aspect and a profound shift in the pastoral associations. On the one hand, drones continue to signify topographical aspects of the space topic: the vast, uninflected expanse of space itself or the vistas of alien worlds. These are landscapes of a sort, but no longer with any strong folkloric associations. However, there is at the same time a sense in which these spacescapes distill an element that was always present in the pastoral: the sublime, indifferent expanse of timeless nature. In many of the Pink Floyd songs discussed earlier, we noted a space/pastoral trope that draws precisely on this zone of overlap. What is happening in more explicitly space-rock songs like "Astronomy Domine" and "Interstellar Overdrive" is that the pastoral trope is rendered at its most implicit, and arguably absent, because there are no longer any overt terrestrial or folkloric reference points. But even so, there are some indirect pastoral holdovers. One of the most important is that many space-rock songs employ some kind of "space-wind" sound effect. This often doubles as UFO noises and could be heard exclusively as interstellar wind or the wind of alien worlds. But it could also be heard as a vague echo of the pastoral. Similarly, in "Astronomy Domine" the vocal doubling at the end of the song, with its thickening and rising effect, can easily be heard as "dawning," whether it is dawn over this planet or another. Maybe the best way to summarize this topical substitution is to recall the point made when we first discussed cinematic topics: the indexicality of a topic can in some cases be to a virtual world rather than to the literal physical world. In the case of space-rock drones, the Terran pastoral has been replaced with a virtual pastoral based on representations of alien worlds.

Morse Code

The last topical sound to discuss in "Astronomy Domine" is one we've already encountered in "Strawberry Fields Forever": the Morse code topic. I want to consider Morse code in detail and in connection with the closely related family of radiophonic sounds. By *radiophonic* I mean in part the sounds and contexts of early radio and telegraphic communications. Along with these, the word also evokes the sound world of the BBC Radiophonic Workshop and of similar sound-effects services, with their profound influence on science fiction topicality. Like many radiophonic sounds, Morse code was connected to a variety of specific contexts and so can be topical in various ways. Common evocations of Morse code include telegraphy, railways, shipping, aviation, and warfare, all in both modernistic and slightly archaic modes. It can also evoke the future and space, given that Morse-like signals were common in early science fiction soundtracks and are also literally employed by some space technologies. Through this wide range of topical associations, Morse code has also come to be associated with a complex range of affects. Philip Tagg has described many of these: "It is conceivable that morse signal and teleprinter rhythms may have undergone a transfer of meaning through their constant use in situations of urgency . . . so that this general feeling and atmosphere of 'important announcement' and 'urgent message' will be the affective content of such musemes rather than the sonic object itself or the cognitive message being transmitted via the object. In other words, it is neither the actual telegraphing nor teleprinting that is represented . . . but the mood of urgency and importance" (2000b, 236).

Related to the connotation of urgency, Tagg and Bob Clarida note how Morse/teletype rhythms resemble a verbal stammer: "We are in no way suggesting that Morse code rhythms *derive* from stammering but rather that the irregular hurry of those telegraphic rhythms and the nervous sense of urgency they are demonstrably presumed to communicate is affectively very similar to the sort of nervous state we all get into when too many important things are happening around us, when there is too much to say, when we get tongue tied and the words come out all wrong" (2003, 489).[2]

To all of this we can add the various cool affects associated with Morse code: a feeling of distance (both spatial and temporal) and of mechanical consciousness. So Morse code qualifies as a topic in terms of its indexicality and is a potentially useful topic because of its affective and referential richness. It also qualifies as a topic because Morse code and telegraphic sounds became highly stylized in their musical signifiers, especially as the actual sounds faded from daily life: "Morse code and Morse code figures in music both feature one-pitch patterns whose internal sound events are presented in alternatingly rapid . . . or very rapid succession. . . . It is in this sense that the musical device can be regarded as a sonic anaphone of telegraphic rhythms" (Tagg and Clarida 2003, 488). The sonic anaphone (roughly, Tagg's term for an icon) functions even without literally being a message in Morse. It doesn't matter from a topical point of view what the code might mean or even if it is really Morse code at all. Although, that being said, trying to decode Morse code snippets in rock songs became a popular theme in fan discussions. And this practice plays into a general psychedelic attraction to puzzles and things that *might* be coded messages, such as hard-to-read lettering, rustling and noisy textures that might contain voices, backward masking, and reversed voices in general.

Tagg's remarks bear on topicality because they involve conventionalization. And in topical terms, this sort of conventionalization is often accompanied by a removal from original context and the passage from one era to another. The late 1960s was a time when Morse code was beginning to fade from everyday life, becoming conventionalized and abstracted as it gradually became archaic. So in order to properly interpret psychedelic Morse code snippets, it is important to ask: How archaic *was* Morse code circa 1967? I suggest that it was in a transitional phase: still able to signify futuristic technology, but at the same time evocative of older telegraphy and of radiophonic-intensive historical moments such as the world wars. The same was true for related sounds such as radio-tuning noises and Theremins, and we could also recall points made in the last chapter about Pink Floyd's clockwork, which sounds at once futuristic and old-fashioned.

This brings us to a larger point, which is that early space rock would often mix futuristic, cutting-edge imagery with historical reflexivity and a sense of the archaic. In the case of Morse code and other radiophonic noises, the dialogic potential is built into the individual sounds. In other cases, the effect is achieved by troping futuristic signifiers with topics such as the epic, western, or spy. And in a looser sense, this duality resonates with the continuing garage rock aesthetic in much early space rock, which tends to attenuate the intellectualist and avant-garde aspect of the electronic elements.

Another important nuance of Morse code and radiophonic noises, one that links them to the pastoral, is that they evoke soundscapes and environments, always having something of a diegetic flavor. They are one of the ways that space rock is spatial, evoking topographic scenarios both literal and imaginary, inner and outer. This topographic tendency of space rock applies not only to the signifieds but also to the signifiers, which often rely on spatializing production effects such as echo and reverberation. In this connection, we can make a lateral connection to Jamaican dub music, which emerged at roughly the same time and which would be explicitly fused with space rock in the 1980s. Michael Veal describes the important similarities:

> [Dub] music actually implies several re-visionings of the concept of space. Dub's sonic effects, somewhat similar to what could be heard contemporaneously in the soundtracks of science fiction film, evoke the dark expanse of outer space. The oft-mentioned meditative quality of the music, on the other hand, resonates with a listener's internal space. The Africa-inspired rhythm structures evoke a mood of historical space.... Even the physical concept of space is relevant here: dub's spatialized songscapes, heard at the extreme volumes of the Jamaican sound system,

simulated an actual physical space within which the "roots" African past and the utopian sci-fi future could be fleetingly experienced as one. (2007, 213)

We will return to these space-related tropes shortly when we discuss Afrofuturist psychedelic funk. But for now I'd like to look at one of the more self-consciously British radiophonic songs: "I Am the Walrus." A great deal could be said about this recording, but I'm interested here in its use of radiophonic sound to portray different kinds of diegetic situatedness.

THE BEATLES, "I AM THE WALRUS" (1967)

- The song presents a mix that layers many different kinds of voices, often densely, although only at the end does it become multiple speaker blur. For the present discussion, the most important vocal elements are the found-audio excerpts from a radio broadcast of *King Lear*, which Walter Everett (1999, 134) suggests might indicate some influence on John Lennon from Yoko Ono and John Cage.
- There is a major discontinuity in the texture at 2:00, just before the slow string interlude. At this point the sound effects suggest several topical signifiers. The texture is very dense, but at a minimum there are elements strongly resembling an alarm clock, a backward half-singing voice, a radio announcer's voice, and a radio tuning shriek.
- Right after that passage, a string theme enters that is similar enough to the opening theme that it feels like an echo or continuation. But because of the equalization and the way the theme is immediately preceded by a dense layering of radiophonic sounds, these strings feel more like an evocation of radio music than do the earlier ones (a hearing that also fits with the "sitting in an English garden" lyric).
- During the very long registral expansion (about the last fifty seconds of the song), with the strings continually rising and the bass continually falling, the radio tuning noises become almost continuous, and the voices finally become multiple speaker blur.

There is no Morse code in this song, but there is a striking use of radiophonic sound to suggest different spatialities (the production space of radio, the theater, the English garden, and a psychological inner space). There is also a mixing of present-moment urgency with a sense of distances both spatial and temporal. Overall, this combines topics of Englishness with affects of both estrangement and transcendence and demonstrates some of the topical nuances possible with radiophonic sounds.

Space Rock: Jimi Hendrix, "Third Stone from the Sun"

While space topics are not the most commonly evoked in discussions of Jimi Hendrix, they formed a consistent if secondary part of his style. Examples of Hendrix songs with clear space themes and sound effects include "EXP" and "Third Stone from the Sun," both released in 1967. I would also include "1983 . . . (a Merman I Should Turn to Be)" from 1968, because while it is not overtly a space-rock song, we saw earlier how nautical topics and space topics were often closely related, and it is certainly a science fiction song, as well as one that powerfully evokes an alien world. If we allow all of these as space-rock songs, then there is exactly one representative on each of his first three albums: enough to make space and science fiction important secondary themes for Hendrix, but not to make them dominant. Another interesting thing about Hendrix's science fiction and space-rock songs is that they are fairly diverse in style. We would not be able to take them collectively as a model for later space rock. But there is one track in particular that does closely resemble later space-rock norms and was likely influential in putting these into place.

JIMI HENDRIX, "THIRD STONEZ FROM THE SUN" (1967)

- In part 1 of the introduction (0:00–0:34) the bass line is a strictly repeated motor rhythm cell with ambiguous harmonic implications (E–D–A–D), similar to a drone but more open-ended (not unlike a modal jazz riff). The guitar plays long atmospheric chords with a somewhat jazz-like sound (they could be spelled Em6–Bm7, but the overall context doesn't provide sufficient cues to fully determine function). There are dropped-pitch spoken vocals that will come and go sporadically throughout the entire piece. The drums here and throughout have a swing feel. They propel the groove largely with the ride cymbal and use many fills, rolls, bombs, and so on to shape the texture and to mark important points in the form.
- In the main theme (0:42–1:20) the bass settles into a new motor rhythm cell, which is repeated quite strictly for a long time (E–E–E–E–E–F♯–E–G♯–B–B–B–B–B–C♯–B). The theme itself presents a leisurely decorated scalar fall from G♯ to B, followed by a slightly more rapid rise to E. This could be seen as a slow-motion turn figure. The floating feeling of this theme is enhanced by the repeated use of quarter-note triplets. There is also frequent use of wide, slow, whammy bar modulation on long notes, which creates a trill that could be linked to the siren trill. The use of octave doubling on the guitar evokes various things, especially the style of Wes Montgomery. Finally, there are very quiet feedback/whammy glisses in the background that foreshadow the much louder space-wind noises that become common later.
- The guitar solo (1:29–1:38) starts out as a typical Jimi Hendrix fuzz solo, but that only lasts a few measures.
- Now a vocal spoken narrative overrides the guitar solo (1:38–1:54). The focus of the mix shifts with the entrance of the most intelligible voice yet, and the guitar retreats somewhat. The first clear-cut entry of space-wind noise is at 1:48.
- There is a reprise of the main theme (1:54–2:11), this time with much louder space-wind noises. The theme is only played once this time.
- Now the sound effects override the theme (2:11–2:27). Although a repeat of the theme might be expected here, there's just a rhythm section with some feedback wash guitar (subtle, but getting louder), space wind, and very quiet vocal sounds. In general, the mix is gradually being taken over by looping riffs and ambient sounds.
- This is the beginning of a long space jam (2:31–3:05). The bass sticks to a very strict and short two-beat riff (an E quarter note followed by B–D eighths). There is a dense layering of obscure voices and space-wind noises, nearly continuous and with constant variations and transformations. The guitar almost exclusively plays extended-technique ambient noises. The drums continue to hold down a swing feel,

with many breaks and fills that blur the metrical groupings and downbeats in a bebop-like manner.
- Lead guitar noise textures (3:05–4:11) continue as described above, with more emphasis on extended-technique ambient guitar noises.
- The vocal spoken narrative returns (4:11–4:40). The voice is quite intelligible here, especially as contrasted with the extended noise passage that has preceded it.
- The texture continues, now with pitch-dropped voice (4:40–4:55). This is the most pitch-dropped and processed voice in the entire piece.
- The texture continues, with the guitar back in the foreground (4:55–5:12).
- The main theme returns over a continuing new vamp (5:12–6:06), with more fuzz on the guitar than in earlier theme statements and also with octave doubling. The extra fuzz allows the whammy trills on long notes to become even more featured, often morphing into feedback. The bass and ambient noises continue as in the preceding jam, so there is a blurring of the main theme's structured character with the space jam's openness.
- The outro is a mostly pulseless noise passage (6:06–6:43), with no rhythm section. Much of it uses the same guitar noises as before, but there is also a mechanical/woody tape loop that enters at 6:11. This could be characterized as construction-like or train-like, and it also resembles clockwork. Some of the very high feedback squeals at the end sound a bit like radio tuning noises.

The first thing to note about this piece is that, compared to all of the other examples we've seen, it is the most uncompromising in its presentation of space-specific elements. It is an instrumental rather than a song and is quite long. It is even more minimal than early Pink Floyd. And it is the most consistent in sticking to a texture of ambient sound effects layered over repetitive rhythm figures. It is also the first to adopt a frankly nonhuman point of view. The voice is difficult to understand, but the few phrases that come through are clearly from the perspective of an alien ("your people I do not understand") in a prophetic and oracular mood ("you will never hear surf music again"). Sonically, the alien quality of the voice is enhanced by equalization, which makes it sound radiophonic, like a transmission from far away. And as with many other space-rock performances, there is a nod to the old-fashioned in the train-like wooden sound effect at the very end. These are all elements that we have seen in other examples, but this recording is the most consistent in highlighting features that would be typical of space rock and removing almost all other reference points.

The one topical complication in this picture comes from the jazz elements, many of which resemble the epic jazz of later John Coltrane projects (especially the long, hanging chords and the slowly unfolding diatonic theme). This overlap between jazz and space rock is not unusual. For example, we have already noted similar elements in "Section 43" and "Eight Miles High." And in a more general sense, there were parallels between the approaches to group improvisation taken in space rock and in certain kinds of jazz (modal and free). The difference, to return to arguments made in connection with psychedelic soul, is that Hendrix's blackness would have been marked in this context and would likely for many listeners have made the jazz elements seem more pronounced and direct. In a broader frame, Hendrix tended to link space and science fiction topics to a more general ideology of spiritual enlightenment and aesthetic freedom, and this made him in some respects an important early Afrofuturist, albeit one with an ambivalent and often reluctant relationship to racial politics. Given that Hendrix himself generally avoided using racial frameworks to situate his music, I wouldn't want to push this point too far. But since Afrofuturism will shortly emerge as a central theme in psychedelic funk, we cannot overlook this aspect of Hendrix's space rock, because it is here that we see some of the most developed early fusions of space topics with jazz and soul.

Space Rock: Further Developments

The creation of space rock as a distinct genre largely had to do with the exaggeration of some elements along with the attenuation of others. Some of the attenuations are explicitly topical and involve minimizing reference to anything too strongly or literally terrestrial, human, and social/historical. So the troping of space topics with those of Orientalism, spy and surf, and folk music all became less common than they had been in earlier psychedelic space performances. Along with this came formal changes that largely hinged on degrees and kinds of stasis. Paul Hegarty has argued that in space rock and jam-based rock styles more generally, "movement continually alternates with stasis, or is caught up with it" (2007, 63). This impulse toward stasis and repetition was present in earlier psychedelic rock when it evoked space topics, but in this earlier music the stasis was usually balanced by other features. When space rock emerged as a relatively autonomous genre, the static and repetitive quality was one of the main things that became exaggerated. One dramatic way to see these changes is to compare later Pink Floyd to the Syd Barrett–era Pink Floyd. Consider, for example, "Set the Controls for the Heart of the Sun."

PINK FLOYD, "SET THE CONTROLS FOR THE HEART OF THE SUN" (1968)

- At 5:27 seconds long, the song is largely static. There is one main motif, which serves both as riff and as principal vocal theme. This riff/theme also appears in transposition, and in addition there is a shorter second theme.
- The first theme is essentially an extended turn, and the second is essentially a single leap followed by a short, descending scale.
- The texture is very consistent throughout. The bass is minimal and repetitive, doubling the main theme. The drums emphasize slow space toms and tympani. There is a continually shifting wash of ambient sound, with special emphasis on the organ, vibraphone, cymbals, and gongs. And there is a great deal of echo and reverberation.
- For a long segment of the instrumental, following the second verse, there is a whispering spoken voice rhythmically repeating "the heart of the sun."

All of these elements were present in the first Pink Floyd album as well, so the main thing is how this song represents a distillation of certain elements and a removal of others, which collectively shifts the signification firmly toward space. One word that could span many of these changes is *ambient*. And indeed, when various genres began to be called ambient in the mid-1970s and later, they were often relatives of space rock to one degree or another. One interesting example from the late 1960s is Donovan's "Atlantis" (1968), mainly in its overall approach to form and in the piano theme. The form is based on many repetitions of a simple folk-pop chord progression, with the extended time-scale allowing for a gradual buildup of density, leading ultimately to an epic chorus. This is not unlike later Pink Floyd in the general formal approach and in the basic flavor of the musical materials. Similarly, the A section piano line is cinematic and ambient, first entering very quietly at 0:30 and then building over a long time (e.g., it begins to be doubled at the upper octave starting at 1:03). This piano theme is spacious and slow-moving, like some of the space-rock themes we have discussed. The song overall shows again how nautical topics and space topics can overlap and how they can be simplified in a general direction of repetitive ambience. This also points out how ambient techniques spread beyond the psychedelic context, but in a way that kept them cognate with psychedelia: "Ambient music should be considered a descendent of psychedelia because it shared three of its defining attributes. First, it is spatial music: Brian Eno developed echo and reverb in order to create an imaginary 'psycho-acoustic space.' . . . Like psychedelic/cosmic rock, ambient is wombing. Second and third, ambient tends to be pastoral and fixated on childhood" (Reynolds and Press 1995, 176–77).

At this point we are looking at a chain of postpsychedelic topicality, from space rock to ambience more generally. Another direction in which the space topic was distilled and troped was toward an even greater focus on technology and mechanism. This trend is especially evident in some German bands of the late 1960s and early 1970s:

> Around 1970, a form of music took off in Germany, with Faust, Can, Neu! and Kraftwerk at its centre. This "kosmische" music aspired, just as psychedelic music, space rock, and a fair amount of 1960s jazz had, to escape the everyday world. The groups cited here are the most well-known, but are also linked through exploration of repetition, stasis and a machinic quality exemplified in the "motorik" beat. . . . Linear beats in bars and the possibility of expressive climaxes are lost, in a "circular" drumming where each beat is both singularity and presence of the whole: in short, little changed, and if it did, it did on glacial time scales compared with either classical or rock expectations. . . . If there is to be exploration in this music, it is not the single-minded adventurer ignoring all else, but part of a system working out its potentials. (Hegarty 2007, 70)

This new style is clearly related to space rock but is not coterminous with it. And like space rock, it grew in part out of psychedelia but is not narrowly psychedelic. I would like to expand a little more on these features by looking at Can's "Father Cannot Yell" (1969).

Music example 4.1 shows the basic texture for much of this song. It is extremely drone oriented and motoric in all instrumental parts. In this texture, the

Music example 4.1. Can, "Father Cannot Yell," introduction (0:00–0:18). Written by Holger Czukay, Michael Karoli, Jaki Liebzeit, Malcom Mooney, and Irmin Schmidt. © Raspe Music Inc. / Better Be Good Music / Spoon Music [GEMA].

balance of movement and stasis is maintained in several ways. For example, the organ presents a sustained drone, but it is animated by tremolo, which creates a sixteenth-note motor rhythm. This is not unlike the technique we saw in earlier space rock, of creating a rhythmic pulse through echo or modulation rather than through retriggering of notes. The bass and guitar are both, in this passage, entirely literal in their repetition of simple cells, and the drums are more varied but still constrained within a strict motor rhythm. While this song is not framed as space rock, it does demonstrate how Can and some other German bands of the time pushed the simplifications and exaggerations of space rock in dramatically extreme directions.

These bands, along with some contemporary space-rock bands, also presented the clearest examples of what I've previously called the developing variation ap-

Music example 4.2. Can, "Father Cannot Yell," A section (beginning) (0:35–0:52). Written by Holger Czukay, Michael Karoli, Jaki Liebzeit, Malcom Mooney, and Irmin Schmidt. © Raspe Music Inc. / Better Be Good Music / Spoon Music [GEMA].

proach to improvisation. This is rooted in the Yardbirds-style rave-up, where short and simple motifs were continually looped and minutely varied so that the improvisational ideas and even the formal structures are marked by continual simple transformation rather than detailed elaboration or sudden contrasts. The main difference is that a developing variation jam as such rarely has the sort of overall direction seen in a rave-up. It is more planar. In the bass line of music example 4.2 we can see a short excerpt of this process. Within the extremely reductive motoric and drone approach, a feeling of constant motion is introduced through a developing variation approach that resembles classical minimalism more than rock jamming. Timbral variations, occasional dissonances, and other enriching elements are constantly introduced and explored, but not in a manner that suggests any definite overall direction. There is not much pretense of song form, but also not an unmeasured noise excursion, since this is a type of formal organization that combines aspects of both form and noise from the outset.

In the case of many German bands of the era, this was all combined with an overt connection to the classical avant-garde, bringing them in some respects closer to the early roots of electronic rock music than to space rock. However, these sorts of textures allowed for an affect of heaviness and menace that also resonated with the garage rock aspect of space rock, and this potential was exploited by some more narrowly space-oriented bands. The best example is Hawk-

Music example 4.3. Hawkwind, "Be Yourself," opening riff (0:03–0:06). Written by David Brock. © EMI Blackwood Music Inc. obo EMI United Partnership Ltd.

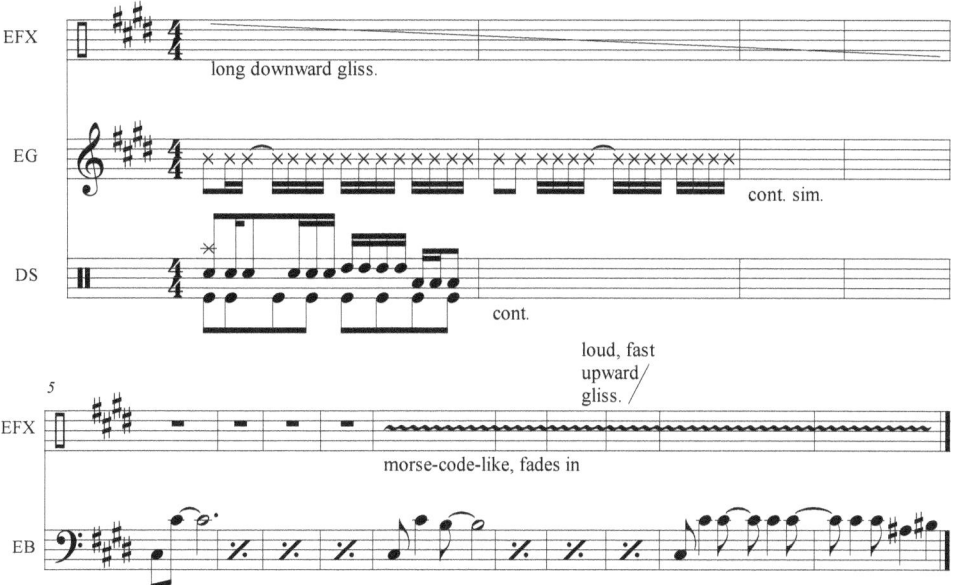

Music example 4.4. Hawkwind, "Be Yourself," space toms (beginning) (1:18–1:45). Written by David Brock. © EMI Blackwood Music Inc. obo EMI United Partnership Ltd.

wind. We can see many of the key features in "Be Yourself" (1970), which employs the minimalist developing variation jam texture to create a dark affect with clear space-rock allegiances. The first riff in "Be Yourself" appears alone for about forty-three seconds (see music example 4.3). Then the voice enters, but only to double this riff, which continues to about 1:17. Then a new pattern is introduced based around toms, a decorated drone bass, and muted rhythm guitar (see music example 4.4). This new pattern is built up gradually and feels complete by about

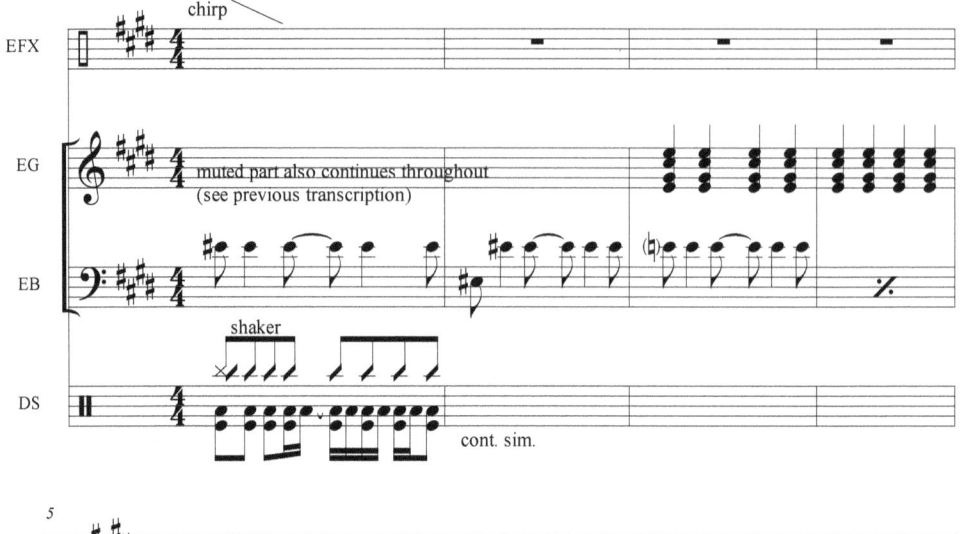

Music example 4.5. Hawkwind, "Be Yourself," new chords (beginning) (5:57–6:11).
Written by David Brock. © EMI Blackwood Music Inc. obo EMI United Partnership Ltd.

1:50. This process of gradually assembling the pattern relies largely on an additive, developing-variation approach in the bass, visible in the second part of music example 4.4. There are also some noteworthy sound effects in this passage, including Morse code, long electronic glisses, and shorter electronic chirps. Then there is a long saxophone solo (fifty-six measures) followed by a guitar solo (fifty-two measures), all based on the same groove and with continual intensive variations. Finally, a new set of chords is introduced at about 5:57: a slow C♯ major-to-minor alternation (see music example 4.5). The change to this chord progression is another example of the developing variation approach, since much of the feel of the previous groove is maintained in the drums and rhythm guitar, with these new elements layered in. After twenty measures of this new texture, there is a structural pause and then a return to riff 1 for the rest of the song.

Songs like "Be Yourself" are striking in the way they stretch a very few simple musical ideas over extremely long time spans. I think it's clear that the droning and temporally extended developing-variation texture has become a prototopic by this point, given the extent to which it has been distilled and isolated. Indeed, it has been foregrounded to such a degree that all of the other topics are subsumed in this glacial and expansive formal approach, which has by now become completely standardized. That being said, there are still traces of earlier space-rock tropes, even if the overall impression is one of extreme homogeneity. For example, jazz is referenced in the saxophone solo. And the epic is evoked in the main riff: regular spaced chords with a gap accompanied by a slow, regular cymbal that sounds a bit like orchestral chimes and a bit like a time-passing motif. There is also an obvious epic reference point in the Zarathustra-like quality of the slow major-minor alternation (music example 4.5). This would stand as an epic topic troped with the prevailing space topic regardless, but its subtle evocation of the soundtrack of *2001: A Space Odyssey* (1968) probably would also have been a factor for many listeners.

Hawkwind is equally a part of psychedelia, space rock, and early heavy metal. In the latter connection, they epitomize one aspect of later space rock: its emphasis on sonic heaviness and a somber, brooding affect. While violence is only one component of this mix, arriving at the end of our space-rock discussion provides a good opportunity for a quick retrospective examination of the relationship between violence and psychedelia more generally. This will help us review a number of previous themes from a new angle and will also set up certain points to be made in later discussions.

Rather than start with outright violence, let's start with control: with the suggestion that control, and the disruption of control, has been a central theme in psychedelia. Among their other effects, psychedelic drugs can destabilize thought and feeling, often weakening self-control and social control. This loss of control was explored by different interested parties in different ways. In the 1950s, for clinical psychiatrists and the CIA, the breakdown of control was studied as a model of psychosis or adopted as a tool for coercion. For humanists such as Aldous Huxley and the psychedelic therapists, loss of control was understood as an opportunity for beneficial personal change. The destabilizing effects of psychedelic drugs could be aestheticized or fetishized as they became widespread with the Merry Pranksters and with psychedelic music and art. These destabilizing effects could also be a tool of social insurrection, as with the Diggers, Yippies, and White Panthers. Control is also a central issue in the class, race, and gender dynamics of psychedelia—for example, the lingering classism of the 1950s salon scene, or the sexism of 1960s radicalism, or the neocolonial entitlement of Goa partiers in the 1990s. I emphasize control not only because it is an important theme in psychedelia but because it is also closely related to violence. Bruce Johnson and Martin Cloonan have made this a central feature in their work on the subject: "The sense of control is central to many negative reactions to music. . . . Much music associated with violence is not in any obvious way physically or aesthetically painful, but its imposition is a matter of power relations" (2008, 24).

The contexts of primary interest to Johnson and Cloonan, where one agent forcibly imposes music on another who does not wish to hear it, are not going to arise in our discussion. However, what Johnson and Cloonan make clear is that any engagement of music with issues of control is on a continuum with the same power relationships as are implicated in more overt acts of violence. Another way to approach this point is through Slavoj Žižek's concept of "objective violence," which is the form of violence enacted in social norms and established institutions. This perspective has been explored in a musical context by Susan Fast and Kip Pegley (2012, especially locs. 111–41). The overarching point is that the manner in which a music symbolizes and enacts aspects of control always has implications for its relationship to violence more generally. In order to build on this perspective and apply it specifically to psychedelia, it is also important to consider the continuum between pain and other forms of discomfort. Outright pain is not foreign to psychedelia but is arguably not central either. However, what is central is something very similar to pain and also closely related to control that I'll call *disturbance*. Disturbance can include pain, but it also includes effects such as disorientation, confusion, and cognitive dissonance. Disturbance is similar to what Johnson and Cloonan call "violation," but in psychedelia the condition is so often self-inflicted, and so often positively or ambiguously valued, that the word "violation" seems to presuppose too much. So without diminishing the importance of pain to the analysis of violence more generally, I'll focus instead on other kinds of disturbance that are equally complicit in violence but are more appropriate to psychedelia as it was often understood by participants.

The period up to the early 1960s is somewhat peripheral for us insofar as no distinctively psychedelic styles of music had yet appeared. Nonetheless, important patterns were set by this early psychedelic culture. What can we say about violence and control in that complicated moment? Perhaps the fundamental thing is what we have already noted: psychedelic drugs introduced profound psychological disturbance. Early psychedelic agendas were all marked by a two-part process: (1) an enthusiasm to explore this disturbance, and (2) a belief that it could be put to the service of some desirable objective. The urge to manage and exploit psychedelic disturbance allowed many existing patterns of domination to persist. For example, the humanistic salon scene was deeply rooted in Orientalism and markedly classist, and it reasserted the discursive authority of academics. Even more obvious were the ways in which CIA research reinscribed the discursive authority of the laboratory scientist, of the state, and of state entitlement to violence. In all of these cases, there are two interrelated moments that are violent in different ways. First, there is the drug-induced disruption itself, which is violent as a kind of deviation from normal psychology. Second, there was a perpetuation of existing hegemonic objective violence when potentially repressive social inequities persisted as a framework for exploring and explaining this disruption.

The most striking change in psychedelic culture and practices in the mid-1960s was the removal of many of these controls and frameworks. In part this was a matter of the breakdown in the 1950s situation as some experimenters abandoned their clinical and academic frameworks. But the change also came about because of shifts in popular culture. The violence of psychedelia at this point became much more a matter of self-infliction, on the one hand, and outright manipulation, on the other. Or, to put it more theoretically, at least on the surface psychedelia's relationship to objective violence shifted from one of subservience to one of critique. As a result, the scope and variety of psychological disturbance increased. Unregulated authority figures began to proliferate, and subcultural participants increasingly exposed themselves to potentially dangerous dosages and situations in an overall atmosphere of marginalization as legal crackdowns intensified. When specifically psychedelic musical styles began to emerge in this context, Anglo-American popular music had a complex relationship to violence. Popular music was employed both in protest against state-sanctioned violence and as a tool of countercultural violence. The place of psychedelia in this picture is especially interesting because of how it was associated in some instances with powerful disruption, while in other cases, and sometimes simultaneously, it was aligned with sentiments of love, pacifism, and enlightenment. Also, it must be noted that as a component of the broader social fabric, psychedelic musics and countercultures could not help but reproduce certain forms of objective violence. Their biases in terms of gender and race, for example, are well known.

In what ways did the new psychedelic music represent or participate in more violent aspects of this situation? In some ways, it served as a potentially oppressive physical force in exactly the manner highlighted by Johnson and Cloonan when they speak of music as a sonic weapon. For example, increasingly high volume levels, especially in combination with potentially harmful visual stimuli such as strobe lights, provided an acoustic icon of the intensity of an acid trip, which could lead to pain or even permanent physical damage for some. But more significant to psychedelic style were the many ways in which the music toyed with expectations and codes, enacting various forms of representational disturbance. We have seen that as a part of this there was often appropriation of older and/or non-Western musical styles in ways that reproduced existing power imbalances. Finally, after intensity of physical stimuli and cultural appropriation, perhaps the other important kind of disruption to be encoded into psychedelic music was disorientation. This was sometimes represented through defamiliarization of various kinds. Timbre, for example, could be defamiliarized through the creation of completely new timbres or through extreme processing of familiar ones. Defamiliarization could also be achieved through the alteration of stylistically expected norms in harmony, rhythm, melody, and acoustic space. Aside from these various sorts of defamiliarization, musical textures could also be mobilized as icons or indices of psychedelic disorientation, for example, through continually rising curves in pitch or volume, or relatively nondirected harmonic progressions, or sudden changes in the entire character of the music. In all of these cases, there is no firm distinction to be made between representation, enactment, and incitement to confusion. In the case of psychedelia, the same stylistic features that represent a particular state of mind can be used to intensify it.

From the perspective of 1960s rock culture participants, most of this was probably not perceived as violent. Or if violence was perceived, it was usually understood as necessary or positive, sometimes in hedonistic terms (as a kick to be desired) and sometimes in heroic terms (as a risky but valuable step toward enlightenment). And indeed, although some early psychedelic music had an aggressive, overwhelming quality, psychedelia was more frequently characterized by relatively passive textures, or quirky humor, or pleasant folk-pop melodies and harmonies. However, as Johnson and Cloonan note, there is no direct correlation between the acoustic violence of a style and the degree of symbolic or objective violence to which it is associated.

Later Psychedelic Funk and Afrofuturism

In a sense, this entire chapter is related to space topics, because as we now pick up the thread of psychedelic funk it is to look at the markedly Afrofuturist variants that arose in the mid-1970s. By this time psychedelic funk was just one of several new, modern funk styles, and the prominence of psychedelia at the vanguard of African American music was much less than it had been in the 1960s. By the early 1970s many of the main features of earlier psychedelic funk and soul had been taken up as general signifiers of urban blackness, for example through their ubiquity in blaxploitation film soundtracks. This is not surprising, since modernism was never a feature exclusively of psychedelia. As Guthrie Ramsey Jr. (2004) has noted, Afromodernism was a sensibility widely distributed in many forms of African American culture throughout the early twentieth century. Even within soul music, it can be found in multiple forms not particularly related to psychedelia, as shown, for example, in Eric Weisbard's (2014) reading of the Isley Brothers. Nonetheless, in the mid-1970s work of Parliament we find a striking continuation of psychedelic Afromodernist themes married to a science fiction mythology that not only brings them closer to space rock but also anticipates the new psychedelic imaginaries that would emerge closer to the end of the decade.

To start, I want to look at "P. Funk (Wants to Get Funked Up)." This is the opening track from *Mothership Connection* (1975), the album that established Parliament as a major commercial force and that also set in place the science fiction mythology that defined the band's later work.

The form is basically an alternation of DJ rap sections and group-sung sections, with some solos thrown in. The more obviously psychedelic elements are confined largely to the DJ sections, which feature a highly pointillistic approach to the mix (see music example 4.6). This strengthens the affect of charged stasis, as elements come forward and recede without a strong sense of overall direction. This sense of kaleidoscopic drifting is not just formal but also topical, since

Facing: Music example 4.6. Parliament, "P. Funk (Wants to Get Funked Up)," introduction (0:00–0:45). Written by George Clinton Jr., William Collins, and Bernard Worrell. © Bridgeport Music Inc. (BMI). Reprinted by permission of Bridgeport Music Inc. All Rights Reserved.

many of the elements evoke different topic and style areas, including funk guitar and bass; jazz/avant-garde piano and saxophone; horns that are located stylistically somewhere between funk and jazz; a string machine providing ambient and spacey textures; and the speaking voice, which evokes psychedelic guide figures and a DJ persona. The only sense of directedness comes from the horns, which, like everything else, are somewhat disjoined but also melodic and trace long, stepwise arcs ending with a long rise. The drums are sparse and repetitive, not unmetrical, but close in effect to the nonmetrical pulses of space rock and to the time-passing motif. In contrast to the DJ sections, the sung sections are based much more in hard funk. They have a less psychedelic flavor, although the synthesizers and the wah bass are relevant here, as are all the general psychedelic-cognate aspects of funk groove and temporality.

Seen as a psychedelic track, there is much repeated here from earlier psychedelic soul. On the other hand, the entire production is more texturally subdued, less sonically adventurous, and more dance oriented. One example of textural simplification is especially important and has to do with the place of electronics. While earlier psychedelic soul and space rock usually displayed their electronic aspect through dense and highly experimental passages of sound collage, in later Parliament the electronic connection is established through the keyboards, especially through string machines and synthesizers. In textural terms this is a more streamlined and concise sort of electronic sound, with none of the earlier sprawling space-trip features. But although 1970s funk synthesizers are less "spacey" in a 1960s sense, they still signify futurity and technology. They just do so in a more controlled and dance-oriented fashion, anticipating genres such as electro funk, techno, and hip-hop. In order to see how general these features might have been, let's compare this track to another Parliament opening track, this time from their next album, *The Clones of Dr. Funkenstein* (1976).

PARLIAMENT, "PRELUDE" (1976)

- This track is clearly an introduction: it is relatively short, presenting an extended narration over a largely ambient soundscape.
- The rhythm and phrasing are difficult to parse. They sound very clear when just listening, but they are actually quite flexible and irregular. The song is not unlike a traditional folk song or a folk blues performance in this respect.
- Overall, there is an interesting mixture of seemingly measured and less clearly measured elements. There is a strong pulse, and in places there are clear metrical groupings. But these never quite settle into a regular or predictable structure. This applies to the string machine and to the sparse, almost-regular percussion.
- The string machine is based on organ-style phrasing and voicings throughout. It evokes both turn-of-the-century theatrical organ music and extemporized gospel organ, exploring dissonances that creep around a variety of tonal implications with occasional cadences that only temporarily create a feeling of arrival.
- The first vocals to enter are backward.
- The backward vocals quickly resolve into the central feature of the song, which is the spoken narrative. This vocal could be heard as a preacher persona, or as an

oracle, or as a simple narrator. This multiplicity of possible personas is intensified by the dual implications of the organ (both gospel and theatrical).
- Near the very end there are a few high-pitched vocal interjections that could be consistent with a variety of hearings: child-like, monkey-like, clown-like.

This track is much closer to earlier forms of psychedelia. But again, it is different in that its main purpose is to present a strange but coherent narrative and to frame the "real" start of the album, which returns us to a less psychedelic hard-funk sound. In this way, the older topical signifiers of psychedelia are constrained to a framing or introductory function, which at once gives them special importance and separates them off from the main event.

Looking at Parliament in broad terms, as with space rock the main procedure relative to earlier psychedelia seems to be removing certain elements so that others can be given a more prominent place. As we will discuss further below, in Parliament the groove elements are simplified and foregrounded even more than they were in earlier funk. This is not unlike the way that space rock converged on the developing variation approach to form as its default, which was texturally more consistent and rhythmically more motoric than earlier psychedelic rock. We should also recall points made previously about the place of unmeasured sound effects passages. In earlier psychedelic soul these were emphasized, being generally extreme and of long duration. This is interesting, because at that time the primary topical association of such passages in rock was with the space topic. However, even though these passages were just as developed and prominent in psychedelic soul, they were not at that time particularly futurist in tone. Then, when psychedelic funk did become markedly futurist in the mid-1970s, the long, unmeasured sound effects passages had largely been abandoned. This is a reminder that not every meaning afforded by a particular texture will be exploited in all cases, even when it would seem entirely obvious to do so.

One of the key similarities between earlier and later psychedelic funk is that both were groove-based musics, and in both cases the distinctive temporal effects of groove were exploited for, among other things, their resonance with psychedelia. But how do the grooves of Parliament compare to those of the 1960s and earlier 1970s? Anne Danielsen can get us started: "With P-Funk the sound of funk has gone through a severe dislocation: the distance from top to bottom has become even larger than in the grooves of James Brown. However, this distance has not dissolved the grooves themselves, which are now, if anything, easier to follow" (2006, 115, 118). One reason that the grooves are easier to follow is that they tend more in the direction of disco—still multilayered and often with polymetrical elements, but generally slower than earlier funk, and over time evolving to emphasize a four-on-the-floor kick drum and the back beat. These changes aside, maybe what's more important is that in musical terms not a great deal needed to change to move from 1960s funk into the more frankly futuristic versions of the 1970s. This is partly because psychedelic soul was from the start inherently modernist and was premised on many of the same cultural values as the later science fiction variants. To single out one especially important feature in this regard, earlier psychedelic soul already enacted forms of alienation and estrangement. So the move to a more explicitly Afrofuturist version was more a matter of refining inherent features than introducing something radically new. And as with the case of space rock, all of the necessary changes involved intensifying elements already present in the space and epic topics: slowing the beat, simplifying the rhythm, and adding new electronic elements (although in this case that meant abandoning the 1960s-style electronics in favor of newer synthesizer textures).

By emphasizing these continuities I do not want to belittle the significance of the new style. Even if some of the changes were subtle, they gain importance through their later effects. By taking psychedelic funk in a clearly Afrofuturist direction, important ground was laid for the later cybernetic psychedelias that have flourished into a major family of styles and subcultures. There are also important updates to our critical theory framework suggested by Afrofuturist psychedelic funk that have to do with how it engages with the markedness of race. So now that we've surveyed some of the musical changes, I would like to move on to these interpretive issues.

We can again start with Danielsen and the way she summarizes Parliament's racial stance. According to Danielsen, "By the mid-1970s, black music's emphasis on black experiences and black values was weakened. According to the critical voices, black music had turned beige," and in this context the two 1975 Parliament albums, *Chocolate City* and *Mothership Connection*, can be taken as "a deeply critical response to the racial aspects of the increasing inequality of power and resources among the different members of American society." But at the same time, Danielsen notes that this critique was expressed in terms of futurism, irony, and surreal psychedelic humor. She also draws attention to the gospel elements: how funk, psychedelia, and other old-school resources were all mobilized in "a clear attempt to revive black music's strong ability to uplift" (Danielsen 2006, 113–15). Danielsen locates some of the key signifiers of this attitude in the groove itself:

> At the level of groove . . . P-Funk clearly was a forceful response to the threat to musical blackness represented by both crossover funk and disco. . . . P-Funk is music that stresses the groove and focuses on the riff as a primary musical entity in a way that constitutes blackness. Its rhythmic design cultivates a micro-rhythmic level and is in this respect almost to be regarded as an anti-crossover demonstration: the One rules; there is no sign of the equally weighed $\frac{4}{4}$ rhythm of disco (at least not until 1977 . . .); there is a total absence of a straight layer of even sixteenths, and the grooves are heavy, almost "anti-light." (2006, 137)

Compared to earlier psychedelic funk, markedness of race is still a key issue and in some ways is even more aggressively engaged. This engagement is still mostly achieved through humor and playfulness, but at the same time the tone is more militant and confrontational. Also as before, the act of occupying a futuristic science fiction persona as a black artist was something of an intervention and an act of resistance. In the 1960s the intervention was largely one of simply choosing to identify as psychedelic, and the futurist implications of this choice were mostly implicit. By the mid-1970s, the intervention had become more specifically futurist and drew more forcefully on science fiction sources. So the rest of my discussion will focus on that aspect: What are some of the implications of this intensification of space and science fiction topics in psychedelic funk?

We know in retrospect that one drift of these topics will be toward cybercultural posthumanism and that this family of ideas will deeply inform psychedelic electronic dance musics. So just as I emphasized modernity in earlier psychedelic funk, in order to show that music's continuity with mid-1970s Afrofuturist funk, I will emphasize the posthuman in Afrofuturism for two reasons: first, because it is both resonant with and distinct from earlier psychedelic imaginaries, and second, because it is a key stepping-stone to later ones.

Kodwo Eshun has been influential in discussions of posthumanist racial politics. But rather than beginning with him directly, I would like to start with Alexander Weheliye, who reiterates Eshun's main themes while at the same time building on them. (The discussion that follows is from Weheliye 2002, 25–30.) As paraphrased by Weheliye, one of Eshun's core insights is that there is "a specifically black constellation of the posthuman in which New World black subjects have privileged access to the posthuman because they were denied the status of humans for so long." According to this view, despite the ways in which black subjects have been systematically excluded from science fiction and other representations of the technological posthuman, they are in fact particularly qualified to explore this area. Insofar as psychedelic cultures are also invested in the idea of expanding or even transcending normal states of human being, it is not surprising to find that many psychedelic subcultural participants identify with themes of exile, the alien, and the posthuman in a way that resembles Afrofuturist sensibilities (St. John 2013, 56). However, as discussed earlier, many topical areas in African diasporic culture are split between features that resonate with psychedelia and those that are more dissonant. The posthuman leanings of Afrofuturism, rooted as they are in the history of slavery and racial terror, are no exception. And indeed, there is often a dichotomy regarding these within contemporary black cultures as well. As Weheliye puts it, there is a tension between tendencies toward a posthuman "Afro-diasporic futurism and the humanist future-shock absorbers of mainstream black culture" (2002, 29). He argues that these tendencies are constantly intermingled and interdependent, rather than separate or antagonistic.

This tension comes about because the basic categories of human and humanism have subtle, layered meanings when read through Afrodiasporic history and experience. Weheliye describes the complex relationship of black intellectuals to the whole idea of humanism and humanity: "Because New World black subjects were denied access to the position of humanity for so long, 'humanity' refuses to signify any ontological primacy within Afro-diasporic discourses. In black culture this category becomes a designation that shows its finitudes and exclusions very clearly, thereby denaturalizing the 'human' as a universal formulation while at the same time laying claim to it" (2002, 27). From the perspective of psychedelic topicality, the most important detail is in the last phrase. Afrofuturist expressions of the posthuman denaturalize the category of humanity, and this is one reason why they are cognate with psychedelia. But at the same time, psychedelic imaginaries generally maintain an optimistic, humanist strain in parallel with their transcendentalist leanings, and so the simultaneous "laying claim" to humanism is also important. In all, this subtle formulation of the human adds another to our earlier list of psychedelia-cognate features in Afrodiasporic cultures, but it also highlights another set of tensions within that category. And as with psychedelia in general, Afrofuturist participation in imaginings of the posthuman can be understood as an intervention. Because despite everything that's been said about zones of compatibility between Afrodiasporic cultures and psychedelia, most representations of the posthuman still tend to be biased toward whiteness and toward an ahistorical futurity and centered on visual representation. So there is an inevitable sense in which having the posthuman expressed by black subjects through musical forms rooted in older African American styles can't help but be a kind of intervention and produce a creative frisson. According to Weheliye, it is especially significant that this should be done through the medium of sound: "Incorporating other informational media, such as sound technologies, counteracts the marginalization of race rather than rehashing the whiteness, masculinity, and disembodiment of cybernetics and informatics" (2002, 25). And in doing so, Afrofuturist funk artists did not assimilate into the dominant modes of behavior associated with the technological and posthuman but instead fused those modes with forms of playfulness and political consciousness more typical of Afrodiasporic expression. A very similar dynamic is noted by Michael Veal in his discussion of Jamaican dub and Afrofuturism: "The science fiction metaphor also has relevance in the irreverent way Jamaican recording engineers utilized their sound equipment . . . which at the very least seemed to problematize the issue of Western technoscience and its network of cultural associations. The genre of dub music is populated with the trope of the 'crazy' sound mixer, as well as the theme of science interwoven with madness" (2007, 212). This sort of practice produces tropes combining a Western notion of rational science and of the future with a Jamaican sense of science as occult knowledge. Likewise, a common move in Afrofuturist criticism is to pick up on Sun Ra's concept of myth-science. As Tobias van Veen puts it, myth-science aims at describing practices that are "capable of representing *but also transforming* the coordinates of the present" (2013, 10, emphasis in original). Apart from the usual truism that by abandoning realism, myths can express a different sort of reality, myth-science emphasizes that myths have the power to shape the future according to mythical patterns of the past. In this sense, the temporality of myth-science is circular, such that, according to Graham Lock, "visions of the future and revisions of the past become part of the same process, a 'politics of transfiguration,' in which accepted notions of language, history, the real, and the possible are thrown open to question and found wanting" (1999, 2).

There are two key ideas here. The first is that the representations are always critical and concerned with possibilities for future change, even when they seem to be focusing on mythical and nonrealistic retellings of old mythologies. And perhaps even more interesting, there is the idea that past and future become very difficult to distinguish. This is a representational framework much more compatible with a circular, cyclical time than with a linear one. The resulting paradox—that a sensibility founded in futurism should fundamentally draw upon ancient mythologies and ultimately lean toward a circular view of time—is clearly cognate with psychedelia on many points. But as with the posthuman, the specific history of black politics and experience means that the relationship between models of temporality and visions of the future is multilayered. Some commentators have noted a dissonance on this point between the Afrofuturist sensibility and traditional forms of religion and spirituality. For example, Paul Gilroy notes that "black Christianity was certainly future-oriented, but its sense of the future was bounded by its eschatology. Its utopia was not of this sorrowful world and required the supercession of modern, that is, of racialized and racializing, time" (2000, 330).

To take one recorded Afrofuturist objection, Lock argues that Sun Ra had powerful disagreements with the Judeo-Christian tradition because he felt that it trapped African Americans in a disempowering version of history (1999, 21). But does that require a critique of the linear view of time often associated with Christianity? Sun Ra's social critique was based in large part on a Nation of Islam viewpoint, which was critical of Christianity but nonetheless enshrined a similar prophetic future orientation. And interestingly from an Afrofuturist perspective, Nation of Islam ideology occasionally placed considerable emphasis on technology, in some cases even using images of UFOs as vehicles for salvation (Zuberi 2004, 80–81). From one perspective this would suggest that a circular view of temporality is not necessary for an Afrofuturist social critique. On the other hand, there were aspects of Nation of Islam thought that also drew upon perennialist sources more compatible with such a circular temporality. Indeed, Gilroy argues that much Nation of Islam thought, in its more occultist moments, "recalls nothing so much as the apocalyptic and equally racialized predictions offered by comparably eccentric occult figures like Helena Blavatsky and Carl Jung, who still remain largely unacknowledged as influences on the development of the NOI and its theology" (2000, 330–31).

For our purposes, the most important thing to note is that a similar conflation of temporalities is found in much of psychedelia. Recall, for example, that we found both apocalyptic and prophetic strains in American imaginaries of the Grateful Dead. What many hippies and Afrofuturists shared is a conviction that a more radical view of temporality is needed in order to resolve persistent social and individual problems. On the one hand, the resulting views of time typical to psychedelic subcultures were often circular, based on Buddhist and Hindu models. But on the other hand, many of the relevant countercultures were attracted to a model of progress and change that had linear characteristics. Ultimately, it is the rich interplay between such views, along with the simple fascination with time and the fluid relationship between past, present, and future, that creates powerful resonances between psychedelic and Afrofuturist perspectives.

At this point we can wrap up both our Afrofuturism discussion and the chapter by asking: What happened to the space topic through the creation of Afrofuturist psychedelic funk? Let's take as a starting point two different critical reactions to the music. One of these is more of a survey, and one is centered on the work of Parliament, but the more interesting difference is in their affective tones. First, regarding the many "deliberately futuristic" black artists of the 1970s, Paul Gilroy has stated: "This period of intense musical creativity arose between the demise of Black Power and the rise of popular Pan-Africanism triggered by Bob Marley. It was dominated by the desire to find a new political and ethical code in which the contradictory demands for blackness on one side and postracial utopia on the other could be articulated together under the bright signs of progress, modernity, and style" (2000, 342). Gilroy's affirmative tone resonates with the generally positive, if sometimes barbed, mood of much psychedelic funk. But then there is an entirely different perspective from Kodwo Eshun:

> P-Funk compels you to succumb to the inhuman, to be abducted and love it. Funk gets drawn out of the body, an entelechy harvested by an alien force.... P-Funk is the gladallover suffusion of *Funkentelechy*, the enjoyment of mutation.... *Funkentelechy* is the process which demands Abduct me! Abduct me! As soon as funk comes from off this world, it collides with common sense.... The vocoder generates a menagerie of machine voices, nonhuman subjects. These voices aren't anempathetic or robotic. Rather they are disconcertingly oral, larynx machines, synthetic pharynxes that stretch the vowels into plastic.... Unlike Kubrick's luminous uteronaut in *2001*, Parliament's Star Child, the Protector of the Pleasure Principle, Dr. Funkenstein's emissary, is disconcertingly creepy. Far from being a body-enhancing, life-affirming soundtrack for young social rebels, '74–'77 era P-Funk is underhand and insinuating, snide, contemptuous. Star Child has a gloating, ultraphonogenic voice, miked so that it's always intimate, tactile.... Star Child sings nursery rhymes, memes that burrow familiar routes into the brain, Trojan horses, pathways used to infiltrate the perceptual apparatus.... It creeps in under the cover of nonsense, rearranges the furniture of your mind, leaving you feeling probed and palpitated. (1998, 140, 143–44)

To some extent, Eshun is probably exaggerating for effect. But at a minimum, it needs to be acknowledged that Parliament enacted a fusion of the bright, optimistic black futurism described by Gilroy and a more dystopian, abject posthumanism. In both respects, blackness is claimed in this music more aggressively than in earlier psychedelic funk. Gilroy characterizes the era as following the demise of Black Power, but the aesthetic force of Black Power is still felt here. On the other hand, there are many positive slogans and lyrics, some of which are markedly inclusive. But if Parliament is integrationist, it is definitely not so in a 1960s civil rights sense. It is more a matter of inviting people to participate in the Parliament party, expanding the tribe on their own terms. Linking this back to our discussion about violence, there is a willingness to entertain and to join in with others, but control is retained by the mother ship. Also in connection with violence, and drawing closer to Eshun, this is a music of disruption on all levels—lyrical, visual, and sonic—that draws upon psychedelic styles and procedures that were, by that point in history, topical. But these psychedelic topical features were also often those that had been widely deployed for the depiction of 1970s social disorientation and critique and for inner-city chaos. The cumulative effect is not unlike early Pink Floyd in the way both affects are fused: whimsy and darkness, transcendence and psychosis.

So what can we say as an overview of changes in the space topic up to the mid-1970s? In the case of rock, the trajectory is fairly simple. Rock versions of the space topic first became common around 1967 as a subpart of psychedelia and then gradually calved off as space rock became a distinct genre and as typical rock signifiers of space became more minimalist and abandoned almost all real-world indexicality. By the mid-1970s the space topic in rock was no longer a subfield of psychedelic topicality so much as a cognate field. This is a fairly simple story of topical field change, but the appearance of Afrofuturist funk enriches the picture greatly. It is a matter of preference whether this addition is best read as all happening within one increasingly complex space topic or whether it is better to think in terms of a family of related space topics by the mid-1970s, with the two major clusters being rock-like and funk-like. Aside from that structural question, the crucial thing is that the indexicality of space topics on the funk side is much richer than in rock, because while it has a virtual component like the space-rock world, this virtual world is troped with indexical connections to markedly Afro-diasporic contexts. This trope adds many layers of political, social, and affective complexity. Where the space topic in funk is concerned, both Gilroy and Eshun are correct insofar as they identify different affective subfields of this increasingly important and layered topic.

Notes

1. Readers interested in more historical context might like to consult the short but sweeping overview of psychedelic space rock from Hayward (2004, 15–20).

2. Morse code and teletype sounds differ insofar as the Morse signifier is based in part on a difference between short and long durations, whereas teletype is not. As usual with such distinctions, the semiotic relevance will depend greatly on context and would need to be judged on a case-by-case basis. But when considering higher-level topical significations, as we are doing here, I will conflate Morse and teletype together into a general family.

5   The 1980s and On

There is a genuine question as to whether any significant new topics were added to psychedelia after the mid-1970s. There were undoubtedly new styles, new contexts, and new combinations, so the specific scope, affect, and other aspects of the old topics shifted. In principle, these kinds of shifts could be sufficient to create altogether new topics, but while some candidates for this sort of process can be identified in post-1970s psychedelic music, none are definitive examples of new topics. In fact, from what we've seen in the 1970s it could be debated whether even the changes in the space topic are best read as the creation of a new topic or as a reweighting of elements and signifiers within the already-existing space topic. What is beyond doubt is that the space topic became much richer in its range of signifiers, its scope of reference, and the variety of its indexical connections. But what is less clear is whether it should be seen as having separated from the psychedelic topical field by that time, to be related as cognate but relatively autonomous, or whether a space topic still invariably evokes psychedelic reference points.

Before going deeper into this question, it is worth briefly reviewing the initial conditions necessary for a new topic to form. One necessity is a new context sufficiently distinct from others so that it can become generally regarded as a unique signified. There should also be something important or noteworthy about that new context so that people will be motivated to signify it. A second necessity is that some genuinely new signifiers must be available that can be indexically linked to the new context. For these to be available for the purpose, they need to be either quite novel or bound weakly enough to any earlier meanings that they can be repurposed. There are various processes that could block the formation of new topics. First, there could be a lack of distinctiveness, either of signifiers or context or both. Second, there could be *capture*, which could also be called *asymmetrical attribution of novelty*. Consider the troping of flamenco and acid rock that is found in much of Robbie Krieger's guitar playing for the Doors. In absolute terms, it doesn't make sense to ask whether this event caused a greater change in flamenco or in acid rock, because the trope is symmetrical insofar as both genres came together to make it happen. However, for particular listeners it may well be the case that the event will be perceived more as an event within rock or as one within flamenco. For example, individual listeners would not necessarily be indifferent if asked to choose between the statements "this style is a new kind of rock music" and "this style is a new kind of flamenco music." Now, if a listener is equally inclined to endorse either statement, then there is no capture taking place. The novelty is equally attributed. But if a listener tends to prefer one statement over the other, then this is what I mean by capture, or an asymmetrical attribution of novelty. The force of innovation is captured by one term over the other, one term is felt to change more than the other. And if a general tendency toward a certain kind of asymmetry develops in a particular interpretive community, then it would make sense to say that capture had occurred in a wider sense, as an event at the level of language rather than just as a description of one listener's reaction. These sorts of event are highly specific to particular listening communities, and a full study would require detailed research. But they are the sorts of dynamics we should keep in mind even when offering initial surveys. At points in this chapter, I will put forward my own impressions about where and when events of capture or failures of novelty might have happened. These should be understood as hypotheses, rather than as assertions of fact.

So did new psychedelic topics emerge in the 1970s? Might we find some in the 1980s? I will not offer an answer to these questions, because I believe that the situation is still in flux. Topic formation requires a removal of signs from their original context and a process of conventionalization, both of which take time. Speaking from the perspective of this writing, one interesting thing about psychedelic topicality is that it offers the full gamut of temporal distance and conventionalization. There are very old and established pre-1960 topics, and even pre-twentieth-century ones, that early psychedelia took up and transformed. There are also psychedelic prototopics of the 1960s that by now have become fully topical and are themselves in the process of being rearticulated in new contexts. And there are developments within psychedelic substyles after the 1970s for which we can make topical observations but that aren't yet old enough to have settled down into conventionalization. So in this final chapter I will back away from even tentative conclusions about large-scale changes in topical fields. Instead, I will focus on contextual and stylistic changes that, at a minimum, represent new ways of presenting and combining existing topics and that have at least the potential to develop into new topics in the future.

The picture is further complicated because many features that were originally linked to psychedelia have become so widely distributed in popular music as to be unmarked. In our discussion up to this point, we have emphasized that style features can become topical over time, but we have not considered how, given even more time, certain topics can become unremarkable and therefore nontopical. This complicates the selection process when deciding which post-1970s musics to discuss, because if we looked only at musical features resembling psychedelia, the scope would be extremely wide, and in many cases the connection to psychedelic cultures and topics would be minimal. So I've made the decision to focus on examples that have a self-consciously neopsychedelic aspect. As a result, the issue of historical reflexivity will be important. We will be looking at cases where the music is presented as something that should be heard within the lineage of psychedelia. So what does this do to the process of topic formation?

Does the historically reflexive impulse dampen the sort of contextual translation necessary to the formation of new topics? This is a question that will be kept in view throughout the chapter.

And there is one other interesting question that follows from all of this and that, like the others, did not come up earlier in the book: To what extent can topics be limited to small specialist communities or to very short time spans? For example, within electronic dance music (EDM) subcultures there are certain fine stylistic differences that some participants associate strongly with particular historical contexts and with ideologies and aesthetic preferences typical of those contexts.[1] Examples include Detroit techno, early Balearic, acid house, and 'ardcore. Within these relatively small circles of aficionados, the relevant categories are topical. But those interpretive habits don't generalize to a larger interpretive community and are often short-lived. The tendency in existing topic theory has been to look only at those topics that hold for larger groups and have demonstrable longevity. This is another issue that I will raise rather than resolve, but it is important to note that the question of scope presents itself strongly in cases like these.

With these general questions in mind, we can move on to look at psychedelic rock music and EDM of the 1980s and early 1990s. The two objectives of these discussions will be, first, to see how various existing psychedelic topics are taken up and transformed in these musics and, second, to highlight features relevant to the question of whether these new musics and contexts seem to be likely breeding grounds for the emergence of new topics.

Rock to the Mid-1980s

We can divide 1980s psychedelic rock into two phases. Up to about 1986 psychedelic rock had little crossover with EDM culture and so is best read mostly as a continuation of earlier rock styles. But in the later 1980s, and especially around 1987–88, there was a wave of rock-rave crossover music in which both the sociological and the topical features are more distinctive relative to earlier rock. While the earlier 1980s rock was an Anglo-American phenomenon, the later rock-rave crossover was more specific to the UK. I will start with the earlier material and then move on to the crossover music.

1960s Retro

By around 1980 the jangly sound of 1960s folk rock, garage rock, and sunshine pop was returning to the foreground in some rock substyles after being largely abandoned for a while. During this resurgence these styles were frequently presented in a self-consciously retro mode, for example, in the way many Los Angeles bands were lumped together under the Paisley Underground genre. In much of this music, psychedelic topics and style features were not specifically highlighted but were part of a broader mix focused on 1960s West Coast pop and rock more generally. As Keir Keightley (2011) notes, by the 1980s the boundaries between categories such as psychedelia, folk rock, and sunshine pop had become extremely porous due to emerging cultures of collecting and connoisseurship and through the influence of various revivals that often freely mixed and matched such styles. But despite this general tendency toward nonspecific mixing of retro styles, there were some artists whose work fitted into a 1980s revivalist strain but who were also more self-consciously situating themselves within a psychedelic lineage. One good example is The Teardrop Explodes and the band's leader, Julian Cope, more generally. "Bouncing Babies" (1979) is one Teardrop Explodes recording that resembles psychedelic garage rock in some of its details. Overall, it is a good example for seeing the kind of stylistic ratio that can function either as neopsychedelia or as a less specific retro statement, depending on the knowledge and priorities of the listener. Some of the song's more psychedelia-specific features include the following:

- The prominent use throughout of a combo organ timbre.
- The open, melodic vocal timbre insofar as it is different from other common voice types of the era, especially from punk.
- The alternating A–F harmonic movement in the A section, with persistent triplets on the F (e.g., 0:00–0:15). This accompaniment figure has a bit of a flamenco/surf flavor both rhythmically and harmonically.
- A B section based around alternating cross-relation chords (E–G), with the organ now on a slow, siren-like, single-note G♯–G alternation (0:15–0:29).
- Overall, a formal/harmonic simplicity that helps create a trancey, pendular affect throughout.

"Bouncing Babies" is rich with references to 1960s psychedelic garage rock, and yet the composite effect is very postpunk as well, perhaps predominantly so. Overall, the song would better be called new wave with a slight psychedelic inflection, rather than psychedelia as such. That being said, it does not sound particularly like pastiche or like a genre experiment. It does demonstrate that certain psychedelic topics can be incorporated into a 1980s rock style in a fairly cohesive manner. Indeed, there were songs in this vein that achieved a much more extended and multifaceted presentation of psychedelic topics. To find examples of such songs, we could look at different material from Julian Cope / The Teardrop Explodes. But in order to broaden our scope I want to focus on someone else: Robyn Hitchcock and his primary band at the time, the Soft Boys.

The Soft Boys, "Underwater Moonlight"

Robyn Hitchcock was considerably less of a psychedelic proselytizer than Julian Cope, but his close stylistic and affective link to songwriters like Syd Barrett, combined with the many retro elements in the Soft Boys' sound, cause a great deal of the band's material to sound self-consciously neopsychedelic but at the same time specific to the early 1980s. One track that encapsulates most of the key features is "Underwater Moonlight." We will see that this song draws upon several established psychedelic topics, presents them in new forms rather than simply reiterating the

Above and facing: Music example 5.1. The Soft Boys, "Underwater Moonlight," introduction and first verse (0:00–0:40). For North America: Words and Music by Robyn Hitchcock. © 1980 Complete Music Ltd. This arrangement © 2015 Complete Music Ltd. All Rights Administered by Universal Music–MGB Songs. International Copyright Secured All Rights Reserved. Reprinted by permission of Hal Leonard Corporation. For World excluding North America: Words & Music by Robyn Hitchcock. ©1980 Cherry Red Music Limited. Complete Music Limited. This Arrangement ©2015 Cherry Red Music Limited. All Rights Reserved. International Copyright Secured. Used by Permission of Music Sales Limited.

1960s and 1970s variants, and tropes the psychedelic elements with features more typical of the 1980s, such as a gothic topic.

THE SOFT BOYS, "UNDERWATER MOONLIGHT" (1980)

- The overall feel of the introduction is bustling yet static (see music example 5.1, mm. 1–4). The harmonic stasis is underscored by the alternating octaves in the guitar and

by the droning trill in the violin. But while these elements maintain harmonic and melodic stasis, they also create a strong motoric pulse. The bass is dub-like: very active and melodic, in-and-out rather than continuous. This dub-like aspect is less evident during the introduction but quite pronounced in the first verse. The drums are very simple, without snare and built on a motor rhythm quarter-note kick. When the melody enters with the verse, it is highly active although largely stepwise, following long arcs (see music example 5.1, m. 5). The rhythm of the melody is quite free, largely based on the highly prosodic rhythm of the lyrics. During the entire verse, the instruments shift the same basic patterns up and down as needed to follow the harmony, continuing their balance between movement and stasis.

- During the transition the vocal timbre becomes more nasal and forced compared to the earlier open sound, and it is doubled by the guitar (see music example 5.1, mm. 21–24).
- The second verse doesn't introduce new topical elements, although it does follow the general psychedelic tendency of gradual thickening around a motoric drone. The bass, for example, moves toward a more continuous motor rhythm (see music example 5.2) and remains that way throughout most of the song. All of these remarks generally hold also for the chorus, subsequent verse, and subsequent chorus.

Music example 5.2. The Soft Boys, "Underwater Moonlight," guitar solo (excerpt) (2:52–2:59). For North America: Words and Music by Robyn Hitchcock. © 1980 Complete Music Ltd. This arrangement © 2015 Complete Music Ltd. All Rights Administered by Universal Music–MGB Songs. International Copyright Secured All Rights Reserved. Reprinted by permission of Hal Leonard Corporation. For World excluding North America: Words & Music by Robyn Hitchcock. © 1980 Cherry Red Music Limited. Complete Music Limited. This Arrangement © 2015 Cherry Red Music Limited. All Rights Reserved. International Copyright Secured. Used by Permission of Music Sales Limited.

- The guitar solo starts at 2:23. It is here that more obviously psychedelic elements begin to come back to the foreground, especially in the second part of the solo (starting at 2:52), which is based strongly on surf/spy elements with psychedelic inflections layered against an intermittent and obscure spoken vocal (see music example 5.2). The other striking element in the solo is the violin figure, which had been present earlier in the song but which becomes increasingly foregrounded (also given in music example 5.2). The violin double-stops resemble the earlier violin trill in their droning aspect but are also evocative of fiddle music or bluegrass.
- At 3:18 the solo ends, and there is a long vamp over which the obscure spoken voice continues. The backing vocals, beginning at 3:25, are repetitive and based on a two-chord figure that is literally F♯–B^7 but is voiced so as to also sound like a major-minor alternation (see music example 5.3). The bass and guitar both settle into slow, repetitive cells based around an alternation of F♯ and B (also given in music example 5.3). The vamp becomes denser, louder, and increasingly motoric before seguing into the final chorus. For example, the violin double-stops now add an alternating element to their earlier droning profile and become more rhythmically complex (see music example 5.3).

"Underwater Moonlight," while sounding like nothing so much as early 1980s rock, is extremely rich with psychedelic topics on many levels. For example, the alternating octave figures evoke clockwork and are also a drone (reinforced by the

Music example 5.3. The Soft Boys, "Underwater Moonlight," vamp before final chorus (3:18–3:28). For North America: Words and Music by Robyn Hitchcock. © 1980 Complete Music Ltd. This arrangement © 2015 Complete Music Ltd. All Rights Administered by Universal Music–MGB Songs. International Copyright Secured All Rights Reserved. Reprinted by permission of Hal Leonard Corporation. For World excluding North America: Words & Music by Robyn Hitchcock. © 1980 Cherry Red Music Limited. Complete Music Limited. This Arrangement ©2015 Cherry Red Music Limited. All Rights Reserved. International Copyright Secured. Used by Permission of Music Sales Limited.

violin). But at the same time this sort of figure was a new wave cliché, especially when combined with the sparse, motoric drums and the vocal style. Similarly, the dub-like bass in the opening has psychedelic associations, and dub was already cognate with psychedelia by the early 1970s, but the specific influence of dub on rock bass is largely a thing of the 1980s and later. We could continue to find other aspects of the music that are at once psychedelic topics and distinctly 1980s rock features, but instead I would like to show how some of the tropes and other nuances in the song resemble those of earlier psychedelia while also managing to be distinctive.

A few of the psychedelic topics in this song are virtually unaltered from their 1960s versions. For example, the sudden new texture of the first transition, along with the fanfare-like figure, mirrors the 1960s device of undermining a fanfare topic with a kazoo. Similarly, the guitar solo with its psychedelic spy and surf mood is strongly retro, especially since it coincides with the obscure spoken voices. But what makes the song interesting is that certain established topics are also presented in new variations. For example, the violin tropes psychedelic topics (largely due to the droning quality) with roots music ones. This is not at all an unusual trope, but earlier examples like those in the Grateful Dead and the Incredible String Band did not usually have the flavor of a fiddle dance tune, as found here. This makes the trope fresh at the same time as it is familiar. Even more complex is the voice. It is difficult to assign a style to the verse melody. The meandering quality and the way the rhythm follows the text together suggest recitative or a traditional ballad. They also evoke psychedelic storyteller songwriting, especially Syd Barrett. But the linear stepwise shape is not unlike Gregorian chant, and the vocal timbre and subject matter suggest more gothic topics. A similar vocal trope is found in the vamp near the end of the song, where the implied minor-major alternation hints at the same Zarathustra-like epic topic we found in Hawkwind, but also has a country-gospel aspect.

The predominant trope in this song is a three-way one, blending the psychedelic, country-gospel, and gothic. We have seen how this is developed in the music, but it can also be found in the lyrics. Like a folk song, these lyrics tell a story. The song speaks of two statues who for fifty years sat "looking stupid by a jar." Then "one night in mid-August, when the moonlight got too strong," something happened. All that's literally said in the lyrics is that the statues climbed down from their places and sang a song (presumably the rest of this song). But then a story unfolds about two people going to a beach and rowing away across the ocean. At first it seems like the ocean-goers are the statues themselves, but later details make this unlikely. These people are pink (the statues were white). They were dragged down and killed by a giant squid, and the statues took their place. So the most likely thing is that the statues, who were once the people, are sometimes moved by intense moonlight to sing a song of their origins.

As with the music, there are many psychedelic themes here: Greco-Roman imagery, a magical transfiguration, a journey, and the ocean. But as in the music, there are counterbalances that prevent the song from being purely psychedelic. In the context of the early 1980s, maybe the most significant are the gothic elements. The statues are dialogic in this sense, and other specifically gothic images include moonlight penetrating through deep water and a death story with some grim lyrics ("why don't you feed the fish?" and "watch your baby drown"). Overall, a song like this not only mobilizes a range of psychedelic topics but in some respects stands in a psychedelic lineage. The topics are not just used as decorative touches, they are woven into the basic formal, compositional, and performative framework. But at the same time, they are combined with decidedly early 1980s elements, so that what is produced in the end is a trope, in this case, psychedelic/gothic and a new kind of psychedelic/roots.

American Independent and Rembrandt Pussyhorse

By the mid-1980s there were also neopsychedelic gestures cropping up in the punk-centered American independent scene. Some of these were more on the decorative side, such as the jangle elements occasionally taken up by Hüsker Dü. But some American independent groups of the era, while largely perceived as punk bands, were also deeply neopsychedelic. To discuss just one example, I want to look at three selected songs from *Rembrandt Pussyhorse* (1986) by the Butthole Surfers. As with Robyn Hitchcock and the Soft Boys, one point of this reading will be to show how the Butthole Surfers found new ways of presenting existing psychedelic topics and did so in a way that seems integral to their contemporary musical context. I also want to draw attention to the band's scope, since they mobilize many contrasting psychedelic substyles and topical areas, rather than just one or two.

THE BUTTHOLE SURFERS, "CREEP IN THE CELLAR"

- The song opens with minimal repetitive drums, not unlike typical Velvet Underground drums, and a similar approach to riffs in general.
- The violin is stereotypically spooky and uncanny in various ways, sometimes playing fast disjointed scales, sometimes processed with deep tremolo, sometimes sounding reversed.
- Verse endings are elongated on subsequent repetitions (e.g., compare 0:19–0:27, 0:45–1:02, and 1:10–1:36).
- There is a long violin solo at the end (1:40–2:02). Compared to the earlier violin parts, the melodic materials here sound much more like a folk ballad, although some of the disjunctive interjections are still present as well.

"Creep in the Cellar" is full of horror movie imagery ("When he starts talking backwards your head starts to spin / And he really freaks me out when he peels off his skin"). This is topical in itself but is also resonant with the more psychotic side of psychedelic garage rock. The violin reinforces the psychotic and horror film aspects but tropes them with roots music and with the avant-garde. Other psychedelic topics with either garage rock or avant-garde tendencies include the minimal drumming and rhythm section figures and certain formal features that resonate with the outward journey expressive genre, such as the elongation of verse endings and the long concluding solo. Relative to earlier psychedelia, the most distinctive thing about this song is how the horror imagery is handled. There were a few gothic and horror elements in 1960s psychedelia, especially in the poster art and other visual designs, but for the most part it didn't draw upon this sort of comic-book or horror movie imagery. So the presence of this kind of imagery is clearly a variant on psychotic garage rock, but it also has a more contemporary feel that is enhanced in retrospect by the way similar themes were elaborated by later artists such as White Zombie. And the psychedelic/horror trope becomes even richer when the horror imagery is further troped with folkloric moments in the violin (mostly in the long solo at the end). This creates, by the end of the song, a specifically rural version of psychedelic psychosis, a creepy American gothic that was not explored to any extent in earlier psychedelic folk.

While a song like "Creep in the Cellar" is topically interesting, a major psychedelic feature of *Rembrandt Pussyhorse* overall is that it moves between a wide variety of different genres from song to song, much like *Sgt. Pepper* or Parliament's *Osmium*. For example, "Sea Ferring" is in another psychedelia-related topical area: pirates and the nautical.

THE BUTTHOLE SURFERS, "SEA FERRING"

- Woozy $\frac{3}{4}$ throughout.
- The voice alternates between drawling folk song and shouting, creating a sense of barely contained chaos.
- There are several long instrumentals, but no solos as such. The instrumental in the middle (1:53–2:28) is most like a typical guitar solo. It relies heavily on slides between frets and is processed with a deep tremolo. It sounds overall like an almost-continuous note sliding gradually up and down long arcs, mostly in a stepwise manner.
- There is a chant-like, extended vocal recitation near the end (2:53–3:20).

In many ways, the topics in this song evoke a drunken sailor more than anything specifically psychedelic. But in the context of the album and of the band's image, the drunken sailor reading does not so much preclude a psychedelic nautical topic as extend its reach. In fact, both of the songs we have looked at so far are similar in that they enact the band's punk identity by taking certain psychedelic topics and making them more sinister both by selectively enhancing features already in those topics and by troping them with related but darker topics such as horror films and drunken pirates. Finally, let's consider one more strongly contrasting piece from the album.

THE BUTTHOLE SURFERS, "STRANGERS DIE EVERY DAY"

- The first sound is a whispery, crackling voice that seems to be coming quietly through a megaphone. Listeners familiar with the band's stage performances will probably hear it as a megaphone, but it could also be heard as a crackly radio, a bad telephone connection, and so on. It is too distorted to be intelligible. This voice comes and goes sporadically throughout the piece. It is not multiple speaker blur at first but a single unsettling voice.
- The organ enters almost immediately, repeating a simple downward sequence with a pipe organ timbre. The nature of the theme and the degree of repetition are not unlike midperiod Pink Floyd or other space rock. The organ is also a little like the string machine in Parliament's "Prelude" in that its phrase structure and meter seem clear on a cursory listen but would be difficult to precisely transcribe. The faster

notes create a sense of regular pulse and grouping, but the long sustained notes blur this considerably. The lack of a rhythm section emphasizes this somewhat drifting, timeless quality throughout the piece.
- At 0:59 an intelligible whispering voice enters, speaking the title of the song. It returns to repeat the single phrase "die every day" at 2:06 and once more at 2:43.
- The vocal texture becomes multiple speaker blur about halfway through (from 1:18), with the entry of a larger number of voices sounding like radio traffic.
- Water sounds enter at 1:44. These are not like running water but more the sound of being inside a submerging vessel.
- At 2:36 the organ drops out, and there are sporadic pitch-shifted sounds, like tape being fast-forwarded at varying speeds, or the time parameter on an analog delay being swept up and down.

This recording deploys many space-rock features but at the same time renders them claustrophobic. This comes about largely through the water sounds, which bring up various submarine images but in an unsettling mode. In structure and affect, the piece is not unlike the sound collages of early Funkadelic, but without the humor or the African American reference points.

While it would be impossible to fully summarize early 1980s neopsychedelic music with this small number of examples, I suggest that the songs we've examined are broadly representative of the ways that psychedelic topics were being used in rock at the time. Particular stylistic details would vary if other examples were brought to bear, but we would not find radically different topical procedures. And regardless of how well the examples generalize, we can still ask of these particular cases: To what extent do they show evidence of new topic formation relative to psychedelia? There is no doubt that songs of this sort developed new stylistic variants of existing psychedelic topics and explored some tropes that, while not completely unprecedented, were quite novel. At the same time, there are factors that limited the topical creativity of early 1980s psychedelic rock and that I suggest prevented it from making fundamental new contributions to the psychedelic topical field. This judgment is based in part on comparison with the even more psychedelic rock-rave crossover music and electronic dance music that came to prominence later in the 1980s. Specifically, if we ask what kind of new musics came to be generally understood as representing psychedelic culture by the 1990s, the answer seems to be musics that sound more like EDM and not as much like early 1980s neopsychedelic rock. Conclusions of this sort are speculative for reasons discussed at the start of the chapter, but I put this interpretation forward as a hypothesis. To the extent that it might be true that these earlier 1980s styles did not widely come to represent psychedelia, they would provide an example of capture. In the case of the Paisley Underground bands and the specific examples from the Teardrop Explodes and the Soft Boys, the main kind of capture involved would be by perception of the psychedelic elements as retro. Although the combinations are sometimes fresh and the stylistic details are often new, there is often a powerful feeling of historical reflexivity and stylistic repetition in this music, enough so that at least to my hearing the novelty is not easily attributed to the specifically psychedelic features. Another kind of capture that I hear working in these examples is the same sort identified earlier with the example of the Doors and flamenco. In the same sense that most listeners likely do not hear the Doors as a flamenco band, my hypothesis is that most would not have heard the Butthole Surfers or the Soft Boys primarily as psychedelic bands but as some other sort of band (new wave, punk, industrial, goth, etc.) that happened to have some notable psychedelic influences. To the extent that this interpretation holds, psychedelic topicality in these cases would be a more passive partner in the meaning making and would not tend to be transformed so much as mobilized in its existing form.

While the force of this reading depends partly on comparison to more obviously neopsychedelic styles that we will soon discuss, it also depends on the other criterion for new topic formation: apart from novel signifiers (and maybe even more important than these), there must be a novel context. Here as well, the early 1980s neopsychedelic bands tended to reiterate existing forms more than to innovate. Some of them had no contact at all with new contexts of performance. Others, for example, American independent bands like the Butthole Surfers, were part of a more distinctive network of indie production and reception, but the ways in which the Amerindie network was distinctive did not tend to be particularly relevant to psychedelic topicality. In short, while individual bands like the Teardrop Explodes and the Butthole Surfers created microscenes with clear psychedelic commitments around themselves, they were not part of a larger neopsychedelic movement. This does not in itself preclude topical innovation, but it could help explain a lack of topical innovation should we decide that we perceive one.

We can combine the point about context and the comparison with more obviously neopsychedelic musics by making a further observation: the new elements brought to bear by rock bands of the earlier 1980s—mostly punk, gothic, and industrial stylistic features—were not particularly consonant with the new psychedelic imaginaries that came to dominate the psychedelic mainstream in the later 1980s and 1990s. These new imaginaries, especially because of their association with rave culture, came to be cemented in the public imagination as the new face of psychedelia, and I suggest that for neopsychedelic bands of the earlier 1980s, being out of step in this way was another constraint on the ability of their stylistic innovations to become widely perceived as permanent additions to the vocabulary of psychedelic topicality. It is not that they didn't create innovations that might have had the potential to more fundamentally alter the topical field, but that their innovations were overshadowed by others that were more aggressively seized on as emblems of the psychedelic.

Some Changes in Psychedelic Imaginaries and Subcultures

Despite extensive psychedelic features in some of the examples we just discussed, they were not generally part of a broader neopsychedelic movement. This is in contrast to the final two styles I want touch on: rock-rave crossover and psychedelic EDM. In both of these cases, the musics were more thoroughly embedded in neopsychedelic subcultures and widely understood as such. So before looking at the musical examples, it might help make a few remarks about what changed and what stayed the same in psychedelic imaginaries of the later 1970s and 1980s. My focus is on factors that could foster the emergence of new topics or major changes in existing topics. These factors include shifts in the contexts, ideologies, practices, and aesthetic preferences associated with self-consciously psychedelic musics.

The 1970s and 1980s were a transitional period for psychedelia. By the late 1980s these changes had culminated in the emergence of various psychedelic EDM styles and their associated party contexts, often bunched together under the *rave* umbrella. One major contributing factor was a shift in the festival and traveler cultures associated with psychedelia, which involved the emergence of a free festival circuit in the early to mid-1970s along with the continuation and gradual transformation of the hippie trail heritage in places like Goa. These contexts provided sites for a gradual musical transition from 1960s psychedelic styles toward the psychedelic EDM styles that had coalesced by the mid-1980s. A second key factor was that drugs other than LSD—most importantly, botanical psychedelics (especially mushrooms) and MDMA/Ecstasy—emerged as the central symbols of these new contexts and were associated with new symbolic priorities. Finally, there were new psychedelic imaginaries promulgated by the generation of myth makers following the 1960s, especially the McKenna brothers. We will only have time to survey the highlights, but providing at least a few details on all of these fronts will be useful in discussing the topical novelty or otherwise of the new rock and EDM styles that emerged from this period.

The new performance and reception contexts that came to define psychedelic subcultures in the later 1980s and into the 1990s—free festivals, beach parties, and raves—are in many respects like psychedelic rock contexts of the earlier 1980s. They recycle elements of earlier situations such as psychedelic ballrooms and happenings, communes, the hippie trail, early rock festivals, and 1970s underground dance culture, combining these in new ways, intensifying some features and attenuating others, but not fundamentally altering the constituent parts. Consider, as one example, the traveler culture that arose in connection with early free festivals. Simon Reynolds argues that "the traveling lifestyle began in the early seventies, as convoys of hippies spent the summer wandering from site to site on the free festival circuit," and that this lifestyle was linked closely to ongoing attempts at forging an economy and network of subsistence parallel to mainstream culture (1998, 163). And as George McKay stresses, "Free festivals in Britain were *not* a central part of the 1960s counterculture—they'd hardly got going when the sixties ended" (1996, 21). This point is supported by Christopher Partridge: "Emerging partly as a protest against the commercialism and capitalism of the large-scale festivals, a *free* festival was initially a festival at which no profit was made by the organisers. However, they quickly became much more than this. The festival became a utopian model of an alternative society. It sought to be what the anarchist thinker Hakim Bey . . . has since termed a 'temporary autonomous zone,' where members freely contribute to an economy based on mutual aid rather than money" (2006, 42). Partridge goes on to explain that this ethic included an ideology of personal freedom, and that "also significant were the spiritual emphases of, particularly, the festivals held at Stonehenge and Glastonbury" (43). While the overlaps with earlier 1950s and 1960s subcultures are clear, Partridge argues that we must maintain "a distinction between the fashionable hippie culture of the 1960s and the much more countercultural, spiritually eclectic free festivals that emerged in the early 1970s" (41). Partridge further explores the connections, many personal and institutional, between these subcultures and later rave culture, for example, in the spiritual significance accorded to places like Glastonbury by some trance producers and the strong links between the early Goa trance scene and earlier psychedelic subcultures (45–46). Finally, these sorts of contexts were shaped by the way they drew together a range of different psychedelic constituencies. They were a nexus of contact and to some degree synthesis between those older 1960s counterculturalists still committed to an alternative lifestyle, various New Age spinoffs of these, elements of the punk-related independent music movement (especially the crust punks), and emergent EDM cultures.

Without denying any of this, it also needs to be considered that the specific novelty of these contexts is not necessarily topical. As we will see when we look at musical signifiers in rock-rave crossover and psychedelic EDM, the situation is similar to what we found in earlier 1980s psychedelic rock: a borderline case where the novelty of style and context might be sufficient to generate significant shifts in the topical field but might also be seen as more like a reshuffling of existing possibilities. Similarly, while the musical styles associated with free festivals in the 1970s and early 1980s were extremely diverse, they generally drew from templates either that were well established or whose innovate aspects were not specifically linked to psychedelic topicality, including neojam bands like Ozric Tentacles, experimental punk and postpunk artists like Crass and the Raincoats, and some contributions from first-generation psychedelic space-jam bands such as Hawkwind and Gong. However, there is a crucial difference between our earlier 1980s examples and the musics that developed within these more self-consciously psychedelic party and festival contexts. By assertively foregrounding psychedelic topicality as a principal frame of reference, these contexts functioned as *anticapture machines*. They created situations in which stylistic innovations that in other circumstances might have been likely candidates for capture were more likely to be specifically understood as psychedelia related.

While the free festivals and similar contexts possibly minimized the chances of capture, the effect of new psychedelic imaginaries was similar but different. I suggest that these new imaginaries had the effect of maximizing the chance that certain stylistic changes that might have seemed minor from some perspectives would be widely perceived as important, insofar as these changes resonated with new foci in the new imaginaries. So what were the points of continuity and difference between typical psychedelic imaginaries of the 1960s and those that became prominent in the 1980s? Unlike a 1960s leader such as Timothy Leary, later figures like Terence McKenna and Daniel Pinchbeck put their primary emphasis on shamanism, with geographical fantasies centered on a variety of locales other than South or East Asia. This shamanistic emphasis went along with enthusiastic promotion of botanical as opposed to synthetic psychoactive substances and was often bolstered by ethnobotany of varying degrees of legitimacy. It also meshed with a perennialist spirituality and a renewed interest in British and Celtic mythology and, in the 1990s, with a proliferation of neotribal design aesthetics. All of these features were throwbacks to the generation of pre-1960s psychedelic researchers and experimentalists, given that much of that earlier activity was also anthropological and ethnobotanical in nature and was linked to perennialist and transcendentalist philosophies of the nineteenth century. But the late 1970s variants were also different, primarily in the way they troped these existing themes with a posthuman cybernetic utopianism and with other pseudoscientific and New Age influences. Also, by the 1980s even the older ideas stood out as fresh insofar as they differed in emphasis from psychedelic imaginaries of the late 1960s, which for a younger generation had come to represent psychedelia as a whole.

Many of these features can be seen to have influenced the free festival traveler culture, but it was with neopsychedelic EDM that the most fully articulated formulations of the new imaginaries were found. As a result, most of the scholarly commentary on these imaginaries is centered around trance subgenres of EDM, but many of the points made there apply more widely: "As trance travelled from the beaches of Goa to the West it became more Pagan/Shamanic and earth-centred, often focusing on the indigenous religious traditions of the area (e.g. Aboriginal in Australia, Celtic in the United Kingdom, Native American in the United States).... Hence, although there was still much that was spiritually Eastern in 'rave' music, increasingly more earth-centric, indigenous, Pagan, and, indeed, eco-conscious content was expressed" (Partridge 2006, 48–49).

Also important was the merger with technoculture, which produced various cross-mappings of neopaganism, cyberculture, posthumanism, and millenarianism. Significantly, this occurred in an increasingly transnational and translocal framework. A fairly affirmative description of this process is offered by Graham St. John: "Throughout the 1990s, psychedelic trance accelerated the interfacing of technology, ecology and spirituality. Psytrance became a transnational context for the growth of a planetary ethos among youth, for the evolution of eco-spiritual commitments expressed and performed through dance" (2004, 213). And a more critical assessment is offered by Arun Saldanha (who is in part paraphrasing Andrew Ross): "Trance is commonly described as a global music, even a global movement.... Naturally, the term 'global' refers to mostly white people in the overdeveloped world, and to the process by which trance draws inspirational sources from the underdeveloped world" (2007, 40).

We have already discussed how this can be seen as the reinscription of a modernist bohemian colonialism. But an interesting further nuance is noted by Hillegonda Rietveld, who describes the perennialist aspect of this worldview in a way that strongly resonates with features we noted in Afrofuturist temporality: "There seems to be a need for a deeper, pre-modern, meaning, which is often invented and constructed to suit present circumstances. Such understanding of the pre-historical could be conceived of as, in fact, being post-historical, not unlike contemporary imagery found in science fiction fantasy.... This longing for pre-modern roots can partially explain the adoption of a 'timeless' or seemingly transcendental shamanism in some of the more countercultural rave scenes" (2004, 47).

I started this discussion by suggesting that new psychedelic imaginaries might have caused certain changes in associated musics to be granted greater significance than otherwise would have been the case. The changes I have in mind will be seen in the case studies below, but there are four in particular to highlight. First and second, the change in exoticist reference points away from the more narrowly Orientalist and toward a wider range of world musics, coupled with the increasingly globalized nature of the trance community, can be linked to a renewed and expanded mythology of global perennialism. Third and fourth, the increasing use of sampling as a production technology, coupled with the emergence of EDM as a dominant framework for neopsychedelia, can be linked to cybercultural and posthumanist leanings of the new imaginaries.

Rock-Rave Crossover

The discussion of new contexts and imaginaries has jumped us forward in time a little, since many of the quintessential formulations are to be found in 1990s trance. But since we started this chapter with rock styles, and since rock-rave crossover predates the emergence of trance, I would like to skip back and pick up the thread of 1980s psychedelic rock. In the late 1980s, especially in the period 1987–88, there was in the UK a crossover between the emergent rave culture and a rock culture based around soccer-centric laddism. This was not entirely unprecedented, since UK psychedelia emerged in the first instance partly from pub rock. Simon Reynolds elaborates: "This interface between soccer fanaticism—with its ritualized inebriation and hand-to-hand combat—and acid house—with its anti-alcohol bias and hippy-dippy pacifism—seems extremely unlikely. But there are actually quite a few parallels between soccer and raving. In the eighties, with mass unemployment and Thatcher's defeat of the unions, the soccer match and the warehouse party offered rare opportunities for the working class to experience a sense of collective identity" (1998, 64). Reynolds goes on to note, however, that "despite the Summer of Love and Unity rhetoric, less than a year into its existence the scene was stratifying" into separate rock and electronic dance contingents (69). If we consult the lineages of individual bands, social groups, and stylistic influences, the most immediate legacy of this crossover is Britpop of the early 1990s rather than any continuing influence on psychedelia. Nonetheless, the short-lived rock-rave crossover is interesting in topical terms because it represented a new way to combine the rock and dance streams into which psychedelia had otherwise stratified. The best-known exemplar of this convergence was the Madchester scene, along with the *baggy* style (both musical and sartorial) associated with it. While many of the artists in question drew upon generalized 1960s stylistic references, much as the Paisley Underground bands had done, none were narrowly rooted in psychedelic rock or space rock as such. Rather, they tended on average toward a broadly groove-centric rock style drawing on diverse sources. There was a fairly broad range in the specific influences and combinations of different bands, for example, the Stone Roses tended toward postpunk and hard rock, Inspiral Carpets were more neogarage (especially due to their emphasis on combo organs), and Happy Mondays were perhaps the most difficult to categorize, although they generally presented a stylistic mix somewhere between the Paisley Underground and New Order.

In many cases, the crossover between rock and rave was more sociological than sonic. Many of these rock bands did play longer songs foregrounding regular grooves that were suitable for a dance club, but there was often little new topicality in evidence. It isn't possible in the available space to cover all the various gradations of dance influence and retro psychedelic influence on this scene, so we'll look instead at one selected example that encapsulates some of the more widespread features.

Primal Scream "Loaded"

As Simon Reynolds notes, some of the more influential rock-rave crossovers were more the result of savvy collaborations than of individual musicians internalizing both styles: "Bands like Primal Scream and Happy Mondays depended on the dance floor savvy of DJ/producers like Andy Weatherall and Paul Oakenfold to overhaul their basically traditional rock songs" (1998, 105). "Loaded" is one of the more commercially successful and artistically influential projects of this sort, being an Andy Weatherall remix of the earlier Primal Scream song "I'm Losing More Than I'll Ever Have." In the details of production, it is very literally a crossover between working methods and formal priorities—those of a rock band and of a dance DJ-producer—and it sounds that way. The same chord changes and versions of the same riff and groove underlie the entire recording. But the effect is not like a space-rock developing variation form. The approach is more terraced and articulated, like contemporary dance music in the formal strategy of juxtaposing long blocks of contrasting textures. Also typical of EDM form, there are a few breakdowns of various density and length. There is nothing that would suggest improvisation and jamming, apart from a DJ-like freedom in bringing elements in and out of the mix and in constantly exploring new combinations of the basic materials.

The overall formal effect is a very evenhanded fusion of rock and dance music features. It could be heard as a large rock band performing an EDM-inspired form or as a producerly remix of materials that originated in rock performance. This overall impression of hybridity is reinforced by the varying connotations of specific components:

- The horns and bass are dub-like and include a slight R&B flavor.
- The main piano riff is very typical of later 1960s and 1970s rock: I–♭VII–IV–IV, with each chord having a midmeasure excursion to its suspended-fourth variation.
- There is a Latin percussion layer, and the drums in general evoke funk and disco.

- There is a gospel choir near the end.
- The slide guitar is a bit folky/country but also evocative of Pink Floyd–style slide textures and similar space-rock guitar.

Many of these topical reference points are loosely cognate with psychedelia, although none are strikingly or narrowly psychedelic. Similarly, while there is a great deal here that is loosely evocative of funk and disco, these styles are hinted at rather than allowed to dominate. In topical terms, maybe the most significant thing is that the distance between the rock region and the funk-dance region is foreshortened, but without the creation of a radically novel hybrid. This mirrors the seemingly spontaneous way in which dance and rock subcultures merged in certain neopsychedelic contexts from the mid-1970s onward.

One further detail of "Loaded" is extremely important: it is the first of my examples to contain an obvious sample. In this case, the sample is a long excerpt from Peter Fonda's "we want to be free" speech in *The Wild Angels* (1966) and is used as an introduction to the song. In many respects it functions like other unmeasured sound effects openings we have considered, but the effect is also different. For one thing, it is an especially concrete manifestation of historical reflexivity. But as with many of the retro gestures we have seen, the meaning is inflected toward contemporary circumstances. In this case, through selection of a sample that leans so heavily toward the simple party aspect of 1960s youth culture and avoids any ideological or mystical elements, the track is positioned in a lineage with 1960s countercultures but is also distinct from them. One reading would be that the sample is ironic, taking a jab at the more pretentious revolutionary claims of the earlier era. Or it could be seen as a statement of difference, claiming a new attitude for the rock-rave generation. Or finally, it could be a statement of selective solidarity, aligning with certain aspects of 1960s youth culture but not with others. In any case, a balance is struck between historical reflexivity and contemporary identity formation.

In some genres, and most notably hip-hop, sampling was a technology that enabled strikingly new approaches to musical production and aesthetics. Some have argued that there was a similar effect of sampling within neopsychedelic musics: "'Sampladelia' is an umbrella term covering a vast range of contemporary *hallucinogenres*—techno, hip-hop, house, jungle, electronica, swingbeat, post-rock, and more. 'Sampladelic' refers to disorienting, perception-warping music created using the sampler and other forms of digital technology" (Reynolds 1998, 41). What kind of "perception warping" is being evoked here? To some extent, the effect can be sonic. Sampling excels at certain sorts of sound manipulation that didn't begin with it but that became widespread in sample-based musics. This includes the creation of quasi-real soundscapes and scenarios that can then be subjected to various counterrealist combinations or transformations. It could also include the creation of sounds that are audibly hybrids of "real" and "synthesized" aspects. But maybe even more significant is that sampling functions as part of a new information ecology brought about by networked digital communications technologies in which older distinctions of space (both geographical and temporal) can be more easily sidestepped and new transversal relationships between previously separated styles and contexts more easily established.

With respect to topicality, there are two features of sampling that stand out. First, when used as a recognizable technique, sampling is itself a good candidate for eventual topicality. For example, some ways of manipulating obvious samples are already hip-hop topics. Second, sampling allows for a particularly literal kind of intertextuality. While in certain respects an intertextual reference created through sampling is not fundamentally different from one created through less literal kinds of quotation, the ubiquity of sampling in some genres has in this regard created a qualitative difference out of a quantitative one. The premier example is again the striking density and sophistication of intertextual relationships in hip-hop. But have these topical potentials of sampling been realized to a comparable extent in neopsychedelic rock music or EDM? With respect to the first sort of sampling topicality, certain kinds of sample-based synthesis, such as granular synthesis, have become staples of some psychedelic EDM genres, especially trance. Whether these will develop into fully topical signifiers remains to be seen (at present they are more on the level of style characteristics). In terms of intertextuality, the case of sample-specific topicality in psychedelia is even weaker. In psychedelic EDM and in rock-rave crossover, sampling is often used to add a few superficial details to a song or, conversely, as a nearly invisible structural production technique. In neither typical use is there a strongly topical effect specific to sampling.

Sampling has become such a rich technique in hip-hop partly because it resonates with tendencies already present in African American and Afrodiasporic musics. Alexander Weheliye has argued that such musics are partly defined by their development of a space he calls "the mix," a strategy and set of practices extending beyond music—into visual art and literature, for example—and present substantially earlier than the sampling era:

> The "mix," as it appears in black cultural production throughout the twentieth century, highlights the amalgamation of its components, or rather the process of this (re)combination, as much as it accentuates the individual parts from which it springs.... As a mode of cultural criticism and practice, the mix brings together disparate elements, but not in the manner suggested by the notions of "pastiche" and "bricolage" as they appear in postmodern literary theory; the mix offers a strategy for the construction of modern temporality that results not from the randomness or irony evoked by these terms. Instead, it creates a transversal, nonempirical space that coexists with its other components. (2005, 73, 83)

The space of the mix is not specific to sampling, since it predates sampling. But sampling is a technique very well suited to it. To an extent, a sample like the one in "Loaded" does begin to achieve the creation of such a space, but in a limited way. Comparison with almost any track from Public Enemy's *Fear of a Black Planet*, for example, also released in 1990, makes the difference immediately evident. This is not to say that more densely layered and ontologically suggestive uses of sampling are not to be found in psychedelic EDM and rock music. The Orb's "Little Fluffy

Clouds," for example, will be discussed soon and offers something closer to the sort of space described by Weheliye. But such examples are not the norm in psychedelic musics.

It might seem that I've devoted considerable space to a discussion of sampling only to argue that, on balance, within psychedelic musics of the 1980s and early 1990s sampling did not have many effects that were, strictly speaking, topical. That is true, but I think it is an interesting result given that sampling certainly does have a special relationship to topicality more generally. In broad terms, this is the result again of capture. Sampling-specific effects tended in these musics to be mobilized as slightly new versions of existing psychedelic techniques—crafting unusual timbres and inserting sound effects—and so didn't tend in that context to develop strikingly new topical features of their own.

Psychedelic EDM

One interesting feature of electronic dance music from the late 1980s to at least the mid-1990s is that while some subgenres are explicitly psychedelic in orientation, they do not necessarily sound any more psychedelic than other forms of EDM. This is not to say that no EDM sounds like a contemporary version of psychedelic music but rather that most of it does. Should the most important psychedelic features of EDM be considered the general ones, rather than the more subgenre-specific ones? Robin Lindop suggests that interest in this question is widespread: "[Among psytrance participants,] dance music in general (i.e., everything from acid house to techno) is often viewed as 'psychedelic,' another development intensely debated on psytrance forums. Users often present the opinion that certain non-psytrance EDM tracks are more deserving of the tag 'psychedelic' than some psytrance tracks" (2010, 118). These sorts of conclusions are often drawn on stylistic grounds, rather than with reference to any kind of psychedelic intent. For example, early Detroit techno pioneered many of the EDM characteristics that came to typify rave music and its neopsychedelic spinoffs. But several of the key innovators of Detroit techno are reported as strongly disavowing any connection to psychedelics: "There was virtually no drug element to the Detroit party circuit. For the DJ/philosopher Derrick May, in particular, the deranged and debauched atmosphere of the British scene was a world away from his vision of the ideal techno audience of urbane aesthetes.... By the early nineties, May's distaste for Brit-rave excesses had hardened into bitter contempt [and] Eddie Fowlkes shares May's resentment" (Reynolds 1998, 71).

For the purposes of this book, rather than resolve the problem of saying which EDM genres and tracks should or should not be regarded as properly psychedelic, I will use the vagueness as a cue to pick questions that keep us focused on the bigger picture, rather than getting too far into detailed discussion of specific subgenres. I will proceed with two main goals in mind: (1) describe why almost all EDM is psychedelic in some broad sense and what this has meant for the topical field of psychedelia; (2) ask which specific signifiers characterize the psychedelic trance genres

(Goa trance and later psytrance), since these are among the most self-consciously neopsychedelic of EDM genres, and ask further whether these distinct features include anything new in terms of topicality.

The Orb, "Little Fluffy Clouds"

This recording is one of three I will consider from early rave music. In terms of its specific significance on the scene, "Little Fluffy Clouds" is a good example of the ambient chill-out subgenre.

Like "Loaded," this track has an unmeasured sound effects introduction that is sample based and focused on realistic-sounding identifiable sources. But unlike "Loaded," the ambient nature of "Little Fluffy Clouds" asserts itself immediately because the samples evoke a soundscape rather than a single source. These sounds include a rooster, a BBC announcer–style voice, an airplane, the brief appearance of another voice asking a question (interviewer voice), the voice of the protagonist, and a harmonica. There is just enough echo and reverberation coming and going at various times to make all of these ordinary sounds seem slightly otherworldly. It's striking how this montage can be realistic, almost documentary in tone, while at the same time evoking a rich tradition of psychedelia. Most of the specific sounds are dialogic in this way:

- The rooster is a conventional sign of rural spaces and also harks back to psychedelic signs of awakening and to specific roosters on specific earlier psychedelic recordings (e.g., "Good Morning Good Morning").
- The BBC announcer voice signals Englishness and helps establish the realist documentary tone, but it also evokes the radiophonic side of psychedelic and space rock.
- The harmonica reinforces the rurality of the rooster but makes this rurality more abstract and epic by evoking the Hollywood western. In doing so, it also links back to western motifs in the very earliest psychedelic recordings.
- The voice of the protagonist is on one level simply autobiographical, adding a layer of personal reflection to the rural imagery. But the tone of voice and almost mystical affect also evoke 1960s psychedelic pastoralism.

Knowing the sources of the samples doesn't alter the basic topical effect, although it does enhance the intertextuality. Some of the specific samples in the introduction include a Rickie Lee Jones interview for the spoken parts and a harmonica from *Once upon a Time in the West*. In the main body of the track there are excerpts from *Electric Counterpoint* by Steve Reich and Pat Metheny. The drums are also likely sampled but are less distinctive and more processed, which lessens their intertextual significance for listeners outside of more specialist circles.[2]

In the introduction, to the extent that these topical references create an abstract mood and a general set of possibilities, they resemble earlier psychedelic sound effects introductions. But to the extent that they create a montage of realist, almost documentary world making, they draw strongly on the intertextual space of post-

Music example 5.4. The Orb, "Little Fluffy Clouds," first sequence/theme (0:36–0:46). Written by Steve Reich, Martin Glover, Duncan Alexander, and Robert Paterson. © Universal Music MGB Songs obo EG Music Ltd. / Hendon Music, Inc. / BMG Monarch obo Chrysalis Music Ltd. UK.

1980s sampling. This provides an important expansion to the description of sampledelia previously quoted from Simon Reynolds. His description emphasized disorientation and experimentalism, which highlights those aspects of sampling most related to the more flamboyant 1960s branches of psychedelia and space rock. But the kind of understated, almost-documentary use of samples found in "Little Fluffy Clouds" is also important. It relates transversally to what was being done in hip-hop, for example. It also highlights the fact that a certain amount of the strangeness in 1960s-era montage came from the realistic elements as much as from the heavily processed or disjunctive ones, from the way things were *almost* as expected, like the nearly normal circus in "Being for the Benefit of Mr. Kite!" or the nearly normal household morning chaos of "Good Morning Good Morning."

"Little Fluffy Clouds" also provides an opportunity to describe the typical EDM approach to formal structure, which is to begin with an unmeasured or rhythmically sparse introduction, build density over an extended period by successively adding layers of sequences, dissolve this density in a breakdown, and repeat that basic arc several times before concluding. As with any formal scheme there are myriad variations, but this basic approach describes the most common underlying logic. For example, the structure of roughly the first third of "Little Fluffy Clouds" runs as follows, with each layer mostly continuing as new ones are added:

- Ambient sounds and vocal samples (0:00–0:27).
- The first sequence enters with a typical acid-house Roland TB-303 timbre. This sequence sounds alone alongside the ongoing ambient sounds (0:27–0:45; see music example 5.4).
- The drums enter from 0:45. They gradually add layers over four measures and reach their full pattern at 0:54 (see music example 5.5).
- By 1:04 it is obvious that the bass has been gradually getting louder.
- The Steve Reich / Pat Metheny sample enters, adding a second foregrounded sequence at 1:13 (see music example 5.6).[3]
- The Reich/Metheny sample drops out, and a new melodic riff is added. The protagonist voice is added back in, this time with extensive editing and layering to repeat "little fluffy clouds" in a rhythmically complex, fragmented manner (1:31).
- The texture thins out considerably (1:49). This is not quite a breakdown but is similar in effect.

Music example 5.5. The Orb, "Little Fluffy Clouds," first drum pattern (0:55–0:59). Written by Steve Reich, Martin Glover, Duncan Alexander, and Robert Paterson. © Universal Music MGB Songs obo EG Music Ltd. / Hendon Music, Inc. / BMG Monarch obo Chrysalis Music Ltd. UK.

Music example 5.6. The Orb, "Little Fluffy Clouds," second sequence/theme (1:13–1:22). Written by Steve Reich, Martin Glover, Duncan Alexander, and Robert Paterson. © Universal Music MGB Songs obo EG Music Ltd. / Hendon Music, Inc. / BMG Monarch obo Chrysalis Music Ltd. UK.

- After this there is a similar buildup to a similar dropping back at 2:44, and then another buildup until the entire texture begins to gradually thin out, leading to the ending (starting at 3:39).

This sort of formal approach is repetitive and groove based, but it is also more linear than earlier psychedelic funk or space rock because of its tendency to follow a thicken-then-break-down template above all others. The form is clearly processual in its origins—like all the EDM examples discussed in this chapter, while "Little Fluffy Clouds" is a studio product rather than the result of live mixing by a DJ, it bears many formal hallmarks of the live dance mix. Form in such a context is generally the result of improvisation, and given that the purpose of the dance mix is to sustain a party, formal events are subsumed to that function. Indeed, there is no form as an independent factor: it is more a side effect of how a DJ needs to perform a balance between continuity and contrast and to manage intensive changes over long time spans. In this sense, the fundamental unit of live EDM is not a song or any other kind of text but a performance event based on improvised mixing. This approach can be seen as the logical extension of the directions taken by space rock and psychedelic funk insofar as they displaced song form in favor of groove. That being said, for many listeners this sort of texture and formal strategy will evoke rave culture and related dance cultures rather than earlier funk or space rock and so is likely well on the way to becoming an independent topic. The case for a prototopic in the typical EDM form is strengthened in that the improvisational practice of EDM DJs has been distilled into a formal structure that mirrors the major features of this practice but that has also become standardized and is now often symbolic of the dance party rather than literally embedded in it.

In "Little Fluffy Clouds" there are other features aside from the ambient introduction and the general formal strategy that are reminiscent of specific psychedelic topics and style features. For example, both of the first themes (see music examples 5.4 and 5.6) are framed around alternating pitches: a bit siren-like, certainly oscillating, and implying a slow alternation between two chords. Both also feature something of a hocket feel without strictly being hocket. In the first case this is largely a result of the way delay is used, and in the second it is more the result of Steve Reich's compositional style. But in both instances some exoticism is introduced through this hocket-like aspect because of the technique's association with some non-Western musical forms. It is also interesting to note the amount of troping that takes place just in the main drum pattern (see music example 5.5). Elements include the following:

- Four-on-the-floor kick drum, which by this point was a prototopic of late 1980s and early 1990s electronic dance music but which also dialogically harks back to disco and also to the more minimalistic motor rhythms in some space rock and psychedelic rock.
- A short (one-measure) snare drum pattern that is somewhat militaristic in its flams.
- A short (one-measure) shaker pattern, which adds a bit of a Latin reference.

- A clacking noise, which sounds especially mechanical given that it is made up largely of eighth notes. It is vaguely reminiscent of earlier clockwork topics. Both this rhythm and the one in the shaker also sound somewhat militaristic in their rigidity, especially when heard against the strict kick drum and in conjunction with the flammed snare.
- The hi-hats are more loose, partly because there are two distinct hi-hat lines present, and partly because they are the most syncopated and least regular component of the drum pattern.

Finally, it is significant that the Orb were known for their incorporation of dub music into ambient techno. "Little Fluffy Clouds" is not the most striking example in that it doesn't contain many specific dub figures or timbres. Compare it, for example, to "Towers of Dub" (1992), which highlights many dub clichés. However, the more general dub influence on EDM is still evident here and is perhaps even more interesting than the more iconic sorts of references. Dub production techniques that became widespread in EDM include adding and subtracting textural layers, extreme timbral separation between parts, the breakdown, and, the reduction of vocals to short snippets that are edited and woven in and out of the mix. Dub was also an influence in its heavy use of spatializing effects. But despite the profoundly cognate nature of dub with respect to psychedelia, Michael Veal suggests that a direct link between the two is an oversimplification. Indeed, when he outlines some of the factors that led to the frequent interpretation of dub as psychedelic, he is almost providing a template for topic formation, whereby dub needed to be removed from its original context and symbolically reinterpreted in order to be assimilated into non-Jamaican psychedelic musics:

> Any interpretation of dub as psychedelic music rests upon (1) an unstable classification of cannabis derivations as hallucinogens; (2) an admission that the question itself is only really relevant in the Euro-American zone within which psychedelic rock music exists as an established genre category; and (3) a demonstrable influence of European and American production trends in Jamaica. In the Euro-American context, drawing such a link seems deceptively easy: with the exception of transplanted sound systems serving immigrant Jamaican communities, fans of dub music in those cultural areas tend to use the music more for reflective listening than dancing—very different than the chaotically external setting of the Jamaican sound system. Furthermore, because of the traditions of psychedelic and progressive rock, dub in England and Europe has tended to be appreciated on purely sonic terms, as opposed to Jamaica where it was largely understood to be a backdrop for deejays. With song lyrics removed, the focus on the soundscaping elements grew much stronger. (Veal 2007, 82–83)

We last discussed dub in connection with the space topic, a discussion that concluded with the idea that by the early 1970s space topicality had divided into two spheres, one centered on funk and one centered on rock. A signal contribution of EDM and of rock-rave crossover is that it closed this rift, bringing psychedelic funk and space rock much closer together. But at the same time, while in EDM the signs of futurism and technology were even more pronounced than in earlier psychedelic funk, the element of racial politics is essentially gone. Some of the topics do have racial markedness at least as part of their range of reference, as, for example, with dub. But this aspect is rarely foregrounded.

The Shamen, "Re-evolution"

The next recording I'd like to discuss is, like "Little Fluffy Clouds," a fairly early ambient rave track. What makes it of special interest is that it sets an extended spoken performance by Terence McKenna, one of the most important figures in developing the new psychedelic imaginaries of the late 1970s and 1980s.

- The introduction, part 1, includes a repeated, slow, rising figure with timbre somewhat resembling an organ. It is also not unlike a Shepard tone.
- The voice enters almost immediately (0:07). This is a recording of Terence McKenna speaking a long, sermon-like statement touching on many aspects of his neopsychedelic, technoshamanistic, posthuman worldview. The material comes and goes, but it forms the backbone of the piece, and the entire composition essentially feels like a setting and interpretation of this material.
- The other sounds that are most important in setting the specific mood (as opposed to more generic rave music features) are the long string melody notes that come and go, often as single-note lines and sometimes in pad textures (first appearance at 0:30).
- Starting at 0:48 there is the almost-subliminal start of a gradual tempo increase, which continues until 1:38, gradually becoming more pronounced.
- The tempo stabilizes with the appearance of a new sequence (1:37). Not only does the tempo stabilize after the long accelerando, but it is striking how this new sequence maintains a fairly high pitch level after the long development of the rising motif. This sense of arrival and height is underscored by timbrally bright hi-hats, which also increase the feeling of rhythmic drive, as well as by the major-third framework of the sequence.
- The track continues for some time (total length 8:22), but by this point all of the major topical materials have been established. A few less dramatic but still-noteworthy features include the breakbeat-like rhythm from 3:24 to 3:39, which strongly resembles the then-recent genre of drum and bass, and the marimbas, which first enter at 4:09.
- Although most electronic dance music sequences and textures share elements in common with the clockwork motif, this track seems to place special emphasis on creating the effect of mechanisms slowing down and speeding up. We have already described the long accelerando, and there is a similarly extended decelerando passage as well (5:58–6:38). Also, at 7:08 there is a sudden doubling in the speed of a sequence.
- Unusually for this genre, it is a very long time before there is anything like a breakdown. There are various more subtle instances of slowing down or thinning out (e.g., 6:06 to about 6:37), but the only breakdown as such is very near the end (7:50).

Compared to similar ambient rave music of the time, the most unusual feature is the voice. But there are a few other things that set this track apart and that create an interesting topical setting. The first thing is that, even by EDM standards, the mood of the recording is especially clinical and mechanical. For example, by resembling a Shepard tone, the opening rising figure suggests a perception experiment in a laboratory. Similarly, the changes of speed at several points in the piece, some subtle and some abrupt, suggest special emphasis on mechanistic topics such as clockwork. At the same time, there are moments of more sweeping affect suggesting contrasting topics. For example, the manner in which the continual rise of the opening peaks into the sequence beginning at 1:37 suggests bustling motion but also wide expanses. Personally, I hear it as evoking a nautical topic, but other topics fitting that general affect would fit as well. And the long string lines evoke the pastoral, as well as space and space rock. In terms of specific timbre, they sound very much like long pad notes as used in more than one *Star Trek* main title theme (especially *The Next Generation*), again suggesting an expansiveness and heroism.

The voice itself produces several effects. Most importantly, it makes the entire recording into a "talking" piece: not an unmeasured sound effects piece, but similar to one in that the voice derails any expectation of normal song form, even at the same time as it positions a singular human subject as the main expressive element. This voice is very clearly a guide figure, in tone both scientific and shamanic. Like a DJ or preacher guide figure from earlier psychedelic soul or funk, and also like the sampling aesthetic discussed earlier, the voice has a realistic quality that links it indexically to particular communicative contexts. But at the same time, it has an otherworldly and fantastic aspect not unlike the voice-overs in *Space Ritual*–era Hawkwind. The documentary aspect of the voice, combined with the way it describes cosmic and ecological scenarios, could be heard as evocative of television nature shows. And if the voice is heard in that way, then the entire recording gains a dimension of culture jamming and perhaps irony as well, a kind of self-awareness in inhabiting a thoroughly naturalistic and rationalist form in order to promulgate such a fringe and speculative message. Overall, "Re-evolution" is a very direct and yet nuanced topical study in music of the new psychedelic imaginaries associated with figures such as McKenna.

The Shamen, "Ebeneezer Goode (Beatmasters Mix)"

Before moving on to a specific discussion of trance, let's consider one last song from the early 1990s rave period: "Ebeneezer Goode," again by the Shamen. One reason for including this song is that it is a faster tempo dance piece, unlike the more ambient examples we've considered so far. Also, this recording is interesting in that it is positioned, in form and in the nature of the material, between live EDM style and pop song style. It is rooted in continuing rave culture, but it was also produced at the beginning of a wave of successful crossover artists who were by the later 1990s marketed under the umbrella term *electronica*.

- The opening theme, made up of long, held vocal notes and small bells, is epic in various ways. It evokes westerns, Orientalist clichés, and other epic/exotic film contexts.
- The first sequence enters with a typical acid-house Roland TB-303 timbre (0:30). Even more than "Little Fluffy Clouds," this displays most of the key features of such a sequence. In addition to the characteristic timbre, there are slow pans, filter sweeps

(both those programmed into the envelope of each note and those applied more gradually), motor rhythm with occasional gaps, a stuttering effect created by strings of repeated notes punctuated by sudden leaps, and deep glissandi applied to only some of the note transitions.
- There is a terraced buildup of density as elements are added, including a return of the opening vocal theme (0:38), loud bass doubled with kick drum (0:45), a midrange-heavy hi-hat pattern (0:53), and a loud backbeat (1:01).
- The main melodic theme—the one that will eventually support the vocal hook—enters with a combo organ sound that is very reminiscent of early to mid-1960s garage rock (1:46).
- A second melodic theme enters, this one more like 1980s electro-pop in timbre, rhythm, and pitch profile (2:02).
- There is a long rap section (2:09–2:40).
- There is also a pop chorus (2:40–2:55). The first melodic theme, originally heard on combo organ, is now doubled with the vocal hook/pun "Eezer Goode, Eezer Goode / He's Ebeneezer Goode."
- The texture drops back slightly with a return to the second melodic theme (2:55), followed by a very short breakdown (2:59–3:03).
- The rest of the track continues by moving between long blocks of previously heard material. For the most part the density and energy level are fairly consistent, although a near-breakdown is achieved with a thinned-out version of the opening vocal theme (4:34–4:49), and there is a short full breakdown with only percussion and a single sequence (5:04–5:20).
- The other topical feature of note is a manic laugh, sounding mostly like a B-movie villain or a mad scientist, that comes and goes throughout the second half of the track (it first appears at 3:03).

Since this example is the closest yet to an even fusion of EDM and pop forms, let's start with topical features that perch on that dividing line. Like any pop song, "Ebeneezer Goode" has several hooks. I will look at three in particular: the main theme (in both instrumental and vocal forms), the lyrical pun, and the presence of a rap. As is often the case, the hooks are also topical, which adds to their effectiveness as attention-grabbers. Let's take them one at a time, starting with the pun. This lyrical pun, like many earlier psychedelic drug references, is thinly veiled but also difficult to miss ("Eezer Goode" = "E's are good," repeated over and over). But is it legitimate to consider this as topical, a procedure as general as the clever use of words to create a double entendre drug reference? I believe that it does have all of the hallmarks of topicality. On the one hand, the specific indexicality necessary for topic formation could be a problem, given that there is a long and varied history of illicit double entendres in popular music. But there is no inherent difficulty in saying that different historical instances of this sort of double entendre could create their own indexical connections, which would then later allow for distinct but related topics. In other words, a contemporary R&B artist singing a sexual double entendre could be understood as evoking a topic rooted in 1940s R&B and its immediate successors. And a neopsychedelic rave producer using a drug-related double entendre would be evoking a related but distinct topic rooted in 1960s countercultural contexts.

The next topical hook is related to the lyrical pun, because it is the catchy four-note figure that is first heard in a retro combo organ setting and is then used to sing the pun. It is only indirectly topical when sung, because in those passages the topicality is in the lyrics. But in the organ version it is a different topic altogether, evoking 1960s garage rock. This example brings up a general point regarding capture. When discussing early 1980s rock styles I suggested that there was a tendency for materials such as this combo organ timbre to be captured by the retro aspect, making it difficult for the songs overall to be heard as primarily psychedelic or at least as any kind of new statement within psychedelia. But in a case like "Ebeneezer Goode" the retro element is free to fully signify 1960s garage rock without forcing the overall recording away from a more contemporary identity. This point is perhaps obvious, but it is worth saying out loud: capture is far more likely when many similar topics are mobilized in the same piece.

The last hook to consider is the rap, delivered by a narrator/guide persona who is giving advice on how to deal with Ebeneezer. How does this rap relate to the psychedelic elements? For the most part, I consider hip-hop in this context as a strong topical reference coming almost entirely from outside psychedelia. This is not an unproblematic claim, because in the early 1990s trip hop was emergent in the UK, and some US artists such as De La Soul had already drawn extensively from psychedelic influences. Beyond this, there continue to be artists in experimental hip-hop whose work could be regarded as psychedelic, for example, Quasimoto. On the other hand, the "trip" part of trip hop was generally linked more to dub than to psychedelia, so Michael Veal's cautions about a psychedelic reading, cited earlier, would apply. Similarly, in the case of many artists such as De La Soul the psychedelic reference points were subsumed under a general 1960s sunshine pop reference. Most fundamentally, the other topical associations of hip-hop were so well established that the genre's primary signification was likely to be regarded by most listeners as nonpsychedelic. On the whole, then, the rap in "Ebeneezer Goode" can be read as drawing on both the availability of hip-hop as a surprising and extrapsychedelic topical reference and at the same time suggesting solidarity with the relatively few areas of overlap between hip-hop culture and psychedelia of the time. This situation means that the rap has several different layers of topical nuance, all available at once. First, insofar as it can be linked to earlier psychedelic style features the rap is a little like a psychedelic narrative or spoken element, especially because the contents of the rap suggest a guide figure. But relative to earlier psychedelic narrative and spoken passages, there is an affective difference. The rap is comparatively faster and more edgy, more evocative of the speedy rave scene. Second, the presence of rap in an EDM rave production draws attention to other areas of EDM, such as the way it has drawn on electro-funk influences. It asserts the importance of topical areas within EDM beyond the psychedelic and so situates psychedelic EDM topicality within a broader context. Finally, despite the strong US associations of hip-hop, this particular rap signifies Britishness because of the notable accent, the specific dialect, and the arguably greater currency at that time of psychedelic hip-hop crossovers in the UK.

All of the features discussed to this point are closer to the pop song aspect of "Ebeneezer Goode." When we consider the more EDM-specific features, one striking thing is how many of the topical and formal aspects are similar to the earlier ambient examples. For example, there is the same basic formal strategy of slow accumulation and a similar TB-303 acid sequence. By contrast, two of the more noteworthy techniques not present in the earlier examples are the long filter sweeps and the fast stuttering/gapped motor rhythms. These were common devices in faster rave EDM productions and have interesting connections to earlier psychedelic style features. But they are also features that emerged as definitive ones of trance, so I'll move on to consider that most self-consciously neopsychedelic of EDM styles.

The Trance Family

To conclude our survey of psychedelic EDM, I will step back from individual examples and consider the broader subgenre of psytrance. I will also simplify the discussion by treating psytrance as inclusive of the earlier Goa trance genre. In considering the broad features of psytrance, we can return to one of our first questions: To what degree do the self-consciously psychedelic EDM genres actually differ from others? Is psychedelic topicality fairly evenly distributed within EDM, or does it cluster more strongly in some subgenres than in others?

Psytrance as a genre is broad and complex. As Graham St. John notes, "Psytrance constitutes a shifting sonic quilt of genre influences as well as a diversity of national/regional populations and scenes in which recognizable sounds have emerged, or distinct fusions formed" (2010, 1). This is one reason why St. John, along with most other researchers in the area, chooses to approach psytrance as a family of practices rather than as a singular style or scene. One of the practices that defines psytrance is a tendency to continually transpose styles, behaviors, and ideas associated with Goa trance into new spaces and contexts. But Goa trance is itself a complicated hybrid, in part because it emerged during a period in which the older rock-based hippie culture was gradually transforming into an EDM-based one: "Early Goa trance came out of a unique amalgamation of psychedelic rockers, acid-head mystics, gay club culture, innovative music producers, and anti-establishment crusties" (Saldanha 2007, 39). Key figures on the scene, such as Goa Gil, often consciously crafted their music and practices in order to form a bridge between 1960s-era psychedelic spirituality and contemporary trance scenes (Davis 2004, especially 264–65). Unfortunately, we are left without any extensive recorded archive of the musical stages involved in this gradual transformation. There are, however, verbal accounts that offer partial descriptions, like this one from Luther Elliott:

> Goa's earliest electronic dance party soundtracks owed few allegiances to any particular generic form. The emergent musical style was cobbled together from what was at that time called new wave, electro(disco), industrial, kraut-rock and synth-pop—

often with the vocal sections edited out. It is perhaps best identified as an assemblage by the emphasis on rhythm and alien, exotic sonic palettes created by synthesizers, a heavy use of effects and the slowing down, speeding up, and reversing of analogue tape playback.... It has often been impressed upon me that the "hard," "industrial," and above all "psychedelic" sounds of these early pioneers had little in common with early Detroit Techno and Chicago House, which supplied many of the anthems for [UK rave]. Prior to that point, though, several key informants have insisted, much of the "Acid House" that was being played in London clubs and warehouses was also finding its way to Goa. The hippie legacy in India invariably dictated that the musical programming at all-night beach parties adhere to the varied sonic and stylistic expectations invoked by the category "psychedelic." (2010, 31–32)

From the perspective of emergent topicality, this picture of Goa as a meeting ground is highly suggestive. It's a picture of diverse social actors interacting in a temporally and geographically specific context and producing a music that is both indexically evocative of that context and at the same time fundamentally dialogic. It also suggests that Goa trance is a context well suited for pushing psychedelic topicality into new directions, because while the common psychedelic interests of the various participants helped ensure that the music was largely framed within a psychedelic topical field, their diverse backgrounds and interests encouraged the development of new stylistic variations, new tropes, and so on. In addition, these varied backgrounds link psychedelic topicality with other new contexts besides Goa itself, such as the gay dance underground and specific cities like Chicago and Detroit. Perhaps most importantly, this rich meeting place did not produce an indistinct mish-mash but for the most part a recognizable new style family, which has already been extensively described in the musicological literature. Let's look at a few such descriptions in order to collect a list of the most distinguishing trance features. We can begin with Robin Lindop, who, while reiterating that psytrance is not amenable to any monologic definition, also reports that many producers adhere to a generic notion of a core style, sometimes called "full-on" psytrance, with the following features (all drawn from Lindop 2010, 115–16):

- A tempo of around 145 beats per minute.
- A four-on-the-floor, "trancey"-sounding bass drum (i.e., the coupling of a sharp attack or "knock" with a low bass "thud").
- A "driving" or "galloping" sixteenth-note-oriented bass line featuring a typical psytrance synth bass sound (generally similar to the Roland TB-303 acid sequence sound).
- A focus on one tonal center or drone (i.e., little or no harmonic variation).
- Use of the flattened second degree of the scale (particularly in bass and lead lines).
- Swirling, "squelchy" synth sounds.
- Quirky sounds and samples, many drawn from science fiction or Orientalist sources. Also incorporation of speech samples, typically those concerning psychedelic experience.
- Frequent use of a "stutter filter" on vocals.
- Synthesis favored over sampling.
- An abundance of breakdowns, stops, and buildups.

According to Luther Elliott, some of these features were of special importance for distinguishing Goa trance from other similarly named EDM subgenres:

> The earlier use of the term "trance" as a stylistic marker for some European dance music, employing anthem-like melodic sections, necessitated some qualification for the more exotic, more Orientalised music associated with Goa. Less likely to include "uplifting" or "triumphant" melodic development (realised generally through use of major scales), the rapidly coalescing Goa trance genre adopted Phrygian and diminished blues scales, setting up the trademark sixteenth (and syncopated thirty-second note) melodic "lead"—often programmed as an automated synthesiser arpeggiation of tonic, flat second, flat seventh, flat third, and perfect fifth. (2010, 34, based in part on Cole and Hannan 1997)

Another detailed description, this time from Arun Saldanha, reinforces some of these points and adds others:

> Goa trance in its heyday, 1995 to 1997, was characterized by a pronounced kick drum, straightforward hi-hat and clap patterns, thumping between 145 and 155 bpm. Significantly, in its purposeful path away from black dance musics . . . Goa trance in a way returned to rock's emphasis on the cerebral, sometimes even integrating heavy metal guitar chords or a $\frac{3}{4}$ rhythm to bring home its intellectuality. . . . The distinctly hallucinatory force of Goa trance (called simply "Goa" in much of Europe) arises from increasing and decreasing the filter cutoff frequency of the bleeps, crunches, and sweeps in raga-like melodies, then passing these through stereo delay and phaser effects. Unlike in house and techno, Goa trance tracks are complete units, and deejays are usually bad at mixing. Tracks sometimes have "ethnic" instrumentation and quirky sci-fi samples scattered over them. (2007, 41)

Saldanha's "bad at mixing" remark resonates with something also observed by Mark Butler, which is that trance might be more sharply articulated in form, and less improvisatory, than some other forms of EDM: "Not only is form in trance typically expressed much more markedly [than in techno], it is also much more commonly built into the record by the producer, whereas techno tracks are often considerably more static and generic prior to their manipulation by the DJ" (2006, 228). This greater emphasis on form does not mean that breakdowns are less common in trance. In fact, they are even more common there than in other genres, and they host some of trance's most distinctive characteristics. Butler offers a few details: "In addition to the removal of the bass drum, breakdowns may be associated with a host of other features, some of which are quite genre-specific. Trance breakdowns, for example, are often quite long, and tend to introduce an 'ambient' feel through the use of sustained synth lines or strings without accompanying drumbeats. Another characteristic of breakdowns common to many genres is timbral manipulation" (2006, 92).

Finally, we should include an observation from Lindop, who argues that such timbral manipulation is one of the more important psychedelic aspects of psytrance:

> Rather than incorporating other EDM subgenres in their purer and more understood forms, psytrance tends to *psychedelicise* these styles.... The process of *psychedelicising* can be understood as a set of production techniques; a musical "code" that is unique to psytrance.... [These elements include] [u]se of playful, intricate, quirky synth sounds that have "texturological" effects (i.e., sounds that have a texture that makes the listener want to touch them); [s]ampled elements from non-Western music, especially vocals (that are frequently cut-up, distorted and transformed, especially with "stutter" filter) and percussion; [a] focus on the creation of atmosphere, achieved via attention to texture rather than melodic or harmonic elements; [v]ery high production values, multi-layered, expansive pieces of music; [u]se of drone effects (single tonal centres in "full on" psy, dub reggae bass lines in "psychill," etc.); [s]peech samples that focus on psychedelic experience, transcendence and the supernatural. (2010, 118–19)

But which of these features are truly unique to psytrance? None completely. Rather than innovating entirely distinctive psychedelic signifiers, psytrance gains its identity within EDM by selecting and emphasizing the more psychedelic features also found in other EDM genres. Most of these are extremely obvious because they are based on the status of the sounds as earlier psychedelic topics. This is especially true of the Orientalist/exoticist and space-rock elements, and the way that these are often used in extremely clichéd forms is a hint that their main job is to evoke existing topics. Similarly, the use of recognizable samples evokes an indexical connection between this music and earlier contexts and texts of the psychedelic in a way more concerned with mobilizing existing topics than transforming them. This isn't to say that new topics do not arise at all in psytrance. What I'm suggesting is that there are two types of psychedelic topicality in this music. The obvious type, which is also the one that underscores the genre's explicit claim to being psychedelic, is the mobilization of existing clichéd psychedelic topics. The second type arises because psytrance is a subgenre of EDM and so displays all of the more subtle relationships to psychedelic topicality discussed earlier in connection with examples from other EDM subgenres. That level is less obvious and is not unique to psytrance, but it is more interesting in terms of the longer-term development of topical fields.

To come full circle: When we look at events in the topical field of psychedelia during the 1980s and early 1990s, how much novelty do we find? On certain points there is no doubt that new things happened. In both rock and EDM there were new stylistic variations on existing topics, and there were striking new tropes. Given time to cover more examples, we would have found similar innovations in psychedelic funk (especially in the work of Prince) and a little later in genres such as freak folk as well. In some cases, these innovations took place in contexts that framed the musics as primarily psychedelic and so can be read as alterations to the topical field of psychedelia itself. In others, it was more a matter of psychedelia exerting an influence in other genres, which alters the psychedelic field more indirectly by changing its positioning and relationships of overlap relative to other topical fields.

In terms of more fundamental changes to the field, we have seen some developments whose significance might prove great over time but where it is too early to make a final judgment. One example is the way that connections between Afrofuturism and the posthuman were minimized in some kinds of EDM. These dance genres further developed the sort of futuristic synthesizer electronics associated with mid-1970s Afrofuturist funk while at the same time deemphasizing the element of racial politics and in many cases even of specific cultural origins altogether. Also, the increasingly global production and consumption base of psytrance might eventually turn out to be a factor in reorienting parts of the field, given the right circumstances. In cases like these there is clear potential for sweeping changes in what psychedelia can mean and what topical resources it draws from, but there is also as yet a lack of definitive evidence that such changes have taken place. Finally, we should note one area in which musical topicality seems to have failed to capitalize on an opportunity. The shift in psychedelic imaginaries of the late 1970s created a new trope of great novelty and significance by combining neoshamanic mythologies and their associated ethnobotanical focus with posthuman cyberculture. But there is little in the music itself that specifically represents this trope. It is hinted at in the frequent troping of EDM and space rock with exoticist topics, but this is a combination that was already being explored by the early 1970s, and the new variants are not nearly as specific or novel as they might be.

The openness of these questions is to be expected, because topical change takes time. At any given moment it is possible to identify variations of style or context that might develop into new topics or into major new possibilities of existing topics, but such variations can only be called topical if they endure, spread beyond their original situation, and become standardized. It is too early to tell which of the new variants discussed in this chapter might become fully topical, but what can be said with certainty is that there is nothing in the recent past to suggest that the psychedelic topical field has become closed or moribund. It is becoming more self-reflexive, but that too is almost a requirement for a developing topical field. It is also perhaps becoming more stylistically conservative, and this poses the most interesting open question: Can a topical field that was originally premised on radical experimentation evolve in a more tradition-bound direction without losing its original identity? Is self-reference and incremental self-revision consistent with psychedelic topicality, or will trends in this direction transform it into something else altogether?

Notes

1. As of this writing, the abbreviation EDM is beginning to acquire negative connotations, since some on the electronic popular music scene regard it as signifying specifically commercial and derivative dance music product. That recent shift of nuance aside, I will use the term as a convenient shorthand and in its original sense to refer to all styles of electronic dance music of the late 1980s and early 1990s.

2. One source where the samples are discussed is http://www.soundonsound.com/sos/aug11/articles/classic-tracks-0811.htm. But some of the material there is questioned else-

where. For example, the claim that one speaker is LeVar Burton has been doubted, and many believe that the drums come from a recording by Harry Nilsson. These counterviews are reported, among other places, at https://en.wikipedia.org/wiki/Little_Fluffy_Clouds #Samples. I last accessed both websites on August 8, 2015.

3. My transcription of this passage treats the Reich sample as part of the present recording, so the notation is selected to show the logic of how it fits into these surroundings and is not necessarily the same as what would appear for this part on Reich's original score.

Epilogue:
Conclusions and Prospects

My goals for this book were fairly modest. Most importantly, I wanted to explore the idea that new topics and new topical fields are always emerging and that contemporary popular genres such as psychedelia are a good place to look for them. In addition, I wanted to demonstrate that topic theory can be a valuable tool for popular music studies—indeed, that a certain amount of popular music studies is already topic theory—and conversely that topic theory can be enriched by the social and critical perspectives of popular music studies. In order to demonstrate all of this, I made adjustments to the standard model of topic theory, bringing it closer to the way scholars of popular music often address questions of musical meaning but hopefully without damaging its core strengths. From existing topic theory I kept the basic structure of the topic, which includes its indexical roots in historical and social contexts, the processes of diffusion and transposition into new contexts, and the emphasis on conventionalization. But I also emphasized the dynamism of topics themselves and the processes through which they emerge and transform. In methodological terms, this involved looking for moments of dialogism, paying special attention to partially formed topics, attending to the way that topics can be arranged into temporally sedimented layers, and finding sites of multiple reading or ambiguity. My orientation also involved putting forward some specific theoretical claims that diverge from conventional topic theory but that are generally well accepted within popular music studies: that competencies are multiple and negotiated rather than universal and that the meaning of topics always needs to be situated relative to particular communities. There was also one theoretical move that proved crucial to my analysis but that sits outside the mainstream of both topic theory and popular music studies: the claim that topics can be indexically connected to both virtual worlds and the literal world and that this sort of indexicality often needs to be treated as equivalent to the more standard kind.

When it comes to findings, the main one is that the primary idea panned out. I believe it's clear that there is a new emergent topical field connected with psychedelia, that it draws upon a wide range of preexisting topics, that it has played a decisive role in shaping new topics, and that it has so far sustained a half-century history of proliferation and change with no signs of immediately coming to an end. None of this will be surprising to readers who know the music, but developing an extended demonstration was still an attractive prospect. In terms of more specific findings, we have seen that the space topic and various exoticist topics—both specifically Orientalist topics and the universal roots topic—are especially active and central subfields of psychedelia. These two subfields were present from the start, have lasted into the present, and have been foundational to most psychedelic styles. We have also had a chance to examine topical subfields that are more patchy in where and how they manifest but are of great overall importance. These include topics of the classical, the belle époque, Tin Pan Alley and other old pop forms, the church and other religious institutions, the martial, the urban, folklore and traditional folk musics, film genres (western, spy, surf, and science fiction), theatrical traditions (opera, Broadway, music hall), jazz, Latin, and the nautical. We have also had the opportunity to describe a few expressive genres of psychedelia—the outward journey and the strange trip—along with a few standardized large forms, including the decorated pop song, the rave-up, the developing variation jam, the funk jam, unmeasured sound effects passages, and the EDM form.

That being said, this book was intended as a pilot project and a proof of concept, so there remains a great deal of work to be done in order to both advance understanding of the psychedelic topical field and expand our knowledge of popular music topicality in general. For one thing, at some point there need to be more topical studies of reception and the experiences of listeners, perhaps along the lines of Philip Tagg's work on intersubjective comparison. In this book, considerations of a social nature were crucial in setting the theoretical agenda, choosing questions, and framing interpretations, but the next step of proper fieldwork still needs to be taken. It will also be important to pursue more intermedia comparisons, building on the findings of the poster art pilot study in order to properly demonstrate how popular musical topicality sits in the larger topical continuum. Attention to film and video would be especially important in this regard. An intermedia perspective of this sort would need to go along with more particularistic and wide-ranging studies of historical and social context. In this book I have had to be very selective, focusing on issues of exoticism and race. Other axes of context and interpretation such as gender, sexuality, and class will also need to be accounted for in future studies. And this should be done not only with respect to the Anglo-American contexts that have been my focus but also with a broader range of translocal and transnational sites and relationships.

This is the second book I have written on popular music signification, and I am keenly aware of how the two fall into certain well-worn binaries. The first, about Neil Young and spatial/energetic metaphors, engaged with more affective and sensual aspects of the music. This present study is more lexicographic, more about items of vocabulary than affect. In each case I aimed to demonstrate some of the intermingling of these modes by exploring the code-like aspects of energetic forms in the Neil Young book and by emphasizing the dynamics of topicality in this one. There might be good reasons why musical meaning seems to invite these two broadly different kinds of approach, but then again, further synthesis might be possible. In any event, I hope that the theoretical models in this book can be taken up by others who would take an interest in putting them together with other sorts of approaches as part of a search for new connections and new points of view. And in that same spirit, I hope that the findings offered here about psychedelia can be part of a broader, ongoing project to map the rich variety of popular music topical fields in the twentieth and twenty-first centuries.

Appendix A:
The Sample and Discography

This appendix is in two parts. The first part names all the songs and instrumentals that were consulted in some detail during research for the book. It is meant to give readers a sense of which artists and pieces were most influential in shaping my generalizations and conclusions. It could also serve as a listening list. The second part of the appendix provides discographic information for those songs whose specific sonic features are discussed in the text.

Part 1: Overall List of Songs and Instrumentals

Not everything on this list is mentioned in the text, and my listening overall was much broader than what could be included here. So the purpose of this list is to give a sense of which particular pieces emerged as important enough to my thinking to receive detailed attention at some point in the research. Pieces are arranged by their year of first release and alphabetically by artist within each year. For pieces also included in the discography, numbers in square brackets indicate which discography entry they correspond to.

1962

Dick Dale, "Misirlou"

1965

The Beatles, "If I Needed Someone," "Norwegian Wood (This Bird Has Flown)" [2], "Think for Yourself" [2]
The Byrds, "Mr. Tambourine Man"
The Kinks, "See My Friends" [23]
The Seeds, "Pushin' Too Hard"
The Yardbirds, "Evil Hearted You" [39], "For Your Love" [39], "Heart Full of Soul" [39], "I'm a Man" [39]

1966

The Beach Boys, "Good Vibrations," "That's Not Me," "Wouldn't It Be Nice"
The Beatles, "I'm Only Sleeping" [3], "Love You To," "Rain" [6], "She Said She Said," "Taxman" [3], "Tomorrow Never Knows" [3], "Yellow Submarine" [3]
The Bees, "Voices Green and Purple"

The Byrds, "Eight Miles High" [8]
The Chambers Brothers, "Time Has Come Today" (first single version)
The Count Five, "Psychotic Reaction"
Country Joe and the Fish, "Section 43" [38]
The Deep, "Color Dreams," "It's All a Part of Me," "Psychedelic Moon," "Shadows on the Wall," "Trip #76," "When Rain Is Black"
Donovan, "Guinevere" [12], "Mellow Yellow," "The Trip"
Bob Dylan, "Rainy Day Women #12 and 35"
The Electric Prunes, "I Had Too Much to Dream Last Night" [37]
The Ethix, "Bad Trip"
Jefferson Airplane, "Blues from an Airplane" [20], "It's No Secret"
Love, "Hey Joe," "Orange Skies," "Seven & Seven Is" [25], "Softly to Me" [24], "Stephanie Knows Who" [25]
Lyme & Cybelle, "Follow Me" [37]
The Magic Mushrooms, "It's-a-Happening"
The Rolling Stones, "Lady Jane" [33], "Paint It, Black" [33]
Sopwith Camel, "Hello Hello"
The 13th Floor Elevators, "The Kingdom of Heaven (Is within You)" [1], "Roller Coaster" [1], "Splash 1 (Now I'm Home)," "Thru the Rhythm," "You're Gonna Miss Me" [1]
The Yardbirds, "Happenings Ten Years Time Ago" [39], "Hot House of Omagarashid," "Lost Woman," "Over, Under, Sideways, Down" [39], "Shapes of Things" [39], "Turn into Earth"
Frank Zappa, "Help, I'm a Rock (Suite in Three Movements)," "Hungry Freaks, Daddy," "Who Are the Brain Police?"

1967

The Beatles, "A Day in the Life" [4], "All You Need Is Love" [5], "Baby You're a Rich Man" [5], "Being for the Benefit of Mr. Kite!" [4], "Blue Jay Way," "Good Morning Good Morning" [4], "I Am the Walrus" [5], "Lovely Rita" [4], "Lucy in the Sky with Diamonds" [4], "Magical Mystery Tour," "Penny Lane," "Sgt. Pepper's Lonely Hearts Club Band" [4], "Strawberry Fields Forever" [5], "When I'm Sixty-Four" [4], "Within You Without You" [4]
The Beau Brummels, "Two Days 'til Tomorrow"
The Chambers Brothers, "Time Has Come Today" (LP version) [10]
The Doors, "Light My Fire," "The End" [13]
Fifty Foot Hose, "If Not This Time," "Red the Sign Post"
The Freak Scene, "Grok!," "The Center of My Soul," "The Subway Ride thru Inner Space," "When in the Course of Human Events..."
The Grateful Dead, "Cold Rain and Snow" [16], "Good Morning Little School Girl" [16], "Overseas Stomp (the Lindy)," "The Golden Road (to Unlimited Devotion)" [16], "Viola Lee Blues"
The Incredible String Band, "Chinese White" [19], "Little Cloud" [19], "The Mad Hatter's Song" [19]
Jefferson Airplane, "She Has Funny Cars," "Somebody to Love," "The Ballad of You and Me and Pooneil," "Today," "White Rabbit" [21]

Jimi Hendrix, "Are You Experienced?," "Burning of the Midnight Lamp," "Castles Made of Sand," "EXP," "One Rainy Wish," "Purple Haze," "The Wind Cries Mary," "Third Stone from the Sun" [22], "Up from the Skies"
Love, "Alone Again Or," "The Daily Planet"
Pink Floyd, "Astronomy Domine" [30], "Bike" [30], "Chapter 24" [30], "Flaming" [30], "Interstellar Overdrive" [30], "Matilda Mother" [30]
The Rolling Stones, "2000 Light Years from Home," "Something Happened to Me Yesterday," "We Love You"
Sly and the Family Stone, "I Hate to Love Her," "Trip to Your Heart" [35]
Tomorrow, "My White Bicycle," "Three Jolly Little Dwarfs"
The Velvet Underground, "Venus in Furs"

1968–1969

Amon Düül II, "Kanaan," "Phallus Dei"
The Beatles, "Revolution 9," "The Inner Light"
Can, "Father Cannot Yell" [9], "Yoo Doo Right"
Donovan, "Atlantis" [12], "Hurdy Gurdy Man"
The Grateful Dead, "Alligator > Caution (Do Not Stop on Tracks) > Feedback" (live, February 24, 1968) [17], "Alligator > Caution (Do Not Stop on Tracks) > Feedback" (live, August 23, 1968) [16], "Alligator > Caution (Do Not Stop on Tracks)" (Anthem of the Sun version) [16], "Dark Star" (single version) [38]
Jimi Hendrix, "1983 . . . (a Merman I Should Turn to Be)"
Pink Floyd, "Set the Controls for the Heart of the Sun" [31]
Sly and the Family Stone, "Dance to the Medley" [35], "Higher" [35], "I'm an Animal"
The Temptations, "Cloud Nine," "Psychedelic Shack," "Runaway Child, Running Wild"
Tyrannosaurus Rex, "Deborraarobed"
The United States of America, "Cloud Song," "Coming Down"

1970–1976

Amon Düül II, "Archangel's Thunderbird," "Sandoz in the Rain," "Soap Shop Rock—Burning Sister," "Yeti"
Fripp & Eno, "The Heavenly Music Corporation"
Funkadelic, "Eulogy and Light" [15], "Free Your Mind and Your Ass Will Follow" [15], "Mommy, What's a Funkadelic?" [14], "Music for My Mother" [14]
The Grateful Dead, "Box of Rain," "Casey Jones," "Eyes of the World," "Uncle John's Band"
Hawkwind, "Be Yourself" [18], "Hurry On Sundown," "Paranoia (Part 1)," "You Shouldn't Do That"
Parliament, "Dr. Funkenstein," "Little Old Country Boy," "Livin' the Life," "My Automobile," "P. Funk (Wants to Get Funked Up)" [29], "Prelude" [29], "The Silent Boatman," "There Is Nothing before Me but Thang" [28]
The Temptations, "Take a Stroll thru Your Mind"

1979–1987

The Butthole Surfers, "Creep in the Cellar" [7], "Sea Ferring" [7], "Strangers Die Every Day" [7]
Ozric Tentacles, "Dots Thots" (live, Reading, September 1985), "Stupid Reggae" (live, Glastonbury, October 1985)"
Prince, "Around the World in a Day," "Tamborine"
The Screaming Trees, "You Tell Me All These Things"
The Soft Boys, "The Queen of Eyes," "Underwater Moonlight" [36]
Spacemen 3, "Walkin' with Jesus"
The Teardrop Explodes, "Bouncing Babies" [11]

1990–1999

Bardo Pond, "Absence," "Amen," "Back Porch," "No Time to Waste," "On a Side Street"
The Chemical Brothers, "Setting Sun"
The Flaming Lips, "Race for the Prize," "Unconsciously Screaming"
Hallucinogen, "L.S.D."
The Orb, "Little Fluffy Clouds" [26], "Towers of Dub" [27]
Primal Scream, "Loaded" [32]
The Shamen, "Ebeneezer Goode (Beatmasters Mix)" [34], "Re-evolution" [34]

Part 2: Discography

The purpose of this discography is to allow readers to consult recordings cited in the book in cases where specific sonic details are given. It makes no claim to being a comprehensive discography of psychedelia, and since the primary purpose is to allow cross-checking of details given in the text, it does not contain information about recordings beyond those that I personally used. Years indicate release of the edition I used and generally do not correspond to original release dates.

[1]. The 13th Floor Elevators, *The Psychedelic Sounds of the 13th Floor Elevators*, CD, Fuel 2000, 2003.
[2]. The Beatles, *Rubber Soul*, CD, EMI, 1965 (CD package does not include CD edition date).
[3]. The Beatles, *Revolver*, CD, EMI, 1966 (CD package does not include CD edition date).
[4]. The Beatles, *Sgt. Pepper's Lonely Hearts Club Band*, CD, EMI, 1987.
[5]. The Beatles, *Magical Mystery Tour*, CD, EMI, 1987.
[6]. The Beatles, *Past Masters Volume Two*, CD, EMI, 1988.
[7]. The Butthole Surfers, *Rembrandt Pussyhorse / Cream Corn from the Socket of Davis*, CD, Touch . . . Go, 1986.
[8]. The Byrds, *The Byrds*, CD boxed set, Columbia/Legacy, 1990.
[9]. Can, *Monster Movie*, CD, Mute/Spoon, 1990.
[10]. The Chambers Brothers, *The Time Has Come*, digital copy purchased from iTunes store, Sony Music Entertainment, 2008.
[11]. Julian Cope, *Floored Genius: The Best of Julian Cope and The Teardrop Explodes 1979. 91*, CD, Island, 1992.

[12]. Donovan, *Troubadour: The Definitive Collection 1964, 1976*, CD, Epic/Legacy, 1992.
[13]. The Doors, *The Best of the Doors*, CD, Elektra, 1985.
[14]. Funkadelic, *Funkadelic*, digital copy purchased from iTunes store, Westbound Records, 2005.
[15]. Funkadelic, *Free Your Mind . . .*, digital copy purchased from iTunes store, Westbound Records, 2005.
[16]. The Grateful Dead, *The Golden Road (1965, 1973)*, CD boxed set, Rhino, 2001.
[17]. The Grateful Dead, *Dick's Picks Vol. 22*, CD, Grateful Dead Records, 2004.
[18]. Hawkwind, *Hawkwind*, CD, EMI, 1996.
[19]. The Incredible String Band, *5000 Spirits / The Hangman's Beautiful Daughter*, CD, Collector's Choice Music, 2002.
[20]. Jefferson Airplane, *The Worst of Jefferson Airplane*, CD, BMG/RCA, 1970 (CD package does not include CD edition date).
[21]. Jefferson Airplane, *Surrealistic Pillow (Expanded Edition)*, CD, RCA/BMG, 2003.
[22]. The Jimi Hendrix Experience, *Are You Experienced?*, CD, Experience Hendrix / MCA, 1997.
[23]. The Kinks, *Kinda Kinks (Deluxe Edition)*, digital copy purchased from iTunes store, Sanctuary Records / BMG, 2011.
[24]. Love, *Love*, CD, Elektra/Asylum, 1988.
[25]. Love, *Da Capo*, CD, Elektra/Warner, 2002.
[26]. The Orb, *the orb's adventures beyond the ultraworld*, CD, Island, 1991.
[27]. The Orb, *u.f.orb*, CD, Island, 1992.
[28]. Parliament, *First Thangs*, digital copy purchased from iTunes store, HDH Records / Invictus, 1995.
[29]. Parliament, *Tear the Roof Off 1974, 1980*, CD, Casablanca/PolyGram, 1993.
[30]. Pink Floyd, *The Piper at the Gates of Dawn*, CD boxed set, EMI, 2007.
[31]. Pink Floyd, *A Saucerful of Secrets*, CD, EMI, 1994.
[32]. Primal Scream, *Screamadelica*, CD, Sire / Warner Bros., 1991.
[33]. The Rolling Stones, *Aftermath*, CD, ABKCO, 2002.
[34]. The Shamen, *Boss Drum*, CD, Epic / One Little Indian, 1992.
[35]. Sly and the Family Stone, *The Collection*, CD boxed set, Sony BMG, 2007.
[36]. The Soft Boys, *Underwater Moonlight and How It Got There*, CD, Matador, 2001.
[37]. Various artists, *Nuggets: Original Artyfacts from the First Psychedelic Era 1965, 1968*, CD boxed set, Rhino, 1998.
[38]. Various artists, *Love Is the Song We Sing: San Francisco Nuggets 1965, 1970*, CD boxed set, Rhino, 2007.
[39]. The Yardbirds, *Ultimate!*, CD, Rhino, 2001.

Appendix B:
The San Francisco Poster Sample

Numbers marked BG follow the Bill Graham numbering system as presented in Lemke and Kastor (1997, 21). The citation format for posters within the BG numbering system is poster artist; event description; event date; BG number. All of these posters can be found in the Lemke and Kastor collection. For the smaller number of posters included from outside this group, the citation format is the same, but the BG number is replaced by the venue. A few of these can be found in the Lemke and Kastor collection, and the rest are included in Owen and Dickson (1999).

Pst1. W. Wilson; The Sound Festival; 9/23–10/2/66; BG 29–1b

Pst2. W. Wilson; Captain Beefheart & His Magic Band / The Chocolate Watch Band / The Great Pumpkin; 10/28–30/66; BG 34–1

Pst3. W. Wilson; The Grateful Dead / James Cotton / Lothar & the Hand People; 11/18–20/66; BG 38–1

Pst4. W. Wilson; Love / Moby Grape / Lee Michaels; 12/2–4/66; BG 40–1

Pst5. W. Wilson; Chuck Berry / The Grateful Dead / Johnny Talbot and De Thangs; 3/17–19/67; BG 55–1

Pst6. W. Wilson; The Chambers Brothers / Quicksilver Messenger Service / Sandy Bull; 4/7–9/67; BG 58–1

Pst7. W. Wilson; Trips Festival; 1/21–23/66; Longshoremen's Hall

Pst8. P. Bailey; Trips Festival; 1/21–23/66; Longshoremen's Hall

Pst9. P. Bailey; Jefferson Airplane; 2/4–6/66; BG 1–1

Pst10. W. Wilson; Batman Dance and Film Festival; 3/18–20/66; BG 2–1

Pst11. W. Wilson; Blues-Rock Bash; 4/15–17/66; BG 3–1

Pst12. W. Wilson; The Blues Project / The Great Society; 4/22–23/66; Avalon Ballroom

Pst13. W. Wilson; Quicksilver Messenger Service / Final Solution; 5/20–21/66; BG 7–1

Pst14. W. Wilson; Quicksilver Messenger Service / The Grateful Dead / The Mothers; 6/3–4/66; BG 9–1

Pst15. S. Mouse, A. Kelley; Big Brother and the Holding Company / Quicksilver Messenger Service; 6/24–25/66; Avalon Ballroom

Pst16. W. Wilson; The Turtles / The Oxford Circle; 7/6/66; BG 15–1

Pst17. S. Mouse, A. Kelley; The Grateful Dead / The Oxford Circle; 9/16–17/66; Avalon Ballroom

Pst18. W. Wilson; Butterfield Blues Band / Jefferson Airplane / The Grateful Dead; 10/7–8/66; BG 30–1

Pst19. S. Mouse, A. Kelley; Daily Flash / Country Joe & The Fish; 10/21–22/66; Avalon Ballroom

Pst20. W. Wilson; Muddy Waters / Quicksilver Messenger Service / Andrew Staples; 11/4–6/66; BG 35–1

Pst21. W. Wilson; Jefferson Airplane / James Cotton / Moby Grape; 11/25–27/66; BG 39-1

Pst22a. M. Bowen, S. Mouse, A. Kelley; The Human Be-In; 1/14/67; the Polo Field, Golden Gate Park

Pst22b. R. Griffin; The Human Be-In; 1/14/67; the Polo Field, Golden Gate Park

Pst23. W. Wilson; Jefferson Airplane / Quicksilver Messenger Service / Dino Valenti; 2/3–5/67; BG 48-2a

Pst24. W. Wilson; Otis Rush / The Mothers / The Morning Glory; 3/3–5/67; BG 53-1

Pst25. W. Wilson; Moby Grape / The Chambers Brothers / The Charlatans; 3/24–26/67; BG 56-1

Pst26. W. Wilson; The Byrds / Moby Grape / Andrew Staples; 3/31–4/2/67; BG 57-1

Pst27. B. MacLean; Jefferson Airplane / The Paupers; 5/12–14/67; BG 63-1

Pst28. B. MacLean; The Doors / Jim Kweskin Jug Band; 6/9–10/67; BG 67-1

Pst29. C. Seeley; Jefferson Airplane / Gabor Szabo / Jimi Hendrix; 6/20–25/67; BG 69-1

Pst30. G. Irons; Chuck Berry / Eric Burdon & The Animals / Steve Miller Blues Band; 6/27–7/2/67; BG 70-1

Pst31. B. MacLean; Bo Diddley / Big Brother and the Holding Company / Quicksilver Messenger Service / Joe Williams; 7/4–9/67; BG 71-1

Pst32. B. MacLean; Butterfield Blues Band / Roland Kirk Quartet; 7/11–16/67; BG 72-1

Pst33. B. MacLean; Sam & Dave / James Cotton / Country Joe & The Fish / The Loading Zone; 7/18–23/67; BG 73-1

Pst34. B. MacLean; The Yardbirds / The Doors / James Cotton / Richie Havens; 7/25–30/67; BG 75-1

Pst35. B. MacLean; Electric Flag / Moby Grape / Steve Miller Band / South Side Sound System; 8/8–13/67; BG 77-1

Pst36. B. MacLean; Paul Butterfield Blues Band / Cream / South Side Sound System; 8/22–27/67; BG 79-1

Pst37. J. Blashfield; Electric Flag / Mother Earth / LDM Spiritual Band; 9/14–16/67; BG 83-1

Pst38. G. Irons; Jefferson Airplane / Mother Earth / Flamin' Groovies; 9/28–30/67; BG 85-1

Pst39. B. MacLean; Quicksilver Messenger Service / Grass Roots / Mad River; 10/5–7/67; BG 87-1

Pst40. B. MacLean; Pink Floyd / Lee Michaels; 10/26–28/67; BG 90-1

Pst41. S. Mouse, A. Kelley, Rick Griffin; Quicksilver Messenger Service / The Grateful Dead / Big Brother and the Holding Company; 10/31/67

Pst42. B. MacLean; Big Brother and the Holding Company / Pink Floyd / Richie Havens; 11/2–4/67; BG 91-1

Pst43. N. Kouninos; Procol Harum / Pink Floyd / H. P. Lovecraft; 11/9–11/67; BG 92-1

Pst44. S. Mouse; Tim Buckley / The Chambers Brothers / The Mothers of Invention; 12/14–16/67; BG 97-1

Pst45. A. Kelley; Buffalo Springfield / The Collectors / Hour Glass; 12/21–23/67; BG 98-1

Pst46. B. MacLean; "Six Days of Sound" series; 12/26–31/67; BG 99-1

Pst47. B. MacLean; New Year's Eve party; 12/31/67; BG 100-1

Appendix C: Some Notes on the Transcriptions

The transcriptions are not intended to substitute for listening to recordings but rather to help direct attention to those aspects of the recordings most relevant to my discussion. They are formatted like performance scores but are actually analytic: even in the more detailed transcriptions, the focus is on how things sound, which usually corresponds to a reasonable guess as to what was physically played by specific instruments, but not necessarily. In order to fit as much material as possible onto single pages, perfect vertical alignment of beats was sometimes sacrificed in favor of note spacing within individual parts.

Most of the notation is entirely standard and hopefully self-evident. I use two different ways of indicating a full measure repeat. The standard symbol indicates an exact repetition. The standard symbol with "sim." written underneath indicates that the repetition is slightly varied, but not enough to require full notation. For the position of individual drums on the drum staff, see table C.1. Other incidental percussion information is indicated with captions on the transcriptions.

The following abbreviations are used to label individual staves:

Table C.1. Drum notation (pitches named as if in treble clef)

High C (two ledger lines)	Splash cymbal	
B	Crash 2	
A	Crash 1	
G	Ride	An x in a circle indicates a bell. (For other cymbals, an x just indicates a half- or whole-note duration.)
F	Hi-hat	Plain x indicates closed hi-hat. Full circle above indicates open hat. Circle with slash indicates half-open. A solid line over the note indicates that the hi-hat has been shut on that strike.
E	Tom 1	An x indicates a rim shot.
C	Tom 2	An x indicates a rim shot.
B	Snare	An x indicates a rim shot.
A	Tom 3	An x indicates a rim shot.
F	Tom 4	An x indicates a rim shot.
E	Kick	
D	Hi-hat pedal	An x in a circle indicates a hi-hat pedal splash.

AG	Acoustic guitar
DS	Drum set
EB	Electric bass
EFX	Electronic sound effects
EG	Electric guitar
Hpschd	Harpsichord
Hrm	Harmonica
Hrns	Horn section (simplified)
Org	Electric organ
PC	Percussion
Pno	Piano
Sax	Saxophone
Sit	Sitar
Syn	Synthesizer (incudes string machines)
Tamb	Tambourine
Vib	Vibraphone
Vln	Violin
Voc	Lead voice (or primary vocal line)
Vox	Multiple voices (generally backing vocals)

Finally, when the letter *n* is given just before or after a crescendo or decrescendo mark, the indication is *niente*.

List of References

Adlington, Robert. 2009. "Introduction: Avant-Garde Music and the Sixties." In *Sound Commitments: Avant-Garde Music and the Sixties*, edited by Robert Adlington, 3–14. Oxford: Oxford University Press.
Agawu, V. Kofi. 1991. *Playing with Signs: A Semiotic Interpretation of Classic Music*. Princeton, NJ: Princeton University Press.
Albanese, Catherine L. 2007. *A Republic of Mind and Spirit: A Cultural History of American Metaphysical Religion*. New Haven, CT: Yale University Press.
Almén, Byron. 2008. *A Theory of Musical Narrative*. Bloomington: Indiana University Press.
Al-Taee, Nasser. 2010. *Representations of the Orient in Western Music: Violence and Sensuality*. Farnham: Ashgate.
Auslander, Philip. 2006. *Performing Glam Rock: Gender & Theatricality in Popular Music*. Ann Arbor: University of Michigan Press.
Barthes, Roland. 1972. *Mythologies*. New York: Hill and Wang.
Bellman, Jonathan. 1998a. "Indian Resonances in the British Invasion, 1965–1968." In *The Exotic in Western Music*, edited by Jonathan Bellman, 292–306. Boston: Northeastern University Press.
———. 1998b. Introduction to *The Exotic in Western Music*, edited by Jonathan Bellman, ix–xiii. Boston: Northeastern University Press.
Bernstein, David, ed. 2008. *The San Francisco Tape Music Center: 1960s Counterculture and the Avant-Garde*. Berkeley: University of California Press.
Bernstein, David, and Maggi Payne. 2008. "Tony Martin (Interview)." In *The San Francisco Tape Music Center: 1960s Counterculture and the Avant-Garde*, edited by David Bernstein, 146–62. Berkeley: University of California Press.
Blake, Andrew. 2007. "Drugs and Popular Music in the Modern Age." In *Drugs and Popular Culture: Drugs, Media and Identity in Contemporary Society*, edited by Paul Manning, 103–16. Portland, OR: Willan Publishing.
Bohlman, Philip V. 2000. "Composing the Cantorate: Westernizing Europe's Other Within." In *Western Music and Its Others: Difference, Representation, and Appropriation in Music*, edited by Georgina Born and David Hesmondhalgh, 187–212. Berkeley: University of California Press.
Bonds, Mark Evan. 2008. "Listening to Listeners." In *Communication in Eighteenth-Century Music*, edited by Kofi Agawu and Danuta Mirka, 34–52. Cambridge: Cambridge University Press.
Boon, Marcus. 2002. *The Road of Excess: A History of Writers on Drugs*. Cambridge, MA: Harvard University Press.
Boone, Graeme M. 1997. "Tonal and Expressive Ambiguity in 'Dark Star.'" In *Understanding Rock: Essays in Musical Analysis*, edited by John Covach and Graeme M. Boone, 171–210. New York: Oxford University Press.
Boyd, Joe. 2006. *White Bicycles: Making Music in the 1960s*. London: Serpent's Tail.

Bromell, Nick. 2000. *Tomorrow Never Knows: Rock and Psychedelics in the 1960s.* Chicago: University of Chicago Press.
Butler, Mark J. 2006. *Unlocking the Groove: Rhythm, Meter, and Musical Design in Electronic Dance Music.* Bloomington: Indiana University Press.
Cavallo, Dominick. 1999. *A Fiction of the Past: The Sixties in American History.* New York: St. Martin's Press.
Cole, Fred, and Michael Hannan. 1997. "Goa Trance." *Perfect Beat* 3 (3): 1–14.
Cooke, Mervyn. 2008. *A History of Film Music.* Cambridge: Cambridge University Press.
Corbett, John. 2000. "Experimental Oriental: New Music and Other Others." In *Western Music and Its Others: Difference, Representation, and Appropriation in Music,* edited by Georgina Born and David Hesmondhalgh, 163–86. Berkeley: University of California Press.
Danielsen, Anne. 2006. *Presence and Pleasure: The Funk Grooves of James Brown and Parliament.* Middletown, CT: Wesleyan University Press.
Davis, Erik. 2004. "Hedonic Tantra: Golden Goa's Trance Transmission." In *Rave Culture and Religion,* edited by Graham St. John, 256–72. New York: Routledge.
DeRogatis, Jim. 2003. *Turn On Your Mind: Four Decades of Great Psychedelic Rock.* New York: Hal Leonard.
Diem, Andrea Grace, and James R. Lewis. 1992. "Imagining India: The Influence of Hinduism on the New Age Movement." In *Perspectives on the New Age,* edited by J. Gordon Melton and James R. Lewis, 48–58. Albany: State University of New York Press.
Doyle, Peter. 2005. *Echo & Reverb: Fabricating Space in Popular Music Recording, 1900–1960.* Middletown, CT: Wesleyan University Press.
Drummond, Paul. 2007. *Eye Mind: The Saga of Roky Erickson and the 13th Floor Elevators, the Pioneers of Psychedelic Sound.* Los Angeles: Process Media.
Echard, William. 1999. "An Analysis of Neil Young's 'Powderfinger' Based on Mark Johnson's Image Schemata." *Popular Music* 18 (1): 133–44.
———. 2005. *Neil Young and the Poetics of Energy.* Bloomington: Indiana University Press.
———. 2006a. "Plays Guitar without Any Hands: Musical Movement and Problems of Immanence." In *Music and Gesture,* edited by Anthony Gritten and Elaine King, 75–90. Aldershot: Ashgate.
———. 2006b. "Sensible Virtual Selves: Bodies, Instruments, and the Becoming-Concrete of Music." *Contemporary Music Review* 25 (1/2): 7–16.
———. 2008. "Subject to a Trace: The Virtuality of Recorded Music." In *Recorded Music: Philosophical and Critical Perspectives,* edited by Mine Dogantan-Dack, 22–40. London: Middlesex University Press.
———. 2011. "Psychedelia, Musical Semiotics, and Environmental Unconscious." *Green Letters: Studies in Ecocriticism* 15:61–75.
Elliott, Luther. 2010. "Goa Is a State of Mind: On the Ephemerality of Psychedelic Social Emplacements." In *The Local Scenes and Global Culture of Psytrance,* edited by Graham St. John, 21–39. New York: Routledge.
Eshun, Kodwo. 1998. *More Brilliant Than the Sun: Adventures in Sonic Fiction.* London: Quartet Books.
Everett, Walter. 1999. *The Beatles as Musicians: "Revolver" through the "Anthology."* Oxford: Oxford University Press.
———. 2001. *The Beatles as Musicians: The Quarry Men through "Rubber Soul."* Oxford: Oxford University Press.

Farber, David. 1994. *The Age of Great Dreams: America in the 1960s.* New York: Hill and Wang.
Farrell, Gerry. 1988. "Reflecting Surfaces: The Use of Elements from Indian Music in Popular Music and Jazz." *Popular Music* 7 (2): 189–205.
———. 1997. *Indian Music and the West.* Oxford: Oxford University Press.
Fast, Susan, and Kip Pegley. 2012. Introduction to *Music, Politics, and Violence,* Kindle edition, locs. 82–826. Middletown, CT: Wesleyan University Press.
Fujita, Tetsuya, Yuji Hagino, Hajime Kubo, and Goro Sato. 1989. *The Beatles: The Complete Scores.* Milwaukee: Hal Leonard.
Gates, Henry Louis, Jr. 1988. *The Signifying Monkey: A Theory of African-American Literary Criticism.* Oxford: Oxford University Press.
Gilbert, Jeremy, and Ewan Pearson. 1999. *Discographies: Dance Music, Culture, and the Politics of Sound.* New York: Routledge.
Gilroy, Paul. 1993. *The Black Atlantic: Modernity and Double Consciousness.* Cambridge, MA: Harvard University Press.
———. 2000. *Against Race: Imagining Popular Culture beyond the Color Line.* Cambridge, MA: Harvard University Press.
Grunenberg, Christoph, and Jonathan Harris, eds. 2005. *Summer of Love: Psychedelic Art, Social Crisis and Counterculture in the 1960s.* Liverpool: Liverpool University Press.
Harris, Jonathan. 2005. "Introduction: Abstraction and Empathy. Psychedelic Distortion and the Meanings of the 1960s." In *Summer of Love: Psychedelic Art, Social Crisis and Counterculture in the 1960s,* edited by Christoph Grunenberg and Jonathan Harris, 9–17. Liverpool: Liverpool University Press.
Hatten, Robert S. 1994. *Musical Meaning in Beethoven: Markedness, Correlation, and Interpretation.* Bloomington: Indiana University Press.
———. 2004. *Interpreting Musical Gestures, Topics, and Tropes.* Bloomington: Indiana University Press.
———. 2014. "The Troping of Topics in Mozart's Instrumental Works." In *The Oxford Handbook of Topic Theory,* edited by Danuta Mirka, 514–38. Oxford: Oxford University Press.
Hayter, Alethea. 1968. *Opium and the Romantic Imagination.* London: Faber and Faber.
Hayward, Philip. 2004. "Sci-Fidelity: Music, Sound and Genre History." In *Off the Planet: Music, Sound and Science Fiction Cinema,* edited by Philip Hayward, 1–29. London: John Libbey / Perfect Beat.
Heelas, Paul. 1996. *The New Age Movement.* Oxford: Blackwell.
Hegarty, Paul. 2007. *Noise/Music: A History.* New York: Continuum.
Holm-Hudson, Kevin. 2002. "The 'American Metaphysical Circus' of Joseph Byrd's United States of America." In *Progressive Rock Reconsidered,* edited by Kevin Holm-Hudson, 43–62. New York: Routledge.
Home, Stewart. 2005. "Voices Green and Purple: Psychedelic Bad Craziness and the Revenge of the Avant-Garde." In *Summer of Love: Psychedelic Art, Social Crisis and Counterculture in the 1960s,* edited by Christoph Grunenberg and Jonathan Harris, 123–54. Liverpool: Liverpool University Press.
Hoskyns, Barney. 1996. *Waiting for the Sun: Strange Days, Weird Scenes, and the Sound of Los Angeles.* New York: St. Martin's Griffin.
Huxley, Aldous. 2004. *"The Doors of Perception" & "Heaven and Hell."* New York: Harper Perennial.

Johnson, Ann, and Mike Stax. 2006. "From Psychotic to Psychedelic: The Garage Contribution to Psychedelia." *Popular Music and Society* 29 (4): 411–25.

Johnson, Bruce, and Martin Cloonan. 2008. *Dark Side of the Tune: Popular Music and Violence*. Aldershot: Ashgate.

Keightley, Keir. 2011. "The Historical Consciousness of Sunshine Pop." *Journal of Popular Music Studies* 23 (3): 343–61.

Kirk, Andrew. 2002. "'Machines of Loving Grace': Alternative Technology, Environment, and the Counterculture." In *Imagine Nation: The American Counterculture of the 1960s and '70s*, edited by Peter Braunstein and Michael William Doyle, 353–78. New York: Routledge.

Laing, Stuart. 2005. "Economy, Society and Culture in 1960s Britain: Contexts and Conditions for Psychedelic Art." In *Summer of Love: Psychedelic Art, Social Crisis and Counterculture in the 1960s*, edited by Christoph Grunenberg and Jonathan Harris, 19–34. Liverpool: Liverpool University Press.

Lattin, Don. 2010. *The Harvard Psychedelic Club*. New York: Harper Collins.

Lee, Martin A., and Bruce Shlain. 1985. *Acid Dreams: The Complete Social History of LSD: The CIA, the Sixties, and Beyond*. New York: Grove Press.

Lemke, Gayle, and Jacaeber Kastor. 1997. *The Art of the Fillmore, 1966–1971*. Petaluma, CA: Acid Test Productions.

Lenson, David. 1995. *On Drugs*. Minneapolis: University of Minnesota Press.

Letcher, Andy. 2007. *Shroom: A Cultural History of the Magic Mushroom*. New York: Harper Collins / Ecco.

Lewis, George E. 2008. *A Power Stronger Than Itself: The AACM and American Experimental Music*. Chicago: University of Chicago Press.

Lindop, Robin. 2010. "Re-evaluating Musical Genre in UK Psytrance." In *The Local Scenes and Global Culture of Psytrance*, edited by Graham St. John, 114–30. New York: Routledge.

Lipsitz, George. 1994. "Who'll Stop the Rain? Youth Culture, Rock 'n' Roll, and Social Crises." In *The Sixties: From Memory to History*, edited by David Farber, 206–34. Chapel Hill: University of North Carolina Press.

Lock, Graham. 1999. *Blutopia: Visions of the Future and Revisions of the Past in the Work of Sun Ra, Duke Ellington, and Anthony Braxton*. Durham, NC: Duke University Press.

Locke, Ralph P. 2009. *Musical Exoticism: Images and Reflections*. Cambridge: Cambridge University Press.

Lovesey, Oliver. 2011. "The 'World' before Globalization: Moroccan Elements in the Incredible String Band's Music." *Popular Music* 30 (1): 127–43.

Lowe, Melanie. 2007. *Pleasure and Meaning in the Classical Symphony*. Bloomington: Indiana University Press.

Manning, Paul. 2007. "An Introduction to the Theoretical Approaches and Research Traditions." In *Drugs and Popular Culture: Drugs, Media and Identity in Contemporary Society*, edited by Paul Manning, 7–28. Portland, OR: Willan Publishing.

Markoff, John. 2005. *What the Dormouse Said: How the Sixties Counterculture Shaped the Personal Computer Industry*. New York: Viking.

Martin, Tony. 2008. "Composing with Light." In *The San Francisco Tape Music Center: 1960s Counterculture and the Avant-Garde*, edited by David Bernstein, 136–45. Berkeley: University of California Press.

McKay, George. 1996. *Senseless Acts of Beauty: Cultures of Resistance since the Sixties*. London: Verso.

Medeiros, Walter. 2001. "Annotated Checklist." In *High Societies: Psychedelic Rock Posters of the Haight-Ashbury*, edited by Sally Tomlinson and Walter Medeiros, 61–88. San Diego: San Diego Museum of Art.

———. 2005. "Mapping San Francisco 1965–1967: Roots and Florescence of the San Francisco Counterculture." In *Summer of Love: Psychedelic Art, Social Crisis and Counterculture in the 1960s*, edited by Christoph Grunenberg and Jonathan Harris, 303–48. Liverpool: Liverpool University Press.

Meyer, Stephen C. 2015. *Epic Sound: Music in Postwar Hollywood Biblical Films*. Bloomington: Indiana University Press.

Middleton, Richard. 1990. *Studying Popular Music*. Philadelphia: Open University Press.

Miles, Barry. 2006. *Pink Floyd: The Early Years*. New York: Omnibus.

Monelle, Raymond. 2000. *The Sense of Music: Semiotic Essays*. Princeton, NJ: Princeton University Press.

———. 2006. *The Musical Topic: Hunt, Military, and Pastoral*. Bloomington: Indiana University Press.

Moore, Allan. 1997. *The Beatles: "Sgt. Pepper's Lonely Hearts Club Band."* Cambridge: Cambridge University Press.

Moser, Richard. 2003. "Introduction II. Was It the End or Just a Beginning? American Storytelling and the History of the Sixties." In *The World the Sixties Made: Politics and Culture in Recent America*, edited by Van Gosse and Richard Moser, 37–51. Philadelphia: Temple University Press.

Nelson, Alondra. 2002. "Introduction: Future Texts." *Social Text* 20 (2): 1–15.

Owen, Ted, and Denise Dickson. 1999. *High Art: A History of the Psychedelic Poster*. London: Sanctuary Publishing.

Partridge, Christopher. 2006. "The Spiritual and the Revolutionary: Alternative Spirituality, British Free Festivals, and the Emergence of Rave Culture." *Culture and Religion* 7 (1): 41–60.

Peirce, Charles S. 1998. *The Essential Peirce: Selected Philosophical Writings, Volume 2 (1893–1913)*. Edited by the Peirce Edition Project. Bloomington: Indiana University Press.

Perry, Charles. 1984. *The Haight-Ashbury: A History*. New York: Random House / Rolling Stone Press.

Pinch, Trevor, and Frank Trocco. 2002. *Analog Days: The Invention and Impact of the Moog Synthesizer*. Cambridge, MA: Harvard University Press.

Pouncey, Edwin. 2005a. "'I Never Stopped Loving the Light': Joshua White and the Joshua Light Show." In *Summer of Love: Psychedelic Art, Social Crisis and Counterculture in the 1960s*, edited by Christoph Grunenberg and Jonathan Harris, 163–78. Liverpool: Liverpool University Press.

———. 2005b. "Laboratories of Light: Psychedelic Light Shows." In *Summer of Love: Psychedelic Art, Social Crisis and Counterculture in the 1960s*, edited by Christoph Grunenberg and Jonathan Harris, 155–62. Liverpool: Liverpool University Press.

Radano, Ronald. 2003. *Lying Up a Nation: Race and Black Music*. Chicago: University of Chicago Press.

Ramsey, Guthrie, Jr. 2004. *Race Music: Black Cultures from Bebop to Hip-Hop*. Berkeley: University of California Press.

Ratner, Leonard G. 1980. *Classic Music: Expression, Form and Style*. New York: Schirmer.

Reck, David. 1985. "Beatles Orientalis: Influences from Asia in a Popular Song Tradition." *Asian Music* 16 (1): 83–149.

Reich, Steve. 2002. *Writings on Music: 1965–2000*. Kindle edition. Oxford: Oxford University Press.

Reising, Russell, and Jim LeBlanc. 2008. "Within and Without: Sgt. Pepper's Lonely Hearts Club Band and Psychedelic Insight." In *Sgt. Pepper and the Beatles: It Was Forty Years Ago Today*, edited by Olivier Julien, 103–20. Aldershot: Ashgate.

———. 2009. "Magical Mystery Tours, and Other Trips: Yellow Submarines, Newspaper Taxis, and the Beatles' Psychedelic Years." In *The Cambridge Companion to the Beatles*, edited by Kenneth Womack, 90–111. Cambridge: Cambridge University Press.

Reynolds, Simon. 1998. *Generation Ecstasy: Into the World of Techno and Rave Culture*. New York: Little, Brown and Company.

Reynolds, Simon, and Joy Press. 1995. *The Sex Revolts: Gender, Rebellion, and Rock 'n' Roll*. Cambridge, MA: Harvard University Press.

Rietveld, Hillegonda C. 2004. "Ephemeral Spirit: Sacrificial Cyborg and Communal Soul." In *Rave Culture and Religion*, edited by Graham St. John, 46–61. New York: Routledge.

Riley, Robert R. 2008. "Liquid to Light: The Evolution of the Projected Image Light Show in San Francisco." In *The San Francisco Tape Music Center: 1960s Counterculture and the Avant-Garde*, edited by David Bernstein, 21–23. Berkeley: University of California Press.

Saldanha, Arun. 2007. *Psychedelic White: Goa Trance and the Viscosity of Race*. Minneapolis: University of Minnesota Press.

Saussure, Ferdinand de. 1959. *Course in General Linguistics*. Translated by Wade Baskin. New York: Philosophical Library.

Scheurer, Timothy E. 2008. *Music and Mythmaking in Film: Genre and the Role of the Composer*. London: McFarland & Company.

Stevens, Jay. 1987. *Storming Heaven: LSD and the American Dream*. New York: Grove Press.

St. John, Graham. 2004. "Techno Millennium: Dance, Ecology, and Future Primitives." In *Rave Culture and Religion*, edited by Graham St. John, 213–35. New York: Routledge.

———. 2010. "Psytrance: An Introduction." In *The Local Scenes and Global Culture of Psytrance*, edited by Graham St. John, 1–17. New York: Routledge.

———. 2013. "The Vibe of the Exiles: Aliens, Afropsychedelia and Psyculture." *Dancecult* 5 (2): 56–87.

Tagg, Philip. 1989. "Open Letter about 'Black Music,' 'Afro-American Music,' and 'European Music.'" *Popular Music* 8 (3): 285–98.

———. 2000a. *Fernando the Flute: Analysis of Musical Meaning in an ABBA Mega-Hit*. 2nd edition, Adobe PDF format. www.tagg.org, Mass Media Music Scholars' Press.

———. 2000b. *"Kojak": Fifty Seconds of Television Music*. 2nd edition, Adobe PDF format. www.tagg.org, Mass Media Music Scholars' Press.

Tagg, Philip, and Bob Clarida. 2003. *Ten Little Title Tunes: Towards a Musicology of the Mass Media*. Adobe PDF format. www.tagg.org, Mass Media Music Scholars' Press.

Taylor, Timothy D. 2007. *Beyond Exoticism: Western Music and the World*. Durham, NC: Duke University Press.

Tomlinson, Sally. 2001. "Psychedelic Rock Posters: History, Ideas, and Art." In *High Societies: Psychedelic Rock Posters of the Haight-Ashbury*, edited by Sally Tomlinson and Walter Medeiros, 14–37. San Diego: San Diego Museum of Art.
Turner, Fred. 2008. *From Counterculture to Cyberculture: Stewart Brand, the Whole Earth Network, and the Rise of Digital Utopianism*. Chicago: University of Chicago Press.
van Veen, Tobias C. 2013. "Vessels of Transfer: Allegories of Afrofuturism in Jeff Mills and Janelle Monáe." *Dancecult* 5 (2): 7–41.
Veal, Michael E. 2007. *Dub: Soundscapes & Shattered Songs in Jamaican Reggae*. Middletown, CT: Wesleyan University Press.
Wagner, Naphtali. 2008. "The Beatles' Psycheclassical Synthesis: Psychedelic Classicism and Classical Psychedelia in Sgt. Pepper." In *Sgt. Pepper and the Beatles: It Was Forty Years Ago Today*, edited by Olivier Julien, 75–90. Aldershot: Ashgate.
Waksman, Steve. 2009. *This Ain't the Summer of Love: Conflict and Crossover in Heavy Metal and Punk*. Berkeley: University of California Press.
Weheliye, Alexander G. 2002. "'Feenin': Posthuman Voices in Contemporary Black Popular Music." *Social Text* 20 (2): 21–47.
———. 2005. *Phonographies: Grooves in Sonic Afro-Modernity*. Durham, NC: Duke University Press.
Weisbard, Eric. 2014. *Top 40 Democracy: The Rival Mainstreams of American Music*. Kindle edition. Chicago: University of Chicago Press.
Whiteley, Sheila. 1992. *The Space between the Notes: Rock and the Counter-Culture*. London: Routledge.
———. 2008. "'Tangerine Trees and Marmalade Skies': Cultural Agendas or Optimistic Escapism?" In *Sgt. Pepper and the Beatles: It Was Forty Years Ago Today*, edited by Olivier Julien, 11–22. Aldershot: Ashgate.
Young, Rob. 2010. *Electric Eden: Unearthing Britain's Visionary Music*. London: Faber and Faber.
Zuberi, Nabeel. 2004. "The Transmolecularization of [Black] Folk." In *Off the Planet: Music, Sound and Science Fiction Cinema*, edited by Philip Hayward, 77–95. London: John Libbey / Perfect Beat.

Index

Music examples in italics.

13th Floor Elevators, The, 29, 64–70, 131; "Kingdom of Heaven," 34, 42, 67; "Reverberation (Doubt)," 93; "Roller Coaster," 34, *35, 62, 68, 69,* 70, 73; "You're Gonna Miss Me," *65, 66,* 70, 72
2001: A Space Odyssey, 215, 226, 236

abjection. *See* psychosis and dark affect; violence, psychedelia and
acid house, 248. *See also* dance music, electronic
Adlington, Robert, 91
African-American expressive culture, 105, 107–109, 118–119, 247
Afrofuturism and modernity, 106–107, 119, 208–209, 218, 221–223, 224–227; human and post-human in, 223–224
Agawu, V. Kofi, 16
Albanese, Catherine, 56, 60, 108
Alice in Wonderland, 137
Almén, Byron, 19
Al-Taee, Nasser, 57, 59
ambient music, 210, 249. *See also* space topic
American imaginaries and Americana, 145, 130, 145
American Independent Network, 1980s, 237, 240
Anthology of American Folk Music, 79
Art Ensemble of Chicago, 107
Auslander, Philip, 135, 154
Austin, Texas, 64
avant-gardes, psychedelia and, 91–92, 144, 205, 212

bad trips. *See* psychosis and dark affect
bands (brass, marching, ragtime), 95–96. *See also* belle époque period
Barrett, Syd, 209, 231, 236
Barthes, Roland, 96
bass, electric, 116
Beach Boys, The, 65; "Good Vibrations," 95
Beatles, The, 90–91; and the avant-garde, 91–94, 200; "Baby You're a Rich Man," 60; "Being for the Benefit of Mr. Kite," 179–180, 189, 250; classicism of, 160–161, 190; "A Day in the Life," 92, 184–185, 186, 189; "Doctor Robert," 43; "Fixing a Hole," 178, 179, 189; "Getting Better," 176–177, 189; "Good Morning Good Morning," 182–183, 189, 249, 250; *Help!,* 90; "I Am the Walrus," 206; "I'm Only Sleeping," 90; "Lovely Rita," 181–182, 189; "Love Me Do," 77; "Love You Too," 26, 61, 76; "Lucy in the Sky with Diamonds," 176, 177, 189; "Norwegian Wood," 15, 60, 61; nostalgia and, 95–96, 98, 118, 188–189; orientalism and, 57–58, 61, 159, 161; "Rain," 29, 90, 91, 169; *Revolver,* 5, 9, 29, 169; *Rubber Soul,* 29; *Sgt. Pepper's Lonely Hearts Club Band,* 90, 94, 103n13, 115, 135, 169–190, 197, 238; "Sgt. Pepper's Lonely Hearts Club Band" and Reprise, 175–176, 178, 184; "She's Leaving Home," 178–179, 181, 189; "She Said, She Said," 52; "Strawberry Fields Forever," 90, 161–169, 204; "Taxman," 42, 184; "Think for Yourself," 62; "Tomorrow Never Knows," 68, 92; vocal doubling effect, 77; "When I'm Sixty-Four," 181, 189; "With a Little Help from My Friends," 176, 190; "Within You Without You," 61, 180–181, 189; "Yellow Submarine," 20–21, 94–95. *See also* names of individual band members
Beatles, The: The Complete Scores (Fujita, Tetsuya et al), 76, 77, 161
Beck, Jeff, 31
Becker, Howard, 12
belle époque period, 6, 95–96, 98, 128, 130, 131. *See also* nostalgia and childhood
Bellman, Jonathan, 59, 60, 61
Bernstein, David, 91
Berry, Chuck, 2, 16, 17, 33
Bey, Hakim, 241
Blacking, John, 23
Blake, Andrew, 12
Blavatsky, Helena, 225
Bloomfield, Mike, 107
Bohlman, Philip, 58, 59

Bolan, Marc, 154
Bonds, Mark, 22
Boon, Marcus, 11–12, 13, 56, 91–92
Bourdieu, Pierre, 19
Boyd, Joe, 8
Brand, Stewart, 200
britpop, 244
Bromell, Nick, 9
Brown, Arthur, 135
Brown, James, 221
Buchla, Don, 91, 144
Butler, Mark, 260
Butthole Surfers, The, 240; "Creep in the Cellar," 237–238; *Rembrandt Pussyhorse*, 237–239; "Sea Ferring," 238; "Strangers Die Every Day," 95, 238–239
Byrds, The, 127; "Eight Miles High," 37, 73–77, *74–75*, *76*, 78, 82, 99, 208; drumming in, 72; exoticism and, 31, 68, 156; folk elements of, 79–80; historical place of, 5, 29

Cage, John, 92, 206
Can, 210; "Father Cannot Yell," 210–212, *211*, *212*
Cavallo, Dominick, 145
Chambers Brothers, The: "Time Has Come Today," 31, 39, *41*, 94, 109–110, 120, 123
Chemical Brothers, The: "Setting Sun," 26
childhood. *See* nostalgia and childhood
Chomsky, Noam, 23
circus topic, 88, 96, 101, 179–180, 182
Clarida, Bob, 18, 33, 82, 96, 204
classical music as a topic area, 77, 80, 137
classicism, 160–161
Clinton, George, 119
clockwork topic, 94, 101, 109, 192–193
Cloonan, Martin, 215–216, 217, 218
Coltrane, John, 67, 76, 82, 208; *A Love Supreme*, 76
competency, semiotic and linguistic, 23–24, 230. *See also* dialogism
Conklin, Lee, 128
Constanten, Tom, 144
Cooke, Mervyn, 37, 40
Cope, Julian, 231
Corbett, John, 61
Country Joe and the Fish: "Section 43," 47, 73, 76, *97*, 98–99, 99–101, *100*, 145, 191, 201, 208
Crass, 242

dance music, electronic, 230, 239, 240–241, 245, 247, 248–258, 262n1. *See also* DJs, musical practices of; groove and temporality
Danielsen, Anne, 113–114, 118, 221, 222

Davies, Ray, 60
Davis, Erik, 258
Deep, The: "It's All a Part of Me," 93, 95; *Psychedelic Moods*, 93
De La Soul, 257
Deleuze, Gilles, 103n5
DeRogatis, Jim, 11, 67
Detroit Artists Workshop, 107
developing variation jam, 70, 211–212, 213–214
dialogism, 7, 20–25, 96, 98, 118–119, 189–190. *See also* competency, semiotic and linguistic; topics, theory of
Diem, Andrea Grace, 56, 57
disc jockey. *See* DJ, radio, vocal persona
dissolve, textural, 112
DJ, radio, vocal persona. *See* guide figures, vocal staging of
DJs, musical practices of, 245, 252, 258–259, 260. *See also* EDM form
Donovan: "Atlantis," 95, 210; "Guinevere," 43, 80, *81*; "Mellow Yellow," 96
Doors, The, 201, 228, 240; "The End," 115
Douglas, Mary, 12
Doyle, Peter, 38–39, 77
dream voices, 172–173
Dr. John, 125
drones, 42, 64, 203. *See also* harmony
drugs, cultural and semiotic aspects, 9, 11–13
Drummond, Paul, 64, 66
drums, 26, 70–73
dub music, 205–206, 253, 257, 235. *See also* Afrofuturism and modernity; echo and reverberation
Dubois, W. E. B., 107
Dylan, Bob, 80, 109; "Mr. Tambourine Man," 156; "Rainy Day Women #12 & 35," 95

echo and reverberation, 33, 36, 37–39. *See also* dub music; space topic
Eddy, Duane, 33
EDM. *See* dance music, electronic
EDM form, 245, 250, 252. *See also* dance music, electronic; formal structure, music
Edwardian topics. *See* belle époque period
Electric Prunes, The: "I Had Too Much to Dream Last Night," 43, *44*, 47, 93
Elliott, Luther, 258–259, 260
Eno, Brian, 210
Eshun, Kodwo, 125, 223, 226, 227
Everett, Walter, 52, 103n12, 164, 169, 178, 182, 186; on harmonic devices, 42, 43, 91, 179–180; on meter and rhythm, 61, 90–91; on production techniques, 77, 90, 163, 206
exoticism. *See* orientalism and exoticism

expressive genres, 19. *See also* outward journey expressive genre; strange trip expressive genre; topics, theory of

Farber, David, 13
Farrell, Gerry, 57, 60, 61, 62, 79
Fast, Susan, 216
Faust (band), 210
festivals, free, 241–242
fiddle and violin, 236, 237, 238. *See also* folk music topics
Fifty Foot Hose: *Cauldron*, 200
film music genres: epic, 33, 40–42, 138–139; psychological thriller and horror, 33, 237; science fiction, 33, 67–68, 100–101; spy, 33, 236; westerns, 32, 37, 101
flamenco, 82, 228–229. *See also* Latin music
folk music topics, 79–81, 203–204, 236–237, 238; The Incredible String Band and, 132, 154, 155–157; the urban and, 116–117; Pink Floyd and, 132, 192–193; signifiers of, 64, 66, 67, 132. *See also* flamenco; Grateful Dead, The; Native American topics
Fonda, Peter, 246
formal structure, music, 92, 186–188; concise song form, 30–31; improvisation and, 152, 193–194; rhythm/meter and, 90–91, 155–156, 157–158, 210; through-composition, 53, 55, 84–85, 138, 155–156. *See also* developing variation jam; dissolve, textural; EDM form; expressive genres; groove and temporality; hymns; regularly spaced chords texture; structural pause
Fowlkes, Eddie, 248
Fuller, Buckminster, 200
Funkadelic, 119, 125, 239; "Eulogy and Light," 116; "Free Your Mind and Your Ass Will Follow," 124; "Mommy, What's a Funkadelic?," 123–124, 125; "Music for My Mother," 125
funk music, 113–119, 221–222. *See also* Afrofuturism and modernity; soul music
fuzz, 31, 35–37. *See also* guitar

garage rock, 30, 81, 231, 237; space rock and, 205, 212. *See also* psychosis and dark affect
garble line, 68
Gates, Henry Louis Jr., 108
Gilbert, Jeremy, 12
Gilroy, Paul, 108, 197n1, 225, 226
Goa Gil, 258
Gong (band), 242
gothic topics, 236–237
Graham, Bill, 128

Grateful Dead, The, 30, 76, 187, 192, 225; "Alligator > Caution > Feedback," 145, 146–153; American roots music and, 118, 140–141, 145, 154, 236; *Anthem of the Sun*, 146; "Beat It On Down the Line," 142; "Cold Rain and Snow," 142; "Cosmic Charlie," 144; "Dark Star > China Cat Sunflower > The Eleven," 146, 149; "Dark Star" single, 26, 142–145, 156; "Drums > Space," 144; "The Golden Road (To Unlimited Devotion)," 142; "Good Morning Little Schoolgirl," 140, 142; improvisation and, 139–140, 146–147, 152–153, 158; "Morning Dew," 142; "Mountains of the Moon," 144; "Sitting on Top of the World," 142; space topic and, 143–145; "Uncle John's Band," 15; "Viola Lee Blues," 142; *Workingman's Dead*, 140
Greco-Roman topics, 130, 236
Gregorian chant topic, 37, 55, 77, 130, 236
Griffin, Rick, 128
groove and temporality, 113–114, 144, 209, 221, 222, 225–226. *See also* formal structure, music
guide figures, vocal staging of, 68, 116, 133, 137, 255
guitar: jangle, 73, 79–80; sitar-like, 31–32, 53, 61, 62, 99; twang, 33–35, 62, 82. *See also* fuzz

Hall, Tommy, 67
Happy Mondays, 245
harmonica, 101, 249
harmony, 42–43, 91, 179–180, 200–201. *See also* drones
harpsichord, 62, 88
Harris, Jonathan, 11, 12
Harrison, George, 5, 60, 61, 161, 181, 189
Hatten, Robert, 15, 16, 17, 19, 20, 23, 27
Hawkwind, 212–213, 236, 242; "Be Yourself," 213–215, *213, 214*; *Space Ritual*, 255
Hayter, Althea, 13
heavy metal, 215
Hegarty, Paul, 52, 209, 210
Helms, Chet, 133
Hendrix, Jimi, 30, 42, 47, 125, 135; "1983 . . . (a Merman I Should Turn to Be)," 95, 206; "EXP," 206; space topics and, 206–207, 208; "Third Stone from the Sun," 76, 206, 207–209
hip-hop, 246, 247, 257–258
hippie trail. *See* traveler culture
historical reflexivity, 25, 205, 229–230
Hitchcock, Robyn, 231
Hollies, The: "Bus Stop," 26
Holm-Hudson, Kevin, 200
Home, Stewart, 79

Hoskyns, Barney, 81, 82, 127
Hüsker Dü, 237
Huxley, Aldous, 1, 12, 215
hymns, 55, 80

improvisation, 139–140, 152–154, 158, 193–194, 211–212, 252. *See also* developing variation jam
Incredible String Band, The, 5, 80, 118, 132, 192, 236; "Chinese White," 154–156, 157; exoticism and, 156–157, 159–160; "Little Cloud," 157–158, 168; "The Mad Hatter's Song," 157–158
indexicality. *See under* topics, theory of
Indian instruments: tabla, 5; tambura, 5, 143; sitar, 5, 26, 31–32, 61; swarmandal, 164
Indian topic, 31–32, 53, 55, 60–61, 76, 79; signifiers of, 5–6, 42, 53, 55, 59–61, 62, 64, 142. *See also* orientalism and exoticism; raga rock
Inspiral Carpets, 245
instruments, musical. *See* bands (brass, marching, ragtime); bass, electric; drums; fiddle and violin; guitar; harmonica; harpsichord; Indian instruments; kazoo; megaphone; mellotron; organ; sampling; synthesizers; Theremin (instrument)

James, William, 56
Jarman, Joseph, 107
jazz, 72, 73, 76, 77, 82–83, 90, 107, 208
Jefferson Airplane: "Blues from an Airplane," 78, 137–139; theatricality of, 134–135, 136, 139; "White Rabbit," 71, 135–138, 139, 168, 201
Johnson, Ann, 29, 30, 36, 45, 49, 93
Johnson, Bruce, 215–216, 217, 218
Jones, Rickie Lee, 249
Jung, Carl, 225

kaleidoscope, 6
Kantner, Paul: *Blows Against the Empire*, 138
kazoo, 147, 181–182, 236
Keightley, Keir, 230–231
Kelley, Alton, 129
Kinks, The: drums in, 72; Gregorian topic in, 37; historical significance of, 5, 29, 31; lyrics, 55, 70, 73; "See My Friends," 53–55, *54*, *55*, 61–64, *63*, 80, 84–85
kosmiche music, 210
Kraftwerk, 210
Krieger, Robbie, 228

Laing, Stuart, 8
Latin music, 82, 135–136, 137. *See also* flamenco

Leary, Timothy, 106, 242
LeBlanc, Jim, 8, 91, 94, 169, 188
Lennon, John, 184, 186, 189
Lenson, David, 13
Lesh, Phil, 144
Lewis, George, 107
Lewis, James, 56, 57
Lindop, Robin, 248, 259, 260–261
Lipsitz, George, 13
Lock, Graham, 224, 225
Locke, Ralph, 59–60, 79
Lomax, Alan, 79
London, 8
Los Angeles, 81–82, 127, 230
Love, 29, 81–90; "Hey Joe," 81, 85; "My Little Red Book," 85; "Seven & Seven Is," 39, 43, 71, 85–86, *86*; "Softly to Me," 82–85, *83*, *84*, 86, 88, 90; "Stephanie Knows Who," 47, 86–90, *87*, *88*, *89*, 98
Lovesey, Oliver, 95, 159, 160
Lowe, Melanie, 22
Lyme & Cybelle: "Follow Me," 80, *94*
lyrics, 29, 93, 139, 159, 208, 236; as distinct level of code, 78; drug references in, 65, 70, 73, 256–257; folklore and, 79

MacColl, Ewan, 79
MacLean, Bonnie, 197n6
Madchester, 244
Magic Mushrooms, The: "It's a Happening," 93
Manning, Paul, 12
Marley, Bob, 226
Martin, George, 184, 188
Mason, Nick, 73
May, Derrick, 248
MC5, The, 107
McCartney, Paul, 182, 184, 188, 189
McKay, George, 241
McKenna, Terence, 254–255
McKenna brothers, 241, 242
McLuhan, Marshall, 200
Meek, Joe, 200
megaphone, 49, 78, 201, 238
mellotron, 162, 198n14
Metheny, Pat, 249
Meyer, Steven, 40, 42
Middleton, Richard, 18
Miles, Barry, 9
military topic, 71–72, 96
modernity. *See* Afrofuturism and modernity
Monelle, Raymond, 13, 16–18, 19–20, 21, 25, 28n5
Moore, Allan, 175, 178, 180, 181, 186, 187
Morrison, Jim, 115

Morse code topic, 162, 204–206. *See also* space topic
Moser, Richard, 145
Mouse, Stanley, 129
Move, The, 8
music hall and Tin Pan Alley, 96

Native American topics, 58–59, 130, 133–134. *See also* orientalism and exoticism
nautical topic, 65, 95, 210, 236, 238–239, 255
Nelson, Alondra, 106, 107
Neu!, 210
New Order, 245
new wave music, 235
nostalgia and childhood, 95–96, 98, 159, 210. *See also* belle époque period
Nuggets, 30

Oakenfold, Paul, 245
Once Upon a Time in the West, 249
Ono, Yoko, 206
Orb, The: "Little Fluffy Clouds," 247–248, 249–253, 254, *250*, *251*; "Towers of Dub," 253
organ, 82–83, 191–192
orientalism and exoticism, 55–59, 62–64, 156–157, 159–160; 1980s and later, 242–244; drumming and, 72; Latin genres and, 137; visual signifiers of, 130–131, 133–134. *See also* garble line; Indian topic; Kinks, The: "See My Friends"; Native American topics; race, markedness of; raga rock
outward journey expressive genre, 167–168, 184, 186. *See also* expressive genres
Ozric Tentacles, 242

Paisley Underground movement, 230, 239, 244–245
Palmer, Christopher, 37
Parliament, 119–123, 124, 218–223, 226–227; *Chocolate City*, 222; *The Clones of Dr. Funkenstein*, 220; *Mothership Connection*, 218, 222; *Osmium*, 119, 123, 238; "P. Funk (Wants to Get Funked Up)," 218–220, *219*; "Prelude," 220, 238; "There Is Nothing before Me but Thang," 119–123, *121-122*
Partridge, Christopher, 241–242, 243
pastoral topic. *See* folk music topics
Paul, Les and Mary Ford, 77
Pearson, Ewan, 12
Pegley, Kip, 216
Peirce, Charles S., 17, 21, 25, 28n2
Perry, Charles, 127, 134, 135, 199, 200
Pinch, Trevor, 91
Pinchbeck, Daniel, 242

Pink Floyd, 9, 73, 191–197, 208, 238; "Astronomy Domine," 194, 201–204; "Bike," 94, 193, 194; "Chapter 24," 192, 196; "Flaming," 191, 192, 193, 194; "The Gnome," 192, 193, 194; "Interstellar Overdrive," 194, 201, 203; "Lucifer Sam," 191, 194; "Matilda Mother," 191, 194–196; pastoralism and, 132, 145, 192–193; "Pow R. Toc H.," 191, 194; "Scarecrow," 192, 193, 194; "Set the Controls for the Heart of the Sun," 210. *See also* names of individual band members
poster art, 126–134. *See also* visual art and design
posthumanism. *See* Afrofuturism and modernity
preacher persona. *See* guide figures, vocal staging of
Press, Joy, 52, 159, 210
Pretty Things, The: *S. F. Sorrow*, 138
Primal Scream: "I'm Losing More Than I'll Ever Have," 245; "Loaded," 245–246, 247, 249
Prince, 261; "Around the World in a Day," 68
production techniques, audio. *See* sound effects and signal processing
psychedelia: definitions of, 10–11, 12–15, 118–119; history of, 8–10, 28, 29, 91–92, 101–102, 196–197, 199, 216–217, 241–244
psychosis and dark affect, 45, 65, 193–194, 237–239; circus topic and, 88; P-Funk and, 226; space rock and, 212–213; troped with positive affect, 81–82, 194; urban topics and, 116–117. *See also* violence, psychedelia and
Public Enemy: *Fear of a Black Planet*, 247
pub rock, 8, 244
punk, 237, 238

Quasimoto, 257

Ra, Sun, 224, 225
race, markedness of, 104–107, 118–119, 208–209, 222–223. *See also* Afrofuturism and modernity
Radano, Ronald, 105
radiophonics, 204, 205, 206
raga rock, 5–6, 60–61, 62. *See also* Indian topic
Raincoats, The, 242
Ramsey, Guthrie Jr., 218
Ratner, Leonard, 15
raves and rave culture, 230, 240–241, 248. *See also* dance music, electronic; rock-rave crossover
Reck, David, 57
regularly spaced chords texture, 39–40
Reich, Steve, 103n9; *Electric Counterpoint*, 249, 250, 252

Index 289

Reising, Russell, 8, 91, 94, 169, 188
repetition, musical, 52, 193–194, 200–201, 209, 210
reverberation. *See* echo and reverberation
Reynolds, Simon, 52, 159, 210, 241, 244, 245, 246, 248, 250
Rietveld, Hillegonda, 243–244
Riley, Terry, 91
rock-rave crossover, 240–241, 244–246, 247, 258. *See also* raves and rave culture
Rolling Stones, The: "2000 Light Years from Home," 198n14; "Lady Jane," 43, 80; "Paint It, Black," 47, 63, 64, 71, 120
rooster topic, 182, 249
Ross, Andrew, 243

Saldanha, Arun, 11, 106, 118, 243, 258, 260
sampladelia, 246
sampling, 246–248
San Francisco, 8, 126–128, 139–140, 199–200
Saussure, Ferdinand de, 16, 18, 21
Scheurer, Timothy, 27, 100–101
Sender, Ramon, 91
sex and eroticism, 125, 132–134
Shadows, The, 33
Shamen, The: "Ebeneezer Goode," 255–258; "Re: Evolution," 254–255
Shankar, Ravi, 5, 76, 161
siren trill, 45, 47, 101
Slick, Grace, 115, 138
Sly and the Family Stone, 114, 120, 124, 125, 143; "Dance to the Medley," 115, 116; "Higher," 112, 115; "I Hate to Love Her," 115; "I'm an Animal," 112; "Trip to Your Heart," 15, 110, *111*, 112, 168
Smith, Harry, 79
Soft Boys, The, 239, 240; "Underwater Moonlight," 231–237, *232–233*, *234*, *235*
soul music, 110, 112–119. *See also* Afrofuturism and modernity; funk music
sound effects and signal processing, 78, 90–95, 112, 114, 123–125, 220, 221, 247–248
space topic, 99–101, 114, 199–201, 209–210, 218, 227, 253, 255; drumming and, 72–73; signifiers of, 100–101, 193–194, 203–204, 205–206, 220, 221–222; violence and, 215; visual aspects of, 131. *See also* Afrofuturism and modernity; developing variation jam; dub music; echo and reverberation; Grateful Dead, The; Hendrix, Jimi
Starr, Ringo, 186, 190
Star Trek, 255
Stax, Mike, 29, 30, 36, 45, 49, 93
St. John, Graham, 223, 243, 258

Stockhausen, Karlheinz, 92
Stone Roses, The, 245
strange trip expressive genre, 158–159. *See also* expressive genres
structural pause, 43–44
styles: base and donor, 14–15, 30, 64; cognate relationships between, 14–15. *See also* topics, theory of
Subotnick, Morton, 91
surf music, 34, 65, 208, 236
synthesizers, 67, 220, 222, 246, 259, 262. *See also* Buchla, Don

Tal, Kali, 107
Taylor, Timothy, 57, 59
Teardrop Explodes, The, 239, 240; "Bouncing Babies," 231
techno, Detroit, 230, 248. *See also* Afrofuturism and modernity
technology, hippies and, 131, 199–200, 243
temporality, musical. *See* groove and temporality
Temptations, The, 120, 125; "Cloud 9," 117; "Runaway Child, Running Wild," 117
Thatcher, Margaret, 244
theatricality, psychedelia and, 134–135, 138–139
Theremin (instrument), 67
tie-dye, 6
time-passing motif, 163
Tin Pan Alley Pop. *See* music hall and Tin Pan Alley
topics, specific. *See* belle époque period; circus topic; classical music as a topic area; clockwork topic; film music genres; folk music topics; funk music; gothic topics; Greco-Roman topics; Gregorian chant topic; guide figures, vocal staging of; hip-hop; hymns; Indian topic; jazz; Latin music; military topic; Morse code topic; music hall and Tin Pan Alley; Native American topics; nautical topic; nostalgia and childhood; rooster topic; sex and eroticism; space topic; soul music; surf music; universal roots topic; urban topics; waltz topic
topics, theory of: context, importance of, 20–24, 140–142; definition, 1–2, 5–6, 13, 15–17; dynamism, emergence, and change, 19–20, 24–25, 117–118, 228–230, 239–240, 242; historical distance and temporal embedding, 117–118, 188; indexicality, 17–18, 25, 28n2, 32, 118–119; prototopics, 27, 28n5; troping, 19, 140–142, 146. *See also* dialogism; expressive genres; styles
Tornados, The: "Telstar," 200

trance (genre), 243, 247, 258–261; Goa, 242, 258–259, 260; psytrance, 243, 248, 258, 259–261. *See also* dance music, electronic
traveler culture, 159, 241–242
Trocco, Frank, 91
trope. *See* topics, theory of: troping
Tyrannosaurus Rex, 154

United States of America, The, 200
universal roots topic, 157
urban topics, 116–117

Veal, Michael, 205–206, 224, 253
Veen, Tobias van, 224
Velvet Underground, The, 91, 127, 201
Victorian topics. *See* belle époque period
violence, psychedelia and, 215–218, 226. *See also* psychosis and dark affect
visual art and design, 6, 8, 31, 141. *See also* poster art
voices and vocal techniques, 77–78, 112, 115–116. *See also* dream voices; guide figures, vocal staging of

Wagner, Naphtali, 188, 190
Waksman, Steve, 30, 49, 127
waltz topic, 88, 96, 238
Warhol, Andy, 91, 127
Weatherall, Andy, 245

Ween: *The Mollusk*, 95
Weheliye, Alexander, 106, 223, 224, 247, 248
Weisbard, Eric, 218
Whiteley, Sheila, 10–11, 14, 188
White Zombie, 238
Whitfield, Norman, 117
Who, The: *Tommy*, 138
The Wild Angels, 246
Williamson, Robin, 160
Wilson, Brian, 127
Wilson, Wes, 132, 133

Yardbirds, The, 29–32, 35–37, 39–40, 43, 45–53, 65, 142; "Evil Hearted You," 39, *40*; "For Your Love," 43, 77; "Happenings Ten Years Time Ago," 36, 39, 45, *46*, *47*, *48*, 49, 70, 71, 78; "Heart Full of Soul," 5, 6, 30–36, *31*; "I'm a Man," 49, *50*–*51*, 52; "Over, Under, Sideways, Down," 62, *63*; rave-ups, 15, 49–52, 212; "Shapes of Things," 29, 36, 71; "Still I'm Sad," 32, *35*, 42; "Turn into Earth," 37
Yes, 95
Young, La Monte, 91
Young, Rob, 79, 95, 159

Zappa, Frank, 78, 91–93, 115, 125, 200; "Who Are the Brain Police?," 15, 93
Žižek, Slavoj, 216
Zuberi, Nabeel, 225

WILLIAM ECHARD is Associate Professor of Music at Carleton University, Ottawa. His early research on spatial and energetic aspects of musical signification led to his book *Neil Young and the Poetics of Energy* (IUP).